RETIREMENT POLICY ISSUES IN CANADA

EDITED BY
Michael G. Abbott,
Charles M. Beach, Robin W. Boadway
and James G. MacKinnon

JOHN DEUTSCH INSTITUTE FOR THE
STUDY OF ECONOMIC POLICY

Queen's
UNIVERSITY

McGill-Queen's University Press
Montreal & Kingston • London • Ithaca

ISBN: 978-1-55339-162-3 (bound), ISBN: 978-1-55339-161-6 (pbk.)
© John Deutsch Institute for the Study of Economic Policy
Queen's University, Kingston, Ontario K7L 3N6
Telephone: (613) 533-2294 FAX: (613) 533-6025
Printed and bound in Canada

Library and Archives Canada Cataloguing in Publication

Retirement policy issues in Canada / editors, Michael G.
Abbott ... [et al.].

Includes bibliographical references.
ISBN 978-1-55339-162-3 (bound).--ISBN 978-1-55339-161-6 (pbk.)

1. Retirement--Government policy--Canada. 2. Pensions--
Government policy--Canada. 3. Retirement income--Canada.
4. Retirement--Canada. I. Abbott, Michael G. II. John Deutsch
Institute for the Study of Economic Policy

HQ1064.C3R48 2009   306.3'80971   C2008-906581-6

Table of Contents

Chapter III:
Policy Levers and the Retirement Process

Chapter IV:
Panel on Replacement Rates and Design
Features of Workplace Pension Plans

Chapter V:
The Retirement Process and Macroeconomic Implications

Chapter VI:
Panel on Risk and Pension Investment Strategies

Chapter VII:
Pension Rules and Retirement

Chapter VIII
Mandatory Retirement and the Changing Prospects of Retirement

Preface

The papers and commentaries in this volume were all presented at the John Deutsch Institute conference on "Retirement Policy Issues in Canada" held at Queen's University on October 26–27, 2007. The conference was organized by Michael Abbott, Charles Beach, Robin Boadway, and James MacKinnon, all in the Department of Economics at Queen's. Funding for the conference came from the John Deutsch Institute, from Mr. William P. Wilder, and from Fidelity Investments Canada Limited. The organizers thank these latter contributors for helping to make the conference possible.

The objectives of the conference were threefold. First was to bring together different perspectives in the retirement area from a range of disciplines to raise public awareness of the issues and problems that are fast approaching with the baby boom generation now beginning the retirement phase of their careers. Second, the conference and this subsequent volume have brought together some major original research studies to help inform the needed public debate on these issues. Third, the studies presented here offer concrete policy options and proposals for reform that will help address these major issues to the benefit of Canadians as a whole and retirees — current and future — in particular.

The editors of this volume and conference organizers benefited from the assistance of a number of people in both the operation of the conference and the production of this volume. We especially wish to thank Sharon Sullivan of the John Deutsch Institute for her assistance throughout the project, for her excellent job in the planning and managing of the conference, and for her exceptional editorial and development work in producing this volume. Marilyn Banting and Mark Howes of the Queen's School of Policy Studies provided excellent creative and editorial services for the volume, and

Stephanie Stone very ably transcribed the discussion and commentaries that have been included. We would specifically like to thank Bob Baldwin and Peter Drake for their very helpful ideas and suggestions in the planning stage of the conference. We also gratefully acknowledge the contribution of a number of others who contributed to this project by providing advice and by chairing sessions at the conference: Keith Ambachtsheer, Barbara Glover, Peter Hicks, Terry Hunsley, Bruce Little, and Richard Shillington.

Finally, we wish to acknowledge the marvellous cooperation we received from the contributors to this volume.

Michael G. Abbott
Queen's University

Charles M. Beach
Director
John Deutsch Institute

Robin W. Boadway
Queen's University

James G. MacKinnon
Queen's University

Introduction

Michael G. Abbott, Charles M. Beach, Robin W. Boadway, and James G. MacKinnon

Economic Context of Retirement

Retirement is a concern of an increasing number of Canadians and the growing focus of attention of federal and provincial governments in Canada. Recent media reports have highlighted public concern on "The Pension Crisis" (Contenta, 2009) and "Retiring into the Unknown" as part of "The New Middle Class Reality" (Campbell, 2009).[1] The beginnings of a tidal wave of on-coming retirements are already upon us, as more than 8 million baby boomers will be leaving the labour force over the next 15 years or so. This will have implications for the economic well-being of these on-coming retirees and the income-replacement rates they can expect, productivity rates and output levels for the Canadian economy, labour market opportunities across the whole age range of workers, revenue and expenditure patterns and hence demands on government budgets at both federal and provincial levels, and the rethinking of Canada's entire pension system. The last decade has also seen a remarkable change in the entire process of retirement. What was once a ratchet-like, and often mandatory, shift from full-time work to full-time retirement at some specific age such as 62 or 65, has now often become a period of transition or phased-in retirement, involving part-time work and perhaps self-employment activity.

---

[1]See also *The Globe and Mail* (2009), *Toronto Star* (2009), Middlemiss (2008), Mazurkewich (2008), and *The Economist* (2009).

This reflects a greater range of choice, often within a family context (Clark *et al.*, 2004; Wise, 2004; Lumsdaine and Mitchell, 1999).

The recent severe and sudden recession and meltdown of global financial markets raise obvious questions about the current incomes of those already retired and the future financial well-being of workers who had planned to retire shortly. To many workers, "Freedom 55" is now looking more like Freedom 75. Many long-run employees covered by workplace pensions in the private sector are having to take major pension reductions and indeed are seriously concerned about whether their pension benefits will even exist when they retire. The proportion of workers indeed covered by workplace pensions has plummeted. Canada's social safety net for the elderly is also looking increasingly under stress and in need of a major review. Indeed, governments have recently set up expert panels to report on older workers (federal)[2] and the pension system (Ontario),[3] and have already begun making changes to Canada Pension Plan (CPP) rules to better address the current economic environment. A flurry of proposals by several provincial governments, think tanks and pension experts will likely lead to the most substantial restructuring of the Canadian pension system seen since the establishment the Canada and Quebec Pension Plans in the 1960s (Ambachtsheer, 2007; Béland, 2009; Cooper, 2008; Munnell and Sass, 2008).

The objectives of this volume are threefold. First, it brings together different perspectives in the retirement area from a range of disciplines to raise public awareness of the issues and problems that are fast approaching and that currently risk being ignored while policy attention focuses on concerns of the immediate economic downturn and its fiscal demands. Second, the various papers in this volume seek to bring current research knowledge — both in Canada and elsewhere — to bear on these issues and to help educate and inform the needed policy debate on these issues. Third, the studies presented here offer options and proposals that will help address these issues to the benefit of Canadians as a whole and of retirees — current and future — in particular. Accordingly, this volume includes contributions from both public sector analysts and policy practitioners, academic and think-tank researchers, and private-sector specialists on retirement and pension issues.

---

[2]See Expert Panel on Older Workers (2008).

[3]See Expert Commission on Pensions (2007, 2008).

Just what is meant by retirement is actually not clear at all. The basic intuitive notion of retirement is the withdrawal of older workers from the labour market. But this withdrawal may be full or partial, permanent or temporary. It is often associated with receipt of a pension or social security benefits. In many cases, it is not a complete withdrawal but rather a major reduction in hours worked, a move to a less demanding job, a move to some form of self-employment, or some combination of the above. Increasingly, this is the more complex phenomenon that we are seeing, so that retirement needs to be understood in a more comprehensive and nuanced way (Madrian, Mitchell, and Soldo, 2007).

Retirement Income Framework in Canada

Retirement and the standard of living of retirees occur within a complex framework of private and public savings and benefit schemes. Saving for one's retirement is a prerequisite to maintaining acceptable standards of living in retirement. This may be done solely out of self-interest. But many workers, especially in the public sector, may also participate in a workplace pension scheme as part of the conditions of their employment. These schemes are encouraged by government through tax sheltering, as are private retirement savings. Governments generally also implement mandatory contributory public pension schemes that force workers to save at least some minimal amount of their earnings for their own retirement, and furthermore they provide transfer payments to the less well-off retired population financed out of general tax revenues. This multidimensional approach to retirement income has been aptly referred to as the three pillars of saving for retirement: public transfers to the needy elderly, compulsory public pensions, and tax-assisted private savings.[4]

In Canada, the first, non-contributory, pillar consists of Old Age Security (OAS) and the Guaranteed Income Supplement (GIS), which are geared-to-income transfers to all persons over 65. The second, compulsory contributory, pillar is the CPP (and its analogue in Quebec, the Quebec Pension Plan). All earnings are subject to a payroll tax, which then goes to a fund that finances future retirement benefits as well as providing other

---

[4]The concept of the three pillars of pensions was proposed in The World Bank (2002).

forms of social protection such as disability insurance and spousal benefits. While in many Organisation for Economic Co-operation and Development (OECD) countries public pensions are pay-as-you-go, the CPP is largely funded, and the fund is managed by an independent body called the Canada Pension Plan Investment Board. The third pillar includes tax-sheltered savings by employees in workplace Registered Pension Plans, by workers in Registered Retirement Savings Plans (RRSP) for the self-employed and those not covered by a workplace pension, and, as of the 2008 federal budget, Tax Free Savings Accounts. The latter differ from both types of registered plans in that they do not give an income deduction for contributions, but simply allow future capital income to be tax exempt, and thus are more favourable savings instruments for persons whose incomes are expected to rise over the life cycle and into retirement. Taken together, these three pillars constitute the main means of retirement income support for the vast majority of Canadians.[5]

Why should firms and governments get so heavily involved in facilitating savings for retirement? In the case of firms, pensions are a form of deferred compensation that benefits both the firm and the employee. Firms are better able to retain employees in whom they have invested skills and training, at least to the extent that pension rights are not fully portable. Employees benefit by having their savings managed by knowledgeable pension fund managers who are able to obtain better returns at lower fees than individual workers can typically obtain on their own. The self-employed must manage their own retirement savings, but they typically obtain the same tax advantages as workers with registered workplace pensions.

The rationales for government intervention are somewhat more diverse.[6] In the case of the first pillar, the motive is primarily redistributive. Income-tested transfer payments to the retired are a backstop form of social protection to ensure that all retired persons have a minimal level of income with which to sustain themselves.

The second pillar involves forcing income-earners collectively to save for their own retirement, reflecting the apparent fact that most people

---

[5]The government, in addition, provides some important in-kind transfers that benefit the elderly especially, such as health care, pharmaceuticals, and home and nursing care facilities, depending on the province.

[6]A more detailed discussion of the rationale for public intervention in retirement savings can be found in Banting and Boadway (1997).

systematically save too little for their own retirement from the point of view of reasonable life-cycle predictions. Some reasons have been emphasized in the recent behavioural economics literature (see, e.g., Diamond and Vartiainen, 2007). People may discount the future excessively because of a sort of time inconsistency in their preferences that has been experimentally verified. The consequence is over-consumption that resembles myopia. Besides this seemingly irrational savings behaviour, they also suffer from what economists call bounded rationality: they do not have the knowledge or training to understand how much saving they should do in order to provide for their future. In both cases, people may welcome being forced to save in a form that is not up to them to decide. They may even under-save deliberately, fully anticipating that the government will come to their aid if they are left with too little in retirement, an expectation that is borne out by the first pension pillar. Finally, long-term capital markets may be imperfect owing to problems of adverse selection. To counter this, a compulsory public pension is itself a form of annuity. Some lifetime risks may be individually uninsurable, particularly those associated with disability, family circumstances, job displacement or inflation. Taken together, these arguments have persuaded most OECD countries to enact compulsory public pensions, whether funded or not, as part of their retirement income policies.

The third pension pillar involves tax assistance for private saving, including that done via workplace pensions. Tax-assisted private pensions can be seen as a complement to public pensions. The more people are induced to save for themselves, the less reliant they will be on public support in retirement. However, there are tax policy reasons for providing tax assistance to savings as well. Sheltering retirement savings from tax in effect converts the tax from one that is based on income as it is earned to one based on consumption that is spread over the life cycle. In so doing, it effectively eliminates differential taxation of future versus present consumption that is a characteristic of the income tax system. Indeed, taken together with the non-taxation of the imputed returns on owner-occupied housing, the so-called income tax system is actually much closer to a consumption-based tax system. Finally, sheltering retirement savings serves to smooth tax liabilities over the life cycle, which reduces the distortions resulting from a progressive tax structure.

Major Themes Underlying Retirement Policy

While many issues are touched upon in the studies in this volume and in the broad debate on retirement policy in Canada, several major themes can be highlighted. The first major theme concerns how retirement patterns in Canada have been changing over the last 20 years or so, and what factors are contributing to these changes. The median age of retirement in Canada had steadily declined for a generation to around 58 by the mid-1990s, but, since 1997, it has reversed directions and has risen to over 61 years of age. This is quite a remarkable turnaround, one shared with several other countries such as the United States and the United Kingdom, around the same time. There has also been a change from the traditional ratchet pattern of retirement, with an abrupt shift from full-time work to full-time retirement at some specified (often mandated) age, towards a phased period of transition into retirement involving part-time work or self-employment activity. Retirement is also becoming a joint endogenous decision, often involving dual-earner coordination, rather than an event largely determined by the employment of male household heads.

Why these changes have occurred may reflect several factors. People are healthier and living longer on average, so there is a need to provide for a longer retirement period by working longer in order to build up more of a retirement fund. A gradual shift from employment in manufacturing and goods production to a service dominated economy opens greater opportunities for older workers. More educated workers tend to retire later, and each successive cohort of workers attains higher levels of education. The inflow of women and immigrants into the Canadian workforce brings in workers who want to work longer in order to build up their own pension entitlements or pension accounts before retiring. Declining interest rates since the 1980s mean that a given retirement nest egg provides a lower annuity, and working longer helps build up this nest egg. Until recently, the Canadian economy had been experiencing over a decade and a half of uninterrupted growth, rising employment, and declining unemployment rates. And there is nothing like a tightening labour market to open up job opportunities for minority and non-prime-age workers. So there have clearly been several factors at work (Schirle, 2008).

A second theme concerns the implications of later retirement and an aging workforce for the macroeconomy and for government fiscal balance. Later retirement means more workers in the economy and hence higher output and higher income per capita. But an aging workforce associated with the advancing wave of baby boomers is likely to have the effect of (perhaps only slightly) slowing down the rate of year-to-year productivity growth. Delaying the average age of retirement is a way of countering the latter on-going demographic effect. Since individuals' incomes are typically higher while working than when retired, delaying the age of retirement helps keep government revenues higher and delays payouts of government transfer expenditures to low-income retirees, so it is also beneficial for the public sector balances (Robson, 2009).

A third theme concerns the effect of job displacements among older workers on retirement outcomes. How do older workers adjust when major industrial restructuring occurs, particularly if plant closings take place in smaller communities where few alternative employment options are available? This is especially important in light of the current severe recession in North America and elsewhere, where major long-run industries such as automobiles, forestry, and natural resources have shed large numbers of jobs, many of which had been held by older workers. A slow recovery from the recession and a rising Canadian dollar may mean that many of these and other manufacturing jobs are not likely to reappear, at least in the near future. In general, a weak labour market and rising unemployment rates make it particularly difficult for older workers to find re-employment. And if new jobs are found, they are typically at a substantially lower wage than before displacement, perhaps more so for older workers than for younger ones. Both these reasons may well cause discouraged job seekers to drop out of the labour market and take earlier retirement than they had planned.

Fourth, to what extent do pension income levels and pension availability affect retirement outcomes? Economic theory predicts that non-wage income options reduce work effort and time spent in the labour market. The major run-up of financial markets in the 1980s and 1990s was indeed associated with generally declining age of retirement. But the rising uncertainty of private pension payouts as major firms go bankrupt or pension underfunding occurs, and the recent loss of over $200 billion of household wealth in Canada associated with the 2008 meltdown of financial markets are likely to result in older workers staying in the labour market longer because they can no longer afford to retire. How major and long-lasting these uncertainty and wealth effects will be is unknown and will clearly need to be the subject of future research. At the very least, there is a need for a timely review of pension regulation and pension availability in Canada.

Fifth, there needs to be better understanding of the retirement incentives built into Canada's private and public pension schemes, and how these might be changed in order to open up opportunities and reduce barriers for workers who wish to continue working longer. Current restrictions in CPP, for example, require a worker to retire from a job before being able to access CPP benefits, whereas a more flexible option could allow one to continue working on the job past the CPP eligibility age, and to continue paying into the plan while also perhaps drawing partial benefits. Many US studies in recent years have established a strong relationship between the economic incentives of retirement policies and the age at which individuals choose to retire from the labour force, and more investigation along these lines needs to be done for Canada. The last 20 years have seen a decline in the incidence of workplace pensions in the private sector and a dramatic shift in the structuring of private-sector pensions away from defined-benefit plans and towards defined-contribution plans. But what are the consequences for retirement of this growing shift of retirement-income risk away from employers and onto workers themselves? And how adequate is the current public/private pension system in Canada in light of the recent recession and financial meltdown of retirement nest eggs? Is there, indeed, a crisis in workplace pensions in Canada resulting from this combination of events (Crossley and Spencer, 2008; Milligan and Schirle, 2008)?

Finally, there needs to be better understanding of the adequacy of and the retirement incentives built into Canada's old-age security, Employment Insurance (EI), and income tax systems. Compared to the United States, surprisingly little research has been done on the effects of these programs on retirement decisions. Considerably more needs to be known just about the broad economic circumstances of older Canadians and whether there is a growing gap between rich and poor in the older generation. Does Canada need a mandatory tax-sheltered savings program to help workers build up (or in many cases rebuild) their retirement nest egg savings? How significant are the retirement effects of the high implicit tax rates in the current GIS system as they relate to other sources of income? And should RRSP cash-out rules be made more flexible to accommodate workers who wish to continue working longer (Gruber and Wise, 2007; Ambachtsheer, 2008; Gustman and Steinmeier, 2008)?

Overview of the Contributing Papers

The first two contributions of this volume identify some major policy concerns relating to retirement: demographics, public health care of the elderly, and pensions. Laurence Kotlikoff addresses the widespread demographic change and its fiscal implications for government treasuries. By 2050, for example, the proportion of the Canadian population age 65 and over will have more than doubled, from 13% to about 27%, with an even larger relative increase in those age 85 or more. The decline in fertility rates the last 60 years is the major source of the aging population, but on-going longevity increases also contribute. Since 1970, the annual growth in public health-care expenditures per elderly recipient exceeded that in gross domestic product (GDP) per capita. The resulting challenge for public health-care spending will be a large problem in the future for Canada, and in the United States will be a crisis. To fix things, Kotlikoff recommends replacing personal income, corporate income and payroll taxes by a single federal sales tax with a rebate to all households, and replacing public (and employer-based for the United States) health-care systems by a voucher to buy health insurance, where the voucher would be individually risk-adjusted and the government spending on vouchers could be a fixed proportion of GDP.

David Dodge's paper raises some challenges to improving the viability of private employer-sponsored pension plans. He argues that such plans are the most effective means to ensure adequate retirement incomes. But finding the right incentives to facilitate an effective plan is critically important. Dodge reviews the key risks faced by workers and employers and the role of incentives to see that these risks can be effectively managed. He argues the importance of being part of a larger pension group so that risks, governance, and transactions costs can be more widely spread. This allows plan members to gain efficient management of funds at wholesale, rather than retail, costs, enables them to purchase a retirement annuity at widely shared group rates, and ensures that the retirement income of individual members does not depend on market conditions at time of retirement. He reviews some of the benefits of defined-benefit pension plans, and poses the challenge of how to preserve the advantages of a defined-benefit pension plan, but make it possible to distribute risk more appropriately and hence enhance the viability of the plans.

The next set of papers set out some of the background information on retirement patterns in Canada, income security of retirees, and key issues in pension reform. Cliff Halliwell examines how retirement may be defined and uses a compound criterion: older workers who have left a job and haven't started another within three years. He cites a study that estimates that two-thirds of job openings over the next decade will result from retirements from the workplace. Halliwell then looks at recent trends in retirement in Canada, and attributes the recent turnaround and rise in participation rates of older workers to: the greater strength of job markets opening up employment opportunities over the period and the cohort effect of aging baby-boomer women who are simply continuing their strong labour market attachment. For older workers who do not continue working full-time, he finds a strong preference for part-time work and flexible work arrangements. Finally, he notes that life expectancies of both men and women are continuing to rise, leading to longer retirement periods than a generation ago. This means that pensions need to last longer, and hence workers need to seek greater wealth at their time of retirement and a higher rate of saving or a higher rate of return during their working years. Low savings rates over the last decade and declining average returns on household wealth thus pose a huge challenge for workers' increasing longevity.

Sébastien LaRochelle-Côté, John Myles, and Garnett Picot compare pre- and post-retirement incomes in order to examine: how well Canada's retirement income system maintains pre-retirement income standards (i.e., *security* of retirement income), and the *stability* of income in retirement years. They make use of Statistics Canada's Longitudinal Administrative Database (or LAD file) of income tax records to calculate income replacement rates for seniors who had significant labour market attachment. For specific cohorts of workers, the authors follow their income streams for 20 years, from ages 55 to 75, to see how income replacement rates unfold over this period. Their measure of income is adult-equivalent-adjusted family income. They find three main results. First, income replacement rates in Canada provide a relatively high degree of income security in retirement — they average around 100% for low-income individuals, close to 80% for middle-income recipients (and overall), and about 70% for high-income workers. Second, there is considerable variation in replacement rates across individuals. For middle-income recipients, the principal factors distinguishing between those with low versus high replacement rates were the maintenance of employment earnings by age 70 and the presence of private pensions and RRSP income by age 75. Third, year-to-year instability of incomes is greater among low-income earners than among middle- and high-income earners (because of unstable employment earnings). But income instability declines with age — more so for low-income earners because of the stabilizing effect of the public retirement income system — such that the gap in income stability between low- and high-income recipients disappears by age 75 as workers age into retirement.

Michael Veall in his contribution looks at inequality in the distribution of seniors' income in Canada since 1992. Using income data also from the LAD file, he measures inequality in seniors' receipts of market income, total income (including transfers), and after-tax income — all adjusted for family size. He finds that income inequality among seniors (age 66 and over), as compared to all ages as a whole, is slightly larger for after-tax income, moderately larger for total income, and vastly larger for market income, where those who continue working have much higher incomes than those who do not. Inequality for all three forms of income increased over the 1992–2005 period covered by the study, with the biggest jump between 1995 and 2000. At the lower end of the seniors' income distribution, immigrants appear disproportionately along with females and unattached individuals.

William Robson's paper focuses on the broad issue of misperceptions about the nature of defined-benefit pension plans and the contribution of regulation and tax provisions in fostering their use. He argues that the design of classic defined-benefit pensions have falsely presumed that equity could reliably earn several percentage points above high-quality debt, a presumption that was fostered in the era of rapid North American growth of the 1950s and 1960s. Moreover, it largely ignored agency problems that were endemic to defined-benefit plans. In the new reality, since the 1980s, of reduced growth and adverse demographic changes, the expectations that were prevalent during the *Golden Age* of defined-benefit plans are no longer reasonable. Robson argues that policies must foster a more balanced approach to pensions, and especially encourage greater use of money purchase plans such as RRSPs. These plans can be designed in a way that addresses the real difficulties that households have in saving enough, in investing wisely and efficiently, and in annuitizing wisely. And policies could be devised that foster such plans through wider pooling of occupational plans and use of default investment and annuitization options.

The next two papers in the volume discuss several policy levers that affect retirement decisions through defined-benefit pension plans in Canada and through personal savings accounts in the United Kingdom. The first paper by Maxime Fougère, Simon Harvey, Yu Lan, André Léonard, and Bruno Rainville reviews the incentive effects incorporated in Canada's current system of public and private defined-benefit (DB) pension plans. The work disincentive effects in a DB plan can be decomposed, according to the literature, into a wealth effect and an accrual or substitution effect. The former reflects the increase in total pension wealth. The latter arises from the difference in pension wealth between retiring at a given age and one year later. Since DB pension benefits depend on age of retirement, DB plans give rise to both a wealth effect and an accrual effect on retirement choice. Defined-contribution (DC) plans, however, depend on the history of contributions and the investment returns on past contributions, and hence have only a wealth effect.

Fougère et al. review the work disincentive effects incorporated in Canada's public pension system consisting of the Canada/Quebec Pension Plan (C/QPP), which is an earnings-based DB pension plan, and the Old Age Security/Guaranteed Income Suppplement (OAS/GIS) programs, which are income support programs. They find that the C/QPP and GIS programs interact to create strong disincentives to work for individuals between 65 and 70 years of age.

The authors also use a dynamic computable general equilibrium model to analyze private DB pension plans as well as Canada's public pension system for workers grouped by education into low-skilled, medium-skilled, and high-skilled. They find that inclusion of private DB plans along with the public pension system substantially strengthens work disincentives, especially after age 61, and for high-skilled and medium-skilled workers. They calculate that eliminating the early retirement incentives in Canada's private DB pension plans would produce labour supply effects for older workers that are several times larger than would the removal of the early retirement incentives in the public pension system.

Richard Disney, Carl Emmerson, and Gemma Tetlow review recent major reforms to the UK pension system with an eye for whether there are any lessons for Canada. The two key reform features they focus on are the introduction of Personal Accounts for retirement saving for workers who are not eligible for employer-provided pension plans, and the incorporation of "default options" in workers' pension choices. The authors begin by examining the concept of income adequacy in retirement and the explanations in the literature for why individuals, on average, do not seem to save "enough" for their retirement. Arguments in favour of compulsory savings are not convincing, they feel. However, evidence from behavioural economics finds that, in the presence of complex choices and imperfect information, inertia or a default option is disproportionately chosen by participants. This suggests an alternative policy approach to compulsory savings. The UK pension reforms of 2007 and 2008 make major use of this default option approach. For employees being offered an employer-sponsored pension plan of a sufficient standard, membership in the plan becomes the default option. For employees who are not members of such an employer-sponsored plan, the legislation sets up new Personal Accounts for retirement saving in which eligible workers will be automatically enrolled, and in which both employers and employees contribute to a total of 8% of earnings. The Personal Accounts will offer a choice of fund types with one of the options designated the default choice. The authors then provide some discussion of who are likely to be most affected by these reforms and the possible effects of the reforms for total level of retirement saving, their macroeconomic impacts, and possible welfare implications.

The next four contributions come from a panel session on income replacement rates and major design features of the two main forms of workplace pension plans — defined-benefit and defined-contribution plans. Peter Drake and Colin Randall consider development of benchmark retirement income replacement rates for Canada. Conventional wisdom in financial circles has cited 60–70% of average pre-retirement earnings as required to live comfortably in retirement. But a number of structural, demographic and attitudinal changes have occurred over the last 20 years with respect to retirement and work patterns of older workers. The Fidelity research group considers whether this is still an appropriate replacement rate in light of these changes. Financial surveys for Fidelity suggest that many higher-income respondents indeed maintained their pre-retirement spending levels; the incidence of doing so, though, declined with pre-retirement income levels. Assuming that retirees are able to maintain their pre-retirement spending levels and that retirement occurs at age 65, the analysts estimate that Canadians will need a replacement rate between 75% and 85% of their pre-retirement income. The specific rates rise slightly with pre-retirement income levels above $50,000 and are higher for individuals than for couples.

Stephen Bonnar discusses the strengths and weaknesses of traditional, single-employer, defined-benefit plans. He compares the principal features of public-sector DB plans, which typically provide workers with strong incentives to retire after their age plus years of service sum to 85 or 90, with those of private-sector DB plans. The latter are considerably less generous. They typically provide lower pensions, are not indexed to inflation (but generally do offer limited protection against inflation), and provide smaller incentives for early retirement. A significant number of unionized employers offer a different type of defined-benefit plan, in which pensions are not directly related to earnings. The legal status of surpluses and deficits in DB plans, though, is not entirely clear. It seems that employers may be liable for all deficits but have limited ability to claim any surpluses from the plan. Lack of legal clarity about who really takes the risk for funding plan deficits makes it difficult for Canada to have an effective, ongoing DB pension system.

David McLellan discusses defined-contribution (DC) pension plans. He first deals with group RRSPs. These have one major advantage over retail RRSPs: they typically involve much lower fees. However, they also have one major disadvantage: it is impossible for employers to prevent employees from withdrawing the contributions that the former have made on their behalf. Conventional DC plans do not suffer from this disadvantage, but they have other ones. In particular, former employees typically remain in the plan when they leave for another employer, so that over time the lion's share of the plan members may no longer be employees. There may be significant costs and ongoing liabilities related to these former, but not yet retired, employees. McLellan points out that there is really no DC pension legislation in Canada, just DB pension legislation turned sideways. The Guidelines for Capital Accumulation Plans, or CAP guidelines, proposed by the Joint Forum of Financial Market Regulators in 2004 provide a good start for such legislation. However, the CAP guidelines stop short in certain important ways, which McLellan discusses. He concludes that there is a place for defined-contribution plans, especially among employers who do not currently offer any sort of plan, and there needs to be DC-specific legislation to help make this happen.

Marcel Théroux discusses recent legal decisions and regulatory changes and their implications for the design of pension plans. He points out that a very high percentage of public-sector workers belong to pension plans, but a much lower percentage of private-sector workers do. In common-law provinces, pension statutes differentiate very poorly between defined-benefit and defined-contribution plans. As a result, it is unclear whether defined-benefit plans should be treated primarily as a contract between a company and its workers or primarily as a trust. Some recent legal decisions have said that they should be treated primarily as trusts. By doing so, the courts have, in effect, passed unforeseen legislation that applies retroactively to pension plans which have been in existence for many years, and this has created a certain amount of chaos.

The next three contributions look at the process of retirement and the macroeconomic implications of population aging on the economy. Robert Clark examines the arguments and experience concerning phased retirement whereby a growing number of older workers are now choosing to work part-time for a few years as a prelude to full retirement. From the employer's point of view, offering a part-time work option is a way of retaining valuable human capital over the period of transition to younger replacements. The evidence in the United States is that the incidence of phased retirement varies substantially across industries and occupations, and is relatively more common in higher education and professional and technical jobs and public administration. From an employee's view, the option of part-time work as a transitional phase between full-time work and full retirement offers an opportunity to continue working longer in order to further build up pension credits and accumulated savings and achieve a higher standard of living when entering retirement. Canadian evidence finds that just under a third of recent retirees have indicated they would have continued working if they had the option of part-time work. The incidence of phased retirement is more common among white-collar workers, highly educated workers and higher-income workers. From the government's perspective, providing incentives for older workers to continue working can help relieve pressure on public retirement programs and continue bringing in earnings-based tax revenue. Thus removing impediments to continued employment of older workers makes a lot of fiscal sense.

Clark then reviews the experience of a phased-retirement plan at the campuses of the University of North Carolina that was adopted in 1998. It was found that the introduction of phased retirement brought about an approximate 10% reduction in the full retirement rate of faculty and a 20% increase in the odds that an older faculty member would enter either full or phased retirement. About one in every five retirements involved phased retirement. The program turned out to be cost neutral to the university, and allowed the university to better plan for future hiring.

The paper by William Scarth analyzes some macroeconomic effects of population aging on overall productivity growth rates and living standards. He begins his review of effects within the framework of traditional neoclassical economic growth theory with exogenous rates of technological change and population growth. He identifies several channels whereby the demographic change of population aging can affect a country's living standards or per capita consumption: (i) increase in the old-age dependency ratio of non-working adults, (ii) increase in rate of saving for retirement, (iii) decrease in overall population growth rate, and (iv) increase in taxes in order to finance health and pension costs of the elderly. In the framework of this traditional growth theory model, he argues that the higher old-age dependency and tax rates effects are likely to dominate the higher saving and lower population growth rate effects, so that his best estimate on balance of the expected population aging is to lower average living standards by a one-time but ongoing amount of about 7%.

Scarth then extends the framework of analysis to incorporate three forms of the more recent endogenous growth theory: growth in knowledge or human capital, endogenous research and development which affects the rate of technological change, and the presence of non-renewable natural resources. Unfortunately, these different models lead to different predicted outcomes for the effect of population aging on living standards. His main conclusion is that population aging does represent a serious challenge, but one where "the hit to living standards may just be manageable".

The paper by Christine Neill and Tammy Schirle looks at the labour market responses of older workers who are laid off or displaced. What distinguishes older from younger workers in their responses is the retirement option. Current evidence for Canada suggests that the incidence of permanent layoff is slightly lower for older than for younger men, but essentially the same for older and younger women. However, older workers experience substantially longer spells of unemployment than do younger workers. Displaced workers in all age groups 25–69 experience large earnings losses in the year of displacement and in the two years following displacement; however, Neill and Schirle find no evidence that the post-displacement earnings losses of older male workers are any larger than those incurred by their younger counterparts.

Neill and Schirle also find that the incidence of participation or enrolment in a formal education program decreases strongly with age. Older workers do not appear to consider education and training to be worthwhile investments. Such evidence implies that policies with a large education or training component are unlikely to be successful in reintegrating older displaced workers into the employed labour force. On the other hand, policies whose main objective is to mitigate the financial hardship arising from the displacement of older workers have generally tended to reduce the labour force participation and employment rates of older displaced workers. One option that might avoid the work disincentive effects of past income support programs is a wage subsidy program that would pay displaced workers who are employed a percentage of the difference between their pre- and post-displacement wage rates. Such a scheme could potentially encourage labour force participation on the part of older displaced workers, while at the same time partially offset the earnings losses associated with displacement.

The next set of papers come from a panel discussion on risk and pension plan investment strategies. Malcolm Hamilton, in his presentation, discusses longevity risk. He points out that, for ongoing plans, longevity risk is greatly dominated by investment risk, but the opposite can be true when plans are to be wound up and their assets used to purchase annuities. If a plan is to be wound up, there is a risk that the mortality rate of its participants may be lower than average. This is a serious risk for universities, for example, where plan members tend to be long-lived. The other major risk is the unknown rate of future mortality improvement. The cost of winding up a pension plan is particularly sensitive to rates of mortality improvement at advanced ages, which are precisely the ages for which existing improvement scales are least reliable. Hamilton then discusses how longevity risk affects individuals. It is not really a problem for low-income seniors, because most of their income comes from government programs, and governments implicitly underwrite this risk. Nor is it a problem for affluent seniors, because they are unlikely to need all their money, and their heirs end up bearing the risk. For middle-income seniors, however, it is a big problem, which most manage by living frugally rather than by buying annuities. Finally, Hamilton discusses how longevity risk affects governments. For governments, the obvious solution to increasing longevity is to postpone the age of retirement. But this ignores the important distinction between life expectancy and healthy life expectancy. If life expectancy is rising much faster than healthy life expectancy, then people are going to spend a larger fraction of their adult lives as retirees.

Sterling Gunn, in his presentation, discusses the investment strategy of the Canada Pension Plan Investment Board, or CPPIB. In recent years, the CPPIB has chosen to become an active asset manager. In addition to holding a reference portfolio of equities and bonds, which is managed passively, it invests in relatively illiquid asset classes, such as real estate, infrastructure, and other long-term commitments. Because of the certainty of the plan's future contributions and the long-term nature of its obligations, the CPPIB is able to make long-term investments that many other investors cannot. If these investments can sustainably add value over a long period of time, the steady-state contribution rate for the plan can be reduced. The Board takes a top-down approach to asset management, always asking how its marginal investment decisions contribute to the risk and return of the total portfolio. It is seeking to build a culture of accountability built around integrity, high performance, and partnership.

Graham Pugh, in his presentation, first gives some background information about the Ontario Municipal Employees Retirement System (OMERS), and then discusses its target asset mix and how that mix is related to the objectives of the plan. The current target is to have 42.5% in illiquid assets. To determine and update its target asset mix, OMERS performs extensive asset mix studies that involve stochastic projections of investment, actuarial, and demographic assumptions. It also takes account of management's views as to where the greatest returns are likely to arise over the next decade. Pugh also discusses regulatory issues. Many rules for defined-benefit plans date back to 1985 and no longer serve a useful purpose. Canada's rules are out of step with those of other jurisdictions, including the United States, the United Kingdom, and Australia. He argues that eliminating regulatory restrictions will result in more investment opportunities and greater pension security.

The next three contributions look at various aspects of pension rules and retirement. Kevin Milligan and Tammy Schirle consider the possible consequences of recent changes in the tax treatment of Registered Pension Plans (RPPs) that, for the first time, allow taxpayers to accrue further tax benefits after retirement. They suggest that this reflects public acceptance that continuing to work while drawing pension benefits, or "double dipping", is quite reasonable. This view is consistent with the economist's view of pensions as deferred compensation, where there is no reason for the deferment to end only when full retirement occurs. Labour market shortages in recent years owing to demographic change and strong economic growth have contributed to this change in attitude. Milligan and Schirle attempt to infer the order of magnitude of the effect of this policy change by looking at three sorts of data. First, they look at long-run trends in elderly employment and pension coverage, and find that recently there has been a modest increase in work among those near retirement age, but also a decline in defined-benefit pension coverage. Second, they document that the proportion of workers who are receiving a pension is very low. Finally, they find from survey data that most retired persons prefer that status to working, and those who would like to work would prefer to do so part-time. They conclude that the empirical relevance of double dipping appears to be marginal, and the changes in the tax treatment of RPPs are unlikely to have much effect.

John Burbidge and Katherine Cuff explore some consequences of another legislative change affecting pensions: the ending of mandatory retirement in several provinces. Their concern is the impact on retirement, particularly how many older workers will opt to continue working past age 65. As they document, the trend later in the twentieth century was for early retirement to increase, especially among more educated workers. However, since 2000, there is indication that the trend is reversing. The participation rate of older workers is increasing both between 60 and 64 and 65 and over. Moreover, the trend is more pronounced in those provinces that already abolished mandatory retirement. The consequence of ending mandatory retirement for the participation rate of older workers is of obvious importance given coming demographic changes. To study this, they develop a life-cycle model of household consumption and retirement in order to simulate the effect of ending mandatory retirement using a particular group of workers — faculty at two Ontario universities with similar defined-benefit pension plans (McMaster and Waterloo). They find that those with lower earnings trajectories will tend to work beyond 65. To estimate how much the option to continue working benefits this type of worker, they calculate that pension benefits would have to increase by something like 20% to induce them to retire at age 65. These results suggest that abolishing mandatory retirement could have a noticeable effect on labour markets.

Rick Egelton and Steven James examine the sustainability of CPP and the stochastic liability model on which their sustainability forecasts are based. The 1997 reforms of the CPP system put CPP onto a sustainable track well into the future and ensured a lower contribution rate than otherwise. The CPP contribution rate is sustainable if plan assets at least match liabilities (i.e., the present value of expected plan benefits minus contributions). If adverse economic, demographic, or asset return shocks occur so as to push assets below liabilities, adjustments will be needed with their corresponding risks. The CPPIB seeks to reduce such adjustment risk through a Stochastic Liability Model which models CPP liability dynamics and risks, and provides input to the CPPIB's Asset-Liability Model. This model involves key demographic, economic (such as long-run productivity growth and rate of inflation) and fund return assumptions (from the Office of the Chief Actuary), and provides mean projections of asset-expenditure ratios and liability-expenditure ratios along with statistical confidence bands. Not surprisingly, the stochastic modeling shows that adjustment risk is sensitive to the above underlying assumptions. Indeed, higher expected returns and rate of productivity growth substantially reduce the level of adjustment risk in their results.

The final set of papers in this volume examine mandatory retirement and changing retirement prospects of several segments of the labour market. Rafael Gomez and Morley Gunderson provide a stimulating discussion of the "myths and realities" that surround the debate on retaining or abolishing mandatory retirement. A number of the myths they discuss include: mandatory retirement means having to retire from the labour force; mandatory retirement is an employer policy forced on employees; mandatory retirement has a disproportionate adverse effect on women and immigrants; and mandatory retirement constitutes age discrimination and fosters labour and skill shortages. Gomez and Gunderson do not favour legislatively abolishing mandatory retirement, but take a "pro-choice" position that it should be allowed in private contractual arrangements agreed to by employers and employees (or their union). The paper enumerates a number of reasons why both sides would want mandatory retirement to be part of a mutually agreed long-term employment arrangement.

Derek Hum and Wayne Simpson's contribution looks at the retirement prospects of immigrants and the pension gap between immigrants and non-immigrants in Canada. Using census data for 1981 to 2001, the authors estimate the difference in earnings profiles between immigrants and non-immigrants for four entry cohorts of immigrant men — those arriving in 1976–80, 1981–85, 1986–90, and 1991–95. They then use these "immigrant integration profiles" to calculate what they term the lifetime pension gap, or retirement gap, between each of the immigrant entry cohorts and comparable non-immigrant male workers. The pension gap is thus the difference between the discounted present value of lifetime Canadian earnings for observationally similar Canadian-born and foreign-born workers. Assuming equal savings rates between the two groups, Hum and Simpson find that a large pension gap indeed exists and the pension gap estimates are larger — on the order of 1.5 to 1.7 times larger — for more recent immigrant entry cohorts than for earlier ones.

Hum and Simpson also use the 2002 Survey of Labour and Income Dynamics (SLID) to provide additional evidence on the difference by age between immigrant and non-immigrant men in Registered Pension Plan (RPP) contributions for workers and private pension plan income receipts for retirees. Their analysis yields two findings. First, the mean annual pension contributions of immigrants are substantially lower than those of non-immigrants. Second, retired non-immigrants receive on average higher private pension income per year than immigrant retirees. They argue that this private pension income gap is likely to increase over time and will thus pose a challenge for the design and funding of Canada's public pension and income support programs.

Casey Warman and Christopher Worswick use Statistics Canada administrative data to provide evidence on how mandatory retirement has affected the salaries of university professors in Canada. Their analysis identifies the effects of mandatory retirement on the age-earnings profiles of university professors primarily from interprovincial variation in legislation governing mandatory retirement and secondarily from inter-temporal variation in the mandatory retirement status of individual institutions. The comparison of age-earnings profiles of professors at universities with and without mandatory retirement produces somewhat different findings for female and male faculty. For female faculty, the two profiles nearly coincide. For male faculty, the two age-earnings profiles are almost identical from ages 30 to 50 years, but then diverge substantially over the age range 50 to 65 years. In particular, after age 50, the profile of male professors at universities without mandatory retirement is below that at universities with mandatory retirement.

References

Ambachtsheer, K. 2007. *Pension Revolution: A Solution to the Pensions Crisis.* Hoboken, NJ: John Wiley and Sons.

_____. 2008. "The Canada Supplementary Pension Plan (CSPP): Towards an Adequate, Affordable Pension for *All* Canadians". Commentary No. 265. Toronto: C.D. Howe Institute.

Banting, K.G. and R.W. Boadway, eds. 1997. *Reform of Retirement Income Policy.* Kingston: School of Policy Studies, Queen's University.

Béland, D. 2009. "The Threat to Retirement Security", *Policy Options.* Montreal: Institute for Research on Public Policy, February.

Campbell, C. 2009. "Retiring into the Unknown", Part V of "The New Middle Class Reality", *Maclean's*, April 6.

Clark, R.L., R.V. Burkhauser, M. Moon, J.F. Quinn, and T.M. Smeeding. 2004. *The Economics of an Aging Society.* Oxford: Blackwell Publishing.

Contenta, S. 2009. "'Freedom 55' Crashes into Reality Check", Part 1 of "The Pension Crisis", *Toronto Star*, March 15.

Cooper, S. 2008. *The New Retirement.* Toronto: Penguin Group (Canada).

Crossley, T.F. and B.G. Spencer, eds. 2008. "Private Pensions and Income Security in Old Age: An Uncertain Future", special supplement of *Canadian Public Policy* 34. November.

Diamond, P. and H. Vartiainen, eds. 2007. *Behavioral Economics and Its Applications.* Princeton: Princeton University Press.

The Economist. 2009. "The End of Retirement: Ageing in the Rich World", June 27.

Expert Commission on Pensions. 2007. "Reviewing Ontario's Pension System: What are the Issues?" Discussion paper available at: www.pensionreview.on.ca (February).

_____. 2008. *Report of the Expert Commission on Pensions.* Toronto: Queen's Park.

Expert Panel on Older Workers. 2008. *Supporting and Engaging Older Workers in the New Economy*. Ottawa: Human Resources and Social Development Canada.

The Globe and Mail. 2009. "Failure to Save — Pensions for the Pensionless", lead editorial, March 21.

Gruber, J. and D.A. Wise, eds. 2007. *Social Security Programs and Retirement Around the World: Fiscal Implications of Reform*. Chicago: University of Chicago Press and the National Bureau of Economic Research.

Gustman, A.L. and T. Steinmeier. 2008. "How Changes in Social Security Affect Recent Retirement Trends", Working Paper No. 14105. Cambridge, MA: National Bureau of Economic Research.

Lumsdaine, R.L. and O.S. Mitchell. 1999. "New Developments in the Economic Analysis of Retirement", in O.S. Ashenfelter and D. Card (eds.), *Handbook of Labor Economics* 3C. Amsterdam: Elsevier Publishing and North-Holland Publishing.

Madrian, B., O.S. Mitchell, and B.J. Soldo, eds. 2007. *Redefining Retirement: How Will Boomers Fare?* Oxford: Oxford University Press.

Mazurkewich, K. 2008. "Faces of Canada's Pension Crisis — Inequities Divide Canadians into 'Haves' and 'Have Nots'", *National Post*, November 29.

Middlemiss, J. 2008. "Pension Crisis Looms: From Surplus to Deficits", *National Post*, December 1.

Milligan, K. and T. Schirle. 2008. "Improving the Labour Market Incentives of Canada's Public Pensions", *Canadian Public Policy* 34(3), 281–304.

Munnell, A.H. and S.A. Sass. 2008. *Working Longer: The Solution to the Retirement Problem*. Washington, DC: Brookings Institution Press.

Robson, W.B.P. 2009. "Boomer Bulge: Dealing with the Stress of Demographic Change on Government Budgets in Canada", e-brief (January 13). Toronto: C.D. Howe Institute.

Schirle, T. 2008. "Why Have the Labor Force Participation Rates of Older Men Increased since the Mid-1990s?" *Journal of Labor Economics* 26(4), 549–594.

Toronto Star. 2009. "Pension Crisis Requires Debate", lead editorial, April 25.

Wise, D.A., ed. 2004. *Perspectives on the Economics of Aging*. Chicago: University of Chicago Press and the National Bureau of Economic Research.

The World Bank. 2002. *Averting the Old Age Crisis*. Washington, DC: The World Bank.

Chapter I

Policy Concerns

The US Fiscal Gap and its Troubling Implications

Laurence J. Kotlikoff

It is a pleasure to be here and I thank the organizers for inviting me. I am going to discuss worldwide demographic change and fiscal insolvency in the United States and other developed countries. But, not to worry. These other countries do not include Canada, which, as far as I can tell, is in excellent long-term fiscal shape.

The United States, Spain, Japan, Norway, and Germany are some of the countries in deepest trouble. The trouble stems from three sources: growth in government spending on retirement and health-care benefits, growth in government purchases of goods and services and changes in demographics.

Demographic change is already here. In Japan, 18% of the population is now 65 and older. America's oldest baby boomer is now eligible for social security. The European and Japanese workforces are already shrinking, and Japan's population growth rate is negative. Europe's population growth rate will turn negative in just four years.

As Table 1 indicates, the United States is now and will remain significantly younger than Japan and Germany. In time, even China, which is now much younger than is the United States, will be older than the United States. Although the United States will be the young kid on the block, even it will look very old. The entire country will be older than current-day Florida. And there will be not just large numbers of oldsters.

Table 1: Elderly Population Shares
(in percent)

Country	2005	2030	2050	2070
Germany	17.1	26.3	30.6	31.3
Japan	18.0	29.9	36.8	37.7
United States	12.4	19.1	21.3	21.6
Canada	13.0	23.6	26.7	27.1
China	7.6	16.3	23.6	n/a

There will be lots of old oldsters — people that are 85 and older. Indeed, in 2050, there will be enough Americans 85 and older to fill up all of New York, Los Angeles, and Chicago. And there will be enough centenarians to fill up all of Washington, DC!

Canada's elderly population share will be similar to that of the United States for the next three decades, but then Canada gets older than the United States. By mid-century, Canada's oldsters will represent 26.7% of the population compared with 21.3% in the United States.

Fertility is the major force determining long-run aging. As Figure 1 shows, postwar fertility changes have been extraordinary. In 1950, the fertility rate in China was 6.22%; now it is about 1.7%. In the United States, it was 3.45%; now it is about 2.11%. And then there are amazing fertility rates in Europe and Russia. Italy's rate is currently 1.2%. In Japan, it is 1.3%. In Russia, it is 1.1%. These incredibly low fertility rates presage, of course, major declines in population.

Longevity increases are also at play and will continue to have an important role in the aging process. Figure 2 shows dramatic change — past and projected — in life expectancy in the United States, China, Germany, and Japan.

Japanese newborns born in 2050 will live, on average, to age 88. In 2050, the median age in Japan will be 52. In 1950, the median age was 22.

Laurence J. Kotlikoff

Figure 1: Fertility Rates

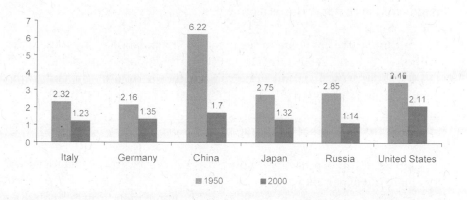

Figure 2: Life Expectancy at Birth

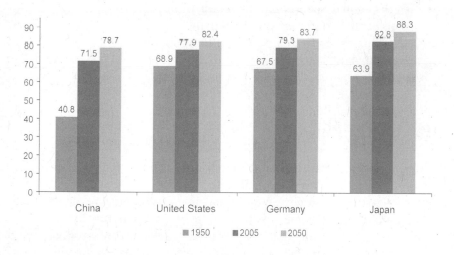

Past and projected fertility and longevity changes have important implications for total population sizes. As Figure 3 shows, the United States' population will expand by about 100 million people through the middle of the century. This is a projected 33% increase compared with the current total.

In Europe, we are going to see a major depopulation — by roughly 80 million — over the same time period. Russia's and Japan's population will fall by about 20%. If fertility rates do not turn around by the end of the century, Russia's and Japan's populations will be roughly half of what they are today.

Here are some other demographic shockers that may be of interest.

- Japanese life expectancy's now 86 — 27 years greater than Russian male life expectancy.
- Minorities now account for 90% of US population growth, including immigration.
- By 2060, US minorities will represent the majority; that is, the majority of the US population will be black and Hispanic.
- By 2050, China will likely constitute two-thirds of the developed world. At that point, the United States will be to China as Canada is to the United States.
- France could become a Muslim country by 2050.
- In the United States, half of 65-year-old couples will have at least one member live to 92; one-quarter will have at least one member live to 97.
- US females in top colleges now outnumber males 1.3 to 1.
- Roughly half of today's US children will live with one parent prior to age 18.

Paying the Piper

These projected demographic changes are fascinating. But what are their fiscal implications? Well, consider the United States, which now spends over $30,000 per old person on Social Security, Medicare and Medicaid. Medicare is the old-age health insurance program run by the federal government. Medicaid is the government's health-care program for the poor; including poor elderly in nursing homes. Thanks to the high costs of nursing homes, about 70% of total Medicaid expenditures is spent on the elderly.

Figure 3: Populating and Depopulating

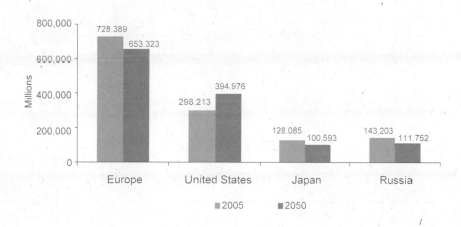

Now, $30,000 seems like a lot of money. It is. It is about 80% of US per capita gross domestic product (GDP). It is higher than the GDP per capita in about 200 of the world's 231 countries. But by 2030, when the boomers are fully retired, the average benefit level per oldster will not be $30,000; it will be at least $50,000 (measured in today's dollars) and represent more than 100% of 2030 per capita US GDP. The remarkably high levels of oldster benefits, current and projected, are due, in the main, to the growth in the health-care component of total Social Security, Medicare, and Medicaid outlays.

Table 2 details real government health-care benefit-level growth in the United States, Japan, Canada, and Germany between 1970 and 2002. In the case of the United States, the real growth rate of the benefit level (measured as Medicare and Medicaid expenditures per person at a given age) averaged 4.61% per year. In Germany, real benefit-level growth averaged 3.3%; in Japan it averaged 3.6%. In the United States, the 1970–2002 health-care benefit level growth rate exceeded the corresponding growth rate of per capita GDP by a factor of 2.3.

The rate of growth of health-care benefit levels in the United States and other countries is clearly unsustainable. But when will it end?

Table 2: Growth in Government Health-Care Benefit Levels, 1970–2002

Country	Annual Growth in Expenditure Per Potential Recipient (%)	Annual Growth in Expenditure Per Capita (%)	Annual Growth in GDP Per Capita (%)	Ratio of Column 1 to Column 3
Germany	3.30	3.62	1.54	2.1
Canada	2.32	3.08	2.04	1.1
Japan	3.57	4.85	2.44	1.5
United States	4.61	5.10	2.01	2.3

The late, great economist Herb Stein was famous for saying, "Things that can't go on will stop." But what Stein left out was that things that cannot go on can stop too late.

In the case of the United States, recent fiscal gap accounting by economists Jagadeesh Gokhale and Kent Smetters suggests that upwards of $70 trillion separates projected total (health-care plus all other) future federal spending from projected future federal receipts when measured in present value. To get a sense of what $70 trillion really means note that closing this gap would require an immediate and permanent doubling of US payroll taxes, which now represent 15.3% of covered wages.

How can the US fiscal gap be so big? Well, when you are projecting paying $50,000, on average, to upwards of 77 million baby boomers, you are talking about spending close to $4 trillion a year in today's dollars. Yes, the US economy will be larger when these payments are made to the boomers, but $4 trillion a year is still a huge expenditure to be making each and every year.

What is particularly troubling is that the $70 trillion fiscal gap calculation was made under quite optimistic assumptions. The calculation assumes the health-care benefit growth rate will be about 3.1% rather than the 4.6% rate recorded between 1970 and 2002. Unfortunately, there is no reason to expect a decline in the growth rate of the combined Medicare and

Medicaid benefit level. Indeed, in the last seven years this benefit-level growth rate has averaged about 5.6% in real terms, not 3.1%!

Macroeconomic Fallout

Any reasonable observer considering the size of the US fiscal gap must conclude that the United States is, quite literally, facing bankruptcy. Bankruptcy is a strong term. In a business context bankruptcy means future earnings cannot cover future costs as well as current unpaid bills. It also means defaulting on creditors. In a government context bankruptcy means future receipts that do not cover future expenditures. It also means defaulting on creditors — all those expecting to receive government health-care, pension, welfare, and other benefits as well as all those expecting to be employed by the government. Government bankruptcy also means jacking up tax rates and printing money to "pay" for what the government spends.

No doubt there are some people who believe that the United States is immune from fiscal meltdown and high inflation, if not hyperinflation. They should think again. Too many countries, big and small, rich and poor, have demonstrated that, sooner or later, fiscal profligacy comes at a very heavy price.

There are increasing signs that Uncle Sam is driving the US economy over the cliff and that the rest of the world is taking notice. The US national saving rate is now running below 3%. In 1960 it was close to 13%. Our incredibly low saving rate has lead to an incredibly high current account deficit, which has led to an incredibly low value of the dollar.

Why is the US saving rate so low? The answer is clear. The counterpart of saving too little is consuming too much. As a share of national income, the federal government is consuming at roughly twice the rate it did a decade ago. But the main explanation for the decline in US saving is not Uncle Sam's spending. It is the spending, the consumption, of households. And among households the group whose consumption has been rising most rapidly is the elderly. Since 1960, average consumption per oldster has roughly doubled relative to average consumption per youngster.

Who is paying for this growth in the consumption of oldsters? The answer, in large part, is Uncle Sam. Take Medicare and Medicaid benefits, the vast majority of which go to the elderly. Every year that Uncle Sam allows these benefits to grow much more rapidly than the economy — and we are talking about virtually each of the past 60 years — the government directly expands the consumption of the elderly and, thereby, national saving. Uncle Sam has also been cutting taxes on the elderly, which has permitted them to consume a lot more.

So Uncle Sam's policy of taking ever larger resources from young savers and handing them to old spenders, increasingly in the form of in-kind medical goods and services, is showing up in the level of consumption of the elderly, in the rate of aggregate US consumption, in the US national saving, in our current account deficit and in the value of the dollar.

Fiscal Gaps in Other Countries

Unfortunately, the recent fiscal gap analyses are not available for other countries to compare with the gap in the United States. But my sense is that the United States is not alone with respect to long-term fiscal insolvency. I suggest that Spain, Japan, Norway, and Germany are also in very bad long-term shape.

But each of these countries has a health-care system directly controlled by its government, meaning that each of these countries is in a much better position to stop, on a dime if need be, excessive health-care spending.

For its part, Canada has a state pension system that appears to be in long-run actuarial balance and one of the lowest real benefit level growth rates in the Organisation for Economic Co-operation and Development (OECD). As Table 2 shows, real government health-care benefit levels are growing in Canada at essentially the same rate as per capita GDP. On the other hand, because of the demographics, total expenditures per capita on health care in Canada have grown more rapidly than has per capita GDP. So Canada also has a health-care spending problem, but it is largely driven by demographics and it is a problem, not a crisis.

The United States Health-Care Crisis

Much of the recent growth in US government health-care benefit levels has to do with the number of people who are collecting benefits at a given age. The benefit level I have been referencing is not benefits per Medicare and Medicaid recipient at a given age, but benefits per person at a given age.

Laurence J. Kotlikoff

Growth in government health-care benefits per person at a given age reflects both the growth in benefits per recipient at that age and the growth in the age-specific participation rate.

There has been an enormous increase in age-specific Medicaid participation rates since 2000. Indeed, overall Medicaid participation has increased by over one-third since President Bush took office. Part of this expansion of Medicaid reflects the recent enrollment of millions of otherwise uninsured children via the SCHIP program. And part reflects the fact that more and more US workers are becoming uninsured, becoming sick, running out of money and going onto Medicaid.

The share of the US workers who are covered under employer health insurance plans has declined from 66% in 2000 to 59% today. Some of this simply reflects employers terminating their health-care plans. But part reflects an increasing practice by employers of shifting the costs of paying health-care premiums onto their employees. Many of these employees are, as a consequence, opting out of their employer's plans.

As I describe in my new book, *The Healthcare Fix*, we have a terrible crisis with respect to health care in the United States. We have companies going broke trying to handle their health-care bills. We have the US government going broke trying to handle its commitments. And then we have 47 million people who are uninsured, living in constant fear that a gall bladder attack or some other malady will put them under financially.

The health-care crisis is not simply a problem on its own. It is a problem that greatly compounds the US fiscal crisis. We now have most of the presidential candidates promising to provide major health-care insurance subsidies to millions of uninsured Americans while simultaneously expanding Medicaid and also leaving Medicare unreformed.

Do not get me wrong. The United States desperately needs universal health insurance. But we need to implement it in a way that does not put the final nail in the US fiscal coffin.

What, Me Worry?

With a $70 trillion fiscal gap, participation and health-care benefit levels growing dramatically and the boomers about to retire, you might think someone in Washington would be starting to watch the shop. But nobody's watching the shop. Since 2000, the Bush administration has cut taxes three times and is now advocating another cut. Meanwhile it has doubled defence spending as a share of GDP and introduced Medicare Part D — the new government prescription drug benefit provided to the elderly at a present value cost of at least $10 trillion.

Fixing Things

Let me close by telling you what I would do were I president for the day. Step one, I would eliminate the US federal personal income tax, the corporate income tax and the payroll tax and replace them with the fairtax — a single federal retail sales tax plus a rebate. The rebate would be paid to each household, including Bill Gates', regardless of its income. The rebate would be set high enough to insulate the poor from paying any taxes on net.

The rebate makes the fairtax quite progressive. Having a single tax rate makes the fiscal system highly transparent. It also makes clear that spending more money on anyone or anything means raising taxes on everyone and everything (every consumption good and service). With the fairtax and a zero fiscal gap (present-value balanced budget) rule, the United States could hope to bring its long-run spending plans in line with its long-run revenue-generating capacity.

Step two, I would eliminate Medicare, Medicaid and the employer-based health-care system and give everyone a voucher to buy health insurance for the year. In October of each year, each American would receive a voucher with its size depending on the person's objective health conditions. If Mr. Jones has cancer, he'd get a big voucher. If he was perfectly healthy, he'd get a small voucher. Each person would be individually risk-adjusted to determine the size of the voucher. And each person would spend the voucher on a health plan, which would cover him/her for the year.

Each insurance company would make a small profit on the vouchers. We would still have private provision, private competition by the hospitals and the doctors, but we would also have socialized finance of health insurance. This is not universal health care per se; it is universal health insurance. And the health care is coming from the private sector.

Now, you might say, "Boy that sounds expensive." In fact, the United States is already spending about 90% of what this voucher plan would cost. So yes, the proposal would cost more to implement in the short term. But in spending more in the short run, we would be implementing a health-care

Laurence J. Kotlikoff

spending structure that would permit the government to limit its annual health-care spending (its annual voucher budget) to a fixed share of GDP. Within a given year, insurers, not the government, would be on the hook to pay, at the margin, all health-care bills.

During my final few hours as president, I would order a withdrawal from Iraq; and a complete overhaul of the social security system in the United States. In particular, I would shut down the existing social security system by promising to pay current workers in retirement only the benefits they have already accrued.

Next I would require all workers to contribute 8% of their salary to what I call the personal security system. Half of a worker's contribution would go to his or her account and half to the spouse's or legal partner's. The government could make matching contributions on behalf of the poor. All account balances would be invested in a global market-weighted index fund of securities routinely traded in the world financial market. At retirement, the government would guarantee that the worker's account balance was at least as large as the sum of her/his past contributions adjusted for inflation. The government would also gradually transform the worker's account balance into an inflation-indexed annuity.

Note that the personal security system is progressive, transparent, protects dependent spouses/partners, limits downside market risk and features real annuitization. Moreover, it entails no participation by Wall Street. All investment and annuitization is done by a single government computer.

Do Cry for Me, Argentina

Unfortunately, I will not be made president for a day. And it is unlikely that the bold reforms I have outlined will carry the day in the political arena. Consequently, I am extremely pessimistic about the long-term prospects of the United States. To me the United States looks like it's about to spend the twenty-first century repeating the mistakes Argentina made in the twentieth, with all the repercussions for Canada and the rest of the world that this will entail.

Pensions Are a Risky Business: Issues in Pension Regulation

David Dodge

The topic of this paper is particularly relevant to me as I approach my own retirement from the Bank of Canada, but it is also extremely important for Canada as a whole as we deal with the impact of demographic changes on our workforce. This volume contains a wide range of interesting topics pertaining to retirement issues. I intend to pose some challenges with respect to the question of ensuring the viability of private pension plans.

We already have a very solid public pension platform to build on, through the Canada Pension Plan (CPP), Quebec Pension Plan (QPP), as well as the Old-Age Security and Guaranteed Income Supplement (OAS/GIS). There are also the tax-sheltered RRSP structures to help people save for their retirement. But for many individuals, neither their public pensions nor their personal savings will adequately replace a significant portion of their employment income. Rather, experience has shown that an employer-based system of contractual savings through a pension plan is really the most effective and important means to ensure an adequate retirement income. Here I would like to consider just how we can get the right incentive structures in place to encourage the private sector to offer well-constructed, voluntary pension plans.

A few of the questions that I will discuss include: What are some of the incentives that drive the creation of an efficient and effective system of private, voluntary pension plans? What are the key risks that face parties to such pension plans, and how can we best manage these risks so they can be tolerated by all? And finally, I will discuss the principle of pooling and how a greater and more effective application of this principle could make risk more manageable in private pension plans.

Finding the Right Incentives to Facilitate an Effective Pension Plan

It is sometimes said in economics that good incentives lead to good outcomes, and this has often been the case with pension plans. Let's consider just a few good incentives, first from the individual's perspective. Protecting and enhancing one's retirement income is certainly a strong incentive to join a pension plan. And a properly structured plan creates the proper incentives to ensure individual choice in terms of when to retire. From the employer's perspective, there have been two longstanding incentives for sponsoring a pension plan. First, a plan can serve as a means to recruit and retain good workers; second, it can ensure that older staff can afford to retire rather than remain at work well past the point of their greatest productivity. A pension plan also removes the need for a firm to make *ex gratia* payments to former employees. Finally, society has an incentive to support a sound system of private, voluntary pension plans. We want to know that our older members have an adequate income when their working days are over. In part, this is because we know that if incomes are not sufficient for the retired, the pressures on government for much greater spending could become significant.

So these are some of the incentives that influence how people save for retirement. It is useful to think of pension plans, which facilitate these savings, as essentially agreements as to who bears the risks — such as market and longevity risk — that are associated with saving for retirement. Given that different people find themselves in different circumstances, it is important that their pension plans can suit their particular needs. The best way to deal with this is through sponsored, private pension plans that are voluntary, rather than mandatory. I realize that this latter point is a contentious issue and that many people I respect would argue for mandatory pension plans. I believe that voluntary plans offer greater choice, but it certainly is an issue for further debate.

Risky Business

It seems clear that understanding the risks involved in a pension plan and getting the incentives right so that these risks can be effectively managed, are really the key points at the heart of the pension debate. I will devote several comments now to this crucial topic, reviewing what risks confront individuals, plan sponsors, and society as a whole; and what incentives can be put in place to mitigate these risks. This is an extremely important issue, because understanding and managing risk is absolutely crucial to protecting the present and future stability of any pension plan.

Pension plans, by their very nature, exist because they are better able to manage risk at a lower cost than an individual can with his or her own savings. For a person who is planning his retirement, there is the tendency to be overly cautious. This inclination would likely lead him to invest too much in low-risk securities relative to the portfolio that would maximize his expected pension while maintaining risk within tolerable bounds. Or, he would try to manage his risk by finding a financial advisor or putting savings into managed, diversified retail investment vehicles such as mutual funds. However, that latter choice can be costly, since an individual outside a pension plan would have to purchase investment advice and ongoing funds management at retail, not wholesale prices. In contrast, the individual's risk could be more efficiently and effectively managed if he were part of a larger pension group, where risks and transaction costs are spread more widely and thus, reduced for each individual.

Without being part of a larger pension group, an individual can face other types of market risk; for example, weak market conditions at the time of retirement could make the value of his assets abnormally low. Or, unusually low interest rates at the time of retirement could make an annuity unusually expensive. In either case, the person acting alone could need to spend a much greater amount to purchase a guaranteed stream of income, compared with a period when market conditions were more favourable.

So there are great advantages for an individual to join an employer-based pension plan. In such a plan, a number of risks are transferred — partially, or in large part — from the individual to the employer. One of the great advantages of a private pension plan, whether a defined-benefit (DB) or a defined-contribution (DC) plan, is that pooling and governance structures allow for the efficient management of funds at wholesale costs. And employer-based plans have another benefit in that members are able to purchase an annuity at group rates that are applicable to the larger pool of members in the plan.

But, of course, not all the risks applicable to the individual are avoided. Defined-contribution plans only partially mitigate risks of adverse market conditions at the time of retirement; risks that I previously mentioned. Hence, there is an advantage to individuals of belonging to a defined-benefit plan. Of course, defined-contribution plans are not risk-free for employers, either. These plans do shift some risk from the individual to the sponsor, creating potential fiduciary and legal risks for that sponsor.

In contrast, an appropriately structured defined-benefit plan, in theory, can provide greater benefits for members, sponsors and, I should mention, society in general. These plans, if made to work effectively, can mitigate various risks. Risks can be spread across plan members — past, present, and future — and this largely ensures that the retirement income of an individual member does not depend on market conditions at the time of his or her retirement. With a defined-benefit pension plan, professional managers have both the ability and the incentive to invest in more risky or longer-duration assets than the DC plan manager would consider. This helps to reduce the risk that these pools of contributions could be invested in a less-than-optimal way, which could eventually reduce the supply of long-term risk capital for the economy. Further, DB pension managers are more likely to invest in alternative asset classes and to engage in arbitrage between markets. These activities can make financial markets more complete, and thus enhance their efficiency. But to achieve these benefits, funding regulations must balance the need to ensure adequate funding by the sponsor, with the sponsor's ability to recoup whatever overfunding may occur.

To be sure, defined-benefit plans do mean greater risk for the sponsor. If a sponsor opts for a DB plan, he must ensure that regardless of market conditions, the company pension plan is adequately funded to pay out agreed-upon benefits. Further, as the workforce ages, the liability associated with a defined-benefit plan can dwarf the sponsors' net worth. And finally, the defined-benefit plan sponsor must make up actuarial deficits in the plan without being assured that he will have equal access to any actuarial surpluses in the future. To avoid these risks, a number of DB plan sponsors have been closing their plans and opting instead to open a defined-contribution plan — or at least considering such action.

However, no matter how good the regulatory framework, there is one risk that no pension plan can eliminate; and that is group-longevity risk. But this risk can be mitigated in a number of ways. For example, contribution rates can be adjusted periodically to reflect changes in average life expectancy. Or, the level of benefits can be adjusted periodically, or the date at which a person becomes eligible to collect a pension can be linked to changes in the life expectancy tables. But legal and contractual obstacles stand in the way of mitigating this longevity risk. It will not be easy to overcome these obstacles, but it is absolutely necessary to do so. Sponsors and plan members both need to have the incentives to deal with group-longevity risk properly.

Those are just a few of the key risks facing pension plan members and sponsors. There would also be risks to society from a lack of private pension plans and in particular, defined-benefit pension plans. For example, younger workers may not be able to generate adequate private savings or even build up enough in a system of defined-contribution plans to fund a sufficient retirement income. That would mean that post-retirement, pressures would be heightened on governments to spend ever greater amounts on income-support programs. Further, there would also be risks to efficient market functioning and long-term risk capital in the economy if there were not enough well-managed, private pension funds able to take a longer view with their investments.

I have discussed a great deal on risk and risk management, and how crucial this is in the planning of pension arrangements. On previous occasions I have argued that an appropriately structured defined-benefit plan can deliver benefits to pension plan members, sponsors and society. But I would like to leave an important question with you: How do we preserve the many advantages of a defined-benefit pension plan but make it possible to distribute risk more appropriately and enhance the viability of these plans?

Why is Pooling so Important? (or Everyone into the Pool)

I would like to pose two further questions. How can we extend the advantages of an appropriately structured defined-benefit plan to small businesses and their employees and to those who do not otherwise have access to a private pension plan? How can we help to make plans more portable, so they do not unduly constrain our flexible labour market?

As I mentioned earlier, pooling is a fundamental risk-management strategy of pension planning, and so creating powerful incentives to encouraging pooling makes a great deal of sense. Taking that logic a step further, we can easily imagine the benefit of a strong incentive to create broader pools comprised of a collection of smaller pension plans and individuals. In the larger pool, the risks and expenses of offering a pension are mitigated by spreading these across a wider collection of employers and plan members.

I will now cite just a few examples of pooling that might be instructive for this discussion and perhaps stimulate further debate on this issue. The Ontario Teachers Pension Plan — a defined-benefit plan — has successfully brought together employees performing the same type of job, but in many different school boards. In the United States, the TIAA-CREF retirement system — a defined-contribution plan — demonstrates the breadth of a membership pool that could be possible. Now, I am certainly not advocating any particular form of pool or suggesting how one might best be structured. Rather, I want to provoke discussion about how pools could be broadened to meet the needs of Canadians.

There are many reasons for workers and plan sponsors to support a properly structured and broader pension pool. It could increase portability and thus remove what has been a disincentive for some to join pension plans. This might also be an incentive for attracting younger workers to a plan. The larger pool could reduce expenses by allowing overhead costs to be spread more widely. The larger investment pool and greater economies of scale could yield greater returns. Further, it could reduce the risk from insolvency of any single employer.

For society, the benefits are similar: larger, more stable pooled pension plans could reduce the risk of retirees facing inadequate pensions. Larger pools of pension funds should also be able to better accept the risk of investing in alternative assets and in infrastructure. This is certainly an area that will require greater amounts of capital investment in future. And indeed, pension and endowment funds are now allocating an increasing share of their portfolio assets to infrastructure investments, in an attempt to ensure reasonable rates of return over a very long time horizon, and to provide a better match to their liabilities.

But there are certainly a great many factors to consider with a broader pension pool; factors that must be dealt with correctly if the wider pool is to be effective. Let me raise just a few examples. There would have to be incentives to ensure that employers, once in a larger pool, would remain current with their contributions. Incentives to ensure good governance and continuing relevance of benefit plans would be necessary. Incentives could also be needed to ensure the pool could expand and diversify.

Finding an appropriate set of incentives for these types of pension plans is extraordinarily difficult. But just because we have not been very successful in the past does not mean that we should not try in the future. And as the CFIB has noted, smaller employers in particular would benefit from a broader pool in which they could participate for the benefit of their own employees. And perhaps it is worthwhile considering the CFIB's suggestion that a voluntary component be added to the CPP, with a segregated fund administered by the CPP Investment Board.

Conclusion

Let me conclude. Regulation can help foster the development of broader, more effective pension pools by reinforcing the right incentives to make private, voluntary plans work, and to ensure choice. I have talked about some of the risks that these pension plans face and have suggested that a greater use of pooling could help to put these plans on a more sustainable footing. This could be particularly valuable in supporting defined-benefit pension plans, which have been under a great deal of pressure in recent years. However, success will hinge on strengthening the legal, regulatory, accounting, actuarial, and economic frameworks that determine how pension plans operate. Reviews are underway, both at the provincial and the federal levels. If collectively we can get it right, these changes would give sponsors the appropriate degree of flexibility needed to manage risk effectively.

I do not have a legislative blueprint to develop the kinds of regulatory changes needed to better balance risk and promote a greater use of pooling. My job here is not to provide prescriptions but rather to challenge you to deal with these issues, during this conference and in the months and years ahead. If you are successful, then Canadians will have a better-managed pension system that is good for members, good for employers, good for the economy and good for society.

Summary of Discussion

David Gray asked of Professor Kotlikoff where he thought the United States' economy was as far as the Laffer Curve is concerned. **Laurence Kotlikoff** indicated that he thought the United States was to the left of the peak so that one could raise taxes and get more revenue as a result, but also generate a lot of distortion at the margin. When you look at all of the different transfer programs and taxes, including the corporate taxes and the states' and federal systems and figure out what the effective tax rates are on working and saving, you see that marginal rates are very high. Almost every American is in a 40% marginal tax bracket, effectively. Of course, it's very non-linear, and in some parts, you have an infinite tax bracket, in effect, when you lose your Medicaid, for example, by earning a little extra money. So people are in very high marginal tax brackets to begin with. Raising taxes will put them in an even higher bracket, so you'll get more revenue, but there's going to be a lot more excess burden. So this is why he feels we need a more efficient tax structure. He also feels the United States needs a more equitable tax structure because we've been shifting the burden from old people onto young people by cutting capital gains tax rates and dividend tax rates. And it's the older people who are primarily paying those taxes.

Robert Clark remarked that in the United States, a great deal of the movement away from defined-benefit plans has come about because of government regulation, and the idea that government regulation might fix that is a little bit strange to him. The fundamental issue about DB plans is, in today's world, why would companies want to bear the particular risks that go with them? Why would a company want to bear the cohort longevity risk? Why would a company want to have a great deal of its future wrapped up in managing a big fund as opposed to doing the business that they're actually in? DB plans are a dying business. No small businesses are operating DB plans now and he doesn't see any fix that would change this. If you go through the fixes that Dodge is suggesting, you change the nature of the plan to individuals. If you say to the individual worker in a defined-benefit plan, "We're not going to tell you the benefit that you get until you get ready to retire and we know what your cohort's going to do", he thinks the worker's interest in such a plan will be a lot less too.

David Dodge responded that Clark was absolutely right. With successive waves of regulation since the 1950s in Canada, we have tipped the balance of risks for the employer very decidedly. And every time a problem arises, we tip the balance further in the direction of the employees so that the expected contribution for an employer goes up. But we can fix that. It's not by new regulation; it's by getting the thing balanced appropriately. It's not easy politically to do so, but this is not impossible to deal with. The first issue, is how you balance these risks much more appropriately. Longevity risk you cannot deal with without some degree of sharing of that risk between the employee, the employer and the state. It's a risk that cannot be managed away. That risk is ever-present. But it does not seem impossible here to devise systems that individuals will think are fair. The retirement age we've left fixed at age 65, while the expected longevity at age 65 has increased. There is no harm in saying to people when they're 20, as long as you're going to honour the promise, that indeed the retirement age when you get out there into your sixties is going to be what the life tables tell us since the expected life has changed. And that would allow that number to automatically march up without governments interfering along the way. That's one way to approach it. As long as the formula by which those things are going to be done is known in advance, he doesn't see that as a particular problem. Devising the formula is a real challenge, but he doesn't see that as an unsurmountable problem.

Finally, Clark raised the issue that risk pooling is critical. And it's been proven very difficult in the private sector in Canada to develop industry pools or geographic pools, more broadly, that would allow smaller employers to join — indeed, allow employers to join in simply by paying the current service costs appropriately year by year. Dodge acknowledged that is a very tricky challenge, but again he thought that it's one that we really do have to look at and think about.

Laurence Kotlikoff added that in the United States, as Robert Clark indicated, the whole DB thing is over. It looks like many companies are freezing their plans. So it looks like what we're going to be left with is 401K plans and without any requirement that people annuitize. And then if they try to annuitize, a host of adverse-selection issues are going to arise. One proposal could be for the government to require that everybody annuitize their pension accounts in an inflation-indexed annuity when they hit retirement, and no annuity insurer could turn anybody down. There would be no ability to rate somebody as a bad risk and give them a much higher premium. That, of course, involves an implicit redistribution, but he thinks it's something that's needed to get around the adverse-selection problem and get everybody covered. Another thing the government could require is that the annuities be geared to decline if the cohort that's being insured lives longer than expected. The cohort risk — the longevity risk of the cohort — which is an aggregate risk, can't necessarily be pooled that well and would thus be put on the annuitants. Individuals would realize that if they lived to 90 and everybody else in their cohort lived to 90, they're going to get a smaller annuity. That could all be done, but it has to be done by government regulation. The private markets aren't going to be able to deal with this.

A participant raised the case of OMERS which is a jointly governed, multi-employer pension plan in Ontario. It has had a lot of success in delivering defined benefit pensions to local government workers in Ontario. Recently, it has been challenged to see whether this template could apply in the private sector. David Dodge in past speeches has indeed suggested that this is a model that might work for smaller employers in diverse sectors so that they can deliver defined benefit pension plans. One of the primary challenges that has been identified by OMERS is that of governance. How would these plans be structured and effectively governed so that all the interested stakeholders are represented?

David Dodge responded that the speaker is absolutely right; it's a *huge* challenge. We've never been very successful in being able to develop this more broadly outside of the public or quasi-public sector. Two big successful plans in Ontario, Teachers and OMERS, are real examples of successful pooling. But how do you structure the plan's governance? That has proven to be a huge problem in the past. But he thinks the speaker is asking exactly the right question. The experience that has been had at OMERS and Teachers, he thinks, really is valuable in terms of how initially you can bring together really rather disparate elements, if you think of the individual municipalities that were the sponsors of their plans prior to OMERS itself.

Chapter II

Background Issues and the Pension Environment

Retirement in Canada: Some Trends ... Some Issues

Cliff Halliwell

Introduction

In this paper I want to start with the question of how we define retirement, not quite as simple as one might first think, address recent trends in retirement in Canada, focus on some of the current work and retirement propensities in Canada and then close with some of the issues this could raise.

Defining Retirement

I want to start with defining retirement. That turns out to not be as easy as one would think. There are several possibilities. First is reaching 65 years. Second is ending a career job. Third is receiving pension income. Fourth is not working at all any more after a career job. I will look at these in turn.

---

* The views expressed in this paper are those of the author and do not necessarily reflect the opinions of Human Resources and Social Development Canada or of the federal government.

Let me start with turning 65. We actually know that it does not have that much to do with retirement, other than being the age of the remaining vestiges of mandatory retirement and a trigger point for some aspects of public policy. That being said, let's look at the trends. The share of the population that is 65 and over is increasing. A quarter century ago it was just over 8% of the population. In 2006 it was around 13%. This rising share is stacked onto a rising population as well, one up by nearly half over the same quarter-century period. Taking the rising share and the rising population together the population aged 65 and over has increased around 2.4 times in a quarter century. At this point I would like to remind you that this is due to greater longevity, not the "pig-in-the-python" effect of aging boomers. The oldest boomers, those born in 1946 will not hit age 65 until 2011.

And, onto another possible definition. Is retirement a case of no longer receiving labour income? Figure 1 shows average labour income per person for the 2004 population by single years of age stacked with average pension income. There is quite a degree of symmetry to the distribution of labour income per person. It starts off quite low and then rises sharply until the mid-30s and then stays relatively flat until the mid-50s. It then starts a steady slide and, by the 60s, is a third or a quarter of that at the peak. By the

Figure 1: Average Labour and Pension Income by Age, 2004

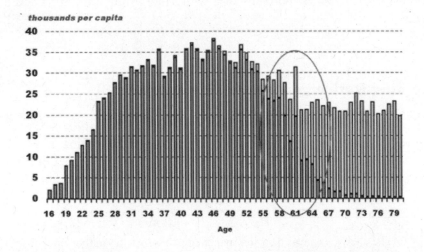

Source: Survey of Labour and Income Dynamics.

Cliff Halliwell

70s there is little labour income per person. Thus, what we observe is a very gradual decrease from high to little labour income, spread across the 50s through the 60s. When switching to average pension income per person by single year of age one sees the converse: a gradual increase starting in the mid-50s and peaking by the mid-60s. Thus, looking just at the ages of the early 50s through the mid-60s, one sees significant amounts of both labour and pension income. This begs an interesting policy question: Is this because people withdraw very gradually from the labour force and get both labour and pension income or because people withdraw very quickly as individuals but at quite disparate times?

Figure 2 looks at the population aged 50 to 69 broken down into those who are in:[1]

- career employment, that is their longstanding employment and labour force attachment (excluding the self-employed);
- bridge employment, which we define as employment performed after receipt of a pension from a career job;
- retirement, which we define as receipt of retirement income without any further employment income at all;
- or the omnipresent "other", which is no earnings and no pension benefits.

As the figure shows, the share of bridge employment, while not tiny, is small at around 8% of those aged 50 to 69 in 1996. This suggests most people are either in their career employment or in their retirement, not in something in between. The "bridge employment" slice has evolved little since 1996 and is still a relatively small, albeit somewhat larger, slice. This is a reminder that receiving a pension does not, as a rule, prevent one from working. When we think about the early retirement incentives in many defined-benefit (DB) plans, we should bear this in mind: they can still work, just elsewhere. This figure also previews some of the trends we will see shortly: a higher proportion of people aged 50 to 69 in their career jobs and a smaller proportion in retirement.

But, for now, back to defining retirement. Is it leaving a job for retirement? Here the Labour Force Survey (LFS) actually captures self-reported retirement. For those who have left a job, the LFS asks why, with

---

[1]The analysis of bridge employment is based on Luong and Hébert (2007).

Figure 2: Labour Market Status of Older (50–69) People

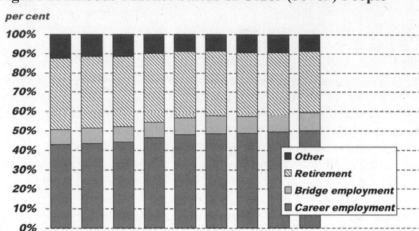

Source: Survey of Labour and Income Dynamics Data and HRSDC calculations.

"retirement" being one possible answer. There are two problems with this self-reporting. First, as we just covered, people can retire and then start work again, in bridge employment. Though small, this would nonetheless result in the LFS *over*-estimating retirement. Second, people can leave or lose a job for other reasons and then never work again. Such people would eventually be "retired" as in never again working but having never "self-declared" retirement as a reason for not working. This would result in the LFS self-reporting *under*-estimating retirement.

The reason for the latter is found in how many older workers (that is 55 and over) leave a job for reasons other than self-reported retirement and then do not find another job. Those who self report retirement as the reason for leaving their job were around one-third of all losers and leavers in the 1970s, a number that has drifted up slightly in the three decades since but is currently only around 40%. Many of the rest are job losers, those laid off from their job, with or without an expectation of return. Many of these older job losers may not find employment subsequently.

We need better estimates for our Canadian Occupational Projection System (COPS) forecasts of labour demand and supply by occupation. We need them because we estimate that two out of every three job openings in the decade ahead will arise because a worker will retire from an *existing* job, rather than because economic growth will create a *new* job (Lapointe *et al.*, 2006).

We constructed a new retirement series from Statistics Canada's Longitudinal Administrative Database, or LAD file (Dunn, 2005). With LAD we can identify those who meet two criteria: they have left a job and have not started another within three years. (We proxy the latter by those having under $500 a year of labour income.) We used a three year cut-off because after three years we see little propensity on the part of older people to re-enter the workplace.

This is the point to turn to the trends we see.

Retirement Trends

Figure 3 shows median retirement ages for both the LFS self-reported series and our measure derived from the LAD. The difference is quite large in the 1980s through to the mid-1990s, by three years initially and then around two. This does indeed suggest that the LFS over-states the effective retirement age by missing large numbers who leave a job or lose a job and then never again generate meaningful labour income. Here we should recall our economic history: the 1980s and 1990s both started with deep recessions and then had sluggish recoveries, likely resulting in layoffs that turned into retirement. But, when we get into the late 1990s the two series are quite a bit closer. Unfortunately, with the LAD-based measure requiring three years or post-retirement retirement to confirm meeting our definition of retirement, we do not have recent data for the LAD-based measure. So, we do not know if the two measures are trending similarly now. We do know that we have been going through a prolonged and ever-strengthening expansion, so they could well be similar.

Figure 4 looks at the LAD-based retirement rates from a different perspective, showing rates by single year of age for three different three-year time periods: 1982 to 1984, 1990 to 1992, and 1999 to 2001. The series for 1992 to 1994 shows retirement rates drifting up during the 50s ages and through the early 60s (related to first Canada/Quebec Pension Plan eligibility) to a peak around the age of 65 (related to Old Age Security/ Guaranteed Income Supplement eligibility) and then dropping down again and staying steady from the late 60s through the 70s. I should add that, although we may look on this as a benchmark for subsequent developments, this does encompass the recession of the early 1980s and its slow recovery.

Figure 3: Median Retirement Age

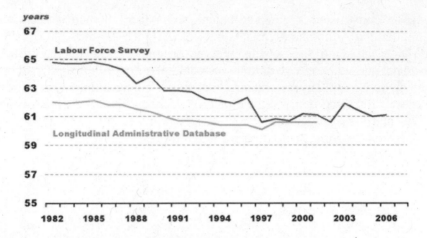

Source: Labour Force Survey and Longitudinal Administrative Database data and HRSDC calculations.

Figure 4: Retirement Rates (LAD-Based) by Age

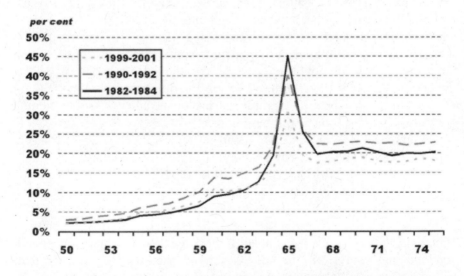

Source: Longitudinal Administrative Database data and HRSDC calculations.

Cliff Halliwell

That being said, the retirement rates from the 1990 to 1992 period, which also overlap a recession (but capturing the pre-recession year of 1990), show a quite different profile. The retirement rates prior to age 65 are quite a bit higher and the peak at 65 somewhat lower and the rates after age 65 somewhat higher. Then, when we overlap some good economic years, specifically 1999 through 2001, we again see a major shift. The whole curve has shifted downwards. Obviously the state of the economy and labour markets matter and retirement is less used to manage the workforce size when the economy is healthy.

I now want to turn to what people do at different ages. Figure 5 shows the population by single years of age for 2006 and what it is doing, including being in the labour force and being employed. The first line, total population, is, of course, a population pyramid that fell over onto its right side: thick at its middle-aged middle, less thick at its younger base, and thinnest at its older ages. The second line is the labour force source population. It by definition only starts at age 15 and is (almost, for statistical noise reasons) below the population curve, because of the usual labour force exclusions. The third line is the actual labour force. Here we see very little labour force in the teen years, when young Canadians are mostly at school. But, looking to the right, one starts to see a considerable

Figure 5: Population by Age: Total, 2006

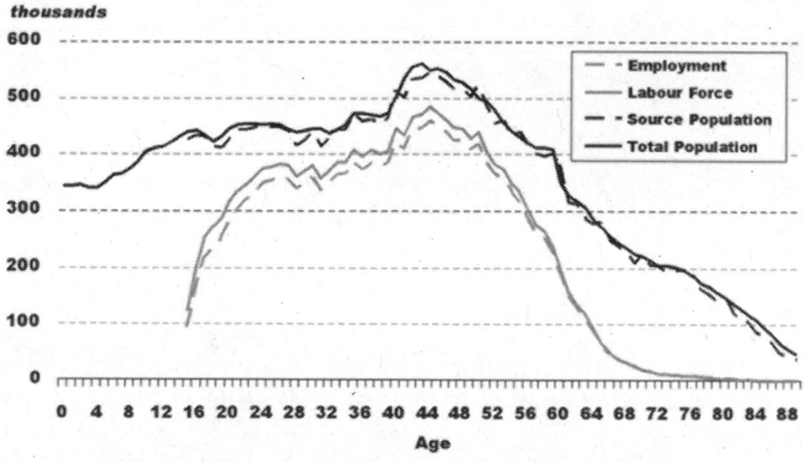

Source: Labour Force Survey.

decline in the labour force that starts in the 40s (around the population mode of the 40s as well) but then accelerates. The final line is employment. It is quite similar to the labour force, but everywhere below due to unemployment. But, the unemployment "wedge" dissipates for those in their mid-50s and virtually disappears by the 60s. This reflects the fact that at those ages leaving the labour force is the predominant alternative to being without work. As an aside, this means that population aging will add a downward trend to the average unemployment rate. But, this is not really more employment, just less employment seeking.

Figure 6 is just another cut on the relationships shown in the previous figure. It shows the participation rate and employment-population ratio by single years of age for 2006. (The wedge between the two would be the unemployment rate again.) What jumps out here is the abruptness of the decline after the mid-50s. Certainly, this suggests that policy action in trying to extend what one could call "work expectancy", that is how long and to what ages people will work, will happen for the 55 to 64 cohort. After 65, notwithstanding the symbolic value of things like ending mandatory retirement, the battle has already been won or lost and people are either staying on or are gone, mostly the latter.

Figure 6: Participation and Employment Rates by Age

Source: Labour Force Survey.

Cliff Halliwell

In the end, we can all discuss retirement at length. But, what interests us most is employment. That is easily measured by the employment-population ratio. This of course encompasses both desire to work and success at finding it, so does have a cyclical aspect. Figure 7 plots the recent increases in that ratio by single year of age since the onset of the 1990s. As you can see, there was little change from 1991 to 1996. Subsequently, that is in 2001 and especially 2006, we have seen quite an increase in the employment-population ratio, especially in the prime working years. This is a combination of both higher participation rates and lower unemployment rates.

We also see that the employment rate increases pushing out into the late 50s and even 60s. It turns out that most of the gains in employment ratios we are seeing are for women (Figure 8). In particular, we are seeing the cohort effects as older women increasingly are baby-boomer women who have had a long standing attachment to the labour force, and are staying in the labour force longer than previous cohorts, but still not as long as men.

Figure 7: Employment Rates by Age: Total

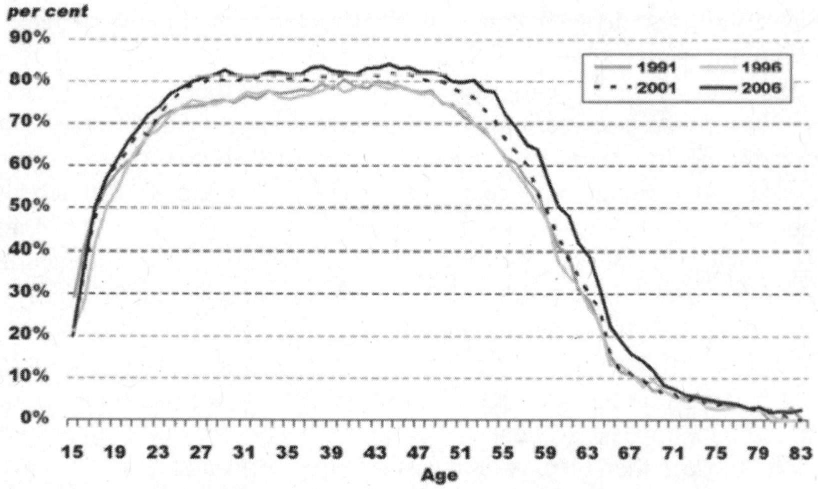

Source: Labour Force Survey.

Figure 8: Employment Rates by Age: Women

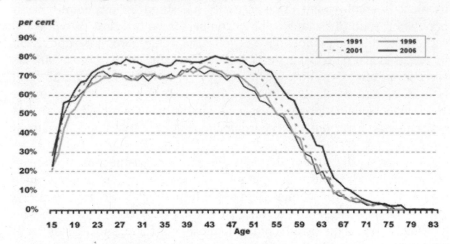

Source: Labour Force Survey.

Work Characteristics by Age

Now I want to turn to some of the other characteristics of the working and the retired. Figure 9 shows, for those aged 50 to 69, the sources of income for those in career employment, bridge employment or retirement. Obviously, those in career employment have — by our definition — no retirement income and mostly earned income, with some transfer income. Those in bridge employment (but recall how few they are) have much less earned income, considerable pension income, some OAS and CPP/QPP, and more transfer income. Interestingly, they have slightly *more* total income. Then, of course, the retired have more pension income and — again by definition here — no earned income.

Figure 10 starts to look at full-time and part-time work, showing the shares by five-year age cohort for 2006. Recall that part-time work is less than 30 hours a week. The data show the highest prevalence of part-time work for those in their teens, who must combine work and school. But, part-time work picks up as a share again starting in the 55 to 59 ages and becomes over 40% for those aged 65 and over. Here, of course, we should not forget how few of those of that age who are working at all. But, many of those who do work do part-time work.

Figure 9: Sources of Income — Aged 55 to 69, 2004

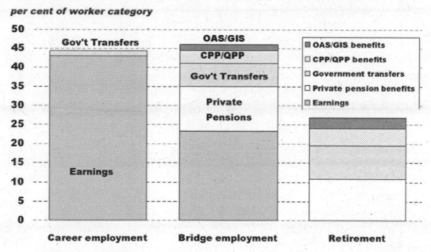

Source: Survey of Labour and Income Dynamics.

Figure 10: Full- and Part-Time Work by Age Group, 2006

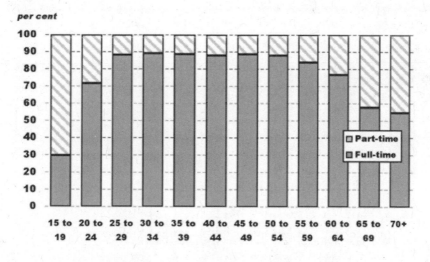

Source: Labour Force Survey.

Is that what they want? Yes, without a doubt. Figure 11 shows the reasons for doing part-time work. The proportion of those working part-time for personal preference just grows and grows by age. Clearly, many of those who wish to work later in life wish work with greater flexibility. This raises some pension issues, as pension plans still largely presume a binary choice: full-time or no work during the course of a year.

Is part-time work easy to find? Figure 12 shows part-time shares by industry for those aged 50 to 59. There is obviously a lot of part-time work in some sectors such as retail. But, clearly, there are some sectors where there is little prevalence of part-time work, in particular a sector that worries a lot and *must* worry about retaining its older workers and the turnover of corporate memory aging is bringing: public administration. Figure 13 shows the same thing, only by occupation. This shows that there are some occupations where there is a lot of part-time work. There are others with little. I would not be surprised if many with little are occupations where employers are worrying about retaining older workers.

There is another metric of the desire of older people for work flexibility. This is the prevalence of self-employment. The various categories of self-employment become a considerable share of total employment by the 60s. Again, I would note that after age 65 there just are not that many Canadians working, period.

Figure 11: Reasons for Part-Time Work by Age, 2006

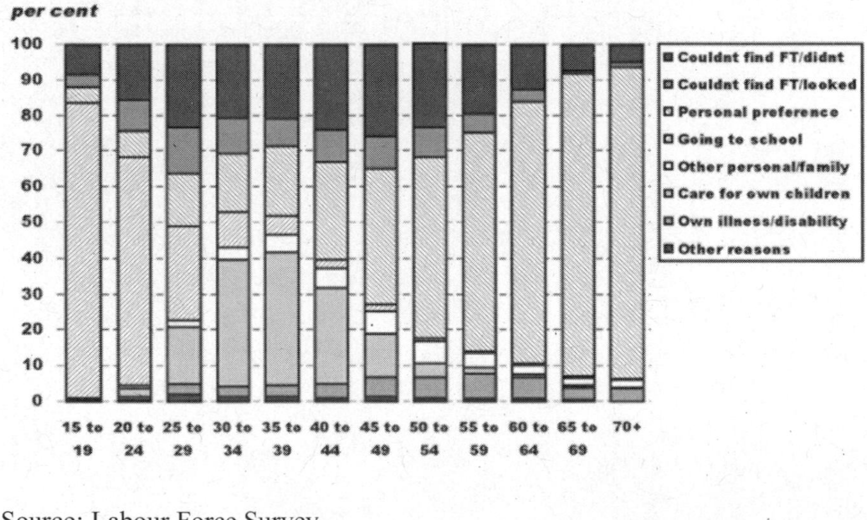

Source: Labour Force Survey.

Cliff Halliwell

Figure 12: Part-Time Work by Industry, Aged 50–59, 2006

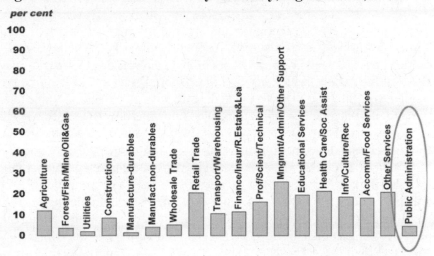

Source: Labour Force Survey.

Figure 13: Part-Time Work by Occupation, Aged 50–59, 2006

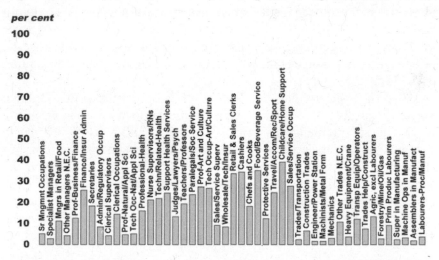

Source: Labour Force Survey.

Retirement in Canada: Some Trends ... Some Issues

Longevity and Its Implications

I want to close by considering longevity and its implications. It is well known that life expectancy at birth has increased markedly in the last half century. It is less well known that a lot of that gain was due to gains at early ages of life when reductions in infant mortality, teenage automotive accidents, or falling into the works at the mill have added considerable total years to life expectancy at birth. Less well known is how life expectancy at any age is also rising. Of course and as always, women are outliving men. But, life expectancies for both men and women are rising and have gone up three and two and a half years respectively in the last quarter-century alone.

This is likely a gross *underestimate* of how long a 65-year-old in 2001 will live. These life expectancies are constructed by cumulating *current* mortality rates (e.g., 2001 rates in the year 2001) by age until you run out of years. But, as noted, those mortality rates are falling and life expectancy continues rising. The 65-year-old in 2001 will get the mortality rates of an 80-year-old in 2021, not those of an 80-year-old in 2001.

What does this greater longevity mean? It means pensions must last longer, especially when combined with earlier retirement. Making pension income last longer requires having more wealth at retirement or a better return. In turn, having more wealth at retirement requires having greater savings (that is foregone consumption) or a higher return. The former is more in our control than the latter and, I suspect, the average rate of return has actually declined in recent years. If so, this triple whammy of greater longevity, earlier retirement and lower returns all act to effectively raise the price of future pension income when converted into foregone consumption out of actual lifetime earned income.

Women especially face this issue, as they both retire earlier and live longer (Figure 14). Thus their pension income has to last even longer. That is why we see more elderly women in financial difficulty, especially in current older cohorts of women who were less likely to have labour market attachment themselves and are thus more likely to be widows on the survivor's benefits of their husband's pensions. That being said, this issue of older women's poverty is likely to diminish, as the boomer cohorts of women will be much more likely to have their own retirement income sources as a consequence of their much greater labour force attachment.

Figure 14: Retirement and Life Expectancy

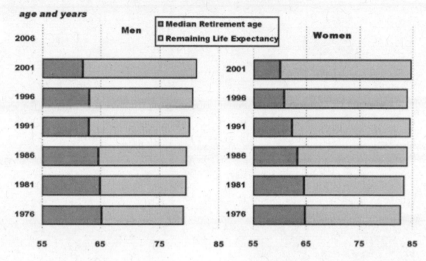

Source: Labour Force Survey and Statistics Canada, Life Tables, Catalogue No. 84–537–XPB.

References

Dunn, K. 2005. *Estimating and Forecasting Aggregate Retirement Flows in the Canadian Labour Market*. Ottawa: HRSDC.

Lapointe, M., K. Dunn, N. Tremblay-Côté, L.-P. Bergeron, and L. Ignaczak. 2006. *Looking-Ahead: A 10-Year Outlook for the Canadian Labour Market (2006–2015)*. Ottawa: HRSDC.

Luong, M. and B.-P. Hébert. 2007. "Bridge Employment: Working in Retirement". Ottawa: HRSDC. Unpublished paper.

Income Security and Stability During Retirement in Canada

Sébastien LaRochelle-Côté, John Myles,
and Garnett Picot

Introduction

As in all western democracies, old-age income support was a top priority on Canada's social policy agenda from the 1950s to the 1970s and had two major drivers. The first of these was the fact that during the postwar decades "old age" was a virtual synonym for poverty. The second was the rapid spread of retirement — the labour force practice of superannuating elderly workers at a fixed age without regard to their physical or mental capacity to continue in employment. High rates of old age poverty were in large measure due to the fact that the elderly of the day had experienced "poor" lives — their peak working years occurred during the Great Depression — and they were beyond the stage when they were able to benefit from the enormous economic expansion that followed the Second World War. But their poverty was accentuated by the drive to create jobs for the young men returning from war and the

This is a revised and much abridged version of Research Paper No. 306 (March 2008) available in the Analytical Studies Research Paper Series, Statistics Canada.

resulting acceleration of mandatory retirement practices in the absence of well-developed pension schemes.

These two features of the postwar world established the two major parameters for social policy debates. How best to deal with the anti-poverty objective? And, how best to provide income security for workers in a world in which mandatory retirement was becoming the norm? The anti-poverty objective dated from the pre-war era, but the income security objective was new for governments (Perrin, 1969). Many workers were happy to embrace retirement but only if retirement was accompanied by a "retirement wage" that allowed them to maintain their pre-retirement living standards. For high-wage, middle-class, workers, simply avoiding poverty was hardly a satisfactory trade-off for giving up their jobs at age 65. Their aim was *income security*, a retirement wage sufficient to maintain pre-retirement living standards in old age. To achieve this objective the Canadian Congress of Labour called for the addition of a universal and publicly administered earnings-related pension in 1953 to supplement the universal flat benefit Old Age Security program adopted in 1951. Their call was met in 1965 with the addition of the Canada and Quebec Pension plans (C/QPP).

How well has the Canadian old-age support system coped with these two objectives — reducing poverty *and* maintaining pre-retirement living standards (*income security*) in retirement. The answer to the first question is well known. Although Canadian public expenditures on old age security is near the bottom of the international league lists, Canada stands near the top among western democracies with respect to reducing old age poverty rates (Smeeding and Sullivan, 1998). But what about income security? How well, for example, do middle-income workers fare when they enter their retirement years?

The question of *income security*, especially for families of "average" workers (the middle class) was the key issue taken up by the Canadian government's Task Force on Retirement Income Policy (1979), probably the most thorough and sophisticated report on Canada's retirement income system ever undertaken.[1]

------

[1] For low-income families, the anti-poverty and income security objectives are virtually synonymous. By 1979, the combination of Old Age Security benefits and the Guaranteed Income Supplement ensured income replacement rates of 100% or more for such families, a finding replicated here. Nor was there particular concern about high-income families who were well-placed to save for their own retirement, especially in light of widespread coverage by private pensions among high earners and their equally widespread

The authors of that report were not optimistic. They concluded (1979, p. 175) that the current system would not maintain "the living standards of those who were middle-income earners during their working years". The income replacement rate for the average worker from Canada's public system (Old Age Security and the Canada Pension Plan) were modest — ensuring only 40% of pre-retirement income — and flaws in private occupational pensions (including inadequate coverage, vesting and portability rules) made it unlikely that they would provide a satisfactory solution for the future. The first best solution according to the task force (and many pension experts) would be a dramatic expansion of the Canada and Quebec Pension Plans to European-like levels that would make private occupational plans redundant. A second-best solution, according to the task force, would be to make occupational plans mandatory for all Canadian workers, a strategy later adopted by countries such as Australia, Denmark, the Netherlands and Switzerland. With onset of recession in the early 1980s, all such plans were abandoned and Canada's retirement income system remains much as it was in 1979.

Since then, of course, Canada's old age pension system has matured (Myles, 2000). In 1979 few retirees were receiving benefits from the Canada and Quebec Pension Plans and the expansion of private occupational plans and Registered Retirement Savings Plans in the post-war decades would only benefit workers retiring in the 1980s or even later. So what has been the outcome?

As the task force (1979, p. 101) observed at the time, there were no (longitudinal) data available to measure the relationship between the living standards of the current elderly and the living standards they experienced during their working years. Ours is one of the first studies to overcome that difficulty. To do so, we use a rich source of longitudinal data (Statistics Canada's Longitudinal Administrative Database based on taxation records, the LAD) and we follow a cohort of individuals over two decades to examine various aspects of income security in retirement. The analysis is restricted to individuals who, at age 55, had a significant

---

use of Registered Retirement Savings Plans. These assumptions reflect the standard result from studies of savings behaviour, namely that the savings to permanent income ratio rises with permanent income but does so in a sharply non-linear fashion (Diamond and Hausman, 1984).

attachment to the labour force.[2] The analysis does not focus on poverty in retirement, about which a lot is known, but rather income replacement among individuals with significant labour market attachment during the working years.

The results (on average) are at odds with the expectations of the task force and other experts of the period, at least for the particular population on which this analysis focuses. We find that by the turn of the century replacement rates for middle-income families are higher than the task force expected. In 2005, the replacement income of retired individuals in their mid-seventies who were in the *middle* of the income distribution at age 55 (in the early 1980s) was between 70 and 80% of their previous incomes some 20 years earlier. This figure is at the high end of the range (65 to 75%) that experts (Schulz, 1992, p. 99) generally consider adequate for middle-income retirees to maintain their pre-retirement living standards. Moreover, it is at the high end of the replacement rates that even the most generous (e.g., Sweden) welfare states offer retired workers through their public pension schemes that the task force sought to emulate.[3] Strikingly, these estimates produced with longitudinal data are not far from cross-sectional estimates of "quasi-replacement rates" based on comparisons of the incomes of the elderly with those of the non-elderly (OECD, 2001, p. 24).

We also show, however, that there is considerable variation among the replacement rates. By age 75, about a quarter of *middle-income* persons had retirement incomes of less than 60% of the income they were receiving in their mid-fifties. This heterogeneity in replacement rates *is* consistent with the expectations of the task force. The main concern of the task force was the uneven coverage of private pension plans and RRSP contributions among Canadian workers with average earnings. And our results show that for middle-income earners, it is largely whether one has income from these two sources that differentiates people with low and high replacement rates after age 70. Had Canada embarked on the more ambitious public pension program

---

[2]For technical reasons related to tax filing behaviour, and outlined in the data section of the paper, the analysis was restricted to individuals who had individual earnings of $10,000 or more at age 55.

[3]The OECD (2001, p. 24) estimates of quasi-replacement rates also confirm that, on *average,* Canada is it at the high end of the international distribution.

Sébastien LaRochelle-Côté, John Myles, and Garnett Picot

proposed by the task force, we would expect much less variation in the replacement rates of middle-income families. Just how much less, however, we are unable to say. Variation in replacement rates also reflects actual differences in employment and earnings histories of individuals who were in the middle of the income distribution by their mid-fifties. Retirement incomes in old age reflect the *entire* employment and earnings history of each individual in our sample and no such data is available. Although income at age 55 provides a reasonable (and previously unavailable) benchmark to estimate income security in old age, it is far from being the ideal benchmark.

We also report income replacement rates for low- and high-income individuals. Among individuals in the *bottom* quintile, median replacement rates remained at about 1.0 (100% of their incomes at age 55) throughout their retirement years. Individuals in the *top* quintile experienced a larger drop in replacement rates, to around 70% since they were starting from a much higher income base at age 55.

We also ask whether income replacement rates have been rising or falling among more recent cohorts of retirees, but we find little change. People aged 55 in 1983 experienced roughly the same median replacement rates in retirement as those aged 55 in 1995. However, family income levels among more recent retirees have been rising, mainly because of higher income from family employment earnings in the early retirement years and private pensions. We do not currently have the data to determine if this trend will continue in the longer run, given the decreased private pension coverage among younger workers, and the shift from defined-benefit to defined-contribution plans.

Finally, we report results about the stability of incomes in the retirement years. Income replacement rates (say at age 75 compared to age 55) are not very useful for evaluating *income security* if the incomes of the elderly fluctuate wildly from year to year, as a result, say, of changes in real interest rates. In fact, we conclude that year to year instability in family income declines for both high- and low-income earners as they age, largely because of the stabilizing effect of public pension income sources.

Data

Statistics Canada's Longitudinal Administrative Database (LAD) consists of a random 20% sample of the T1 family file, a yearly cross-sectional file of all taxfilers. Individuals selected for the LAD are linked across years to create a longitudinal profile of each individual. The LAD contains demographic, income and other taxation information for the period from 1982 to 2005, which makes it possible to track individuals for a maximum of 23 years. As a result, it is possible to follow the evolution of the financial situation of individuals after retirement over a long period. Our focus is on six cohorts of Canadians who were aged from 54 to 56 years in 1983, 1986, 1989, 1992, 1995 and 1998 and who earned at least $10,000 at this age (in 2005 constant dollars). We exclude individuals earning less than $10,000 at age 55 since many of them did not file a return at the time.[4] This implies that our focus is on individuals who had a significant degree of attachment to the labour market when they were in their mid-fifties.

Our six samples (one for each cohort) were constructed as follows. First, individuals who were still alive in 2005 were included if they filed an income return for every year of the period of analysis.[5] For instance,

---

[4]With the introduction of the Goods and Services Tax in 1986 and the Child Tax Credit in 1992, low-income individuals became more likely to file an income tax return in order to apply for various tax credits. Prior to 1992, low-income individuals had fewer incentives to file. We get similarly defined cohorts by excluding all individuals with less than $10,000 in earnings, which is close to the basic exemption amount that was used for most years in federal tax returns and above which most individuals should be expected to file (which corresponds to approximately 50% of all individuals aged 54 to 56 years old in every cohort). One alternative could have been to include individuals with positive earnings. If this had been the case: (i) coverage would have increased by a little, albeit unequally across cohorts (from 53.1% among those aged from 54 to 56 years old in 1983, to 58.6% in 1998); and (ii) our results would have been essentially the same, although replacement rates among low-income individuals would have been slightly higher.

[5]It was necessary to exclude these individuals for reasons of consistency. Naturally, fewer individuals were lost in more recent cohorts because individuals were followed over a shorter period of time. In 1983, about 68,800 individuals were included in the final sample (out of 78,900 individuals aged 54 to 56 with at least $10,000 in earnings), which means that about 10,100 were excluded because of reporting problems (12%). In 1998, only 7,800 were

individuals from the 1983 cohort were included in the sample if a return was filed every year from 1983 to 2005. Second, individuals who died before 2006 were also included if a return had been filed for all years until the year before they died. For instance, consider an individual who was aged 55 in 1983 and who died in 1995 at the age of 67. To be included in our first sample, a return must have been filed for each of the years 1983 to 1994, which was the last complete year of his/her life. As a result of this process, we obtain six samples with a number of observations ranging from approximately 70,000 in 1983 to 100,000 in 1998 (see Table 1 for more information). Women comprised one-third of the sample in 1983, but this share rose to more than 40% in 1998, which is consistent with the higher rates of labour market participation seen among younger cohorts of women. In this paper, we use our first cohort of 1983 most often because it covers the longest time period (20 years). The other samples are used only to examine differences across cohorts.

Our measure of income is based on adult-equivalent-adjusted (AEA) *family* income (on a constant basis), which includes the income of the spouse and all other family members in the census family unit. For the

Table 1: Sample Characteristics

| Cohort | Aged 54 to 56 | Total Number of Observations | Men | | Women | |
			Number of Observations	Share of Total (%)	Number of Observations	Share of Total (%)
1	1983	68,735	46,345	67.4	22,390	32.6
2	1986	73,790	48,735	65.9	25,235	34.1
3	1989	75,930	47,800	63.0	28,130	37.0
4	1992	76,970	46,705	60.7	30,265	39.3
5	1995	85,440	50,700	59.3	34,740	40.7
6	1998	100,565	58,530	58.2	42,040	41.8

Note: The numbers might not add up due to rounding.
Source: Statistics Canada, Longitudinal Administrative Database.

excluded, out of 108,400 individuals (about 7% of individuals with at least $10,000 in earnings).

most part, we use family income after tax because this measure of income is the best approximation of the level of financial well-being experienced by individuals. Our family income values are then adjusted by dividing total family income by the square root of family size to take account of economies of scale that accrue to people who live together in families.[6] Finally, income levels by age are calculated on a "permanent" basis, in order to account for temporary fluctuations that might not be representative of the true financial situation of the family. For example, the permanent income of someone aged 54 was calculated by dividing the sum of income levels reported at age 53, 54 and 55 by three.[7] We also tested several alternative definitions of income to assess the robustness of our conclusions. All income figures are expressed in 2005 dollars adjusted with the consumer price index.

The income replacement rate is the standard indicator of welfare loss associated with retirement. We compute replacement rates by age, using permanent income at the beginning of the period (age from 54 to 56) as a benchmark when earnings are typically at their peak.[8] In addition to median replacement rates by cohort, we also compute replacement rates across key points in the income distribution, again using permanent income at the beginning of the period as a benchmark to classify individuals across income groups.

We have not attempted to pursue one of the more important dimensions of income security in old age, namely the effects of widowhood on the income trajectories of the elderly, especially among elderly women. Early on we determined that estimating the effects of widowhood required a more complex research design than that employed here and would be taken up in a separate paper. And, ideally, we would want to track individuals into their eighties, a task that will become feasible as more data points are added to the LAD file in future years.

---

[6]Changes in the family composition over time are taken into account in our calculations.

[7]Individuals with less than $1,000 in permanent adult-equivalent adjusted income were excluded from our sample, but these amounted to a very tiny portion of the final sample (less than 0.1%).

[8]Earnings peak at age 55, but total family income peaks around 60 years of age (see Figure 5).

Results

Replacement Rates

Family-income replacement rates represent the percentage of permanent family income at age 55 "replaced" by the sources of income that are available during retirement and can be used as an indicator of welfare "loss" associated with retirement. Based on the assumption that family expenses will be lower in retirement than before retirement, it is generally agreed that 100% income replacement in retirement is not necessary. In the absence of children, expenses for goods and services are lower; work-related expenses disappear; there is no longer a need to save for retirement; and, where home-ownership rates are high (as in Canada), housing costs tend to be lower in the retirement years.

Policymakers in the rich democracies have typically set a target replacement rate from 65% to 75% for the average worker (Schulz, 1992, p. 99). In Canada, Old Age Security and the Canada and Quebec Pension Plans were designed to replace about 40% of pre-retirement earnings for the average worker and it was assumed the balance would come from private pensions and personal savings. Low-income families who are already living on the margin are assumed to require higher replacement rates (close to 1.0) while high-income families are assumed to require less.

Figure 1 shows that median replacement rates for the entire sample remain close to 1.0 until around age 60, then decline to about 0.8 around age 65. Furthermore, longer time series from older cohorts indicate that replacement rates remain relatively stable until late in life. The main implication of this is that the Canadian pension system appears to be doing relatively well in ensuring basic standards of well-being among seniors who had a substantial attachment to the labour force, at least for individuals near the median.[9]

---

[9]Recall that these results are based on family income, which is more indicative of the level of financial well-being enjoyed by individuals over the course of the retirement period. The median replacement rate after age 65 is about ten percentage points lower when individual income is used instead of family income, at approximately 0.7 (see Appendix A of the original research paper, No. 306 in the Analytical Studies Research Paper Series, Statistics Canada, for more detail).

Figure 1: Median Replacement Rates of Adult-Equivalent-Adjusted Family Income after Taxes

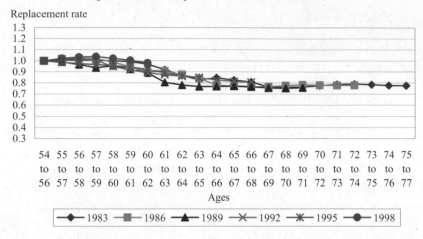

Source: Statistics Canada, Longitudinal Administrative Database.

However, there is considerable variation in replacement rates both within and between pre-retirement income levels as shown in Table 2 for the 1983 cohort.[10] Almost 50% of individuals had a replacement rate above 1.0 at age 59 to 61. This proportion fell to 35% at age 64 to 66 and to 23% at age 69 to 71. Conversely, the share of individuals with a replacement rate of 0.6 or less increased from 10% at age 60 to 21% by age 75.

Are these results a cause for concern? In other words, do individuals have low replacement because of limited access to retirement income, or simply because their permanent income was initially high? If low-income individuals aged from 54 to 56 consistently had replacement rates above 1.0 in the following years, this would suggest that the pensions system is relatively effective in preserving the living standards of low-income seniors. Conversely, if low-income individuals had lower

---

[10]Results for the other cohorts are not shown, but showed similar results when comparisons could be made. Readers interested in other cohorts will find a complete description of these results in Appendix B of the original research paper (see note 9).

Sébastien LaRochelle-Côté, John Myles, and Garnett Picot

Table 2: Distribution of Individuals Across Replacement Rate Categories, All Individuals

| | Distribution of Replacement Rates by Age (%) | | | | |
	54 to 56 years old	59 to 61 years old	64 to 66 years old	69 to 71 years old	74 to 76 years old
All individuals					
<= 0.4	0.0	2.3	2.9	2.4	2.7
> 0.4 and <=0.6	0.0	7.2	14.8	19.0	18.4
> 0.6 and <=0.8	0.0	16.2	26.7	34.1	32.4
> 0.8 and <=1.0	100.0	25.5	21.0	21.5	22.4
> 1.0 and <=1.5	0.0	38.9	24.0	17.2	18.0
> 1.5	0.0	10.0	10.6	5.7	6.0
Bottom quintile					
<= 0.4	0.0	3.4	1.6	0.1	0.1
> 0.4 and <=0.6	0.0	5.3	5.2	1.4	1.8
> 0.6 and <=0.8	0.0	10.6	16.1	19.4	18.3
> 0.8 and <=1.0	100.0	18.5	21.8	28.1	28.9
> 1.0 and <=1.5	0.0	42.9	33.4	35.0	35.1
> 1.5	0.0	19.4	21.8	16.0	15.8
Middle quintile					
<= 0.4	0.0	1.7	2.2	1.0	1.1
> 0.4 and <=0.6	0.0	7.0	15.9	23.3	23.6
> 0.6 and <=0.8	0.0	16.8	31.5	38.8	36.7
> 0.8 and <=1.0	100.0	28.3	21.9	21.4	21.6
> 1.0 and <=1.5	0.0	39.9	21.6	12.9	14.2
> 1.5	0.0	6.4	7.0	2.6	3.0
Top quintile					
<= 0.4	0.0	2.9	6.2	7.5	7.7
> 0.4 and <=0.6	0.0	10.2	21.2	28.7	26.2
> 0.6 and <=0.8	0.0	19.8	26.7	34.6	31.7
> 0.8 and <=1.0	100.0	25.9	17.7	14.8	17.5
> 1.0 and <=1.5	0.0	31.8	19.5	10.2	12.1
> 1.5	0.0	9.3	8.7	4.2	4.9

Note: Based on a cohort of individuals aged from 54 to 56 in 1983.
Source: Statistics Canada, Longitudinal Administrative Database.

and lower replacement rates as they age, this would raise serious questions about the ability of the pensions system to maintain their living standards in retirement. One way to deal with this is to control for initial income levels. We do so by dividing the population into five quintiles (for each cohort) based on their permanent adult-equivalent-adjusted income at age 55 and by examining the distribution of replacement rates in the first, third and fifth quintiles of permanent income. Results for individuals in the bottom quintile are shown in Figure 2.

For the majority of low-income families (the bottom quintile), median replacement rates were generally high, and remained close to, or above 1.0.[11] The 1989 cohort, which was undoubtedly affected by the

Figure 2: Median Replacement Rates of Adult-Equivalent-Adjusted Family Income after Taxes, Bottom Quintile

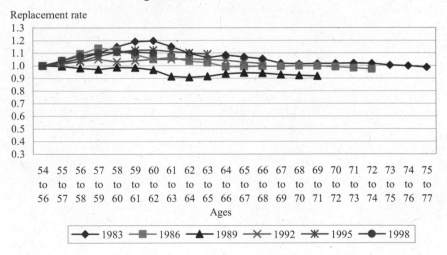

Source: Statistics Canada, Longitudinal Administrative Database.

---

[11]Recall that we have excluded persons earning less than $10,000 around age 55.

1990-to-1992 recession, is the exception.[12] These are encouraging results but if many low-income seniors had replacement rates much below the median, there would be cause for concern. Hence, it is also important to examine the distribution of individuals across categories of replacement rates within the bottom quintile as well.[13]

The results are shown in the second panel of Table 2 and indicate that about half of all individuals in the bottom quintile enjoyed full replacement rates until late in retirement. Four out of five had replacement rates above 0.8 at age 75. Nevertheless, nearly 20% of the bottom-quintile seniors aged 70 had replacement rates below 0.8, which suggests that a sizeable number may face financial stress.

Figures 3 and 4 show median replacement rates among individuals in the middle and top quintiles, respectively. Median replacement rates among individuals in the middle quintile closely resembled those of the cohort as a whole with replacement rates between 0.7 and 0.8 for most cohorts after age 65. After age 70, however, about a quarter of middle-income seniors have replacement rates below 0.6 (Table 2, last column). Replacement rates among individuals in the top quintile declined to approximately 0.7 after age 65.

The replacement rate patterns are similar for men and women, largely because the analysis is based on family income, and not individual earnings. Hence, a man and a woman in the same family will have exactly the same family income replacement rate trajectory in retirement. Both had higher replacement rates if they were in the bottom quintile of the income distribution and lower replacement rates if they were in the top quintile. Similar results were also found in terms of the distribution of replacement rates (results not shown, but available in the original research paper).

---

[12]These results are consistent with Gower (1998), who also finds higher replacement rates among low-income individuals.

[13]The distribution of replacement rates within quintiles is also based on our first cohort of individuals aged from 54 to 56 in 1983. Other cohorts have shown similar distributions (see Appendix B for details).

Figure 3: Median Replacement Rates of Adult-Equivalent-Adjusted Family Income after Taxes, Middle Quintile

Replacement rate

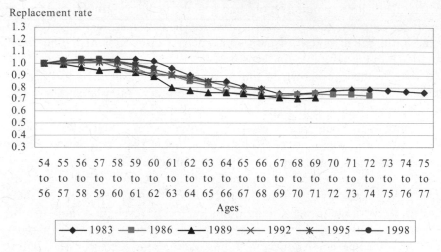

Source: Statistics Canada, Longitudinal Administrative Database.

Figure 4: Median Replacement Rates of Adult-Equivalent-Adjusted Family Income after Taxes, Top Quintile

Replacement rate

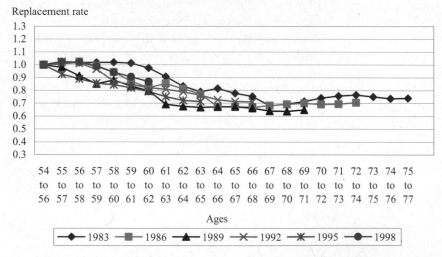

Source: Statistics Canada, Longitudinal Administrative Database.

While replacement rates vary across the income distribution, with generally higher replacement rates among individuals with lower family incomes at age 55, they also vary among individuals with generally the same income at age 55. Why do two individuals who have the same income levels at age 55 end up with very different replacement rates in retirement? Is it simply the case that one has a private pension, and the other does not? Or do other sources of income significantly affect the outcome?

To address this issue we focus on individuals from the 1985 cohort (age 55 in 1985) who were in the middle family-income quintile at age 55. We divide this group into those with high replacement rates (> 1.0), and low replacement rates (< 0.6) at various ages in retirement. We then determine the contribution of each income source to the difference in family income between the low and high replacement rate groups. The results are in Tables 3 and 4.

The average family income at age 55 of the groups with low and high replacement rates were virtually identical at around $38,000 (adult equivalent adjusted, Table 3). Hence, differences in replacement rates in the retirement years were not due to differences in income at age 55.

Table 3 shows that at age 64 to 66, differences in employment earnings is the major factor differentiating those with high replacement rates from those with lower ones, accounting for 57% of the $44,000 difference in income between these two groups. And as the cohort aged from 69 to 71, some maintenance of employment earnings remained the largest single factor, accounting for 40% of the still very large $42,000 difference in family income between the low and high replacement rate groups. Differences in private pension income (occupational pensions and RRSPs) start to become important at this age — accounting for 34% of the difference — as does investment and capital gains, together accounting for about 27% of the difference. By age 74 to 76, employment earnings remain significant, accounting for 29% of the difference, but the money received from private pensions (including RRSP and RIF income) becomes the major contributor (45% of the difference).

These results are based on family income so that the earnings reported under "employment earnings" for an individual aged, say from 64 to 66, may not have been earned by that particular individual, but by someone else in the family, possibly younger. Hence, it is difficult to determine to what extent remaining in the labour market during the older years accounts for the differences in outcomes between the low and high replacement rate groups.

Table 3: Average Family Income Before Tax by Source, Middle Income Quintile (in thousands of 2005 constant dollars)

	Replacement Rates				Difference (High-Low)	
	Low (<60%)	Medium Low (60% to 80%)	Medium High (80% to 100%)	High (>100%)	($000)	Share of Difference (%)
Age from 64 to 66						
Average income at age 55 ($'000)[1]	38.9	38.7	38.7	38.6	...	...
Distribution (%)	18.1	31.5	21.9	28.6	...	...
Earnings ($'000)	1.8	5.2	12.1	26.9	25.1	57.2
Private pensions ($'000)	6.4	11.6	13.2	12.4	6.0	13.7
Investment gains ($'000)	1.6	2.4	3.1	6.0	4.4	10.0
Capital gains ($'000)	0.1	0.4	1.2	10.3	10.2	23.2
OAS/GIS[2] ($'000)	3.5	3.4	3.3	2.5	-1.0	-2.3
C/QPP[3] ($'000)	6.7	7.0	6.6	5.5	-1.2	-2.7
Other ($'000)	0.9	1.0	1.1	1.1	0.2	0.5
Total before tax ($'000)	20.9	30.8	40.6	64.8	43.9	100.0
Age from 69 to 71						
Average income at age 55 ($'000)	38.9	38.7	38.6	38.6	...	...
Distribution (%)	24.3	38.8	21.4	15.5	...	...
Earnings ($'000)	0.3	1.4	4.5	17.3	17.0	40.3
Private pensions ($'000)	5.2	11.7	17.0	19.6	14.4	34.1

(continued)

Investment gains ($'000)	1.0	2.2	3.5	7.6	6.6	15.6
Capital gains ($'000)	0.1	0.2	0.6	5.0	4.9	11.6
OAS/GIS($'000)	7.0	6.8	6.7	5.8	-1.2	-2.8
C/QPP($'000)	7.5	8.2	8.2	8.0	0.5	1.2
Other ($'000)	0.3	0.2	0.2	0.3	0.0	0.0
Total before tax ($'000)	21.4	30.6	40.9	63.6	42.2	100.0

Age from 74 to 76

Average income at age 55 ($'000)	38.9	38.7	38.7	38.6	...	...
Distribution (%)	24.7	36.7	21.6	17.2	...	...
Earnings ($'000)	0.1	0.9	2.7	12.0	11.9	28.6
Private pensions ($'000)	4.4	11.1	17.6	23.3	18.9	45.4
Investment gains ($'000)	0.8	1.8	3.0	8.3	7.5	18.0
Capital gains ($'000)	0.1	0.2	0.5	4.0	3.9	9.4
OAS/GIS ($'000)	7.3	7.1	7.1	6.4	-0.9	-2.2
C/QPP ($'000)	7.6	8.3	8.4	8.2	0.6	1.4
Other ($'000)	0.3	0.2	0.1	0.2	-0.1	-0.2
Total before tax ($'000)	20.7	29.5	39.5	62.3	41.6	100.0

Notes: Numbers may not add up due to rounding.
... not applicable
[1]Total income after taxes.
[2]Old Age Security/Guaranteed Income Supplement.
[3]Canada and Quebec Pension Plans.
Source: Statistics Canada, Longitudinal Administrative Data base.

Table 4: Average Individual Income Before Tax by Source, Middle Income Quintile (in thousands of 2005 constant dollars)

	Replacement Rates				Difference (High-Low)	
	Low (<60%)	Medium Low (60% to 80%)	Medium High (80% to 100%)	High (>100%)	($000s) Difference	Share of Difference (%)
Age from 64 to 66						
Average income at age 55 ($'000)[1]	38.1	38.2	37.9	37.8	…	…
Distribution (%)	26.3	34.3	19.5	20.0	…	…
Earnings ($'000)	0.9	3.7	12.7	24.0	23.1	54.0
Private pensions ($'000)	5.8	12.3	11.9	10.7	4.9	11.4
Investment gains ($'000)	1.8	2.2	3.0	6.7	4.9	11.4
Capital gains ($'000)	0.1	0.4	1.4	12.3	12.2	28.5
OAS/GIS[2] ($'000)	3.2	3.2	2.9	2.2	-1.0	-2.3
C/QPP[3] ($'000)	7.2	7.6	6.4	5.5	-1.7	-4.0
Other ($'000)	0.7	1.1	1.3	0.9	0.2	0.5
Total before tax ($'000)	19.7	30.4	39.7	62.5	42.8	100.0
Age from 69 to 71						
Average income at age 55 ($'000)	38.2	38.1	37.7	37.7	…	…
Distribution (%)	36.5	43.2	13.5	6.8	…	…
Earnings ($'000)	0.0	0.5	2.6	13.1	13.1	27.6
Private pensions ($'000)	5.1	12.8	18.0	20.5	15.4	32.5
Investment gains ($'000)	1.0	2.0	4.2	13.0	12.0	25.3

(continued)

Capital gains ($'000)	0.1	0.2	1.0	8.3	8.2	17.3
OAS/GIS ($'000)	6.4	6.0	5.8	4.8	-1.6	-3.4
C/QPP ($'000)	7.9	8.4	8.5	8.5	0.6	1.3
Other ($'000)	0.2	0.2	0.2	0.2	0.0	0.0
Total before tax ($'000)	20.9	30.1	40.2	68.3	47.4	100.0
Age from 74 to 76						
Average income at age 55 ($'000)	38.2	38.1	37.8	37.7	…	…
Distribution (%)	37.9	39.7	14.1	8.3	…	…
Earnings ($'000)	0.0	0.3	1.1	6.5	6.5	13.4
Private pensions ($'000)	4.7	12.9	19.5	28.8	24.1	49.7
Investment gains ($'000)	0.8	1.7	3.8	12.6	11.8	24.3
Capital gains ($'000)	0.1	0.2	0.7	7.0	6.9	14.2
OAS/GIS ($'000)	6.3	5.8	5.7	4.9	-1.4	-2.9
C/QPP ($'000)	7.8	8.3	8.4	8.5	0.7	1.4
Other ($'000)	0.2	0.1	0.0	0.1	-0.1	-0.2
Total before tax ($'000)	19.9	29.3	39.2	68.4	48.5	100.0

Notes: Numbers may not add up due to rounding.
… not applicable
[1]Total income after taxes.
[2]Old Age Security/Guaranteed Income Supplement.
[3]Canada and Quebec Pension Plans.
Source: Statistics Canada, Longitudinal Administrative Data base.

To overcome this shortcoming, we replicate the analysis based on individual, not family, income. In this case, all reported incomes are received by the individuals themselves, not by others in the family. The results (Table 4) indicate that employment earnings is not as dominant as a source of difference, but investment and capital gains play a very large role. At age 64 to 66, remaining active in the labour market with significant earnings accounted for 54% of the difference in income between the low- and high-replacement rate groups, and investment and capital gains about 40%. But by age 69 to 71, investment and capital gains together accounted for the largest part of the income difference (43%), followed by private pensions (33%) and earnings (28%). By age 74 to 76, it is private pensions and RRSP income that primarily explains the difference in income (about 50%) between the low- and high-replacement rate groups, followed by investment and capital gains (39%) and employment earnings (13%).

To summarize, when replacement rates are computed at the family level, employment earnings is the single most important factor differentiating persons with low-income replacement rates from those with high-income replacement rates until the cohort enters their seventies. After that age, the difference in income from private pensions, including RRSP income, is the most discriminating factor. When computed at the individual level, the importance of employment earnings declines significantly, and investment and capital gains play a large role, accounting for around 40% of the difference between the high- and low-replacement rate groups at all reported ages. Remaining at work is the most important factor for those aged from 64 to 66, but by their mid-seventies, private pensions and RRSPs become the most important source.

Income Levels Among more Recent Cohorts of Retirees

Are more recent cohorts doing better or worse financially than their predecessors as they enter the retirement years? Figure 1 shows remarkable stability in replacement rates across cohorts. People age 55 in 1983 experienced roughly the same replacement rates as those age 55 in 1995 or 1998. However, the story is somewhat different if one turns to actual income levels.

Figure 5 shows that more recent cohorts, such as those age 55 in 1995, are enjoying higher after-tax family income in their early retire-

Figure 5: Family Income after Taxes, Excluding Capital Gains, in 2005 Constant Dollars per Year, Adult-Equivalent Adjusted (AEA), Various Cohorts

Total income, excluding capital gains (AEA)

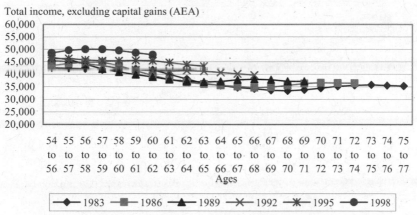

Source: Statistics Canada, Longitudinal Administrative Database.

ment years than their earlier counterparts. For example, at age 64 family income was $35,000[14] in the 1983 cohort (i.e., those age 55 in 1983), but had risen to around $43,000 in the 1995 cohort. This increase was related both to increases in family earnings (see Figure 6) and income from private pensions (see Figure 7).

Although replacement rates have not increased among recent cohorts of retirees, family income has risen simply because income at age 55 is higher among more recent than earlier cohorts.

---

[14]This is after-tax family income in constant dollars, adult equivalent adjusted. To convert adult equivalent adjusted income to actual family income for a family of two, one multiplies by approximately 1.4. Hence, actual family incomes for a family of two in this case would be about $50,000 for the 1983 cohort, rising to $60,000 in the 1995 cohort. Note that capital gains are excluded here, simply because of a discontinuity in the way capital gains are reported associated with a legislative change in 1994. This discontinuity renders the figure less clear, but does not affect comparisons among cohorts.

Figure 6: Earnings by Cohort, in 2005 Constant Dollars per Year, Adult-Equivalent Adjusted

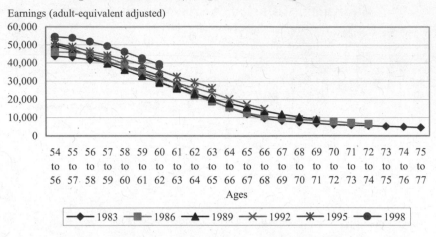

Source: Statistics Canada, Longitudinal Administrative Database.

Figure 7: Income from Private Pensions (and RRSPs) by Cohort, in 2005 Constant Dollars per Year, Adult-Equivalent Adjusted

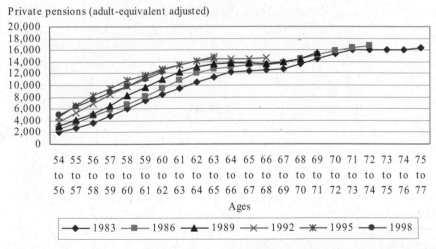

Source: Statistics Canada, Longitudinal Administrative Database.

Sébastien LaRochelle-Côté, John Myles, and Garnett Picot

Income Stability

The core idea underlying the concept of income stability is the notion of predictability (the reduction of uncertainty) in year-to-year income flows at the individual family level. Instability in year-to-year family income may affect the well-being of individuals in that family in many ways, most notably by affecting consumption levels and by creating uncertainty. High levels of income instability in the retirement years are likely to create a good deal of stress and anxiety among seniors.

One very intuitive means of assessing income instability at the individual level is to compute the mean absolute deviation (MAD).[15]

The MAD measures the average deviation, in percentage terms, of actual income from mean income levels during the observation period. For instance, if an individual has a MAD of 0.2 (or 20%), it means that his/her annual family income level during a given period of time, say

---

[15]The mean absolute deviation is computed using the following formula,

$$MAD = \left(\frac{1}{N}\right) \sum_{i=1}^{N} \left[\left(\frac{1}{T}\right) \sum_{t=1}^{T} \left| y_{it}^* - \overline{y}_i^* \right| \right].$$

where N = number of individuals

T = number of years over which the mean deviation is computed

y*(i,t) = the residuals (e(i) + u(i,t)) from a regression of y(i,t) on a vector of observable characteristics, including age, where y(it) is the log of family income. Using the residuals from this regression in essence "detrends" the income variable to account for trends in the age income profile over the five-year period. The regression assumes a common slope for the age-income profile of all individuals, but allows for a distinct intercept for each individual (hence the u(it) residual term). For more detail on this approach, see the original research paper from which this paper is an excerpt, *Income Security and Stability During Retirement in Canada*, Research Paper No. 306, Analytical Studies Research Paper Series, Statistics Canada.

There is an alternative methodology used to study income instability, developed by Gottschalk and Moffitt (1994). It essentially separates the income variance into two components: (a) *permanent* differences in income *between* individuals, and (b) *transitory* differences in annual income for individuals. The (b) component is a measure of income instability. This approach was also used in the original research paper, and can be found there. The results were very similar to those observed using the less complex "mean absolute deviation" approach.

five years, deviated from its mean income level during the five years by 20% each year, on average.

Table 5 shows the levels of income instability experienced by individuals who were in the bottom, middle and top tertiles of the income distribution, using results from the MAD.

There are two major observations: (i) income instability declines as the cohorts age, and (ii) instability was higher among low-income individuals (bottom tertile) than among middle- and higher-income people at the beginning of the period, but became very similar to the instability levels of the other two groups after age 65. From age 55 to 59, in any given year, individuals in the bottom tertile diverged from their mean income by an average 25%, while individuals in the middle and the top tertiles typically diverted by 16% and 18%, respectively. Annual income deviation became much lower after age 70 (below 10%) and did not vary significantly across income groups. These results indicate that the higher levels of instability experienced by low-income individuals (due to unstable employment earnings) are eventually dampened by the stable influx of cash provided by public pensions. The main implication of this is that the pensions system not only provides income security to low-income individuals, but also significantly reduces their degree of income instability.

Table 5: Family Income Instability (mean absolute deviation) by Income Tertiles[1]

Age	All	Bottom Tertile	Middle Tertile	Top Tertile
		Mean absolute deviation		
55 to 59[2]	0.199	0.250	0.162	0.182
60 to 64[2]	0.216	0.257	0.188	0.201
65 to 69[2]	0.126	0.138	0.115	0.124
70 to 74[2]	0.095	0.096	0.086	0.103
75 to 79[3]	0.080	0.081	0.074	0.085
80 to 84[3]	0.085	0.080	0.077	0.097

Notes: [1]Includes all individuals with positive income after taxes in all five years of the interval studied.
[2]Results based on a cohort of individuals aged 55 in 1985.
[3]Results based on a cohort of individuals aged 65 in 1985.
Source: Statistics Canada, Longitudinal Administrative Database.

To assess the extent to which different sources of income dampen income instability among older individuals, we re-estimated the mean absolute deviation (MAD) using a number of different income concepts, starting with: (a) *market income*, including income from earnings, private pensions, investments and capital gains; then moving onto (b) *market income plus public pensions*, including benefits from the Old Age Security, the Guaranteed Income Supplement and the Canada and Quebec Pension Plans; followed by (c) *total income* (market income plus all transfers) before taxes; and finally (d) *total income after taxes*.[16] The results are shown in Table 6. Moving from one income concept to the next allows one to determine the effect of the various income components on income stability. For example, for the 65 to 69 age group in Table 6, public pensions reduced income instability (i.e., the mean absolute deviation) by 15 percentage points as income instability fell from 29% based on market income alone, to 14% based on market income plus public pensions.

In general, the results show that it is the public pension system that is the main source of the reduction in income instability, and that the pension system plays a much larger role in reducing instability for lower- rather than higher-income individuals. This is simply because public pensions, for which annual income instability is extremely low, is a greater share of income among lower- than among higher-income individuals.

For example, among 70- to 74-year-olds, instability falls by 13.2 percentage points as one moves from market income alone (MAD of 22.8%) to total family income after taxes (9.6%). Of this 13.2 percentage point decline, 12.1 percentage points are associated with the public pension system and the remainder with other transfers and taxes. This result is for all individuals. The effect of the pension system on instability in the bottom tertile is even greater, reducing income instability (the mean absolute deviation) by 20.7 percentage points (32.1–11.4). In the top tertile, in contrast, the pension system improved income instability by only 6.5 percentage points (17.6–11.1).

The end result is that, after age 65, income instability is very similar for people at the top and bottom of the distribution (mean absolute deviation of around 10%). The larger effect of the public pension system

---

[16]For convenience, Table 5 only includes individuals who had positive market income in all years, but individuals were similarly classified across tertiles (similar boundaries).

Table 6: Family Income Instability (mean absolute deviation) Based on Various Income Definitions[1]

	Mean Absolute Deviation			
	All	Bottom Tertile	Middle Tertile	Top Tertile
55 to 59 years[2]				
Market income	0.236	0.300	0.206	0.206
Market income + public pensions	0.215	0.262	0.186	0.196
Total income before taxes	0.200	0.238	0.172	0.190
Total income after taxes	0.187	0.218	0.159	0.181
60 to 64[2]				
Market income	0.304	0.379	0.287	0.255
Market income + public pensions	0.228	0.261	0.212	0.213
Total income before taxes	0.210	0.232	0.194	0.204
Total income after taxes	0.200	0.216	0.183	0.200
65 to 69[2]				
Market income	0.290	0.396	0.275	0.217
Market income + public pensions	0.140	0.154	0.132	0.138
Total income before taxes	0.138	0.149	0.129	0.137
Total income after taxes	0.123	0.132	0.113	0.124
70 to 74[2]				
Market income	0.228	0.321	0.205	0.176
Market income + public pensions	0.107	0.114	0.097	0.111
Total income before taxes	0.106	0.112	0.095	0.111
Total income after taxes	0.096	0.100	0.085	0.103
75 to 79[3]				
Market income	0.218	0.315	0.201	0.155
Market income + public pensions	0.091	0.092	0.085	0.094
Total income before taxes	0.090	0.091	0.084	0.094
Total income after taxes	0.080	0.082	0.074	0.085
80 to 84[3]				
Market income	0.217	0.297	0.198	0.173
Market income + public pensions	0.095	0.091	0.085	0.105
Total income before taxes	0.094	0.089	0.084	0.104
Total income after taxes	0.085	0.081	0.076	0.096

Notes: Market income includes earnings, private pensions (including registered retirement saving plans), investment and interest gains and capital gains.
[1]Includes all individuals with positive market income in all five years of the interval studied.
[2]Results based on a cohort of individuals aged 55 in 1985.
[3]Results based on a cohort of individuals aged 65 in 1985.
Source: Statistics Canada, Longitudinal Administrative Database.

among the lower income offset the higher instability in market earnings among this group.

But *average* income instability can also be misleading. Around this average of, say, 20% mean absolute deviation, is a distribution. Some people may have very low levels of instability and some very high.

In Figure 8, we follow the cohort of individuals aged 55 in 1985 to study the changes in the distribution of instability over four age periods: from 55 to 59, from 60 to 64, from 65 to 69 and from 70 to 74. The results clearly show that the distributions move to the left after age 64, indicating that income levels became increasingly stable (instability as measured by the MAD declined) for most seniors as they advanced into their retirement years. At age 60 to 64, there is considerable dispersion of instability, with a significant proportion registering a MAD between 3% and 12%, but also a large proportion beyond 25% and even over 60% mean absolute deviation. By age 70 to 74, the population was heavily concentrated around very low instability levels of less than 10%. These findings suggest that the pension system not only reduces income instability for individuals as they age, but also the *variation* in income instability among retired people. That is, income instability is both lower, and more similar among seniors as a result of the public pension system. This is in addition to providing minimum levels of income security, especially among low-income seniors.

Conclusion

Creating a retirement income system that would generate replacement rates between 65 and 80% of pre-retirement incomes was a widespread goal during the postwar decades in the affluent democracies. Some nations (Germany, Sweden) moved quickly in the late 1950s to establish universal earnings-related pension schemes that would reach that target. In Canada, policymakers chose a more modest route. In 1965, the Canada and Quebec Pension Plans were added to the flat-benefit Old Age Security program created in 1951. Together, the two programs would replace about 40% of the income of the average worker. The expectation then was that the difference for most workers would be made up by private occupational pensions (then rapidly expanding) and personal savings (e.g., in RRSPs).

Figure 8: Percentage Distribution of the Population by Mean Absolute Deviation Levels, and by Age Group

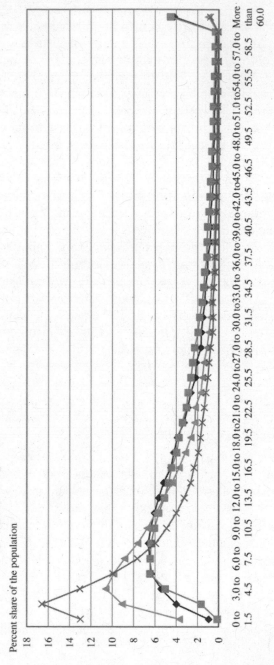

Source: Statistics Canada, Longitudinal Administrative Data base.

Sébastien LaRochelle-Côté, John Myles, and Garnett Picot

By the end of the 1970s, however, scepticism that the desired replacement targets would be reached under existing arrangements was widespread in Canada and in countries with similar designs, largely due to inadequate coverage by private pensions. In the 1980s, Australia, Denmark, the Netherlands and Switzerland all adopted the second option proposed by the Task Force on Retirement Income Policy and made occupational pensions mandatory for all employees.

Recent research, however, has begun to cast doubt on these earlier expectations. An influential report prepared by the Organisation for Economic Co-operation and Development (OECD, 2001) concluded that levels of income replacement in most of the affluent democracies were quite high and similar despite widely divergent pension designs and levels of public benefits. Those results, however, are based on estimating "quasi-replacement" rates, that is, by comparing the incomes of the elderly to those of the non-elderly with cross-sectional data.

Recent longitudinal data produced by Statistics Canada allow us to estimate true replacement rates during their sixties and seventies for individuals with significant labour force attachment. Our main conclusion is that, on average, Canada's income retirement system provides relatively high levels of income replacement for elderly Canadians who had significant attachment to the labour force in their fifties: 100% or more for low-income individuals, close to 80% for those in the middle, and about 70% for those with high incomes.

Averages, of course, do not tell the whole story. Roughly a quarter of middle-income individuals (in their mid-fifties) had income replacement rates of less than 60% by their mid-seventies. By the time they reached their seventies, access to a private pension and RRSP income was the main factor differentiating people with low- from those with high-income replacement rates. This is important, since both the coverage and type of private pensions are undergoing change.

Our analysis of income stability also confirms that the retirement income system yields very stable year-to-year flows of income over the retirement years, due largely to the stabilizing effects of public pensions. Generally speaking, we find that poorer individuals have higher levels of income instability than richer individuals during their late fifties and early sixties, largely because of greater instability in employment income. As the cohorts age, however, the more stable benefits from the public pension system lead to more income stability among low-income individuals and the gap in income stability between the rich and the poor disappears.

But the retirement income system is continuously changing. The results reported for the cohorts included in this analysis, people entering the retirement years during the late 1980s and 1990s, may or may not hold for future cohorts.

In the short term, there are a number of reasons to believe that economic outcomes for most retirees with significant labour market attachment will not be any worse than those reported here. The educational attainment of retirees is increasing dramatically. In 1990, around one-quarter of Canadians aged 55 to 64 had completed some form of postsecondary education; by 2006 this had risen to around one-half. This likely means that the lifetime earnings of future retirees will be higher, and the desires and opportunities for some employment earnings during the retirement years may be greater than among their predecessors.

The opportunities for employment are also likely to be greater for retirees in the future. Many analysts are predicting labour shortages as the workforce ages and labour supply declines. This increased demand will likely result in increased employment opportunities for seniors, if they wish to pursue them and are healthy enough to do so. Furthermore, with the rise in the two-earner family during the 1970s and 1980s, more women entering retirement will have worked a significant portion of their lives, meaning an increased contribution to the retirement income in many families.

But there remain a number of areas for concern regarding income maintenance. Replacement rates may continue to be an issue for families without a private pension or significant RRSP savings — the widowed, divorced or separated women — and possibly immigrants who enter Canada in their later years and do not have time to accumulate savings prior to retirement.

As one moves further into the future, possible outcomes regarding replacement rates are, of course, even less certain. Private pension coverage has been falling among younger people, and in some industries a shift from defined-benefit to defined-contribution plans is underway. These and other changes may significantly affect replacement rates in the more distant future.

References

Diamond, P. and J. Hausman. 1984. "Individual Retirement and Savings Behavior", *Journal of Public Economics* 23, 81–114.

Gottschalk, P. and R. Moffitt. 1994. "The Growth of Earnings Instability in the U.S. Labor Market", *Brooking Papers on Economic Activity* 2, 217–272.

Gower, D. 1998. "Income Transition Upon Retirement", *Perspectives on Labour and Income* 10(4), 18–23. Catalogue No. 75-001-XIE1998004. Ottawa: Statistics Canada.

Myles, J. 2000. "The Maturation of Canada's Retirement Income System: Income Levels, Income Inequality and Low Income Among the Elderly", *Canadian Journal on Aging* 19(3), 287–316.

Organisation for Economic Co-operation and Development (OECD). 2001. *Aging and Income: Financial Resources and Retirement in 9 OECD Countries*. Paris: OECD.

Perrin, G. 1969. "Reflections on Fifty Years of Social Security", *International Labour Review* 99, 249–290.

Schulz, J.H. 1992. *The Economics of Aging*. 5th ed. New York: Auburn House.

Smeeding, T. and D. Sullivan. 1998. "Generations and the Distribution of Economic Well-Being: A Cross-National View", Working Paper Series No. 173. Luxembourg: Luxembourg Income Study.

The Distribution of Seniors' Income in Canada

Michael R. Veall

Introduction

The income distribution of the older population in Canada might be of special policy interest for two key reasons. First, some of Canada's most important transfer programs, Old Age Security and the Guaranteed Income Supplement, are targeted at this population, as of course is the Canada Pension Plan/Quebec Pension Plan. At the same time, the older population has a number of special tax measures, from the clawback of Old Age Security to the recent allowance of pension income splitting for tax purposes. Second, and perhaps related to the first reason, labour supply by the older population is smaller, and hence the efficiency/equity trade-off with respect to labour income may be arguably less important for that group, leading to a greater focus within that group on equity or at least on poverty reduction. (However, note that a number of policy proposals designed to reduce the public burden of income support for seniors focus on

I am grateful for the support of the research program on the Social and Economic Dimensions of an Aging Population (SEDAP) and of the Social Sciences and Humanities Research Council of Canada and for the assistance of Deb Fretz and Simo Goshev, as well as Tom Swoger, André Bernard and Habib Saani of Statistics Canada. Charles Beach and conference participants provided helpful comments.

postponing retirement and hence increasing labour supply by the older population.)

In an important study of recent trends in Canada's all-ages family income distribution, Frenette, Green, and Picot (2004) emphasize the use of taxfiler data as opposed to survey data (the Survey of Consumer Finances and its successor the Survey of Labour and Income Dynamics). They point out that since 1992, the coverage rate of the tax data has been 95% or better, because low-income individuals who would not pay tax increasingly have found filing advantageous because of refundable tax credits. These high coverage rates compare to coverage of about 80% for the corresponding surveys, where much of the coverage gap appears to be in the lower tail. Hence inequality measures using survey data are biased downwards.[1]

Saez and Veall (2005, 2007) also used taxfiler data to study the Canadian all-ages individual income distribution, following other studies such as Piketty and Saez (2003) for the United States and Atkinson (2007) for the United Kingdom by focusing on the very top end, that is, the percentage of pre-tax income received by the top 5%, 1%, 0.1%, and 0.01% individuals in the population. One of the findings of Saez and Veall is that there has been a recent surge in these top shares. For example, between 1980 and 2000, the share of the pre-tax income received by the top 5% recipients rose from 22.7% to 29.0%, the top 1% share rose from 8.1% to 13.6%, the top 0.1% share rose from 2.0% to 5.2%, and the top 0.01% share rose from 0.5% to 1.9%.[2] While many measures of inequality (such as the log of the ratio of the 90th percentile of income to the 10th percentile of income) are not affected by these top shares and others such as the Gini coefficient are relatively insensitive to changes in the tails, these top shares might nonetheless be of interest to students of the income distribution.[3]

---

[1]Survey data may also undersample those at the top end because such individuals may successfully avoid participation. It is possible that such individuals may under-report by not including less transparent sources of income. There may also be topcoding.

[2]Murphy, Roberts, and Wolfson (2007) find similar results when the sample is extended to 2005.

[3]Indeed Frenette, Green, and Picot (2004) exclude the top and bottom 0.1% of incomes from all of their calculations. This is often done with survey analysis to exclude large outliers; they make the same exclusions for taxfiler data for comparability.

Michael R. Veall

The current study therefore uses Canadian taxfiler data to study the income distribution of the older population in recent years, with some additional discussion of the bottom and top ends of the income distribution. This discussion includes reference to such variables as immigration status, age, gender, and marital status.

The next section will briefly describe the data. The third section will give the results. The last section concludes.

The Data

The data source is the Longitudinal Administrative Databank (LAD), which is a replenished, longitudinal sample for 20% of all taxfilers in Canada (so that for 2005 it has over 4 million records). The variables available are confined to those available from tax records, so that there is no information on health or education (except as those variables may affect certain tax deductions or credits). However, Statistics Canada, using information provided directly on the form as well as other methods such as address matching, does link individuals into families.

The LAD begins in 1982. However, the analysis here does not begin until 1992. One reason is that it was not until 1992 that the LAD included data for the Guaranteed Income Supplement (GIS) and the Spousal Allowance (SpA). There would be little point in proceeding without these important sources of income included.

It might be possible to impute GIS and SpA for earlier years, but there is another reason for beginning the analysis in 1992. Since 1992 LAD coverage rates have been 95% or higher, suggesting that the selection bias associated with income distribution bias is probably small. In the early 1990s, refundable tax credits began to bring the lower tail of the income distribution into the filing population. Of these, the most universal incentive is the Goods and Services Tax Credit, a refundable credit first paid in late 1990. In addition, filing an income tax return for 1992 made one potentially eligible for the 1993 Child Tax Benefit, also paid to families even if they had no earnings. As noted in the introduction, Frenette, Green, and Picot (2004) find that coverage biases are likely empirically important.[4]

---

[4]Frenette, Green, and Milligan (2007) provide an all-ages income distribution analysis of the 1980s and the 1990s using census data (thereby solving the coverage problem), where they impute taxes using an econometric equation based on the taxfiler data.

Three types of family income are examined. The first is market income, defined as total income excluding government payments such as Workers' Compensation, the Child Tax Benefit, the Goods and Services Tax Credit, Employment Insurance, Canada Pension Plan/Quebec Pension Plan (CPP/QPP), Old Age Security (OAS), the Spousal Allowance, and Guaranteed Income Supplement (GIS). It does include Alimony and Support Income, pensions, income from Registered Retirement Savings Plans withdrawals as well as all income derived from employment (including self-employment and business income), net rental income, and all capital income.

The second is before-tax income, defined as income including government payments with no subtraction of any type of tax. It is market income as defined above but with government payments included.

The third is after-tax income, defined as before-tax income less federal and provincial personal income taxes. The Quebec Abatement (a rebate on federal tax) is included in this measure. Quebec provincial income taxes are estimated in the LAD data. Federal or provincial payroll taxes, employment insurance premiums and CPP/QPP premiums are not deducted, nor is there any deduction for sales taxes.

Capital gains are included in all the income definitions. In part this is for simplicity: if capital gains were to be excluded then ideally the tax paid on capital gains should also be excluded and this would require an estimate of the marginal tax rate paid on those capital gains, which is not entirely straightforward. Second, it is not entirely clear that capital gains during retirement should be treated differently than other types of capital income. In any case, a version of the key table (Table 1) is provided with capital gains excluded (but no adjustment to taxes) as Appendix Table A1. Saez and Veall (2005, 2007) also include three- and five-year moving averages in their work with the all-ages income distribution, without any important change in the results. This is consistent with Beach, Finnie, and Gray (2001).

Following Frenette, Green, and Picot (2004), zero incomes are included in all samples. Indeed those with negative incomes are also included, although their incomes are set as zero as, for example, is required for the calculation of Gini coefficients. Individuals who die, immigrate or emigrate in the sample year are excluded.

In all cases, the relevant income measure is at the family level. In the vast majority of cases for those 66+, this is either individual income (for an unattached individual) or the combined income of a couple (often the sum of the incomes from their individual filings, but in those cases where the

Table 1: Income Inequality Indices, Canada, Population 66 Years of Age or Older
(Selected years)

Market Income

Year	Log (95/5)	Log (90/10)	Log (50/10)	Gini
1992	n.a.	n.a.	n.a.	0.61631
1995	n.a.	n.a.	n.a.	0.62934
2000	n.a.	n.a.	n.a.	0.66981
2005	n.a.	n.a.	n.a.	0.66957

Total Income (including transfers)

Year	Log (95/5)	Log (90/10)	Log (50/10)	Gini
1992	1.76724	1.48646	0.52343	0.37584
1995	1.76235	1.49924	0.53757	0.36742
2000	1.90892	1.60293	0.58896	0.42504
2005	1.91944	1.61755	0.60169	0.42206

After-tax Income

Year	Log (95/5)	Log (90/10)	Log (50/10)	Gini
1992	1.52719	1.27855	0.47047	0.32015
1995	1.50164	1.27139	0.47324	0.30738
2000	1.65986	1.38454	0.51937	0.36712
2005	1.71450	1.43096	0.54186	0.37319

Notes: Sample sizes are 573,810 for 1992, 628,951 for 1995, 710,409 for 2000 and 778,856 for 2005. There are no log ratio values for market income because the denominator percentiles do not exceed zero.

spouse earns little and does not file, any reported spousal income is nonetheless included). However, there are some cases where there are income-earning children in the census family, and their income is included. Children in such families may be children still living with their parents or adopted children, such as adopted grandchildren.

To convert these family incomes to single equivalents, something very close to the Statistics Canada family-size adjustment is used. Family income is divided by the sum of one plus 0.4 if a spouse is present and 0.3×(the number of children). This would be exactly the Statistics Canada adjustment if adult children were given a weight of 0.4 rather than 0.3. A rival adjustment, used, for example, in Frenette, Green, and Milligan and most calculations involving the Luxembourg Income Study, is to divide by the square root of the number of individuals. Counts and calculations are by individual, where if there is a couple both 66 or over, both are included in the calculations, but if only one has attained the age of 66, only he/she is included. There are a small number of cases where individuals 66 years of age or over live with their older parents and these children are included in the calculations.

Results and Discussion

Table 1 presents some basic measures of inequality, the log of the ratio of the 95th percentile of income to the 5th percentile of income (log (95/5)) as well as log (90/10) and log (50/10), similarly defined. The table also presents the Gini coefficients. All results are presented for all three income measures although for market income, none of the log ratio values are defined as the denominator percentile does not exceed zero.

It is easy to summarize the results of the table. The measures of inequality suggest that for market income, total income and after-tax income, all became more unequal, with the biggest jump between 1995 and 2000. The timing and size of the changes appear to be broadly comparable across income definitions. Given the relatively short time period of this analysis, guesses at causality are particularly speculative, but 1995 to 2000 was a period associated with very strong increases in employment and with substantial financial market returns. These may have disproportionately benefited high earners. Both of these indicators slowed somewhat over 2000 to 2005.

The values for log ratios tend to be smaller than comparable ratios presented in Frenette, Green, and Milligan for the all-age population while the Gini coefficients tend to be a bit larger for after-tax income (compare a year 2000 value of about 0.367 here to 0.322 from their study), moderately larger for total income (0.425 versus 0.357) but much, much larger for market income (0.670 versus 0.439). Our after-tax income Gini values[5] are also somewhat higher than the values presented in Brown and Prus (2004, 2006) which use the Luxembourg Income Study (LIS) data (and hence for Canada the Survey of Labour and Income Dynamics, which is the Canadian dataset used in the LIS).[6] This is consistent with a very strong polarization of market income and the Frenette, Green, and Picot point about coverage. Hence, I will turn to a brief discussion of the top end of the income distribution as well as the bottom end.

Figure 1 illustrates one aspect of the upper end of the senior income distribution. It can be seen that market income is quite concentrated so that in 2002, about 21% of all market income accrued to the top 1% income recipients in Canada. The comparable value for the top 1% of income recipients at all ages is 13%.

Employment income is even more concentrated, with the top 1% of non-self-employment income earners receiving about 68% of all non-self-employment income and only a slightly smaller concentration for employment income.

What explains this? It is possible that senior income support programs may be a cause of the concentration, in that it may only be worthwhile for a small number of seniors with high earnings to pursue high-income employment given the support amounts and the clawbacks on additional earnings. But that seems unlikely to be the sole explanation because as will be discussed below, this concentration is now at income levels well above the clawback range.

Another reason for the concentration of senior employment income is surely health effects. Some seniors who would like to work cannot because of poor health.

But the income support and the health explanations are not fully satisfying. During this period, senior income support programs were relatively stable and senior health (at least at the low end of the senior age range) was probably improving. Yet employment income concentration increased throughout. Hence it seems plausible that the root causes of this

---

[5]Table A1 presents the results with capital gains excluded on the income side. These values predictably estimate a greater degree of equality, but the overall trends are similar, with perhaps less evidence of a jump between 1995 and 2000.

[6]Frenette, Green, and Milligan (2007) do not include capital gains in their income tax measure. Brown and Prus (2004, 2006) include capital gains in their income measure and subtract all personal income taxes. Both subtract all personal income taxes in calculating after-tax income.

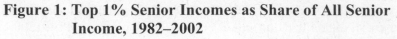

Figure 1: Top 1% Senior Incomes as Share of All Senior Income, 1982–2002

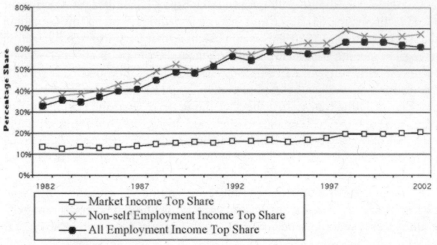

Source: Veall (2006).

change are related to those of the increase in income concentration in the general population.

While these causes are a matter of debate, one type of explanation emphasizes technical change.[7] Katz and Murphy (1992) highlight skill-biased technical change: they argue that the technology improvements over this period (such as those associated with computers) improved the productivity of workers with high skill and education relative to those with low skill and education. It can be further argued that those improvements particularly affected those at the top end of the income distribution so that for example, e-mail and cell phones permit a high-flying, specialized salesperson to service more territory or a top manager to have direct contact with more employees. Thus, continuing improvement in these types of technologies concentrates the income distribution over time.

There are other possible explanations based on technological change. For example, Beaudry and Green (2005) build on work by, among others,

---

[7]Explanations such as the decline of unionization (DiNardo, Fortin, and Lemieux, 1996) are probably not relevant for the concentration of employment income among seniors.

Michael R. Veall

Acemoglu (1998) and highlight the role of technological change and the increased number of highly educated workers in the establishment of new organizations that employ new technology. They argue that the amount of physical capital has not kept pace with these developments, reducing the wages of unskilled workers. In their model the new technology requires less capital to produce a unit of output, leading to an increase in the wage differential between skilled and unskilled workers.

Another class of explanations is institutional, arguing that changes in corporate governance and culture may have led to increased payments for CEOs and other top executives. (This change could also have technological roots, in that innovations in capital markets allowed the development of leveraged buyouts, which may have put a premium on top managerial talent.) This type of explanation may be arguably more consistent with the evidence adduced by Saez and Veall (2005, 2007) that income concentration in Canada is a spillover from income concentration in the United States, perhaps because US opportunities led to the salaries of Canadian executives being bid up, or perhaps because US executive salary outcomes were mimicked by Canadian corporations.

Regardless of the exact impact of technological/institutional change, it clearly could improve the relative incomes of some senior-aged managers and other sorts of senior-aged "white collar" workers who remain in the labour force while other senior-aged workers drop out. Moreover, the pace and type of technological change may make it hard for all workers at all ages to "keep up" with an increasing number of senior-aged workers over the period, electing to retire rather than to continue to adapt.

In passing, I note that such a concentration of employment income makes it difficult to imagine that the aggregate effect on employment income of incremental changes in GIS or OAS clawback ranges could be very large. The threshold level for the top 1% of senior employment income earners is about $130,000: such individuals are well beyond the reach of these clawbacks and, as demonstrated, the aggregate labour income earned by others is small. Hence it may be appropriate that analysis of the disincentive effects of these clawbacks has concentrated on the savings disincentive (see, e.g., Shillington, 1999; Kesselman and Poschmann, 2001).

Finally, Tables 2, 3, 4, and 5 all examine factors that may be associated with either tail of the income distribution. (See Veall, 2007, for a more explicit discussion of poverty in this context involving a larger set of possibly associated variables.) Very briefly, from Table 2 it can be seen that immigration status is very important: immigrants are strongly over-represented in the lower income tail because they do not qualify for senior income support. In Table 3, it can be seen that the older old (those 80 years and over) were mildly over-represented at the bottom end of the senior income distribution in 1992, but that is no longer the case by 2005. The change is due to improved pension earnings for this group, including CPP/QPP earnings. Tables 4 and 5 show that for men and particularly for women, unattached individuals (single, separated or divorced, as opposed to married or in a common-law relationship) are over-represented in the lower tail and under-represented in the upper tail. In addition, women are over-represented in the lower tail and under-represented in the upper tail. For example, in 2005 about 57% of those 66 years or over were women and this same proportion holds in the middle 90% of the income distribution. In the lower 5% tail of the distribution, however, 63% are women while in the upper end, about 51% were women.

Table 2: Immigration and the Top and Bottom Ends of the Senior After-Tax Income Distribution in Canada, 2005

	Year	% in Bottom 5%	% in Middle 90%	% in Top 5%
Immigrants (landed in previous ten years)				
	1992	51.7	46.4	1.9
	1995	60.6	38.7	0.7
	2000	61.7	37.2	1.1
	2005	70.7	28.6	0.7

Table 3: Age and the Top and Bottom Ends of the Senior After-Tax Income Distribution in Canada, 2005

	Year	% in Bottom 5%	% in Middle 90%	% in Top 5%
Individuals 80 years of age and over				
	1992	8.1	88.3	3.6
	1995	6.3	90.1	3.7
	2000	5.2	90.7	4.1
	2005	5.0	90.9	4.1

Note: Rows may not add to 100% due to rounding.

Table 4: Marital and Parental Status and the Top and Bottom Ends of the Senior After-Tax Income Distribution in Canada, Men, 2005

	Year	% in Bottom 5%	% in Middle 90%	% in Top 5%
Attached men with kids				
	1992	4.8	85.9	9.3
	1995	4.5	86.3	9.2
	2000	3.6	88.1	8.2
	2005	3.2	88.9	8.0
Attached men without kids				
	1992	2.6	91.2	6.2
	1995	3.3	90.5	6.3
	2000	4.7	89.0	6.3
	2005	3.9	89.8	6.3
Unattached men with kids				
	1992	6.1	85.6	8.3
	1995	6.4	84.8	8.8
	2000	5.9	86.9	7.3
	2005	5.4	87.5	7.1
Unattached men without kids				
	1992	6.8	89.6	3.7
	1995	5.9	90.5	3.6
	2000	5.4	90.9	3.8
	2005	5.9	90.5	3.7

Note: Rows may not add to 100% due to rounding.

Table 5: Marital and Parental Status and the Top and Bottom Ends of the Senior After-Tax Income Distribution in Canada, Women, 2005

	Year	% in Bottom 5%	% in Middle 90%	% in Top 5%
Attached women with kids				
	1992	4.3	86.5	9.2
	1995	2.8	87.7	9.6
	2000	2.6	89.3	8.0
	2005	1.9	90.4	7.6
Attached women without kids				
	1992	2.5	91.2	6.3
	1995	2.7	90.9	6.4
	2000	4.4	89.6	6.1
	2005	3.3	90.5	6.2
Unattached women with kids				
	1992	5.5	87.2	7.4
	1995	5.7	87.7	6.6
	2000	5.0	89.5	5.5
	2005	5.1	89.9	5.0
Unattached women without kids				
	1992	8.6	89.3	2.1
	1995	8.2	89.8	2.0
	2000	6.1	91.5	2.4
	2005	7.8	90.0	2.3

Note: Rows may not add to 100% due to rounding.

Conclusions

Using log ratio or Gini measures, the income distribution of the older population in Canada has become more unequal over the period 1992 to 2005, with the largest jump between 1995 and 2000. Over this same period there has been a continuing surge of income concentration: the share of the top 1% of senior income earners of after-tax income is 20%. Employment income is even more concentrated with the top 1% earning close to 70%. The low end of the income distribution is very disproportionately immigrant and somewhat disproportionately female and unattached (divorced, separated or single as opposed to married or in a common-law relationship).

Michael R. Veall

Appendix Table A1: Income Inequality Indices, Canada, Population 66 Years of Age or Older (Selected years, capital gains excluded from income distribution)

Market Income

Year	Log (95/5)	Log (90/10)	Log (50/10)	Gini
1992	n.a.	n.a.	n.a.	0.6018
1995	n.a.	n.a.	n.a.	0.6189
2000	n.a.	n.a.	n.a.	0.6366
2005	n.a.	n.a.	n.a.	0.6443

Total Income (including transfers)

Year	Log (95/5)	Log (90/10)	Log (50/10)	Gini
1992	1.72204	1.46042	0.51931	0.3594
1995	1.73489	1.48128	0.53396	0.3552
2000	1.79085	1.53204	0.57411	0.3814
2005	1.82139	1.55701	0.58747	0.3877

After-tax Income

Year	Log (95/5)	Log (90/10)	Log (50/10)	Gini
1992	1.47521	1.25039	0.46706	0.2994
1995	1.46451	1.25045	0.47034	0.2924
2000	1.52480	1.30613	0.50650	0.3167
2005	1.59287	1.36089	0.52803	0.3310

Notes: Sample sizes are 573,810 for 1992, 628,951 for 1995, 710,409 for 2000 and 778,856 for 2005. There are no log ratio values for market income because the denominator percentiles do not exceed zero.

References

Acemoglu, D. 1998. "Why Do New Technologies Complement Skills? Directed Technical Change and Wage Inequality", *Quarterly Journal of Economics* (November), 1055–1089.

Atkinson, A.B. 2007. "The Distribution of Top Incomes in the United Kingdom, 1908–2000", in A.B. Atkinson and T. Piketty (eds.), *Top Incomes Over the Twentieth Century*. Oxford: Oxford University Press.

Beach, C., R. Finnie, and D. Gray. 2001. "Earnings Variability and Earnings Instability of Women and Men in Canada", School of Policy Studies Working Paper No. 25. Kingston: Queen's University.

Beaudry, P. and D.A. Green. 2005. "Changes in U.S. Wages 1976–2000: Ongoing Skill Bias or Major Technological Change?" *Journal of Labor Economics* 23 (July), 609–648.

Brown, R.L. and S.G. Prus. 2004. "Social Transfers and Income Inequality in Old Age: A Multi-national Perspective", *North American Actuarial Journal* 8(4), 30–36.

_____. 2006. *Income Inequality over the Later-Life Course: A Comparative Analysis of Seven OECD Countries*. SEDAP Research Paper No. 154. Hamilton: McMaster University.

DiNardo, J., N. Fortin, and T. Lemieux. 1996. "Labour Market Institutions and the Distribution of Wages, 1973–1992: A Semiparametric Approach", *Econometrica* 64 (September), 1001–1044.

Frenette, M., D.A. Green, and G. Picot. 2004. *Rising Income Inequality in the 1990s: An Exploration of Three Data Sources*. Analytical Studies Research Paper Series No. 219. Ottawa: Statistics Canada.

Frenette, M., D.A. Green, and K. Milligan. 2007. "The Tale of the Tails: Canadian Income Inequality in the 1980s and 1990s", *Canadian Journal of Economics*, 743–764.

Katz, L.F. and K.M. Murphy. 1992."Changes in Relative Wages 1963–1987: Supply and Demand Factors", *Quarterly Journal of Economics* 107 (February), 35–78.

Kesselman, J. and F. Poschmann. 2001. *A New Option for Retirement Savings: Tax Prepaid Savings Plans*. Commentary. Toronto: C.D. Howe Institute.

Murphy, B., P. Roberts, and M. Wolfson. 2007. "High-Income Canadians", *Perspectives on Labour and Income* 8(9). Ottawa: Statistics Canada.

Piketty, T. and E. Saez. 2003. "Income Inequality in the United States, 1913–1998", *Quarterly Journal of Economics*, 1–39.

Saez, E. and M.R. Veall. 2005. "The Evolution of High Incomes in North America: Lessons from Canadian Evidence", *American Economic Review*, 831–849.

_____. 2007. "The Evolution of High Incomes in Canada, 1920–2000", in A.B. Atkinson and T. Piketty (eds.), *Top Incomes Over the Twentieth Century*. Oxford: Oxford University Press.

Shillington, R. 1999. *The Dark Side of Targeting: Retirement Saving for Low-Income Canadians*. Commentary. Toronto: C.D. Howe Institute.

Veall, M.R. 2006. "The Top Shares of Older Earners in Canada", SEDAP Working Paper No. 156. Hamilton: McMaster University.

_____. 2007. "Which Canadian Seniors Are Below the Low-Income Measure?" SEDAP Working Paper No. 186. Hamilton: McMaster University.

Pension Reform in Canada:
Getting from Denial to Acceptance

William B.P. Robson

Introduction: The Five Stages of Dealing with Bad News

The key theme of my contribution to this volume is the need to get over false nostalgia for a "golden age" of pensions — the heyday of the classic single-employer defined-benefit (DB) plan — that really never was. Those plans were built on a false premise: that sizeable premiums in returns on financial assets different from those that would match pension liabilities — returns that became more certain as time horizons extended — would allow guaranteed deferred compensation at low cost. We need to put that hope, and the problematic compensation arrangements it fostered, behind us if we are to focus on a critical task for the future: fostering work-related pension plans that will give the average saver low-cost accumulation and annuitization, without the agency problems that have undermined the classic DB plan.

That summary makes clear, I hope, my motive in drawing from what has become pop psychology for my title — the five stages of dealing with catastrophic loss outlined in Elisabeth Kubler-Ross's book *On Death and Dying* (Kubler-Ross, 1969). While clinicians have reservations about this taxonomy, the idea that catastrophe puts us through, in turn, denial, anger, bargaining, depression, and acceptance has entered popular imagination.

Anyone who has recently tried to start a car with a dead battery or get a balky laptop computer to show presentation slides probably has a recent five-stage episode fresh in mind.

The Bad News about DB Pensions

The plight of the classic single-employer DB pension plan in Canada is more complicated than a dead car battery or laptop, partly because there's no consensus on the problem. We tend to regulate and litigate compensation, and deferred compensation all the more, because of the extra information and agency problems that can creep in when payments are well off in the future. So a lot of regulation, tax provisions, and case law have accreted around pensions, and many people understandably look at regulation, taxation and case law to figure out why these plans are in trouble and how we help them out.

I would argue that the problem — the catastrophic news — is the faulty premise of these plans. The premise was that employees could give up modest current compensation and get a rich and secure deferred compensation. In the public sector, the tax base would provide. In the private sector, the idea was that a long-term investor could ride out equity-market cycles and earn returns several percent above those available on a portfolio that matched the liabilities of a typical pension plan.

Why did people think that? The immediate postwar period provided some compelling numbers. Rapid growth of the working-age population *and* rapid growth of output per worker drove rapid real growth. And yields on high-quality debt were low — around 3% nominal for the first decade, and rarely much above 5% for the decade after that.

Economic growth exceeding returns on low-risk debt means good times for holders of residual claims. At the beginning of that period, holders of lower-priority claims such as common shares got a current yield that reflected higher perceived risk after the turbulence of the 1930s and 1940s. Dividend yields on common shares were higher than bond yields. The "go-go" 1950s and 1960s turned that view upside-down: the premium of dividend over bond yields reversed and common shares earned compound returns well above those on low-risk, fixed-income instruments.

So the view spread that investors with long time horizons could reap a reward by investing in equities. Consultants helped set up pension plans based on this idea. Employees and their representatives gave up little for their employers' rich promises. Managers assumed that risk diminished with time. And accommodating regulators and accountants built projected returns well above the low-risk rate into pension-plan balance sheets.

The story of the recent "perfect storm" of demographic and economic developments afflicting DB plans has been well told elsewhere.[1] It has many elements: "old economy" industries that thrived during the go-go years and made promises they could not sustain when they passed their peak; regulations and case law that eroded sponsors' ability and incentives to fully fund their plans; the combination of earlier retirement and longer life that undermined the demographic assumptions on which many DB plans were based. My summary would be the old maxim that when things look too good to be true, they usually are. The fact that returns on equities had consistently and significantly outpaced returns on long bonds was revealed to be an observation about specific countries during specific periods of time, rather than a universal truth. And people who criticize the move to more market-oriented pension-plan valuations are shooting at a messenger who took too long to arrive. We now have the catastrophic news. My hope is that Canadians will move quickly, if not easily, through denial, anger, bargaining and depression. We need acceptance, and the clearer, forward-looking vision that goes with it, to get on with reforms that will:

- address policies that needlessly aggravate the DB problem;
- make the world of RRSPs and other money-purchase plans more congenial for the majority of Canadians who, for the foreseeable future, will save for retirement in them; and
- foster the growth of new pooled occupational pension plans that will make more realistic promises at reasonable cost.

Denial

Saying that many pension experts and advocates are in denial is not putting up a straw man. The Arthurs Commission in Ontario is a current example

---

[1]Clark and Monk (2006) provide a useful international perspective; Laidler and Robson (2007) summarize some key Canadian experiences.

of an official effort with a mandate explicitly to promote DB pensions.[2] David Dodge (2005) held defined-benefit plans up as the desirable model. And many regulators and advocates want more accommodative reporting and funding requirements to make the bad news easier to ignore.

This last point is, I hope, easiest to dispose of. Another maxim applies here: what gets measured gets managed. Balance sheets of plans with big asset-liability mismatches will show more volatility. If people want more security, they should match better. And if discounting obligations at the low-risk rate makes them look expensive, that is because they are expensive. Guarantees cost money. Higher than low-risk returns are something you book when — we should really say "if" — you earn them, not before.

In many respects, in fact, denial still affects financial reporting. Ontario regulations do not require the balance sheet to reflect the indexed portion of pension benefits. They should, and until more real-return securities exist to discount them, the real return bond (RRB) yield is the apt market measure. Valuing indexed liabilities at that rate produces startling numbers — the last actuarial valuation of the federal public-service plan showed that at the then-current yield of 1.73%, the plan was worth more than 33% of pay.[3] That is the cost of that guarantee — a good thing for taxpayers to know.

Anger

Since those taxpayers who have money-purchase individual accounts cannot contribute more than 18% of pay, that point is a convenient one from which to segue to the next stage: anger. Mounting evidence that the classic DB plan is disappearing in the private sector is making some of its advocates louder in asserting its superiority.

---

[2]Expert Commission on Pensions (Ontario), "Terms of Reference". Available at www.pensionreview.on.ca/english/termsofReference.html.

[3]OCA, 2006, p. 59. A quadratic interpolation of the sensitivity of the plan's normal cost to the real-return bond rate suggests that discounting at the yield prevailing at the time of writing — marginally more than 2% — would produce a contribution rate of exactly 30%.

It is true that many workers with individual retirement accounts do not know how much to save, invest poorly, pay high fees, cash out ineptly, and outlive their assets. But arguing that these defects make the case for the old DB model is to let emotion overrule reason. The misleading promise of DB pensions — combined with perverse tax law, regulation and court decisions — led to underfunding. And underfunding led to broken promises. Not every Ontario steelworker got the implicit return on foregone current compensation that his plan promised. Other DB plan members are discovering that their pension is worth less, or is less secure, than they thought. There's anger at bargaining tables and in court rooms.

Bargaining

So what about the next stage: bargaining? Let me deal mainly with the bargaining actual and would-be DB plan sponsors and participants might undertake with policymakers. What might they ask for?

If we stay agnostic on the equity premium and related issues, and take for granted that plan managers will, or even should, mismatch assets and liabilities, a number of tax laws, regulations and court decisions need revision.

On the tax side, we need higher — or no — limits on overfunding of pension plans. Fluctuations in asset prices and discount rates like those over the postwar decades will cause a plan with a "standard" asset-liability mismatch that is unconstrained by contributions to show assets well over 110% of liabilities on a regular basis. Tax laws that forbid contributions when assets are above that level will cause such plans to have more frequent and larger deficits (Banerjee and Robson, 2008).

Tougher would be to get contribution limits on both DB plans and RRSPs raised. At the risk of prompting a reversion to anger, I'll ask rhetorically why, if the federal public service gets pensions worth more than 30% of pay, they limit the rest of us to 18%?

Bargaining the legal status of surpluses is also tougher. Pension obligations ought to be in law what most of us would say they are in fact: title to periodic payments, not the assets that back them. But that case has to be made courtroom by courtroom and legislature by legislature.

Other less happy kinds of bargaining with policymakers are also in prospect. Some sponsors and participants want government bailouts. Ontario has a guarantee fund, and a sad story it has been. Pressure for a federal one has not gone away. The US Pension Benefit Guaranty Corporation looks to me like a back-door to nationalizing declining industries. The recently established UK fund seems quickly to have created a larger subsidy from well- to badly-run plans than expected, with the prospective premium cost worsening the disincentive to creating new DB plans.

Others want infrequent reporting, long amortization periods, and valuations involving smoothing and judgement. As I remarked earlier, this also is the wrong emphasis. People cannot manage risks they cannot see. In Canada, the distribution of realized equity premiums over overlapping ten-year periods since 1970 shows an average difference between total equity and long-bonds returns of 1.4 percentage points, with a standard deviation of 3.8 percentage points (Laidler and Robson, 2007, p. 11). The realized premium over these ten-year periods was negative more than one-third of the time.

People who insist that the future offers big premiums on equity — or infrastructure or real estate — have also to confront the fact that prices for these assets are being bid up because other people believe the same thing. In the long run, real growth in the economy constrains real returns on our saving, and we need to make sure that pension managers react to disappointments of their more extravagant hopes in a timely way.

Depression

A common objection to high-frequency reporting of pension-plan balance sheets using current interest rates and asset values is the volatility it will add to the bottom line. Reducing that volatility will require managers to match assets more closely to liabilities. And — the influence of the equity premium on thinking being what it is — closer matching will raise the apparent cost of the benefit. So a DB pension becomes a less attractive part of the compensation bargain, and we move on to depression.

Some current DB plan participants would probably be better off letting the sponsor lay their obligations off on an insurer while the plan is still a going concern. But they might get 80 cents for every dollar they are currently expecting — a depressing prospect. So they will hang on, risking a smash and litigation that leaves them with less than 80 cents on the dollar — another depressing prospect.

The fact that the last stronghold of the classic DB plan is the public sector is also depressing. The accrual patterns that promote early retirement and push hidden costs forward will persist in the public service, health, education and so on even as they disappear elsewhere. Taxpayers will get a larger bill than they're expecting, since government financial statements understate the true costs of compensating their workers. The people who make the rules, moreover, don't play by the rules they make.

That is particularly depressing because most Canadian workers will end up in individual money-purchase accounts, where they will save too little, invest badly, and draw their savings down ineptly. The public sector workers who could improve the environment for those plans have less first-hand experience of them, and no direct interest in improving them.

Acceptance

Getting a handle on depression and beginning the transition to acceptance and moving along may be easier if we understand that the problems of DB plans are not confined to Canada. They are also widespread in the United States and the United Kingdom. Moreover, more than just a few economic and financial accidents and policy mistakes got us where we are now. Recent financial-market trends have put many DB plans on a better financial footing (Watson Wyatt, 2008), and regulatory and tax changes would help. But the decline in coverage of employer-sponsored DB plans began many years before the crisis that started us into the five stages I have just outlined. So rather than struggling with denial, anger, bargaining and depression, people concerned with the future of work-related pensions in Canada ought to be thinking about alternatives.

The Sixth Stage: Innovative Response

The most persuasive element in the case for the DB model is the difficulty most people have in saving, investing, and annuitizing. People as individuals and as participants in a more efficient economy gain from pooling and delegating the management of these things to specialists.

The good news, though, is that the classic DB plan is not the only conceivable way to get these things. For example:

- Money purchase plans can have default contribution rates — either fixed, or escalating, or connected by formula to a target payout rate — that will protect unsophisticated workers from saving too little.
- Money-purchase plans can pool the savings of workers in many employers, creating the economies of scale that give access to non-retail investments and lower administration costs.
- Money-purchase plans can provide default investment vehicles, protecting unsophisticated investors from trading too much and taking inappropriate risks.
- Money-purchase plans can have default immunization and annuitization options, protecting unsophisticated savers from market risk as they approach retirement and unsophisticated dis-savers from outliving their funds. With scale, moreover, such plans can annuitize internally or get better terms from annuity providers.

This list is not just hand-waving: plans with one or more of these elements exist already, both in Canada and abroad. In my view, the constructive response to the bad news about the classic DB plan is to focus on making those options more widely available to Canadians who, if they save for retirement at all, do it in individual and group RRSPs. Keith Ambachtsheer (2006) has advocated models drawing on Dutch and Australian experience, arguing that mandating coverage can get us past the coordination problems that currently prevent potential users and providers from getting together. While I think mandatory coverage merits consideration, my preference would be to work three fronts:

- Legislate "safe-harbour" provisions that would protect plan sponsors who provide plans with default contribution rates, investment vehicles and annuitization from lawsuits launched by (former) participants who, despite good faith efforts on the sponsor's part, ended up disappointed (Robson, 2008).
- Remove or liberalize provisions that currently force many members of money-purchase plans to annuitize or otherwise draw down their savings outside the plan, rather than staying in a structure that can offer the advantages of scale and pooling throughout the life cycle.
- Harmonize regulations among the federal and provincial governments that would foster the availability of these plans on a national scale.

William B.P. Robson

Recap

To close, let me underline that seeking to recreate a "golden age" of DB plans that never existed would be to return to denial. More anger, fruitless bargaining, and depression would surely follow. Far better would be to think about a sixth stage for dealing with the bad news on pensions: innovations to help Canadians pool their resources and save for retirement, cushioned not only from financial risk and longevity risk, but from agency risk as well.

Managing the problems afflicting existing DB plans is an important task. But policymakers must not fixate on the plans that most resemble their own: doing so would neglect the well-being of the majority of Canadians who will do most of their retirement saving in money-purchase plans. The most critical challenge for the future is fostering the growth of pooled hybrid plans that will offer more realistic promises than classic DB plans and better returns than RRSPs.

References

Ambachtsheer, K. 2006."Building Better Pensions on a 'Fair Value' Foundation", in N. Kortleve, T. Nyman, and E. Ponds (eds.), *Fair Value and Pension Fund Management*. Amsterdam: Elsevier.

Banerjee, R. and W. Robson. 2008. *Lifting the Lid on Pension Funding: Why Income-Tax-Act Limits on Contributions Should Rise*. C.D. Howe Institute ebrief. Toronto: C.D. Howe Institute. April.

Clark, G. and A. Monk. 2006. "The 'Crisis' in Defined Benefit Corporate Pension Liabilities Part I", *Pensions* 12(1).

Dodge, D. 2005. "Economic and Financial Efficiency: The Importance of Pension Plans". Speech to l'Association des MBA du Québec (AMBAQ), Montréal, Quebec, 9 November.

Kubler-Ross, E. 1969. *On Death and Dying*. New York: MacMillan.

Laidler, D. and W. Robson. 2007. *Ill-Defined Benefits: The Uncertain Present and Brighter Future of Employee Pensions in Canada*. Commentary No. 250. Toronto: C.D. Howe Institute.

Office of the Chief Actuary (OCA). *2006. Actuarial Report: Pension Plan for the Public Service of Canada as at 31 March 2005*. Ottawa: Office of the Superintendent of Financial Institutions.

Robson, W. 2008. "Safe Harbours: Providing Protection for Canada's Money-Purchase Pension Plan Sponsors". Backgrounder. Toronto: C.D. Howe Institute.

Watson Wyatt Worldwide. 2008. "Canadian Pension Funded Ratios Post Net Improvement in 2007". Available at www.watsonwyatt.com/canada-english/news/press.asp?ID=18493 .

William B.P. Robson

Summary of Discussion

Kevin Milligan posed a question for Michael Veall about the effect of immigrants. You're using tax filing data, where the unit of analysis is the tax filing family. His suspicion is that you might get a different answer if you had a look at the *household* level for low-income or poverty measures. He suspects a lot of people who are coming over as older immigrants are coming to live with the rest of their family, providing child care, providing household support and other things, and living perhaps in a household where lots of other people are working so that it isn't a low-income household. But they themselves don't have a lot of income. So you might get a different picture if you were able to look at the household level, which one might argue is the right level to look at as a measure of poverty. Veall agreed that that's possible. The same pattern shows up in other data sets, though.

    Jonathan Kesselman asked of Garnett Picot whether we might not get a better view of the relative well-being of different groups by focusing more on consumption than on income? **Garnett Picot** responded that if we had longitudinal consumption data similar to the longitudinal tax data that we have, that would be great. But we don't have it, so it's hard to look at those issues from a consumption point of view.

    He also added that he was a bit surprised at how high the replacement rates are with a mean of .75 to .8. He recalled back years ago that people were said to be aiming for income replacement rates of .65, .7, or .75. And here we are, showing rates of .75 to .8, and 1.0 at the bottom, which he found quite high. So one would want to go back and do some sensitivity tests on the results to see how sensitive they are, for example, to the adult-equivalent adjustment. It could be, for instance, that you have a family of four, at age 55 with a couple of kids still at home; but by the time you get to 65, you're down to a family of two of, say, just the two adults. Even if your income falls by half, your replacement rate is not going to fall by half because of the adjustment for differences in family size. So there may be these kinds of things going on that are leading to these relatively high replacement rates reported.

Tony Deutsch indicated that he had recently supervised a master's thesis on Canadian pension plans that discovered that if you look at defined-benefit plans as a group in Canada and defined-contribution plans as a group in Canada, the "Dodge Hypothesis" holds: the long-term investment is more in the DB plans. However, if you cut out the five largest plans in Canada, that would include OMERS and Teachers' and so forth, all of which happen to be DB plans, of the remaining DC plans and DB plans, there isn't much difference in the share of long-term investments. So he suspects what makes pension plans invest in long-term issues is their size, not the definition of the benefits. Furthermore, Keith Ambachtsheer has argued that the optimal size for managing investments is about $10 billion. There are very few plans in Canada that are that big.

Malcolm Hamilton made some comments about the Ontario Teachers' Pension Plan. He's had the honour of being the actuary of that plan for the best part of 16 years now. It has a well-deserved reputation for excellence and is really well managed. But he thinks the board of directors of that plan would be surprised to find out that it is being held up as an example for other plans to follow. The reason is not because they're doing anything wrong, but because it's very much a work in progress. This is a plan that 17 years ago, had $20 billion and no equities. It now has $105 billion and $55 billion of equities. And nobody sees any viable way to manage that risk right now. If you have $55 billion of equities, you're getting investment gains and losses on the order of $8 billion a year. And $8 billion a year, to put it in perspective, is 70% of the gross pay of Ontario's teaching profession. You take a model where your annual shock is 70% — plus or minus — of pay and try to figure out how smooth you can make the contribution rates by ignoring that, or by amortizing it, or by spreading it, or by doing anything else, this is a challenging problem. So the bottom line is we don't know how we're going to manage the risk. We know it's going to be a challenge. The Dutch, when they looked at similar problems, reached the conclusion that there is no known way to do this without sharing the risk in a big way with retired members, which the Ontario public sector plans do not do. But once you start sharing investment risk with retired members, it really isn't a defined-benefit plan any more. It becomes a collective defined-contribution plan, where investment risks are flowed back into benefits. That may be a very good way to organize pension plans — that's how they do it in the Netherlands — but it's not a defined benefit model that we find today in Canada.

Larry Kotlikoff suggested that what is needed is greater transparency and the government to come in and try and provide good investment alternatives for workers for the DC plans and also good annuities — to really organize the investment part for ordinary workers. For example, the US government or the Canadian government could say, here's a global index fund at very low cost, at 2 basis points, that any Canadian can invest in. Bring your money here, we'll invest it for you by computer in a global index fund; you get the return, and you don't have to deal with the industry, investment, insurance, and financial conglomerates. Plus, we're going to set up an annuity for you folks. You can annuitize through the government's annuities system. Send us your money, we'll do it at very low cost, and we'll try to make it fair for the different cohorts so that it's going to be one of these annuities that's going to vary through time depending on the longevity of your cohort. The government can set a standard, and then if private industry wants to compete, they're going to have to compete with something that is hopefully quite transparent.

Armine Yalnizyan remarked that we're talking about a really serious intergenerational issue that's emerging. René Morissette's work shows that the coverage for younger people is quite low in terms of private pensions. It's about one-quarter, about 27%, of the population, or so. And even for the general population, it's not that much higher. It's in the order of 33%. So whatever discussion we have today around private pensions, we're excluding the majority of Canadians. And we're really not paying attention to the next generation, which has an even more precarious foothold in the labour market, with greater variability of earnings and less permanent earnings as well as less coverage for pension benefits.

Chapter III

Policy Levers and the Retirement Process

Incentives for Early Retirement in Canada's Defined-Benefit Public and Private Pension Plans: An Analysis with a Dynamic Life-Cycle CGE Model

Maxime Fougère, Simon Harvey, Yu Lan, André Léonard and Bruno Rainville

Introduction

Canadians are retiring when they are younger than the statutory retirement age of 65, the age at which they become eligible for unreduced public benefits. According to Statistics Canada, the average age of retirement has declined steadily in Canada over the 1976 to 1998 period from around 65 for men and 64 for women during the second half of the 1970s to 61.5 years and 60 years respectively by the late 1990s. However, since 1998, the trend in retirement seems to have halted. In fact, from the lowest level observed in 1998, the average retirement age has tended to increase somewhat, ranging between 62 and 62.5 years in 2003–2005 for men and around 61 years for women.

We wish to give a special thanks to Alain Denhez (PRI) and Geoff Rowe (Statistics Canada) for allowing us to use LifePaths to help calibrate the CGE model. We also wish to thank Yves Carrière, Roman Habtu, Cliff Halliwell, Thomas Shephard and Ryan Smith for useful comments. All remaining errors are ours.

Some studies have shown that the cost of early retirement is substantial in terms of unused productive capacity and hours of work (e.g., Fougère *et al.*, 2005; PRI, 2005; Rowe and Nguyen, 2003; Herbertsson and Orszag; 2001). Also, in the context of population aging, the negative labour supply shock due to early retirement will intensify given that there will be more and more people in the 55–64 age group. According to Human Resources and Social Development Canada, Policy Research Directorate's demographic projections, the proportion of the population 55–64 will increase by about 50% between 2000 and 2020.

Canada's public pension system generates work disincentives for older workers. Although it is generally acknowledged that these disincentives are small compared to many other Organisation for Economic Co-operation and Development (OECD) countries (Gruber and Wise, 2004), several commentators have suggested that the C/QPP system should be reformed (Guillemette, 2004; Milligan, 2005).

There is also some evidence that defined-benefit (DB) employer pension plans in Canada provide incentives to retire before the age of 65. According to Pescarus and Rivard (2005), of the 13 private pension plans they examined, all of them offer the strongest incentives to retire before age 60.

The objective of this article is three fold. First, it reviews the incentive effects of Canada's public pension system and defined-benefit private pension plans on early retirement behaviour. Second, it uses a dynamic applied general equilibrium overlapping generations (OLG) model of the type developed by Auerbach and Kotlikoff (1989) to quantify their impact on labour supply, productive capacity and economic welfare. Third, it evaluates some options to reduce early retirement incentives.

The OLG model used in this paper captures the economic impact of projected future demographic changes and the incentive effects of policy through the life cycle. Moreover, in the spirit of Becker (1965), the model uses a time allocation structure where labour supply, human capital and leisure/retirement decisions are endogenous. We also innovate by modeling the retirement incentives from Canada's public and private pension plans. The incentives are expressed as implicit tax rates for workers and are derived from a pension calculator that takes into account the interactions between the various elements of Canada's Public Pension System and defined-benefit employer pension plans. The LifePaths model from Statistics Canada was also used to generate detailed information on Registered Pension Plan (RPP) and Registered

Retirement Savings Plan (RRSP) contributions and benefits to help calibrate the OLG model.

Simulation analysis indicates that eliminating the main work disincentive effects of the Canadian public pension system on retirement decisions would have a moderate positive impact on the labour supply of older workers in low- and medium-skilled occupations, but a marginal effect on high-skilled workers. The impact on high-skilled workers comes mainly from the elimination of the OAS clawback. Eliminating early retirement incentives in public pensions would also be welfare enhancing. Although lifetime leisure would decrease, it is generally more than compensated by increases in lifetime consumption. Several reform options are also examined to make the program near incentive-neutral. Among those, raising the actuarial adjustment in C/QPP has the most favourable impact.

The analysis also shows that the main distortionary effects of defined-benefit private pension plans are significantly larger than those in public pensions and generate more work disincentive effects on older workers in high-skilled occupations. The cost of early retirement in terms of unused productive capacity associated with DB employer pensions is about seven times larger than that in the public pension system. Finally, it must be noted that since the mid-1980s, the proportion of members of private plans which are covered by DB plans has decreased from 95% in 1984 to 84% in 2006. This reduction in the proportion of members in DB plans has likely contributed to an overall reduction in work disincentives. A continued declining trend in the proportion of DB plans over the next decades, if it materializes, could also help to further reduce the impact of early retirement incentives.

The remainder of this paper is divided as follows. The next section presents an overview of early retirement incentives from the Canadian public pension system and private pension plans. The third section provides estimates of early retirement incentives from both public and private pension plans in the form of implicit tax rates using a pension calculator. Section four describes the CGE model used for the analysis and discusses the key parameter values. Section five presents simulation results of the impact of early retirement incentives from both public and private pension plans on the economy and labour market, simulates some policy options to eliminate work disincentive effects in public pension plans and examines a likely scenario of further reduction in the proportion of defined-benefit private pension plans. The following section presents some sensitivity analysis. The final section provides some concluding remarks.

Incentives to Early Retirement

This section provides an overview of early retirement incentives in both Canadian public and private pension plans. Following Stock and Wise (1990), retirement incentives inherent in defined-benefit pension plans can be decomposed into wealth and accrual (substitution) effects. First, pensions increase an individual's wealth. Assuming leisure is a normal good, an increase in pension wealth — the present value of future retirement benefits — will lead an individual to consume more of every thing, including leisure. Second, an accrual or substitution effect exists when pension wealth varies according to the retirement age. The accrual effect can be defined as the difference in pension wealth between taking retirement now and one year later. When it is positive, meaning that working one additional year increases pension wealth, there is an incentive to continue working; when negative, there is an incentive to retire.

If retirement benefits are based solely on contributions and do not depend on the age of retirement, the accrual effect is zero and the retirement decision is entirely based on the trade-off between additional leisure and consumption. Accordingly, defined-contribution pension plans have no accrual effect, only a wealth effect.

In the remaining parts of this section, we will discuss in more detail the source of early retirement incentives in both Canadian public and private pension systems.

Canada's Public Income Security System

Older individuals face financial disincentives to continue working originating from the public pension system, which is primarily composed of two program groups: Old Age Security (OAS) programs and Canada/Quebec Pension Plans (C/QPP).[1] The combined OAS programs represent a similar share of retirement income as C/QPP. For example, net C/QPP payments represented $33.5 billion in 2006, compared with $31.0 billion for all OAS programs.[2]

---

[1] Quebec workers do not participate in the CPP, but rather in the Quebec pension plan, which is very similar to the CPP.

[2] Data for this subsection come from Human Resources and Social Development Canada (2007).

The basic OAS pension is offered to all individuals 65 years of age and older who meet residency requirements. The maximum benefit was $497.83 per month in July 2007 (benefits are adjusted quarterly reflecting changes to the Consumer Price Index). Continuing to work past age 65 does not affect OAS benefits, unless the individual's annual income (other than from OAS pension programs) is higher than $63,511 (in 2007), in which case 15% of the excess income is clawed back. This mainly affects highly-skilled individuals.

On top of the Old Age Security basic pension, the Guaranteed Income Supplement (GIS) provides additional money to low-income individuals 65 years of age and older. In July 2007, the maximum monthly benefit was $414.96 for each member of a couple and $628.36 for singles. The GIS is reduced by 50 cents for singles and 25 cents each for couples for every dollar of family income excepting OAS. This means that GIS benefits are zero when monthly family income (excepting OAS) is higher than $1,256.72 for singles and $1,659.84 for couples. Continuing to work past age 65 will reduce GIS for all workers. However, highly-skilled workers are more likely to have income from other sources (savings, private pensions, RRSPs, etc.). Thus, whether they work or not, they will not likely receive the GIS. Therefore, the GIS will be a greater disincentive to work for low-skilled individuals (starting at age 65).

The OAS system also has another feature, the Allowance (formerly known as the Spousal Allowance), which is paid to low-income 60–64 years-old spouses of GIS recipients, widows and widowers. In July 2007, the maximum monthly benefit was $912.79 for a spouse or partner and $1,011.80 for a survivor. The maximum monthly Allowance is reduced by 75 cents for every dollar of other income. The Allowance is a disincentive to work, mainly for low-skilled workers aged 60 to 64 years old. However, the uptake of this program is very low (94,000 recipients in 2006 compared with 4.3 million for OAS and 1.5 million for GIS), since its requirements apply to few individuals.

The C/QPP is an earnings-based pension plan. It is compulsory from age 18 and covers almost all workers in Canada. It is funded by a payroll tax. In 2007, contributions for both the employee and the employer were 4.95% of annual earnings between $3,500 (the year's basic exemption) and $43,700 (the year's maximum pensionable earnings), for a maximum annual contribution of $1,989.90. Benefits are calculated as 25% of a person's pensionable earnings over the period the individual is aged 18 to 65, with the lowest-earning 15% of months in that period being dropped from the calculation. Therefore, someone with earnings above the maximum pensionable earnings for at least 85% of the 47 years between 18 and 65 will earn the maximum benefit of $863.75 per month in 2007.

The normal uptake for the C/QPP is age 65, although retirement pensions can begin between ages 60 and 70. Early retirement is penalized by 0.5% a month, so that if C/QPP is taken at age 60, benefits are decreased by 30%. Similarly, retiring after age 65 increases the benefits by 0.5 % a month, for a maximum of 30% if C/QPP is taken at age 70. Individuals have to stop working if they want to claim early C/QPP.

Before age 60, C/QPP constitutes an incentive to work, since working one additional year will increase future benefits for most workers because of the possibility of dropping the 15% worst months in terms of earnings from the calculation of benefits. Between age 60 and 65, working one additional year means losing one possible year of C/QPP benefits. On the other hand, it also means that benefits will be increased by 6% over the rest of the individual's lifetime (because of the accrual adjustment), maybe more considering working one more year would help increase the number of years with high income (the 15% drop rule). However, this 6% rate is insufficient to compensate for the lost year of benefits, so overall, between ages 60 and 65, C/QPP offers a disincentive to continued work.

Overall, the public system offers positive work incentives until age 60, because before this age, working longer increases future C/QPP benefits. At age 60, disincentives begin, caused by the possibility of collecting C/QPP benefits, in which case the person has to stop working. At this age, working one more year does not increase future benefits enough to compensate for the loss of one year of benefit. The interaction between C/QPP and GIS is a major disincentive to continue working between age 60 and 65: working one additional year increases the value of future C/QPP payments, mainly because of the actuarial adjustment, but at the same time diminishes future GIS benefits by 50 cents for every dollar of increased C/QPP benefits. The Allowance is also a disincentive to work between age 60 and 64, but the effect is very small as few people benefit from it. At age 65, OAS and GIS programs start. The basic OAS pension is reduced for high-income individuals who continue working. GIS, which is intended for low-income individuals, is also reduced by 50 cents for every dollar of income earned.

Registered Private Pension Plans (RPPs)

RPPs are retirement income plans provided by employers or unions. These plans are provided voluntarily, and take two basic forms: defined benefit (DB) and defined contribution (DC).

DB plans are funded by contributions of employers and employees, and are based on the cost of providing future benefits, which are defined in the plan text. The benefits are normally based on the number of years of service with the employer, and are often a percentage of the earnings of the individual during his whole career, or the best or last years of the worker's career. Benefits normally start at a certain age or after a certain number of years of service with the employer (or a combination of the two). There can be penalties for those who choose to retire before they reach the required number of years of service or age. Therefore, DB benefits vary according to retirement age.

A DC plan is a retirement plan wherein a certain amount of money is set aside by employers every year. Employees can also contribute as much as they want. The benefits are not specified and are based on the return on investment and how much each employee contributed. Since benefits are not determined by rules linked to retirement age, as in DB plans, DC plans do not have accruals. They affect retirement decisions only through the wealth effect.

The percentage of beneficiaries of private pension plans (DB or DC) starts to be significant in the 53–56 year old group (9%), becomes stronger (around 26%) in the 61–64 group, and is highest among high-skilled individuals.[3]

In 2006, 84% of members of private pension plans were covered by DB plans. As shown in Figure 1, the proportion of members of a private plan covered by a DB plan (rather than a DC plan) has steadily declined since the mid-1980s. This shift towards DC plans was also experienced in the United States, but to a much larger extent. Munnell and Perun (2006), using the US Survey of Consumer Finances, illustrate that the proportion of members of private plans covered only by DB plans decreased significantly, from 62% in 1983 to just 20% in 2004.

---

[3]The data source for the coverage by skills level and age group is the 1999 Survey of Financial Security.

Figure 1: Proportion of Private Pension Plan Members Covered by a DB Plan, Canada, 1974–2006

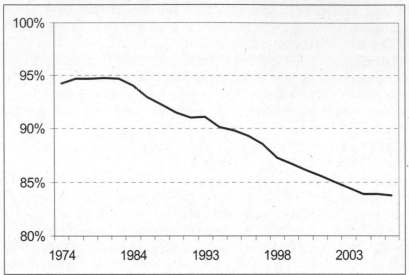

Source: Statistics Canada, Pension Plans in Canada Survey.

Estimates of Incentives to Early Retirement from Public and Private Pension Plans

This section provides estimates of early retirement incentives from both public and private pension plans, in the form of implicit tax rates, using a pension calculator to estimate pension accruals. Please note that the accrual effects are calculated by skill level since the CGE model used in this paper has three representative workers by skill: low-, medium- and high-skilled workers.

This type of pension calculator was introduced by Stock and Wise (1990) and was recently used by Baker, Gruber and Milligan (2003) and Milligan and Schirle (2006). Pension accruals are expressed as implicit tax rates by dividing the accrual for one particular retirement age by average earnings at that age.

In this exercise, we first calculate Income Security Wealth (ISW) from public sources. The pension calculator incorporates all of the rules used to calculate C/QPP, GIS and OAS entitlements in 2001. The

Allowance is not included in the pension calculator, because it is only paid in very specific situations; the uptake of the Allowance is also quite small, so incorporating this program would have a negligible effect on work disincentives in aggregate.

Data from the 2001 census are used to construct age-specific lifetime earnings profiles for the different workers by skill levels in the model. Earnings data are for full-time employees. We assume smooth earnings profiles and calculate predicted earnings rather than actual earnings by estimating a simple regression of earnings on a constant, age and age squared as independent variables. These earnings profiles are used to calculate C/QPP, GIS and OAS entitlements for retirement at each age starting at age 53. C/QPP payments are received starting at age of retirement or age 65, whichever is earlier. GIS is received at retirement age or age 65, whichever is later. OAS always begins at 65, because all seniors start receiving at least some OAS benefits at this age, unless their income is very high (more than $100,000 in 2007 — which is greater than the income of our representative high-skilled worker). Lifetime pension receipts are then discounted for time-preferences and survival probabilities to give a measure of ISW at each potential retirement age. The individual rate of time preference is set at 0.03, which is common in the literature, and survival probabilities come from Statistics Canada's Life Tables (2002). ISW is compared between subsequent retirement ages to determine raw accruals, which are then divided by age-specific earnings to express them as an implicit tax on earnings.

Table 1 shows the average implicit tax rates by age group and skill level. A negative sign means there is a disincentive to continue working at this age. Implicit tax rates are generally positive before age 60, as continuing to work increases future C/QPP benefits.

Starting at age 60, disincentives arise because of the possibility of taking early C/QPP. This is mainly the case for low- or medium-skilled individuals because their earnings are lower, and because the lost year of C/QPP benefit represents a higher share of their earnings. Also, contrary to the high-skilled individuals, they are more likely to receive GIS in the future. Therefore, continuing to work, while increasing their C/QPP entitlement, will also decrease their GIS entitlement. The disincentive usually grows from 60 to 65 because the penalty for taking C/QPP before age 65 decreases: the lost year of C/QPP becomes of a higher value. In the meantime, future GIS entitlements decrease to a greater extent because every dollar of increase in C/QPP entitlement reduces future GIS benefits by 50 cents.

Table 1: Average Implicit Tax Rate, by Age of Retirement and Skill Level
(Public pensions only)

Age	Low-Skilled	Medium-Skilled	High-Skilled
55–56	2.3	2.4	2.4
56–57	2.2	2.2	2.2
57–58	1.7	1.8	1.6
58–59	1.7	1.8	1.6
59–60	1.8	1.9	1.7
60–61	-3.6	-3.5	2.7
61–62	-6.9	-7.2	1.5
62–63	-9.7	-10.0	0.0
63–64	-12.1	-10.8	-1.2
64–65	-14.8	-5.4	-2.7
65–68	-1.7	0.0	-2.8
69+	-1.9	0.0	-2.2

Note: The implicit tax rate is the difference in income security wealth if retirement occurs at age x and at age x-1, divided by earnings at age x-1. A negative sign means there is a disincentive to continue working.

After age 65, the disincentives are the following: for the low-skilled, the only disincentive is the loss of one year of GIS benefit. For the medium-skilled who take their retirement after age 65, the C/QPP benefit is high enough that they do not get any GIS benefit, so there are no more disincentives. The high-skilled do not receive any GIS benefit as well, but their OAS benefits are reduced if they continue to work because their earnings are higher than the threshold of $63,511.

We then introduced private plans in the pension calculator. Since there is not one unique private pension plan but thousands of them, we had to illustrate the disincentive effect of such plans for a representative agent, using the average benefit received from private plans by age group and skill level, from the Survey of Financial Security of 1999. We then multiply these numbers by the proportion of beneficiaries of DB plans in each age group and skill level. Table 2 shows the results of this calculation. We start by measuring the work disincentives at age 55, which is the normal uptake in many pension plans; data also show that the uptake starts increasing within the 53–56 age group. The disincentive reaches a maximum at age 61–64, and we keep it constant afterwards, even though data show that benefits decrease after this age. We believe this observed decline in the data reflects the financial situation of older cohorts rather than an actual decrease in benefits after age 64.

Table 3 shows the new implicit tax rates when both public and private plans are included, as well as the difference between these new implicit tax rates and the rates from Table 1, where only public plans were included. This difference can be roughly seen as the effect of private plans on implicit tax rates (a negative sign means the disincentive increases).

Including private pension plans in the pension calculator increases to a great extent the work disincentives, especially after age 61, and more so for the high- and medium-skilled than for low-skilled workers. This is because a higher proportion of high-skilled workers are covered by such plans and their benefits are higher.

Table 2: Average Benefits from DB Plans for Representative Agents, by Age Group and Skill Level

Age Group	Low-Skilled	Medium-Skilled	High-Skilled
55–56	$894	$2,039	$4,175
57–60	$1,474	$2,696	$6,287
61 and more	$3,208	$4,702	$9,454

Source: Statistics Canada (1999).

Table 3: Average Implicit Tax Rate, by Age of Retirement and Skill Level, Private and Public Plans and Difference with Table 1
(Public plan only)

Age Group	Public and Private Plans			Private Plans Only		
	Low-Skilled	Medium-Skilled	High-Skilled	Low-Skilled	Medium-Skilled	High-Skilled
55–56	-0.5	-2.7	-4.4	-2.8	-5.1	-6.8
56–57	-0.6	-2.9	-4.7	-2.8	-5.1	-6.8
57–58	-3.2	-5.6	-8.9	-4.9	-7.3	-10.4
58–59	-3.1	-5.5	-8.8	-4.9	-7.3	-10.4
59–60	-3.1	-5.4	-8.8	-4.9	-7.3	-10.4
60–61	-8.5	-10.9	-7.8	-4.9	-7.3	-10.4
61–62	-18.5	-21.6	-14.8	-11.6	-14.4	-16.2
62–63	-21.2	-24.4	-16.3	-11.6	-14.4	-16.2
63–64	-23.7	-25.2	-17.4	-11.6	-14.4	-16.2
64–65	-26.4	-19.8	-18.9	-11.6	-14.4	-16.2
65–68	-14.8	-17.3	-20.0	-13.1	-17.3	-17.2
69+	-16.5	-20.2	-20.2	-14.6	-20.2	-18.0

Note: The implicit tax rate is the difference in pension wealth if retirement occurs at age x and at age x-1, divided by earnings at age x-1. A negative sign means there is a disincentive to continue working.

The Model

The analysis is based on a dynamic computable general equilibrium model with an OLG structure. The model is calibrated to represent the Canadian economy. In this section, we present a detailed description of the model.

Household Behaviour

The population is represented by 16 representative Canadian-born agents and 16 representative immigrants agents, structured in an Allais-Samuelson OLG structure. Consequently, at each period of time, 16 Canadian-born plus 16 foreign-born generations live side by side. At any period t, a new generation is born and the eldest dies. Each native-born agent enters the labour market at the age of 17 and dies at the age of 81. This implies that each period of the model corresponds to four years. Younger individuals are assumed to be dependent on their parents (the representative agents), implying that they play no active role in the model. The population growth rate and immigration are exogenous. The model also distinguishes between four categories of agents in each immigration class: three different skill levels of workers (high, medium and low) and a fourth category of adults who are unattached to the labour market (inactive).

Canadian and foreign-born agents optimize a CES type inter-temporal utility function of consumption and time allocation subject to lifetime income and time constraints. The household (or agent)'s optimization problem consists of choosing the consumption and savings pattern over the life cycle, as well as the allocation of time between work, education and leisure. Time spent in education is considered to be human capital investment. Human capital gains also raise effective labour supply and the quality of leisure. For each of the eight different types of agents, the inter-temporal utility function takes the following form:

$$
U_{qual,nat} = \frac{1}{1-\sigma} \sum_{g=17}^{80} \left(\frac{1}{1+\rho} \right)^g (C_{qual,nat,g,t+g-1}^{1-\theta}
$$

$$
+ \phi_{qual,nat,g} \ell_{qual,nat,g,t+g-1}^{1-\theta})^{\frac{1-\sigma}{1-\theta}},
$$
(1)

$$0 < \theta < 1.$$

$C_{qual,nat,g,t}$ and $\ell_{qual,nat,g,t}$ are respectively consumption and leisure activity of an agent of qualification *qual*, nationality (Canadian-born or foreign-born) *nat*, age group g at time t; ρ the pure rate of time preference; σ the inverse of the inter-temporal elasticity of substitution ε ($\varepsilon = 1/\sigma$); θ the inverse of the intra-temporal elasticity of substitution between consumption and leisure activity η ($\eta = 1/\theta$); and $\phi_{qual,nat,g}$ the leisure activity preference parameter.

Notice that as the fourth category of agents is inactive, their inter-temporal problem is simplified by assuming that they consume what they receive in transfers from the government. Consequently, their wealth (Ag, t) remains equal to zero at all times and their time allocation is exogenous. The human capital technology is described by a well-behaved function, linear in the stock of human capital h, but strictly concave with respect to educational and training time.

Human capital production is individualized, and total production of new human capital in the economy is simply the sum of all generations' production. The specification chosen is similar to that in Lucas (1988, 1990). The technology for the production of human capital takes the following form:

$$h_{qual,nat,g+1,t+1} = \frac{h_{qual,nat,g,t}}{1+\delta} + \beta h_{qual,nat,g,t} z_{qual,nat,g,t}^{\gamma} \\ + Exp_{qual,nat,g,t} \tag{2}$$
$$\beta > 0,\ 0 < \gamma < 1,\ \delta > 0,$$

where z is the fraction of time allocated to the production of human capital, δ the human capital depreciation rate, γ the elasticity of human capital production, β a production parameter and Exp an experience variable that evolves exogenously with age. Each agent is endowed with one unit of time for each period of life. As time can be allocated to leisure activity and the production of human capital, what is left for labour market participation ($Lpar$) is:

$$Lpar_{qual,nat,g,t} = 1 - z_{qual,nat,g,t} - \ell_{qual,nat,g,t} \tag{3}$$

The representative agent of each type optimizes equation 1 subject to 2, 3 and to the budget constraint. The representative agent budget constraint in each period of life is:

$$A_{qual,nat,g+1,t+1} - A_{qual,nat,g,t} = \\ w_{qual,t} h_{qual,nat,g,t} Lpar_{qual,nat,g,t} (1 - \tau_t^w - cr_t - dbcr_t) + \\ r_t a_{qual,nat,g,t} (1 - \tau_t^k) + Tr_{qual,g,t} (1 - \tau_t^w) \\ + OAS_{qual,g\geq13,t} (1 - \tau_t^w) + GIS_{qual,g\geq13,t} \\ + C/QPP_{qual,nat,g\geq12,t} (1 - \tau_t^w) \\ + RPP_{qual,nat,g\geq10,t} (1 - \tau_t^w) - (1 + \tau_t^c) C_{qual,nat,g,t}, \tag{4}$$

where $A_{qual,nat,g,t}$ represents the assets accumulated by skill level, immigration status at age g and time t, cr_t the contribution rate to public pensions, $dbcr_t$ the contribution rate to defined-benefit private pensions, τ^w the tax rate on labour income, τ^k the tax rate on capital income and τ^c the tax rate on consumption expenditures. Government transfers are represented by $Tr_{qual,g,t}$, $OAS_{qual,g,t}$, $GIS_{qual,g,t}$ and $C/QPP_{qual,nat,g,t}$. Tr represents government transfers excluding public pensions, OAS is Old Age Security, GIS includes Guaranteed Income Supplement and Spouse's Allowance. C/QPP is Canada and Quebec Pension Plans' (C/QPP) benefits and $RPP_{qual,nat,g,t}$ is benefits from a defined-benefit registered pension plan (private pension plan). Both C/QPP and RPP benefits are a fraction of lifetime best labour earnings and are determined respectively by the pension replacement rate $CQPP\_rr$ and $RPP\_rr_{qual,g}$ (see Table 4). In equations (5) and (6), the left-hand side is total pension benefits to be paid and the right-hand side is workers' contributions.

$$\sum_{qual,nat,g} POP_{qual,nat,g \geq 12,t} C/QPP_{qual,nat,g \geq 12,t} =$$

$$cr_t \cdot \sum_{qual,nat,g} POP_{qual,nat,g,t} w_{qual,t} h_{qual,nat,g,t} Lpar_{qual,nat,g,t} \tag{5}$$

$$\sum_{qual,nat,g} POP_{qual,nat,g \geq 10,t} RPP_{qual,nat,g \geq 10,t} =$$

$$dbcr_t \cdot \sum_{qual,nat,g} POP_{qual,nat,g,t} w_{qual,t} h_{qual,nat,g,t} Lpar_{qual,nat,g,t} \tag{6}$$

Also, as discussed in the second section, the public pension system and defined-benefit pension plans have two types of effects on the individual's retirement decision: a wealth effect and an accrual (substitution) effect. However, they are modeled to capture only the wealth aspect of the incentives to individuals, as it is computationally difficult to include the pension rules that give rise to the accrual effect in the overall model. To circumvent this problem, we develop an external pension calculator to calculate pension accruals, and express these as implicit tax rates which directly affect the price of leisure expressed in forgone wages for older workers.

Differentiating the household (or agent) utility function with respect to its lifetime budget constraint yields a reserve wage, $Wres$ for each generation:

$$Wres_{qual,nat,g,t} = w_{qual,t} \cdot h_{qual,nat,g,t} \cdot Lpar_{qual,nat,g,t}$$
$$\cdot (1 - \tau_t^w - cr_t - dbcr_t - a_{qual,g,t}) + \mu_{qual,nat,g,t} \qquad (7)$$

where $\mu_{qual,nat,g,t}$ is a Kuhn-Tucker multiplier and differs from zero if and only if the agent chooses to retire in year t and represents the extra money the individual would require to leave retirement and supply labour. The presence of cr_t and $dbcr_t$ in the equation means that workers consider C/QPP and RPP contribution rates as marginal tax rates on labour. This implies that an increase in payroll taxes to finance income security reduces the price of leisure or the reserve wage. Also, note that $a_{qual,t,g}$ is the implicit tax rate representing the accrual effects of defined-benefit public and private pension plans. For example, for an individual aged 60, if working one more year reduces the discounted sum of future pension benefits, a becomes positive and distorts the labour-leisure decision in the same manner as a rise in τ^w, cr and $dbcr$.

The intra-temporal first-order conditions of the household problem can be written as:

$$LA_{qual,nat,g,t} = \left[\frac{\phi_{qual,nat,g}(1 + \tau_t^C)}{Wres_{qual,nat,g,t}} \right]^\eta C_{qual,nat,g,t} \qquad (8)$$

As shown in equation (8), an increase in the reserve wage $Wres$ causes a decline in leisure relative to consumption. In fact, a one-unit change in the leisure-consumption ratio following a change in the reserve wage is equal to the intra-temporal elasticity of substitution η. Also, looking at equations (7) and (8), an increase in τ^w, cr, $dbcr$, or a reduces the reserve wage, which in turn raises leisure activity relative to consumption.

The Production Sector

A representative firm produces a unique good. Its production technology is represented by a Cobb-Douglas production function. The national firm hires labour and rents physical capital up to their marginal products. Effective labour is a composite factor of the three skill levels that takes into account both quality and quantity dimensions. It is represented by a constant elasticity of substitution (CES) function. With Y_t representing output at time t, K_t the capital stock, L_t the effective labour force, and A the scaling variable, we have:

$$Y_t = AK_t^{\alpha} L_t^{1-\alpha} \tag{9}$$

where α is the share of capital in value added. Firms are assumed to be perfectly competitive and factor demands follow from profit maximization:

$$re_t = \alpha A \left(\frac{K_t}{L_t} \right)^{\alpha-1} \tag{10}$$

$$w_t = (1-\alpha) A \left(\frac{K_t}{L_t} \right)^{\alpha} \tag{11}$$

where re_t is the rental rate of capital and w_t the wage rate per unit of effective labour.

The labour force is a CES function of labour by skill level. Consequently, the demand for labour of a given skill level equals:

$$L_{qual,t} = \varsigma_{qual} \left(\frac{w_t}{w_{qual,t}} \right)^{\sigma^L} L_t \tag{12}$$

where $L_{qual,t}$ is the effective labour force by skill level, $w_{qual,t}$ the wage rate per unit of skilled effective labour, ς_{qual} a constant parameter and σ^L the elasticity of substitution of the CES function for labour demand. Given equation (4), the wage rate per unit of effective labour w_t becomes a CES function of the wage rate per unit of skilled effective labour $w_{qual,t}$:

$$w_t^{1-\sigma^L} = \sum_{qual} \varsigma_{qual} w_{qual,t}^{1-\sigma^L} \tag{13}$$

Investment and Asset Returns

The accumulation of the capital stock (K_t) is determined by the following equation:

$$K_{t+1} = Inv_t + (1 - \delta)K_t \ , \tag{14}$$

where Inv_t represents investment made at time t and δ is the depreciation rate of capital. The rate of return on capital R_t is a function of its rental rate re_t minus the depreciation rate:

$$1 + R_t = (1 + re_t - \delta) \tag{15}$$

Since bonds and capital shares are perfect substitutes, the expected return on capital also equals the expected return on bonds:

$$1 + R_{t+1} = 1 + ri_t \tag{16}$$

where ri_t is the rate of return on bonds issued at time t.

The Government Sector

The national government issues bonds to finance the public debt and to satisfy its budget constraint. It taxes labour income and taxable transfers, capital income and consumption expenditures. It spends on public expenditure, health care, education and interest payments on the regional government public debt. It also provides transfers to agents through social transfers.

The government budget constraint is defined as:

$$
\begin{aligned}
&Bond_{t+1} - Bond_t \\
&+ \sum_{qual,nat,g} (Pop_{qual,nat,g,t}(\tau_t^w(w_{qual,t}h_{qual,nat,g,t}Lpar_{qual,nat,g,t} \\
&+ Tr_{qual,nat,g,t} + OAS_{qual,g \geq 13,t} \\
&+ C/QPP_{qual,nat,g \geq 12,t} + RPP_{qual,nat,g \geq 10,t})) \\
&+ \tau_t^c C_{nat,g,t} + \tau_t^k ri_t a_{nat,qual,g,t}) = (Gov_t + GovH_t + GovE_t) \\
&+ \sum_{qual,nat,g} Pop_{qual,nat,g,t}(Tr_{g,t} + OAS_{qual,g \geq 13,t} + GIS_{qual,g \geq 13,t}) \\
&+ ri_t Bond_t
\end{aligned}
\tag{17}
$$

On the left-hand side of the above equation, $Bond_t$ is the stock of debt accumulated by the government at time t and $Bond_{t+1} - Bond_t$ is the government deficit. The three remaining terms on the left-hand side are government revenues from taxes levied on labour income (plus taxable transfers), consumption and capital income. On the right-hand side of the equation, Gov_t is public expenditure, $GovH_t$ health-care spending and $GovE_t$ education spending. The remaining terms include total transfer payments (Tr, OAS and GIS), which evolve with demographic changes and interest payments on the public debt.

Market and Aggregation Conditions

The model assumes perfectly competitive markets and agents with perfect foresight. The equilibrium condition for markets of goods states that total output must be equal to total demand:

$$Y_t = \sum_{qual,nat,g} (Pop_{qual,nat,g,t} C_{qual,nat,g,t}) \\ + InvI_t + Gov_t + GovH_t + GovE_t \qquad (18)$$

There is a demand for labour by level of qualification. The stock of effective skilled labour supplied is the number of workers in each skill category multiplied by their corresponding human capital stocks and labour force participation rates:

$$L_{qual,t} = \sum_{nat,g} (Pop_{qual,nat,g,t} h_{qual,nat,g} Lpar_{qual,nat,g}) \qquad (19)$$

Bonds and physical capital ownership are considered perfect substitutes, hence total supply of assets must equal total demand:

$$\sum_{qual,nat,g} Pop_{qual,nat,g,t} A_{qual,nat,g} = K_t + Bond_t \qquad (20)$$

Behavioural Parameters

Table 4 reports key behavioural and government program parameter values. The value of the inter-temporal elasticity of substitution is 0.9 and the value of the intra-temporal elasticity of substitution between consumption and leisure is 0.8. These values are similar to those used by Altig *et al.* (1997); Kotlikoff, Smetters, and Walliser (1999); and Baylor (2005). The C/QPP replacement rate is 0.2. RPP replacement rate varies

Table 4: Behavioural and Government Program Parameters

	Symbol	Value
Inter-temporal elasticity of substitution	ε	0.9
Intra-temporal elasticity of substitution	η	0.8
CPP/QPP replacement rate	$CQPP\_rr$	0.2
RPP replacement rate	RPP_rr	0.02 - 0.14
Elasticity of time allocated to the production of human capital	γ	0.7
Elasticity of human capital already acquired to the production of human capital	ψ	1.0
Elasticity of substitution for labour demand across qualification	σ^L	1.5
Production share of physical capital	α	0.3
Rate of interest	ri	0.04
Depreciation rate of physical capital	δ	0.051
Labour income tax rate	τ^w	0.318
Capital income tax rate	τ^k	0.352
Consumption tax rate	τ^c	0.11

by age and skill and ranges between 0.02 and 0.14.[4] The elasticity of substitution for labour demand across qualification is set to 1.5. This is based on a survey of recent studies which estimated the long-run elasticity of substitution between more educated and less educated workers.[5] The elasticity of human capital technology is equal to 1.7 (ψ + γ) and is taken from Fougère and Mérette (1999, 2000) and Heckman, Lockner, and Taber (1998).[6]

Measuring Lifetime Economic Welfare by Cohort and Level of Qualification

We calculate the impact of population aging and alternative public pension options on lifetime economic welfare by cohort and level of qualification. The measure is calculated as follows. First, according to equation (1), we calculate the level of utility $U^I_{qual,t}$ before the demographic shock by cohort and level of qualification, which depends on lifetime consumption and leisure activity, where I indicates the level of utility in the initial steady state, for cohort t and level of qualification *qual*. Next, we recalculate utility levels by cohort and level of qualification, $U^F_{qual,t}$ and report the percentage difference, ($U^F_{qual,t}$ - $U^I_{qual,t}$)/$U^I_{qual,t}$. The same calculation is made to evaluate the economic welfare effect of alternative public pension plan scenarios. Also, we decompose the change in economic welfare into two parts: lifetime consumption and leisure.

---

[4]The RPP replacement rate of representative individuals is positively associated with age and skill level. It reflects the fact that the proportion of Canadians who receive benefits from a DB private pension plan increases with age and that average and median benefits from such plans increase with skill levels.

[5] These studies are Ciccone and Peri (2005); Krusell *et al.* (2000); Caselli and Coleman (2000); and Katz and Murphy (1992).

[6] Heckman, Lockner, and Taber (1998) have estimated the value of γ and ψ to sum to 1.8.

Simulation Analysis

As indicated in the introduction, here we analyze the impact of eliminating early retirement incentives in public and defined-benefit private pension plans and examine alternative policy options to make the public pension system "near" incentive neutral. Also, for DB private pension plans, we examine the likely scenario that the recent declining trend in the proportion of DB private pension plans observed since the mid-1980s continues until 2030.

Impact of Eliminating Early Retirement Incentives in Public and Private Pensions

The simulations of eliminating early retirement incentives in public and private pension plans are undertaken separately. We first discuss the impact on the labour supply of older workers, followed by an analysis of the impact on key economic indicators. Lastly, we discuss the economic-welfare implications.

Public Pensions

To apply the shock of eliminating early retirement incentives in the current public pension system, we set the implicit tax rates from Table 1 to zero in the CGE model. Table 5 presents the impact of the shock on the labour supply of older workers by age group and skill level.

As can be seen, for age groups 53–60, the labour supply impact is slightly negative as hours of work fall by one or two weekly hours. Under the current system, before age 60, workers are encouraged to continue working to obtain more C/QPP benefits. Removing early retirement incentives thus eliminates this effect early on. At age 61–64, the impact on the labour supply of low- and medium-skill workers is positive as they increase weekly hours by six to eight hours. However, there is virtually no effect on high-skilled workers.

After age 64, high-skilled workers have somewhat more incentive to work, since the OAS clawback is eliminated. According to the model result, the highly skilled would raise their labour supply by about two weekly hours. There is no impact on medium-skilled workers, since they are not affected by the OAS clawback. Finally, low-skilled workers

**Table 5: Impact of Removing Early Retirement Incentives
in Public Pensions: Change in Weekly Hours
by Skill Level**
(Level difference relative to benchmark scenario)

High-skilled workers	2006	2010	2018	2026	2034	2050
53–56	-1.3	-1.3	-1.3	-1.4	-1.4	-1.7
57–60	-1.4	-1.4	-1.4	-1.4	-1.5	-1.8
61–64	0.3	0.4	0.4	0.4	0.3	0.3
65–68	2.3	2.2	2.4	2.3	2.4	2.5
69–72	1.9	1.8	1.9	1.9	1.9	2.1
Medium-skilled workers	2006	2010	2018	2026	2034	2050
53–56	-1.5	-1.5	-1.5	-1.5	-1.6	-1.8
57–60	-0.6	-0.6	-0.6	-0.6	-0.7	-0.8
61–64	5.9	5.9	5.9	5.8	5.9	6.4
65–68	-0.1	-0.4	-0.3	-0.3	-0.3	-0.4
69–72	-0.2	-0.1	-0.4	-0.3	-0.4	-0.4
Low-skilled workers	2006	2010	2018	2026	2034	2050
53–56	-1.8	-1.8	-1.8	-1.8	-1.9	-2.1
57–60	-0.9	-0.8	-0.9	-0.9	-0.9	-1.0
61–64	7.6	7.5	7.5	7.5	7.6	8.3
65–68	1.2	0.8	0.9	0.8	0.8	1.0
69–72	1.4	1.3	0.9	1.0	1.0	1.2

aged 65+ increase their labour supply slightly after age 64 because of the elimination of the work disincentive effect of the GIS.

Private Pensions

Table 6 presents the impact of removing early retirement incentives from DB private pension plans on the labour supply of older workers by age group and skill level. To apply the shock of eliminating early retirement incentives in private pension plans, the implicit tax rates in Table 3 for private pensions only are set at zero in the CGE model.

Table 6: Impact of Removing Early Retirement Incentives in DB Private Pensions: Change in Weekly Hours by Skill Level
(Level difference relative to benchmark scenario)

High-skilled workers	2006	2010	2018	2026	2034	2050
53–56	-0.6	-0.5	-0.5	-0.4	-0.5	-0.7
57–60	3.5	3.4	3.4	3.4	3.5	3.6
61–64	8.0	7.6	7.4	7.4	7.6	8.1
65–68	10.0	9.3	8.6	8.6	8.8	9.5
69–72	11.5	10.7	9.5	9.3	9.5	10.4
Medium-skilled workers	2006	2010	2018	2026	2034	2050
53–56	-0.1	-0.1	-0.1	-0.1	-0.2	-0.4
57–60	2.4	2.3	2.2	2.2	2.2	2.2
61–64	7.5	7.2	6.9	6.8	6.9	7.5
65–68	10.7	10.1	9.4	9.3	9.4	10.3
69–72	12.1	11.4	10.3	10.0	10.1	11.1
Low-skilled workers	2006	2010	2018	2026	2034	2050
53–56	-1.1	-1.1	-1.1	-1.1	-1.2	-1.5
57–60	0.9	0.8	0.7	0.6	0.6	0.6
61–64	6.8	6.5	6.3	6.2	6.2	6.7
65–68	8.5	7.9	7.4	7.3	7.3	7.9
69–72	10.2	9.6	8.7	8.5	8.5	9.3

As can be seen, the labour supply impact of removing early retirement incentives in private pensions is several times larger than in public pensions. Across all skill levels, the labour supply of older workers begins to rise at age 57 and continues to increase until they eventually fully retire. High-skilled workers increase their labour supply from 3.5 weekly hours at age 57–60 to 10.4 hours at age 69–72. In comparison, changes in weekly hours for medium- and low-skilled workers range from 2.2 hours to 10 hours and from 0.8 hours to 9 hours, respectively, between ages 57 and 72.

Finally, when work disincentives are removed, workers are expected to work longer. Accordingly, they change work behaviour earlier in their life. For example, at age 53–56, there is a small reduction in their labour supply and a corresponding increase in leisure.

Long-Term Economic Impact of Removing Early Retirement Incentives

We now present the long-term economic impact of removing early retirement incentives in both public and private pension plans. Table 7

Table 7: Impact of Eliminating Early Retirement Incentives on Key Economic Indicators
(Percentage point difference relative to the benchmark scenario)

	2006	2010	2018	2026	2034	2050
Real GDP per-capita						
Public pensions	0.3	0.3	0.4	0.5	0.6	0.7
DB private pensions	2.4	2.7	3.4	3.9	4.3	5.2
Effective labour supply per-capita						
Public pensions	0.5	0.5	0.5	0.6	0.6	0.7
DB private pensions	3.9	4.0	4.4	4.8	5.3	6.1
Physical capital per-capita						
Public pensions	-0.1	0.0	0.2	0.3	0.5	0.9
DB private pensions	-1.2	-0.4	0.6	1.1	1.4	2.2
Capital-labour ratio						
Public pensions	-0.6	-0.5	-0.5	-0.4	-0.3	-0.1
DB private pensions	-5.0	-4.5	-4.2	-4.6	-5.3	-6.3
National savings per-capita						
Public pensions	1.0	0.8	0.7	0.7	0.8	1.2
DB private pensions	7.7	6.6	4.8	3.7	3.2	3.9
Real wages (high-skilled)						
Public pensions	0.0	0.0	0.1	0.1	0.2	0.4
DB private pensions	-3.0	-2.8	-2.8	-3.1	-3.4	-4.1
Real wages (medium-skilled)						
Public pensions	-0.2	-0.2	-0.1	-0.1	0.0	0.1
DB private pensions	-2.3	-2.1	-2.1	-2.2	-2.4	-2.9
Real wages (low-skilled)						
Public pensions	-0.5	-0.5	-0.6	-0.7	-0.7	-0.9
DB private pensions	-2.0	-1.8	-1.6	-1.7	-1.8	-2.1

provides an overview of the results on key economic indicators, including the impact on real gross domestic product (GDP) per capita, effective labour supply per capita, the capital-labour ratio, national savings per capita and real wages by skill level.

As can be seen, the impact of removing early retirement incentives from public pension plans has a small positive impact on real GDP per capita. By 2050, real GDP per capita is 0.7% higher relative to the benchmark scenario. The real GDP gain comes from both an increase in effective labour supply and an increase in physical capital. However, there is a slight decline in physical capital intensity.

Although households do not have to save as much for retirement since they work longer, national savings per capita increases. The effect on national savings is induced. The policy change stimulates total income and raises the overall tax base somewhat. If the government chooses to keep expenditures and tax revenues constant, the government balance improves, thus raising public savings. If, on the other hand, the government chooses to lower taxes (in this scenario, we assume taxes on labour are reduced), this stimulates private savings and consumption.

Finally, low-skilled workers are the most affected with a greater labour supply increase than medium- and high-skilled workers. As a result, their real wage declines by 0.9% in the long run, while real wages for medium- and high-skilled workers do not change much.

The economic impact of eliminating early retirement incentives in DB employer pension plans is much larger. As shown in Table 7, the increase in effective labour supply per capita is quite significant and the impact on real GDP per capita is about seven times larger. By 2050, real GDP per capita rises by 5.2%, compared with 0.7% when we eliminate early retirement incentives in public pensions. National savings per capita also increases substantially, but the capital-labour ratio diminishes, compared to the benchmark. The significant rise in the labour supply of older workers across skill levels reduces real wage pressures. For example, high-, medium- and low-skill real wages fall by 4.1%, 2.9% and 2.1%, respectively in 2050. This in turn encourages firms to substitute away from physical capital towards labour.

Figure 2 also illustrates the change in labour market behaviour over the life cycle for high-skilled and medium-skilled cohorts who enter the labour market in 2006. For high-skilled workers, the impact of removing early retirement incentives in public pensions has virtually no effect on their labour supply until age 53. Between 53 and 60, they reduce their

Figure 2: Weekly Working Hours of Cohorts Who Enter the Labour Market in 2006

High-Skilled Workers

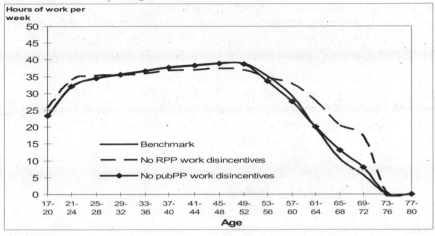

Medium-Skilled Workers

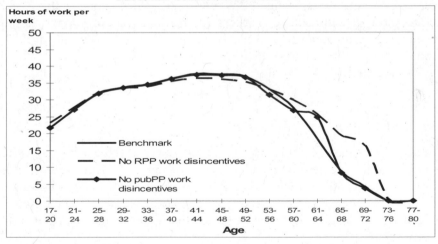

labour supply somewhat, since the elimination of the accrual no longer encourages them to work more intensively to receive C/QPP benefits. Between 61 and 64, their labour supply remains unchanged because the accrual effect is virtually zero. Finally, after 64, the elimination of the OAS clawback encourages them to work more.

Eliminating early retirement incentives in DB private pension plans 'has a much larger impact on high-skilled workers over the life cycle. Under this scenario, high-skilled workers significantly increase their labour supply when they are older. They also expect real wages to grow more slowly and they adjust their labour supply accordingly over their working life. For example, the expected return to education is smaller, so they choose to spend less time in school and to work more between ages 17 and 24, which has a small negative impact on human capital investment. During middle age, they also reduce their labour supply and choose to spend more time in leisure. Finally, after age 57, they significantly increase their labour supply.

For medium-skilled workers, removing work disincentives in public pensions has no impact on their labour supply until age 57. Between ages 57 and 61, they reduce weekly hours just like high-skilled workers. The elimination of accruals between ages 61 and 64 encourages them to work more during those years, while at age 65 and over, their labour supply remains virtually unchanged. When RPP work disincentives are eliminated, medium-skilled workers reduce their labour supply during middle age and spend more time in leisure. However, around age 57, they significantly increase their labour supply, just like high-skilled workers, until they fully retire.

Impact on Economic Welfare

Figure 3 presents the impact of removing early retirement incentives in public and private pension plans. As can be seen, the elimination of early retirement incentives in both public and private pension plans raises economic welfare. Not surprisingly, the positive impact is much greater when we eliminate early retirement incentives in private pensions than in public pensions.

Eliminating early retirement incentives in public pensions has a marginally small negative impact for existing cohorts of low-skilled workers. Even though lifetime consumption increases, it is more than compensated by a fall in lifetime leisure. For future cohorts of low-skilled workers, the effect is slightly positive and is dominated by a rise

Figure 3: Change in Lifetime Economic Welfare and Lifetime Consumption by Cohort Eliminating Early Retirement Incentives in:

Public Pensions

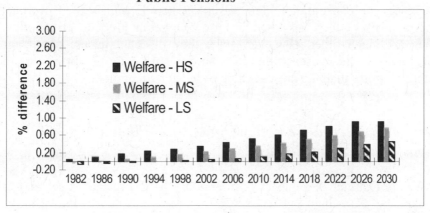

DB Private Pensions

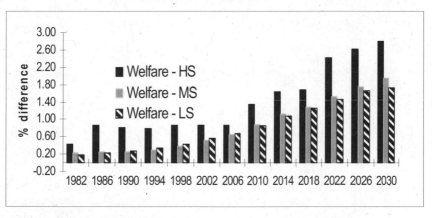

in lifetime consumption. In comparison, both medium and high-skilled workers enjoy a greater increase in economic welfare. Both groups of workers do not increase their lifetime labour supply as much and do not suffer from real wage decreases.

In comparison with public pensions, all three types of workers across cohorts benefit from an economic welfare increase when we eliminate early retirement incentives in private pensions. However, for both low-

and medium-skilled workers, the economic welfare increase is explained mainly by an increase in lifetime consumption, while lifetime leisure decreases. Finally, high-skilled workers benefit the most from the removal of early retirement incentives in private pension plans. For high-skilled workers, the economic-welfare increase comes from both increases in consumption and leisure. Overall, high-skilled workers increase leisure activities when they are younger and reduce leisure when they are much older. However, since they discount leisure over their working life, the present value of leisure when young is worth more in lifetime utility than the present value of leisure when older.

Impact of Alternative Policy Options to Make Public Pensions Incentive Neutral

We now examine the impact of alternative policy scenarios seeking to make the Canadian public pension system incentive neutral. Five scenarios are examined:

- Raising the actuarial adjustment in C/QPP from 0.5% per month to 0.8%.
- Eliminating early eligibility age in C/QPP.
- Using unadjusted value of C/QPP benefits to determine GIS payments.
- Removing the OAS clawback.
- Increasing the statutory retirement age in OAS/GIS and C/QPP from 65 to 66.

The economic impact of each scenario is summarized in Table 8. As shown in the table, of all five scenarios, raising the actuarial adjustment in C/QPP from 0.5% to 0.8% has the largest positive impact on real GDP per capita, which rises by 1.1% in 2050. However, this scenario is somewhat more than incentive neutral, since high-skilled workers now have a net positive incentive to work more between age 60 and 64. Recall that under the current regime the accrual effect on high-skilled workers is near zero.

Table 8: Impact of Alternative Policy Options to Make the Public Pension System Incentive Neutral on Key Economic Indicators
(Percentage point difference relative to the benchmark scenario)

	2006	2010	2018	2026	2034	2050
Real GDP per capita						
Raise actuarial adjustment on C/QPP from 0.5% to 0.8%	0.5	0.6	0.8	0.9	1.0	1.1
Eliminate early eligibility age to C/QPP	0.4	0.4	0.5	0.5	0.6	0.8
Use unadjusted value of C/QPP benefits to determine GIS payment	0.3	0.4	0.5	0.5	0.6	0.7
No OAS clawback effect	0.1	0.1	0.1	0.1	0.1	0.2
Moving the statutory retirement age in OAS/GIS and C/QPP from 65 to 66	0.4	0.5	0.6	0.6	0.7	0.8
Effective labour supply per capita						
Raise actuarial adjustment on C/QPP from 0.5% to 0.8%	0.9	0.9	1.0	1.0	1.1	1.2
Eliminate early eligibility age to C/QPP	0.6	0.6	0.6	0.5	0.6	0.7
Use unadjusted value of C/QPP benefits to determine GIS payment	0.5	0.5	0.6	0.6	0.7	0.7
No OAS clawback effect	0.1	0.1	0.1	0.2	0.2	0.2
Moving the statutory retirement age in OAS/GIS and C/QPP from 65 to 66	0.6	0.6	0.6	0.5	0.5	0.4
Physical capital per capita						
Raise actuarial adjustment on C/QPP from 0.5% to 0.8%	-0.3	0.0	0.3	0.5	0.7	1.0
Eliminate early eligibility age to C/QPP	-0.2	0.0	0.1	0.5	0.6	0.9
Use unadjusted value of C/QPP benefits to determine GIS payment	-0.2	0.0	0.2	0.3	0.3	0.5
No OAS clawback effect	0.0	0.0	0.0	0.0	0.0	0.1
Moving the statutory retirement age in OAS/GIS and C/QPP from 65 to 66	-0.1	0.1	0.6	1.0	1.4	2.0
Capital-labour ratio						
Raise actuarial adjustment on C/QPP from 0.5% to 0.8%	-1.1	-1.0	-0.8	-0.8	-0.8	-0.7
Eliminate early eligibility age to C/QPP	-0.7	-0.6	-0.5	-0.1	-0.2	0.0
Use unadjusted value of C/QPP benefits to determine GIS payment	-0.7	-0.6	-0.5	-0.5	-0.6	-0.6
No OAS clawback effect	-0.2	-0.2	-0.2	-0.2	-0.2	-0.2
Moving the statutory retirement age in OAS/GIS and C/QPP from 65 to 66	-0.8	-0.5	-0.1	0.3	0.7	1.5
National Savings per capita						
Raise actuarial adjustment on C/QPP from 0.5% to 0.8%	1.7	1.5	1.1	1.0	1.0	1.1
Eliminate early eligibility age to C/QPP	1.1	1.0	0.8	0.4	0.6	1.1
Use unadjusted value of C/QPP benefits to determine GIS payment	1.0	0.9	0.7	0.6	0.5	0.6
No OAS clawback effect	0.2	0.2	0.1	0.1	0.1	0.1
Moving the statutory retirement age in OAS/GIS and C/QPP from 65 to 66	1.5	1.5	1.5	1.5	1.5	1.5

Eliminating the early eligibility age in C/QPP and using the unadjusted value of C/QPP benefits to determine GIS payments have virtually the same economic impact (0.8% and 0.7% by 2050 respectively) on real GDP per capita. These two options would also bring the program much closer to being incentive neutral for retirement decisions and have little impact on high-skilled workers.

Removing the OAS clawback on high-income earners has a small positive impact on real GDP per capita (0.2% by 2050) and mainly affects the labour supply of high-skilled workers aged 65+. It is also interesting to see that removing the OAS clawback accounts for nearly one-third of early retirement incentives in public pensions. One important drawback, however, is that this policy change would raise OAS payments to individuals and would need to be financed through a tax increase or an expenditure cut, although this remains a small expenditure amount.

Finally, raising the statutory retirement age in OAS/GIS and C/QPP pushes early retirement incentives by one year. However, negative accruals become larger when they are delayed. This happens for two reasons: first, by delaying retirement, older workers receive more C/QPP benefits when they retire; second, past a certain age, wages start to decrease and thus raise negative accruals. Because of that, the change in accruals is positive for certain age groups and negative for others. Overall, the impact on GDP per capita is positive (0.8% in 2050). This positive impact essentially comes from the fact that older workers start receiving benefits one year later, which represents a negative wealth effect, resulting in increased labour supply and savings. However, the labour supply impact is smaller than in other scenarios since a significant part of the real GDP gains comes from higher savings and physical capital.

Further Decline in the Proportion of Defined-Benefit Private Plans

As indicated earlier, between 1984 and 2006 the proportion of members in defined-benefit private pension plans as a proportion of total employer pension plans declined from 95% to about 84%. In this last scenario, we simulate a continued decline in the proportion of members in defined-benefit private plans and a gradual shift towards defined-contribution plans until 2030. This would represent a 14 percentage point reduction in the share of DB plans to about 69% by 2030.

As shown in Table 9, the impact on real GDP per capita is small but positive. By 2050, real GDP per capita rises by 0.6% relative to the benchmark and is explained entirely by an increase in effective labour supply per capita, but is partly offset by a small decline in physical capital per capita. The rise in the labour supply of older workers leads to some real wage reduction for high-skilled, medium-skilled and low-skilled workers. This in turn encourages firms to substitute away from physical capital into labour.

Sensitivity Analysis

As discussed earlier, the value of the intra-temporal elasticity of substitution determines the sensitivity of changes in the leisure-to-consumption ratio. This implies that the magnitude of the impact of a change in accruals or implicit tax rate on labour supply and productive capacity is dependent on this value. The greater the value of the elasticity, the more sensitive the leisure decision will be to a change in the implicit tax rate. As given in section four, the value used in this paper (0.8) is well accepted in the literature. For example, Altig *et al.* (1997)

Table 9: Impact of a Continued Decline in the Share of Defined-Benefit Private Pension Plans on Key Economic Indicators
(Percentage point difference relative to the benchmark scenario)

	2006	*2010*	*2018*	*2026*	*2034*	*2050*
Real GDP per capita	0.0	-0.1	0.1	0.3	0.5	0.6
Effective labour supply per capita	0.0	0.0	0.2	0.6	0.8	1.0
Physical capital per capita	-0.1	-0.2	-0.4	-0.5	-0.4	-0.1
Capital-labour ratio	0.0	-0.2	-0.7	-1.2	-1.5	-1.5
National savings per capita	-0.2	-0.4	-0.3	0.0	0.2	0.3

and Kotlikoff, Smetters, and Walliser (1999) use an intra-temporal elasticity of substitution of 0.8 in their dynamic OLG models of the US economy. For Canada, Baylor (2005) also uses an elasticity of substitution between consumption and leisure for Canada of 0.8, while Baylor and Beauséjour (2004) use 0.7.

This section presents two alternative scenarios to evaluate the sensitivity of the results of eliminating early retirement incentives in public and private pension plans to the value imposed on the intra-temporal elasticity of substitution. One scenario imposes an intra-temporal elasticity of substitution of 0.6, while the other imposes a value of 1.0.[7] Along with the original scenarios shown in the last section, Table 10 presents the impact of the accrual shock on real GDP per capita under alternative values of the elasticity of substitution.

As can be seen, a difference of ± 0.2 on the elasticity of substitution changes the impact of eliminating early retirement incentives in public pension plans on real GDP per capita by ±0.1% to ±0.2%. Accordingly, the sensitivity of the impact on real GDP per capita for private pension plans would range between ±0.5% and ±0.8%. For example, using an

Table 10: Impact of Removing Early Retirement Incentives In Public and Private Pension Plans on Real GDP Per Capita, Under Alternative Values of Intra-Temporal Elasticity of Substitution (η)
(Percent difference relative to the benchmark scenario)

		2006	2010	2018	2026	2034	2050
Public pensions	$\eta=0.6$	0.2	0.2	0.3	0.4	0.5	0.5
	$\eta=0.8$	0.3	0.3	0.4	0.5	0.6	0.7
	$\eta=1.0$	0.3	0.4	0.5	0.6	0.7	0.9
DB private pensions	$\eta=0.6$	2.2	2.3	3.0	3.3	3.9	4.4
	$\eta=0.8$	2.4	2.7	3.4	3.9	4.3	5.2
	$\eta=1.0$	2.6	3.1	3.8	4.5	5.1	6.0

---

[7]These alternative scenarios are performed by creating first a new benchmark scenario with the new elasticity of substitution and then applying the accrual shock.

elasticity of substitution of 0.6 (1.0), for public pensions the real GDP per capita impact would reach 0.5% (1.1%) by 2050, compared with 0.9% using a value of 0.8. For private pensions the real GDP impact would reach 4.4% (6%), compared with 5.4% using a value of 0.8.

Accordingly, we feel confident in saying that reforming the Canadian public pension system would have a small positive impact on retirement decisions, and that the potential gains to be achieved with private pension plans are far greater.

Conclusion

As indicated in the introduction, early retirement incentives from the Canadian public pension system are small compared to most OECD countries. Using a dynamic CGE model we estimate that the cost of early retirement associated with public pension plans likely represents less than 1% of GDP.

We have also examined alternative policy options to make the program near incentive neutral to retirement behaviour. Among those, raising the actuarial adjustment, eliminating early eligibility age to C/QPP, using unadjusted C/QPP benefits to calculate GIS payments, and delaying the statutory retirement age in OAS/GIS and C/QPP would make the regime near incentive neutral.

We also clearly demonstrate that there are much greater work disincentive effects present in DB private pension plans than in public pensions. According to our model calculations, the loss in productive capacity could be as much as seven times larger than in public pension plans. However, the recent decline in the share of RPP members covered by DB plans since 1984 has likely contributed somewhat to reducing early retirement incentives over the past two decades. A continued downward trend decline over the next several years, if it materializes, should bring some additional gains.

References

Altig, D., A. Auerbach, L. Kotlikoff, K. Smetters, and J. Walliser. 1997. "Simulating US Tax Reform". NBER Working Paper No. 6246. Cambridge, MA: National Bureau of Economic Research.

Auerbach, A. and L. Kotlikoff. 1989. *Dynamic Fiscal Policy.* Cambridge: Cambridge University Press.

Baker, M., J. Gruber, and K. Milligan. 2003. "The Retirement Incentive Effects of Canada's Income Security Programs", *Canadian Journal of Economics* 36(2), 261–290.

Baylor, M. 2005. "Government Debt, Taxation, and the Economic Dynamics of Population Ageing". Paper presented at the Annual Meeting of the CEA, Hamilton, May.

Baylor, M. and L. Beauséjour. 2004. "Taxation and Economic Efficiency: Results from a Canadian CGE Model". Working Paper No. 2044–10. Ottawa: Finance Canada.

Becker, G. 1965. "A Theory of the Allocation of Time", *The Economic Journal* 75(299), 493–517.

Caselli, F. and W. Coleman. 2000. "The World Technology Frontier". NBER Working Paper No. 7904. Cambridge, MA: National Bureau of Economic Research.

Ciccone, A. and G. Peri. 2005. "Long-Run Substitutability Between More and Less Educated Workers: Evidence from US States, 1950–1990", *The Review of Economics and Statistics* 87(4), 652–663.

Fougère, M., S. Harvey, J. Mercenier, and M. Mérette. 2005. "Population Ageing and the Effective Age of Retirement in Canada". Working Paper No. 2005 A–03. Ottawa: Skills Research Initiative, HRSDC-IC-SSHRC.

Fougère, M. and M. Mérette. 1999. "Population Ageing and Economic Growth in Seven OECD Countries", *Economic Modelling* 16, 411–427.

_____. 2000. "Population Aging, Intergenerational Equity and Growth: An Analysis with an Endogenous Growth Overlapping Generations Model", in G. Harrison, S.E. Hougaard Jensen, L. Haagen Pedersen, and T. Rutherford (eds.), *Using Dynamic General Equilibrium Models for Policy Analysis.* Amsterdam: North Holland.

Gruber, J. and D.A. Wise, eds. 2004. *Social Security and Retirement Around the World: Micro-Estimation.* Chicago: University of Chicago Press.

Guillemette, Y. 2004. *Follow Quebec's Lead: Removing Disincentives to Work After 60 by Reforming the CPP/QPP.* Commentary No. 199. Toronto: C.D. Howe Institute.

Heckman, J., L. Lockner, and C. Taber. 1998. "Explaining Rising Wage Inequality: Explorations with a Dynamic Equilibrium Model of Labor Earnings with Heterogeneous Agents", *Review of Economic Dynamics* 1, 1–58.

Herbertsson, T.T. and J.M. Orszag. 2001. "The Costs of Early Retirement in the OECD". Working Paper No. W01:02. Reykjavik, Iceland: Institute of Economic Studies, University of Iceland.

Human Resources and Social Development Canada. 2007. *The CPP & OAS Stats Book 2007*. Ottawa: HRSDC.

Katz, L. and K. Murphy. 1992. "Change in Relative Wages 1963-1987: Supply and Demand Factors", *Quarterly Journal of Economics* 107, 35-78.

Kotlikoff, L., K. Smetters, and J. Walliser. 1999. "Privatizing Social Security: A Simulation Study", in K. Schmidt Hebbel (ed.), *Pension System: From Crisis to Reform*. Washington DC: The World Bank.

Krusell, P., L. Ohanian, V. Rios-Rull, and G. Violante. 2000. "Capital-Skill Complementarity and Inequality: A Macroeconomic Analysis", *Econometrica* 68, 1029–1053.

Lucas, R. 1988. "On the Mechanics of Economic Development", *Journal of Monetary Economics* 22(1), 3–42.

_____. 1990. "Why Doesn't Capital Flow from Rich to Poor Countries", *American Economic Review* 80(2), 92–96.

Milligan, K. 2005. *Making It Pay to Work: Improving the Work Incentives in Canada's Public Pension System*. Commentary No. 218. Toronto: C.D. Howe Institute.

Milligan, K. and T. Schirle. 2006. "Public Pensions and Retirement: International Evidence in the Canadian Context". Working Paper No. 2006 A–13. Ottawa: Skills Research Initiative, HRSDC-IC-SSHRC. At: http://strategis.ic.gc.ca/epic/site/eas-aes.nsf/en/ra02019e.html.

Munnell, A.H. and P. Perun. 2006. *An Update on Private Pensions*. An Issue In Brief, Center for Retirement Research at Boston College, August, Number 50.

Pescarus, C. and M. Rivard. 2005. "Régimes de retraite d'employeur et incitations à la retraite anticipée au Canada". Working Paper No. 2005–02. Ottawa: Department of Finance.

Policy Research Initiative (PRI). 2005. *Encouraging Choice in Work and Retirement — Project Report*. Ottawa: Policy Research Initiative.

Rowe, G. and H. Nguyen. 2003. "Early Retirement in Perspective: Insights from the LifePaths Microsimulation Model". Report prepared for Human Resources Development Canada.

Statistics Canada. 1999. *Survey of Financial Security*. Ottawa: Statistics Canada.

_____. 2002. *Life Tables, Canada, Provinces and Territories, 2000–2002*. Catalogue No. 84–537–XIE. Ottawa: Statistics Canada.

Stock, J. and D. Wise. 1990. "Pensions, the Option Value of Work and Retirement", *Econometrica* 58(5), 1151–1180.

Personal Accounts, Changing Defaults, and Retirement Saving in the United Kingdom: Are there Lessons for Canadian Pension Policy?

Richard Disney, Carl Emmerson, and
Gemma Tetlow[1]

Introduction

In countries such as the United Kingdom (UK) and Canada, retirement incomes are derived both from contributions to publicly-provided (social security) programs and from private saving; the latter predominantly through employer-provided pension plans and individual pension accounts. Mixed provision or multi-pillar systems of this type (as advocated by the World Bank, 1994) contrast with so-called Bismarckian

Financial support from the ESRC-funded Centre for the Micro-economic Analysis of Public Policy at IFS (grant number RES–544–28–5001) is gratefully acknowledged. The British Household Panel Survey data used in this paper were collected by the Institute for Social and Economic Research at the University of Essex, funded by the ESRC, and were supplied by the ESRC data archive. Any errors and all opinions expressed are those of the authors.

[1]Since the writing of this paper, the provisions discussed have been enacted in the Pensions Act of 2007 and the Pensions Act of 2008 – the editors.

programs for retirement income provision where the responsibility for providing pension benefits rests almost wholly with the state.

In several respects, the Canadian and UK retirement income programs are closely related: in both countries, the social security component of the program contains three parts — a long-established contributory component providing flat benefits, an earnings-related component, and a means-tested component.[2] And in the field of private provision, both Canada and the UK have employer-provided pension plans as well as various tax-relieved individual retirement saving provisions.[3] So it would appear that the policy issues facing Canada and the UK concerning pension provision should be fairly similar, subject to the particular idiosyncratic features of the national programs.

One of the questions that most vexes policymakers in countries such as Canada and the UK, which rely in large part on voluntary saving arrangements to provide incomes in retirement, is whether or not, left to their own devices, individuals will save "enough" for their retirement. This simple statement of course raises a host of questions; in particular about the decision-making capacities of individuals and also about how *adequacy* is defined and who defines it. Such questions have generated a good deal of debate in the UK and have led to a series of policy initiatives in recent years (reforms were announced in Pensions Green Papers of 1998 and 2002 and the Pensions White Paper of 2006). As in Canada, the UK has considered, and so far rejected, the arguments for a greater emphasis on mandatory private saving for retirement on top of publicly-provided social security programs. However, current UK legislation (described in this paper), which will lead to the vast majority of employees being defaulted into a private pension plan with a compulsory employer contribution, represents a major step towards a

---

[2]In Canada these are, respectively, Old Age Security, the Canada/Quebec Pension Plan and the Guaranteed Income Supplement. In the United Kingdom, these are, respectively, the Basic State Pension, the State Second Pension (S2P) (and its predecessor the State Earnings-Related Pension, SERPS), and the Pension Credit.

[3]Employer-provided plans are known as Registered Pension Plans in Canada and as occupational pensions in the United Kingdom. Individual retirement accounts are known in Canada as Registered Retirement Saving Plans (RRSP) and in the UK as Personal or Stakeholder Pensions. For a general discussion of the relevant issues for this paper in a Canadian context, see Hoffman and Dahlby (2001) and Milligan (2003).

more prescriptive approach. As such, the proposed UK reforms may be of interest to Canadian policymakers and analysts who have been considering the issue of retirement saving adequacy in that context.

The plan of this paper is as follows. In the next section, we discuss measures of the adequacy of retirement saving, and how levels of retirement saving which are perceived to be "too low" have motivated the UK debate. In the following section, we consider the issue of whether the standard "life-cycle" model of saving adequately describes saving behaviour, and in particular the idea that "default options" may prove a major factor in determining household saving decisions. This issue has been raised in the UK in the context of the debate on whether private retirement saving should remain voluntary or whether the government should mandate greater private pension saving. In the fourth section, we describe the current UK reforms, focusing in particular on how changing the default options in the retirement saving regime have been seen as a halfway house between voluntary and mandatory approaches to retirement saving. Finally, in the last section, we provide some evidence on the characteristics of individuals who are most likely to be affected by these reforms, and draw out some issues that arise from the proposals.

The Adequacy of Retirement Saving in the UK

The issue of whether or not individuals will voluntarily save enough to provide a sufficiently generous retirement income has been central to the recent debate about retirement and pension policy in the UK and elsewhere. Indeed, the presumption that many individuals do not save enough for retirement, for whatever reason, has been central to the rationale for public intervention, including the case for direct provision of contributory social security programs, as in the seminal paper by Diamond (1977).

Once there *is* a social security program in existence, however, it becomes harder to prove or disprove the argument that individuals (would) fail to save enough for retirement. This is simply because the existence of a social security program in part crowds out private retirement saving; the extent to which this will happen depends somewhat on the program's overall generosity and other design features.[4] Nevertheless, even with public provision of social security benefits, governments (and taxpayers) may still be interested in individual retirement saving decisions. This is true not just because policymakers have redistributive goals, but also for the pragmatic reason that inadequate retirement saving implies low incomes in retirement which thereby increases entitlements to public programs when, as in both Canada and the UK, there is a large income-tested component to the program of retirement income provision.

Given the existence of public programs, how might retirement saving *adequacy* be defined? The standard approach relies on positing a target replacement rate at retirement (typically defined as retirement income net of taxes and benefits divided by current income net of taxes and benefits) and examines whether or not a significant fraction of individuals would fail to achieve that target given observed or projected individual or household saving rates. In determining this target, the traditional approach of the policymaker has been to set as the benchmark a replacement rate that is related to indicators such as past replacement rates, current replacement rates in comparable countries, survey responses to qualitative questions and/or stylized actuarial calculations. Economists, in contrast, might consider that an approach based on direct evidence on individual households' preferences for consumption now *versus* consumption in the future predicated on the standard forward-looking model of life-cycle consumption (as in, for example, Deaton, 1992) would be a more appropriate benchmark.

The Pensions Commission in the UK, which was set up to advise on the direction of pension reform by the Labour government then led by Tony Blair, in its first report (2004) took the more traditional replacement-rate indicators into account when examining the extent of undersaving for retirement among the UK working population. In its own benchmark definition (which related to gross pension income in retirement as a share of current gross earnings), the Pensions Commission concluded that a "replacement rate" of pension wealth to earnings of around 67% at retirement for average earners constituted adequacy although the program as a whole should aim for higher replacement rates among lower earners and lower replacement rates for

---

[4]Disney (2006) compares saving rates across a number of OECD countries with differing pension program design features.

higher earners (ibid., p. 142).[5] Using a mixture of evidence on actual saving rates by different age groups and stylized simulations, it then concluded that around 60% of people were saving at an insufficient rate to achieve this target (ibid., Table 4.13).[6] This, in the Pensions Commission's view, underscored the fact that the status quo was not working and that a more interventionist approach to individual retirement saving was needed.

One difficulty with using a target replacement-rate approach, as Banks *et al.* (2005) point out, is that households with high current earnings are more at risk of having low replacement rates than, say, households that have low earnings relative to an *absolute* threshold such as an official poverty benchmark. In their own work, Banks and his co-authors identify two possible criteria for being at risk of insufficient resources in retirement. One criterion is that a household belongs to the group of those who are "lifetime poor" and who are likely to be eligible for income-tested benefits after retirement. The second group comprises those who are likely to fail to achieve the Pensions Commission target replacement rate (67% on average, somewhat higher for lower earners). They show that there is *not* a great deal of overlap between these groups among individuals aged 50 and over in English survey data. Only 55% of individuals identified as potentially eligible for income-tested benefits on the grounds of low income in retirement are identified as saving "inadequately" by the Pensions Commission's replacement-rate benchmark. Almost 75% of those who fail the saving adequacy test by the Pensions Commission's criterion are not likely to have inadequate incomes in retirement according to the eligibility threshold for income-tested benefits.

---

[5]Note that the benchmark definition of *adequacy* by the Pensions Commission, which is put in terms of gross replacement of earned income (and which was incidentally primarily derived from a commissioned survey which asked people what they thought a sensible replacement rate should be), is not the same as, or as appropriate as, a definition in terms of *net* replacement of *total income*.

[6]This calculation excluded all people aged under 35; a group that is likely to exhibit even lower retirement saving rates. In its later report (and in response perhaps to the implicit criticism that this calculation overstates the fraction of undersavers), the Pensions Commission implied that its first report had derived an undersaving fraction of 40%. Although this fraction docs not appear in the first report of the commission, it could be derived in various ways.

In addition, Banks and his co-authors show that "few personal characteristics are significantly associated with being more at risk of having a low replacement rate" (ibid., p. 100). This implies that using a replacement rate benchmark for saving adequacy based on observed incomes at a point in time generates a somewhat random set of individuals perceived as at risk of inadequate retirement resources. Despite these reservations, however, a replacement-rate target does have the advantage of establishing a clear benchmark for focusing policy discussion on the retirement saving issue, which has proved attractive to policymakers.

An alternative criterion for examining retirement saving adequacy is to back out a measure of adequacy from an explicit model of life-cycle optimization of the household's consumption path given lifetime resources, along the lines of Yaari (1965). Given explicit and plausible preference parameters and observations on underlying life-cycle income profiles and saving rates, it should be possible to estimate the optimal trajectory for the accumulation/decumulation of wealth for each household and to simulate or calculate actual wealth at, say, retirement relative to the target wealth that should be accrued at that date given preference parameters. Although the data requirements of such an approach are substantial, the results derived, at least to the economist, would seem to be less arbitrary than an aggregate target replacement-rate approach.[7]

In a recent paper, Scholz, Seshadri and Khitatrakun (2006) undertake such an exercise using data for the United States. They find that in "making use of household-specific earnings histories, that the model accounts for more than 80% of the 1992 cross-sectional variation in wealth. Fewer than 20% of households have less wealth than their optimal targets, and the wealth deficit of those who are undersaving is generally small" (ibid., p. 607). This is a very different conclusion from the Pensions Commission's report for the UK, but confirms earlier work in this vein by Engen, Gale, and Uccello (1999) for the United States, although contrasting with earlier results presented by Bernheim (1992), who *did* conclude that there was an undersaving problem in the United States. So either US households are more financially savvy than UK

---

[7]However, even this approach falls short of a more data-intensive benchmark for saving adequacy that incorporates *ex ante* expectations as well as *ex post* outcomes, since *ex post* outcomes are still subject to unanticipated negative shocks.

households (or the US system is considerably easier to understand), or there is a major discrepancy in terms of methodology and credibility of the different approaches.

A key issue in understanding these discrepancies concerns what resources are included in the definition of adequacy. Focusing on pension wealth alone may be too narrow if households are also accruing other wealth, such as financial assets and housing equity, which they are prepared to use to finance expenditures in retirement. In its second report (2005), the Pensions Commission partially accepted this argument, in particular in response to work on actual wealth distribution among those approaching retirement in England. This work by Banks *et al.* (2005) had suggested that, if the definition of retirement wealth was extended to include not just wealth in pension plans, but also financial wealth and half of housing wealth, the proportion of undersavers fell to around 18%, which is much closer to the figures quoted by Scholz, Seshadri, and Khitatrakun (2006).[8] In fact, Scholz, Seshadri, and Khitatrakun incorporate *all* housing wealth in their measures of household saving adequacy and, in common with other studies that use a broad definition of wealth in the adequacy calculation (e.g., Scobie, Gibson, and Le, 2005 for New Zealand) this fact alone (rather than the methodological issues or differences in financial acumen) probably explains why measures of "saving adequacy" differ across studies.[9]

Nevertheless, the UK government accepted the broad argument put forward by the Pensions Commission and others that many households were not saving enough for retirement, and that a new framework was

---

[8]Banks *et al.* also used family level wealth rather than individual level wealth. Since many low-earning (largely part-time) individuals have partners with greater earnings, they assumed that such families would need a lower replacement rate (since the higher earnings are, the lower the rate needed).

[9]The Second Report of the Pensions Commission argued against including housing wealth in its core measure of adequacy: "On average, pension wealth and non-pension wealth do not act as substitutes for each other" (ibid., p. 78). It supported this by citing the known correlation between levels of pension wealth and non-pension wealth across households (see, e.g., Disney, Johnson, and Stears, 1998, and the aforementioned research by Banks *et al.*, 2005). In ongoing research using household panel data, however, Disney and Gathergood (2008) find evidence of a degree of substitutability, insofar as households' holding of housing wealth appears to affect their active level of retirement saving.

needed in which retirement saving should operate. To understand the main drivers of the reform that has ensued, however, it is important to understand another line of research which has gained prominence in recent years — the notion of default options — and how, perhaps uniquely, at least in terms of policy towards pension provision, this has motivated the recent pension reform in the UK.

Do Default Options Matter in Retirement Saving?

The paradigm of the representative consumer optimizing over the life cycle which underlies the orthodox approach to retirement saving has received its share of criticism in recent years, most notably from economists who believe that the behaviour of economic agents cannot be adequately described by the standard textbook model of consumer behaviour. Low levels of retirement saving can easily be explained (especially among young people) within the standard paradigm by high rates of time preference and/or informational imperfections. As the Pensions Commission noted, the UK's pension program is one of the most complex pension programs in the world, but complexity, to a risk-averse consumer, may not of itself predict undersaving. Indeed, where future outcomes are unknown and households are risk averse, standard economic theory predicts greater precautionary saving, not less. However, if responses to complexity are characterized by behavioural inertia, procrastination and inconsistent decision making, as is argued by some psychologists and behavioural economists, policies for dealing with saving inadequacy (so it is argued) should take these behavioural responses into account.

The traditional approach to certain types of market failure is compulsion. Indeed certain *lock-ins* and compulsion in saving may be regarded as desirable by individuals who know that they are liable to procrastination or time inconsistency (as argued by Laibson, Repetto, and Tobacman, 1998), and some individuals do appear to act accordingly in some circumstances. However, such consumers may well also resist compulsion given preferences for current consumption over self-control mechanisms and may be able to unwind the impact of compulsion by reducing voluntary saving/savings or increasing debts. In addition, governments also provide for compulsory social insurance through the

Richard Disney, Carl Emmerson, and Gemma Tetlow

public social security program and may be unwilling to advocate programs that require additional compulsory saving for retirement.

The evidence that households would prefer compulsion is not convincing in the UK. Survey findings cited by the Pensions Commission show that just over 40% of people *who were already active pension members* agreed "that all employees should be forced to contribute to a pension". But only just over 20% of those who were *not* contributing to a pension agreed with that statement. In another study: of those not currently contributing to a pension, around 20% agreed strongly that "the government should make it compulsory to pay into a pension" and another 32% agreed slightly. The rest — almost half — disagreed (UK Pensions Commission, 2005, Figure 1.28). That the proportion arguing for compulsion was higher among those who already contributed to a pension might not be surprising; such a requirement might be relatively costless (or even cost reducing) for such a group. Overall, this evidence of public antipathy, especially among those who are not currently engaged in pension saving, poses one problem for a strategy of further compulsion.

A second problem for a strategy of compulsion is that, if compulsion is applied to a particular type of pension plan (for example, to saving in an individual retirement account such as a RRSP or a Personal Pension), households, however rational, would inevitably substitute the compulsory component for other types of saving if they are undertaking some saving already. Since the other saving may be on more attractive terms, such as in an employer-provided pension plan, total saving may not rise by as much as was hoped, and some households might in welfare terms be worse off. In addition, and related to this point, if the compulsory saving *rate* becomes a new benchmark for what is perceived as the government's view of what constitutes adequate saving, those who are contributing more than the compulsory amount may consider that they are saving too much, and so reduce their saving.[10]

If compulsion is ruled out and the existing arrangement under which individuals can choose how much, if anything, to invest in their pension does not seem to generate adequate saving, policymakers face a dilemma. Results from the recent analysis of behavioural economists have therefore proved attractive to policymakers when considering alternative strategies.

---

[10]In other words, appeals to the findings of behavioural economists can cut both ways.

One such finding from behavioural economics suggests that peoples' choices are affected by the number of options available. In investment allocations, for example, where a disproportionate number of choices were offered in a particular form (for example, in stock-dominated portfolios relative to bond-dominated portfolios) investors tended to choose the commonest option. And where too many investment allocation choices were offered, participation in the exercise fell, indicating that greater complexity of choice may indeed induce greater non-participation (Thaler and Benartzi, 2001, 2004).

A second even more pertinent finding is that, with inertia, the default option is disproportionately chosen by participants. For example, in a US retirement saving plan where the plan automatically enrolled people unless they deliberately and explicitly opted-out of the plan into some other arrangement (or no arrangement), the participation rate was around 30 percentage points higher, even after 48 months, than in a similar plan where there was no automatic enrolment (Madrian and Shea, 2001; see also Choi et al., 2004). Though enrollment rates were higher, these researchers show that the contribution rate chosen by participants is likely to peak at the default rate at which the participant is automatically enrolled in the plan, whereas with voluntary enrolment there is greater variability in contribution rates. The presence of a default investment fund is also found to affect the allocation of portfolios in a similar way, with individuals being less likely to choose a different investment strategy when a default is made available. Evidence from the UK cited by the Pensions Commission (2005) from the Government Actuary's Department (GAD) data on plan membership for 2004 shows that joining rates among eligible members are around 90% for defined-benefit (DB) plans and 85% for defined-contribution (DC) plans where employees are "auto-enrolled" whereas the proportions are around 68% and 58% respectively when employees are not auto-enrolled. However, caution should be exercised in interpreting this last finding as an appropriate treatment since pension scheme membership may be more appropriate for those employees who are auto-enrolled into a scheme than for those employees who are not auto-enrolled.[11]

---

[11]This evidence from GAD does not tell us whether those plans which auto-enrolled offered similar generosity of treatment to members as those that did not. Most public sector DB pension plans, for example, seem to offer a form of auto-enrollment and are generous to participants relative to employee contributions. In contrast, private sector DC plans, where plan participants are likely to contribute a greater proportion of total plan contributions may also be

Richard Disney, Carl Emmerson, and Gemma Tetlow

Note that the standard textbook model of consumer behaviour *with full information* and no transaction costs predicts that default options should not affect choices — individuals will choose whether to save and how much to save, on the basis of their intertemporal preferences and expectations. However, it is not clear that the findings of these various studies necessarily refute a model where consumers have imperfect information — default options, enrollment strategies, and other such devices may be seen by individuals as signalling information about optimal behaviour for agents of their type. Indeed, as Carroll *et al.* (2005) point out in a recent contribution in this field, requiring individuals to make an explicit choice, or at least increasing the cost to them of not making an explicit choice, rather than automatically enrolling them into a particular choice should be sufficient to overcome the inertia problem. Nevertheless, whether or not such findings form an effective critique of the traditional textbook model of consumer choice, they raise interesting issues in several policy contexts — not least that of finding a method of increasing saving for retirement without requiring compulsion that forces certain arrangements on all participants.

The Pension Reform Agenda in the UK

Background

The UK's pension program is complex; a complexity that has been heightened by frequent pension reforms (although a notable recent exception was much of the Pensions Act of 2004). One consequence of these reforms has been to widen considerably the choice of retirement saving options available to UK households. The reform trajectory has involved a number of policy initiatives and tax reforms designed to increase the incentives to save for retirement among some or all of the working population (for an overview and overall evaluation, see Chung

---

less likely to offer auto-enrollment. In addition, employers with a greater proportion of employees for whom pension saving is appropriate are more likely to be asked by their employees to enrol automatically relative to those who have a greater proportion of employees for whom retirement saving is not appropriate. But the former would have higher pension membership rates even in the absence of auto-enrollment.

et al., 2008). These incentives have included the introduction of new tax-relieved retirement saving accounts (such as Personal Pensions from April 1987 and Stakeholder Pensions from April 2001), as well as changes to the regime of tax relief underpinning retirement saving (as in 1987, 1997, 2001, and 2006).

Despite, or perhaps because of these many reforms, the evidence suggests that pension coverage, at least among men, has been falling in recent years. As shown in Figure 1 the percentage of working-age men thought to have been contributing to a private pension fell from 54% in 1996–97 to 43% in 2005–06. In contrast, among women coverage appears to have been extremely stable over this period. In addition employee contributions to funded pension schemes are estimated to have barely grown in recent years, with the UK's Office for National Statistics estimating that these totalled £15.2 billion in 2000 but had reached just £15.6 billion in 2005, that is, a fall relative to both inflation and (especially) average earnings (Wild, 2007).

The Pensions Commission (2004) pointed to a combination of over-complexity in the pension program, inertia, and procrastination among households, disincentives arising from the expected future availability of

Figure 1: Current Private Pension Coverage of Working Age Individuals 1996–97 to 2005–07

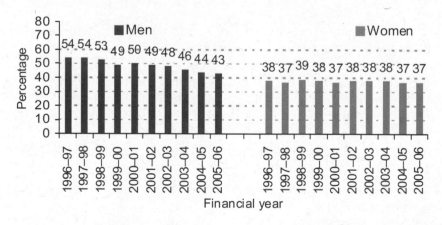

Source: Office for National Statistics, *Pension Trends*, using data from the *Family Resources Survey*.

means-tested benefits for lower-income households, and the lack of trustworthy and independent advice on saving as among the factors that caused this downward trend (ibid., Chapter 6). With its enthusiasm for the insights of behavioural economics, the Pensions Commission did not pay a great deal of attention to the econometric evidence which suggests that individuals *did* respond to retirement saving incentives such as additional tax reliefs.[12] Whether households responded or not, however, it is perfectly plausible to argue that, given the difficulties in targeting incentives on the "marginal saver", these policies could not have delivered (at reasonable expense to the taxpayer), levels of retirement saving that would eliminate what the Pensions Commission believes is a sizeable problem of saving inadequacy.

In light of these trends, and with greater compulsory retirement saving not on the political agenda, the recommendations of the Pensions Commission for an alternative approach found a willing audience among UK government officials (and many others). The government adopted a new approach to retirement saving with fresh legislation being enacted in 2007 and 2008. To understand these reforms, and in particular the shift in "default options" at the centre of the reform, it is useful to summarize briefly the UK's pension regime as it existed in the period since 1987, and the proposed regime as should exist when the latest reforms are fully implemented. This can best be illustrated by two stylized *schema* of the various tiers of the pension regime and the choices available to households within those regimes before and after 2007.

The UK's Pension Regime 1987 to 2007

As mentioned earlier, the UK pension program contains several tiers of public provision and a wide choice of pension strategies for individuals. A crucial part of the program, as it existed from the late 1980s until the proposed legislation of 2007 and 2008, is illustrated in *Schema 1*.

A key starting point in understanding the choice structure is whether the individual is offered the chance to join an employer-provided pension plan. This determines the first part of the decision tree. If the employer offers a pension plan, whether of the defined-benefit (DB) or defined-contribution (DC) type, the individual employee can choose whether to

---

[12]For evidence from the UK, see, for example, Disney, Emmerson, and Wakefield (2001, 2007).

join that plan or not. Membership of an employer-provided pension plan has not been a compulsory condition of employment (if offered) since 1987. Some employer-provided plans auto-enrol employees: that is, new employees are informed that they will be enrolled in the plan unless they explicitly request to opt out. One private sector example of this is Tesco, a large UK supermarket group, which auto-enrols employees after one year of service (unless they are aged under 21) into its occupational defined-benefit pension plan. Other employers simply inform their employees that there is an employer-provided plan available that they can join if they wish; for these employees the default option (i.e., the "do nothing" strategy) is to opt out. Data from the British Household Panel Survey show that, in 2005, roughly 50% of employees in the UK were offered an employer-provided pension plan, of which roughly a quarter did not join.

Employees who choose to enter their employer-provided pension plan then pay a minimum (typically earnings-related) contribution to the plan, usually supplemented by a contribution from the employer. The employee then has the option to supplement these minimum contributions with additional voluntary contributions (AVC) to the plan (for example, to make up for lost years of service). As the name suggests, these AVCs are wholly voluntary and the default option is just to pay the required minimum contribution.

For employees who choose *not* to join their employer-provided plan, there is a choice of retirement saving arrangements. They can purchase (or continue to contribute to) an individual retirement account such as a Personal Pension. Established in 1987, Personal Pensions are tax-relieved individual retirement accounts provided by insurance companies. They were originally introduced as an alternative to the earnings-related part of the social security program, permitting individuals to opt out of this part of the social security program (SERPS until 2002, replaced by S2P thereafter), but the legislation also allowed individuals to opt out of an employer-provided plan in order to purchase instead a Personal Pension.[13]

---

[13]This option might have been attractive for an employee who intended to leave the company for which he or she was working and wanted a more "portable" type of pension; see Disney and Emmerson (2002). For a full discussion of the incentives to opt out of SERPS into a Personal Pension, and how these incentives have changed over time, see Chung *et al.* (2008).

Alternatively, the employee could choose not to make any private retirement arrangement having opted out of their employer-provided pension plan. Such employees would accrue entitlement to the second tier of the social security program (i.e., SERPS until 2002 and S2P thereafter). There is still a first tier to the social security program: the basic (flat) state retirement pension, from which employees and the self-employed cannot contract out.

For employees *not* offered an employer-provided pension plan, the decision tree is somewhat different. Since 2001, employers employing five or more employees who do not offer a pension plan have had to offer their employees the chance to purchase a "Stakeholder Pension" from a specified provider who has negotiated terms with that company. The Stakeholder Pension is a "no frills" individual defined contribution retirement account with capped administrative charges and limited choice of investment strategies (unlike the variable charging structure and wider choices available through a Personal Pension provider). The reform was designed to introduce a basic retirement saving vehicle through (but not provided *by*) employers for those employers unwilling to offer their own pension plan. Collectively, these Stakeholder Pensions and existing Personal Pensions, which are offered through the employer by an insurance company, are termed Workplace Personal Pensions.

Therefore, for employees who choose not to take up the Workplace Personal Pension arrangement, there is the same set of choices as an employee who has chosen not to join an employer-provided pension plan. The individual employee can purchase (or continue to contribute to) his or her own Personal Pension, with the choice of paying in the minimum rebate of social security contributions if they are "contracted-out" of SERPS/S2P (again, for further details, see Chung *et al.*, 2008) or supplementing these by his or her own extra contributions. Alternatively, the individual can make no private retirement saving arrangement, in which case they will again be defaulted back into the second tier social security program.

In examining this rather complex set of choices in *Schema 1*, we have delineated the default options by the bold lines and arrows. Note that there is a bold dashed line for those employees whose employer offers a pension plan, since some employers default their employees into the plan and some do not. Individuals who are not offered an employer-provided pension plan and take no other action, however, are defaulted in to the second-tier social security program. The key point is that, for many employees, the default option is not to engage in active private retirement saving. It was this point which was addressed by the reforms announced in 2006 (UK. Department for Work and Pensions, 2006a, 2006b) in the light of the concern over retirement saving inadequacy and the apparent importance of the default option; both discussed earlier in this paper.

The UK's Pension Regime from 2008 Onwards

Under the legislation proposed by the Department for Work and Pensions, which was introduced to Parliament in 2007 and (at the time of writing) set to be passed in 2008, the choice schema available to employees takes on a rather different complexion. It is depicted in *Schema 2*.

For employees whose employer offers them a pension plan of a certain standard ("compliant" employers in the new jargon), the change is, at least from the point of the view of the employee, relatively straightforward. The government intends that all such employers should make membership of the employer's pension plan the default option. Employees can still choose not to join the employer's plan, in which case they would be defaulted into S2P. They may also choose to purchase their own retirement saving account such as a Personal Pension. It is of course possible that "reluctant" plan providers, who have not previously been encouraging employees to default into their pension plan, may use this opportunity to withdraw their offer of a pension plan completely (although we might expect that they would already have done so). This change to the mandating of a default option for employer-provided pension plans is indicated by the shift from a dashed bold line/arrow to a continuous bold line/arrow between *Schemas 1* and *2*.[14]

For employees who are not defaulted into an employer-provided pension plan, the proposed reform is more complex. First, all such employees become members of the second tier of the social security program automatically. On top of this, the government will initiate a new set of Personal Accounts for retirement saving for all such eligible employees. All employees aged 22 and over but below State Pension Age will be automatically enrolled into these accounts if they earn over £5,035 a year, and will pay 4% of their gross earnings between £5,035

---

[14]The government has also announced (May 2008), after some concerns over the implications of European Law, that "Workplace Personal Pensions" can also implement auto-enrollment of employees into such plans (which, as we mentioned before, are offered through, but not operated by, the employer).

and £33,540 a year into their account (values in 2006/07 terms). This contribution rate will be matched by a contribution of 3% of earnings from the employer plus 1% in the form of basic rate income tax relief on the employee contribution from the government, making an 8% contribution rate in total.

The Personal Account holder will be offered a limited choice of fund types (asset mix) in which to invest these contributions. There will be a default choice of fund if the employee does not make an active choice of fund. There will also be a cap on administrative charges. The fund can be accessed from age 55 onwards and must be accessed by age 75: the funds should be taken as a (taxable) pension annuity with up to 25% as an income tax-free lump sum (this follows existing UK practice with private retirement saving accounts).[15] The funds will be managed privately, but with the Department for Work and Pensions operating as the clearing house for contributions and also as monitor of fund performance and administrative charges. Employees who remain enrolled in the Personal Account can subsequently change their plan type or increase their contribution rate. However, they could lose the entire employer's contribution if they contribute below the 4% rate or, of course, if they opt out completely.

As this last point implies, membership of a Personal Account is not compulsory; employees who do not wish to participate can formally opt out by writing to the Department for Work and Pensions. If they do decide to opt out, they will be re-enrolled in the Personal Account system every three years unless they continue explicitly to opt out of the program (or unless they become covered by the employer-provided pension plan of a *compliant* employer). Thus the new default option is to save through a Personal Account (as well as being a member of the second tier of the social security program) for those who are not covered by an employer-provided pension plan.

For those who choose to opt out of a Personal Account the choices are as before. By simply making no other arrangement, they remain members of S2P, the second tier of the social security program. They can also initiate (or continue to contribute to) another retirement saving account such as a Personal Pension or a Stakeholder Pension. Whilst a

---

[15]So, unlike IRAs in the United States or, say, the National Provident Fund in Singapore, the accumulated fund cannot be used for investment types other than providing a pension annuity and a limited cash lump sum at age 55 or beyond.

Personal Pension may offer advantages over a Personal Account (for example, a wider range of investment strategies), it is hard to see that Stakeholder Pensions will long survive this proposed reform, even though the introduction of Stakeholder Pensions was the "flagship" innovation of the 2001 reforms.

The new proposals are described in *Schema 2* and it will be seen that the most striking changes from *Schema 1* are the introduction of Personal Accounts and the change in the default option so that both employer-provided plans and Personal Accounts provide a default opt in to retirement saving that was absent from the previous pension regime. And, referring back to the discussion in the third section, this change in the default option is likely to have a substantial effect on retirement saving behaviour if the arguments of the behavioural economists about the importance of the default option are accepted. In contrast, the "traditional" model of consumer behaviour where individuals save optimally subject to full information and no transactions costs would suggest that individual employees would simply opt in whatever direction enabled them to continue to maximize lifetime utility. However, there are significant other changes between the old and new regimes — not least the introduction of a compulsory employer contribution — which do not permit such a "clean" test of the predictions of economic theory (as described in the next section). The Department for Work and Pensions "estimates that personal accounts could have between 6 and 10 million members with private pension saving of around £8 billion a year, of which approximately 60% will be new saving" (2006b, p. 21), but this of course hinges on assumptions made about the extent of opting-out of the default option and about the trend in employer-provided pension plan coverage, among other things.

Evaluation

The main purpose of this paper has been to identify the elements of the recent pension reform process in the UK which might be of interest to other countries with mixed public-private provision and where the adequacy of retirement savings and the issue of voluntary versus mandatory employee coverage by retirement saving plans are being debated. However, at the time of writing, several important details of the UK reform have not yet been settled and there is a transition period for several key components of the "package", so it is obviously far too early to carry out any serious evaluation of the reform.

In this last section, therefore, we identify some preliminary issues that will be worthy of consideration during the subsequent evaluation process. We first consider who might be affected by the reform (i.e., those who currently do not choose to save in a private pension). We might consider that these data give an upper bound to the effects of the reform on savers insofar as the reform only affects the saving behaviour of this subset of the population. On the other hand, this upper bound will vastly overstate the effects of the reform on retirement saving if the traditional life-cycle model of behaviour characterizes employee behaviour and these employees are able to offset any changes in the default option simply by opting-out of the default (as they are free to do) and/or to offset any saving in the new Personal Accounts by altering their other saving arrangements. Moreover, we are thereby assuming that the reform has no effect on the fraction of employers willing to provide pension plans that are compliant with the new regime (which would then affect the proportions of the population potentially affected by either the change in defaults for employer schemes or the introduction of the new Personal Accounts).

We also consider briefly how we can evaluate the effects of the reform on retirement saving given that it is a "noisy" reform in the sense that several changes are introduced simultaneously — this is not simply a "treatment" characterized by a change in the default option as in some of the US examples in the literature. Thus, even if we did not believe the findings of behavioural economics on inertia, the power of default options, decision-making and so on, we might expect an impact on total retirement saving from this reform simply from other components of the "package"; for example: requiring employers to contribute to Personal Accounts when these employers had not previously contributed to their employees' pension provision. This leads onto our final point, which is how we evaluate the effects of this reform on the macro-economy and on social and individual welfare. Again, at this stage, we can only provide some speculative comments.

Who Might Be Affected by the Change in Defaults and the New Personal Accounts?

Figure 2 examines the proportions of various employees in different earnings bands by their pension coverage using the 2005 wave of the

Figure 2: Pension Status of those Aged 22 to the State Pension Age in 2005–06

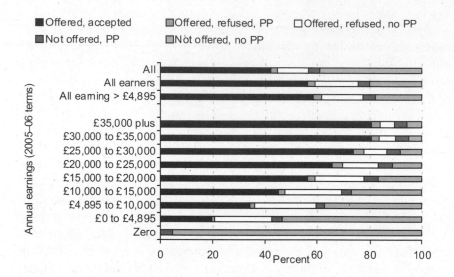

Notes: Individuals aged between 22 and the State Pension Age only.
Sample size = 8,916 of which 6,700 had positive earnings and 6,309 had earnings in excess of £4,895.
PP = Personal Pension.
Source: Authors' calculations from the 2005 British Household Panel Survey.

British Household Panel Survey, which is the most recent wave of the survey with comprehensive coverage of wealth and pension variables. The lower earnings band is chosen to be comparable to the current proposed floor — earnings of £5,035 in 2006/07 (the proposed floor) is roughly equivalent to £4,895 in 2005/06.

If we take these responses at face value (for example, that individuals do not misclassify existing Workplace Personal Pensions as "employer-provided pension plans"), then it is apparent that over 80% of workers earnings over £20,000 are either members of, or have refused membership of, an employer-provided plan and thereby might not be expected to be affected by the introduction of Personal Accounts. However, some of those who opted *not* to join their employer-provided plan *and* who had not made some other pension arrangement might be affected by the change in the default option for employer-provided

Richard Disney, Carl Emmerson, and Gemma Tetlow

pension plans if their decision not to join had been influenced by their employer plan previously having had a "not join" default option. The magnitude of the effect on this group will at least in part depend on the extent to which this change in default matters.

The target group for Personal Accounts therefore looks likely to be the significantly larger share of employees earning between £4,895 and £20,000 who were not offered an employer-provided pension plan and who chose not to make any other private arrangement such as a Personal Pension (in other words, in Figure 2, "not offered, no PP"). This group, which comprises nearly 40% of those earning between £4,895 and £10,000, would now start contributing to a Personal Account *unless* they explicitly enforce their right to opt out of the Personal Account. The fraction that is likely to choose to remain in depends on whether we believe that the evidence from US studies of default options is pertinent here. For example, if we believe the result of Madrian and Shea (2001) that a "pure" change in the default option raised the probability of membership by 30 percentage points, then this may be the appropriate benchmark for how many of this fraction might choose to remain in Personal Accounts. However, we have to reiterate that the reform is not purely a default option switch — contributors to Personal Accounts will also receive (perhaps for the first time) a contribution from their employer to their account. On its own this extra incentive would be likely to induce a far higher proportion of this group to remain in the Personal Account program.

The hardest group for which to evaluate the possible effects of Personal Accounts on saving are the group that were not offered an employer-provided pension plan but who chose to buy some form of Personal Pension. There are a variety of potential responses to the introduction of Personal Accounts among this group. Some of these respondents may belong to Workforce Personal Pensions which are treated as "compliant" and will thereby be exempt from the Personal Accounts; some may choose to substitute the new Personal Accounts for their existing Personal Pension account (especially if the latter had a small or zero employer's contribution); some may opt out of the new Personal Account; and some may even reduce their total saving if the new combined 4%+3%+1% contribution is treated as the new benchmark of saving "adequacy" within their existing scheme.

Table 1 examines the characteristics of those who have and who do not have a private pension. Not surprisingly, those with a private pension are more likely to work in the public sector, be more educated, have higher earnings, be homeowners, be full-time, and also to report that they

Table 1: Characteristics by Pension Status

	No Private Pension (34%)	With a Private Pension (66%)	All (100%)
Male (%)	48.8	51.2	50.3
Age (mean years)	37.3	41.6	40.1
Couple (%)	68.5	77.9	74.6
Employment			
Public sector (%)	16.0	49.4	37.9
Full-time (%)	79.1	86.7	84.0
Ann. Pay (median £)	13,998	21,617	18,044
Education			
Higher (%)	46.8	64.4	58.3
Middle (%)	14.9	12.5	13.3
Lower (%)	38.3	23.2	28.4
Assets and saving			
Regularly saves? (%)	38.0	59.0	51.7
Net financial wealth (median £)	0	3,000	1,000
Owner occupier (%)	71.7	89.0	83.0
Sample size	2,163	4,116	6,279

Notes: Individuals aged between 22 and the State Pension Age earning more than £4,895 in 2005/06.
Source: Authors' calculations from the 2005 British Household Panel Survey.

save regularly. They are also more likely to be older, male and to be in a couple. What is perhaps most striking is, amongst those who do not have a private pension, the median level of liquid financial wealth is £0, compared to £3,000 among those who do have a private pension. Whether this group remain opted-in to either their employer pension scheme or the new program of Personal Accounts or opt out because they perceive their financial constraints as limiting their capacity to engage in retirement saving, will be crucial to the success or otherwise of the new program in increasing both retirement saving and overall saving.

Richard Disney, Carl Emmerson, and Gemma Tetlow

Finally, to formalize these differences across characteristics, Table 2 provides maximum likelihood probit estimates where we test for differences in characteristics between those currently contributing to a private pension and those not currently contributing to a private pension. Broadly speaking, these tests for differences in characteristics confirm the comparisons of means in Table 1. Large and statistically significant

Table 2: Multivariate Analysis of Pension Status

	Marginal Effect (Estimated at Median Characteristics)	Standard Error of Marginal Effect
Male	−0.013	(0.016)
Aged 30 to 39	+0.131***	(0.017)
Aged 40 to 49	+0.210***	(0.022)
Aged 50 to SPA	+0.149***	(0.018)
Couple	+0.019	(0.018)
Public sector worker	+0.258***	(0.018)
Full-time worker	−0.023	(0.022)
Ln (annual pay)	+0.347***	(0.022)
Degree	+0.020	(0.016)
O level	+0.028	(0.021)
Regularly saves?	+0.117***	(0.015)
Net financial wealth £0 to £1,000	−0.020	(0.021)
Net financial wealth £1,000 to £10,000	+0.036*	(0.018)
Net financial wealth £10,000 plus	+0.072***	(0.018)
Owner occupier	+0.140***	(0.020)

Notes: Sample size = 6,135. Individuals aged between 22 and the State Pension Age earning more than £4,895 in 2005/06. Marginal effects calculated at the median characteristics. This is a man in a couple aged 40 to 49, working full-time in the private sector, earning £18,200, has degree, regularly saves, has liquid financial wealth worth between 0 and £1,000, and is an owner-occupier. Standard errors reported in parenthesis.
Statistical significance at the 1%, 5% and 10% levels denoted by ***, ** and * respectively. Controls for missing whether working part-time or full-time, and missing whether or not they regularly save, also included.
Source: Authors' calculations from the 2005 British Household Panel Survey.

positive marginal effects are found for age, earnings, working in the public sector, regularly saving and being an owner-occupier.

The Macroeconomic Effects of Personal Accounts

To examine the effects of this reform on total retirement saving clearly requires a set of heroic assumptions about behaviour in response to changing default options, substitutability among different types of pensions (and indeed saving more generally), and so on. Furthermore, the reform takes place against a changing background of public pension provision which will also affect behaviour. For example, the current legislation includes the provision that the age at which individuals can receive their state pension will rise from its current level (65 for men and 60 for women — already planned to rise to 65 between 2010 and 2020) to age 66 in the year 2026, 67 in 2036 and 68 in 2046.

The government estimates that annual contributions to the new Personal Accounts will total around £7–8 billion in steady state of which around 60% will be "new saving", the remaining 40% being accounted for by substitution of saving in the new accounts for existing saving in other forms. This implies that total annual saving will increase by around £4.5 billion. There is little discussion in government documents of how this number is derived. Even if the analysis of the previous subsection gives a guide to who is perhaps most likely to be affected and to their existing savings levels, we still do not have a clear guide to the extent of substitutability of saving, the impact of default options on individual behaviour, and the effect of additional employer contributions on retirement saving.[16]

Nevertheless, taking this value for increased total saving as the benchmark, efforts have been made to explore the possible macroeconomic implications of an increase in saving of this magnitude. A technical report from the Department for Work and Pensions (2006c) argues that the hypothesized increase in saving coupled with the corresponding short-term fall in consumption spending will initially reduce national income slightly and then raise it slightly above the level that it would otherwise have reached since lower consumer spending induces a slight fall in interest rates and the exchange rate which thereby

---

[16]However, see Hawksworth (2006).

stimulates economic activity (ibid., p. 31). This increase in national income is treated as a further positive impact of the reform.

Attempts to estimate the macroeconomic impact arising from changes in the intertemporal allocation of spending must, however, be weighed against the huge uncertainty surrounding the magnitude of the additional saving effect. The macroeconomic scenario advanced in the department document also fails to model the impact of the increased cost to employers both of providing the additional 3% contribution to Personal Accounts and the administrative and regulatory burden of the new program. The impact of the additional contribution rate depends crucially on where it is ultimately incident (i.e., on consumers, employees or shareholders). In addition, since the whole package is not revenue-neutral to the government, there will be additional macro-economic effects arising from the change in the net tax burden and how the government chooses to finance it (and, in turn, how the latter affects consumers). The uncertainty over the saving magnitude and the impli-cations of the change in costs to both employers and taxpayers would seem to dwarf any macroeconomic effects arising from changing interest rates.

It is even harder to assess the welfare implications arising from the pension reform. At the heart of the reform is the assumption that it will shift consumption from the working life into retirement by encouraging greater saving. It is worth remembering that the rationale for this change, and in particular the use of changing default options as the mechanism, is a model based on behavioural economics in which individuals exhibit inertia, procrastination etc., which cause them to save less than is desirable either socially or to themselves in the long run. Taken at face value, it is very hard to utilize standard measures of individual consumer welfare to analyze the type of model provided in, say, Laibson, Repetto, and Tobacman (1998) in which individuals have a "long-run" self and a "procrastinating" self, since the former might apply a standard discount rate to evaluate the gain from greater postponement of consumption whereas the latter would almost certainly prefer immediate consumption (i.e., would potentially value future consumption at zero). A transfer of resources from now to the future for a highly impatient consumer, for example, would leave that individual worse off from that individual's point of view whilst perhaps leaving society better-off if there are adverse externalities to the consequences of that individual's impatient actions. All of which suggests that an appropriate method of valuing the extra saving is to take a *social* welfare function based on a view about what the optimal level of saving in society is, as in the seminal paper of

Phelps (1961) and in standard texts such as Blanchard and Fischer (1989).

In contrast, Department for Work and Pensions (2006c) takes a slightly odd approach to evaluating the welfare gain from the extra saving hypothesized to arise from the introduction of Personal Accounts. They set the discount rate equal to the assumed rate of return so that the (discounted) gain in future consumption relative to present consumption is zero. The welfare gain therefore arises from improved *consumption smoothing*. Assuming that the target replacement rate in retirement is 67%, as argued by the Pensions Commission (see the second section), the loss of utility from an individual's replacement rate being below this target is proportional to that consumption deficiency in retirement. By simulating consumption profiles under the *status quo*, comparing these with the hypothesized consumption profiles under the assumed saving through Personal Accounts (which should get the individual closer to the target) and valuing these consumption deficiencies with an explicit utility function — that utility is a function of log(consumption) — the report calculates the welfare gain arising from this change. Aggregating up across various representative consumer-types, the report concludes: "even the simple method set out above produces an estimate of a welfare gain equivalent to £30 billion in NPV terms. This means that people over time could feel as if they had £30 billion more in lifetime income. Using the most optimistic of the assumptions gives a gain which could be as large as £60 billion" (ibid., p. 56).

Unfortunately, this reasoning is muddled. If consumers are genuinely financially constrained, in the sense that they are unable to access saving arrangements, then there is a welfare gain to be obtained from improving access to the credit market. If we could agree on appropriate measures of preferences and about what would be an optimal consumption profile (subject to the major difficulties described earlier), then improved access would indeed provide a gain from increased consumption smoothing. But the argument here is not that consumers are financially-constrained, but that they have non-standard preferences which imply that they do not take advantage of available saving instruments. We cannot use the standard tools of consumer theory to evaluate welfare gains if the reasoning behind the reform is non-standard, that is, drawn from other models of economic behaviour. If, for example, the inert consumer currently places a high premium on consumption now (however much he or she might regret that decision later), then any consumption-smoothing program of this type could arguably induce a large loss in welfare (evaluated at current preferences). However, it is precisely because consumers are perceived to be inconsistent in their behaviour that the social case for interventions such as mandating or the intermediate step of default options becomes stronger. But this requires, as suggested earlier, an argument for applying a *social* welfare function based on consideration of what the social planner considers the optimal saving rate rather than a hybrid analysis based on applying various inconsistent stories about consumer behaviour to the problem.

All this is not to suggest that the current reform proposals are wrong or inconsistent. The analysis merely serves to show not just that the current proposals provide a novel approach to some old questions of pension reform (such as retirement income adequacy and voluntary versus mandatory components of retirement saving regimes) but also serves to provide challenging questions about how the reform will be evaluated. This will give analysts many fruitful issues to research in the future.

Schema 1

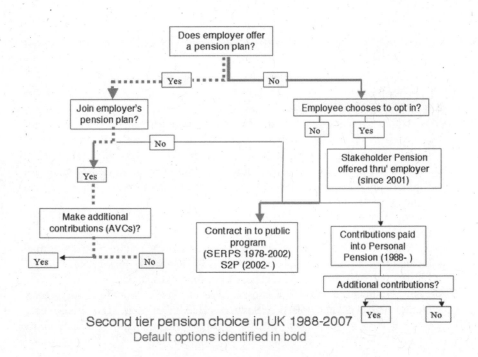

Second tier pension choice in UK 1988-2007
Default options identified in bold

Schema 2

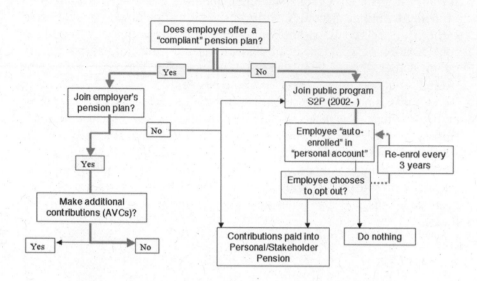

Second tier pension choice in UK after 2007
Proposed Default options identified in bold

References

Banks, J., C. Emmerson, Z. Oldfield, and G. Tetlow. 2005. *Prepared for Retirement? The Adequacy and Distribution of Retirement Resources in Britain*, Institute for Fiscal Studies Report No. 67. London: The Institute.

Bernheim, B.D. 1992. "Is the Baby Boom Generation Preparing Adequately for Retirement?" Technical Report, unpublished paper, New York: Merrill Lynch (September).

Blanchard, O. and S. Fischer. 1989. *Lectures on Macroeconomics.* Cambridge, MA: MIT Press.

Carroll, G., J. Choi, D. Laibson, B. Madrian, and A. Metrick. 2005. "Optimal Defaults and Active Decisions", NBER Working Paper No. 11074. Cambridge, MA: National Bureau of Economic Research.

Choi, J., D. Laibson, B. Madrian, and A. Metrick. 2004. "For Better or Worse: Default Effects and 401(k) Savings Behaviour", in D. Wise (ed.), *Perspectives in the Economics of Aging.* Chicago: Chicago University Press, 81–121.

Chung, W., R. Disney, C. Emmerson, and M. Wakefield. 2008. "Public Policy and Saving for Retirement in the UK", in R. Fenge, G. De Menil, and P. Pestieau (eds.), *Pension Strategies in Europe and the United States*. Cambridge, MA: MIT Press, 169–209.

Deaton, A. 1992. *Understanding Consumption*. Oxford: Oxford University Press.

Diamond, P. 1977. "A Framework for Social Security Analysis", *Journal of Public Economics* 8, 275–298.

Disney, R. 2006. "Household Saving Rates and the Design of Public Pension Programs", *National Institute Economic Review* 198 (October), 61–74.

Disney, R. and C. Emmerson. 2002. "Choice of Pension Scheme and Job Mobility in Britain", Working Paper No. W02/09. London: Institute for Fiscal Studies.

Disney, R., C. Emmerson, and M. Wakefield. 2001. "Pension Reform and Saving in Britain", *Oxford Review of Economic Policy* 17(1) (Spring), 70–94.

_____. 2007. "Tax Reform and Retirement Saving Incentives: Evidence From the Introduction of Stakeholder Pensions in the UK", Working Paper No. W07/20. London: Institute for Fiscal Studies.

Disney, R. and J. Gathergood. 2008. "Housing Equity and Retirement Saving in the British Household Panel Survey", unpublished paper. University of Nottingham.

Disney, R., P. Johnson, and G. Stears. 1998. "Asset Wealth and Asset Decumulation Among Households in the Retirement Survey", *Fiscal Studies* 19 (May), 153–175.

Engen, E., W. Gale, and C. Uccello. 1999. "The Adequacy of Household Saving", *Brookings Papers on Economic Activity* 2, 65–165.

Hawksworth, J. 2006. "Review of Research Relevant to Assessing the Impact of the Proposed National Pensions Savings Scheme on Household Savings", Research Report Series No. 373. London: Department of Work and Pensions.

Hoffman, M. and B. Dahlby. 2001. "Pension Provision in Canada", in R. Disney and P. Johnson (eds.), *Pension Systems and Retirement Incomes across OECD Countries*. Cheltenham: Edward Elgar, 92–130.

Laibson, D., A. Repetto, and J. Tobacman. 1998. "Self-Control and Saving for Retirement", *Brookings Papers on Economic Activity* 1, 91–196.

Madrian, B. and D. Shea. 2001. "The Power of Suggestion: Inertia in 401(k) Participation and Savings Behavior", *Quarterly Journal of Economics* 116(4), 1149–1187.

Milligan, K. 2003. "How Do Contribution Limits Affect Contributions to Tax-Preferred Saving Accounts?" *Journal of Public Economics* 67, 253–281.

Phelps, E.S. 1961. "The Golden Rule of Accumulation: A Fable for Growthmen", *American Economic Review* 51, 638–643.

Scholz, J.K., A. Seshadri, and S. Khitatrakun. 2006. "Are Americans Saving 'Optimally' for Retirement?" *Journal of Political Economy* 114(4), 607–643.

Scobie, G., J. Gibson, and T. Le. 2005. *Household Wealth in New Zealand.* New Zealand: Institute of Policy Studies, Victoria University of Wellington.

Thaler, R. and S. Benartzi. 2001. "Naïve Diversification Strategies in Defined Contribution Saving Plans", *American Economic Review* 91(1), 79–98.

_____. 2004. "Save More Tomorrow: Using Behavioral Economics to Increase Employee Saving", *Journal of Political Economy* 112(1), 164–187.

The World Bank. 1994. *Averting the Old Age Crisis.* Oxford: Oxford University Press.

United Kingdom. Department for Work and Pensions. 2006a. *Security in Retirement: Towards a New Pensions System,* Cm 6841. London: The Stationary Office.

_____. 2006b. *Personal Accounts: A New Way to Save,* Cm 6975. London: The Stationary Office.

_____. 2006c. *Estimating Economic and Social Welfare Impacts of Pension Reform*, Pensions Technical Working Paper. London: The Stationary Office.

United Kingdom. Pensions Commission. 2004. *Pensions: Challenges and Choices.* The First Report of the Pensions Commission. London.

_____. 2005. *A New Pension Settlement for the Twenty-First Century.* The Second Report of the Pensions Commission. London.

Wild, R. 2007. *Private Pension Contributions: Updated Estimates 1996–2005.* London: Office for National Statistics.

Yaari, M. 1965. "Uncertain Lifetime, Life Insurance and the Theory of the Consumer", *Review of Economic Studies* 32 (April), 137–158.

Summary of Discussion

John Stapleton remarked that conspicuous by its absence was any discussion of persons with disabilities, especially for people between 50 and 65, insofar as that's when people start to contract various sorts of chronic and episodic disabilities. Some of the options discussed, especially for this age group, should incorporate options for people with disabilities — retention strategies as well as strategies for going back into the labour force.

Kevin Milligan agreed with Maxime Fougère that he's likely right that the incentives in the private systems for exit from the workforce are larger than the public system. But an important difference is that in the private system, these are incentives to leave a particular job; in the public system, they're incentives that affect you no matter what job you're in. So they're more pervasive.

Malcolm Hamilton raised the observation concerning two different messages that we get consistently from the federal government on early retirement. The first is that there are likely severe workforce shortages coming; the population's growing older; no stone should be left unturned in our effort to eliminate any incentive for people to retire early. The second message we get is that the federal government is the proud sponsor of a defined-benefit pension plan that's hugely expensive; costs, if properly reckoned to the taxpayer are about 25% of pay. It has in it a 55-and-30 provision, which means any public servant, upon attaining age 55 with 30 or more years of service, can retire with an unreduced pension, and indeed, would be a fool not to. If you work out the total compensation impact of that, it's basically that your pay is cut in half the day you qualify if you fail to retire. So he wonders if there comes a day when the federal government, or someone from it, will turn up at a conference and say, "This is a serious problem; we're going to lead by example".

Chapter IV

Panel on Replacement Rates and Design Features of Workplace Pension Plans

Retirement Income Replacement Rates: Responding to Changing Attitudes and Needs

Peter Drake and Colin Randall

This paper describes the research done by Fidelity Investments Canada on retirement income replacement rates and the Fidelity Retirement Index™, which projects the median retirement income replacement rate in Canada.

Background

The research by Fidelity Investments into retirement income replacement rates in Canada was initiated against a background of structural and attitudinal changes to retirement. Both have important implications for financial preparation for retirement.

Among the structural changes are the longer lives and earlier retirements that, combined, mean longer retirements. Between 1979 and 2004, life expectancy at birth in Canada increased by 5.3 years, while life expectancy at age 65 increased by 2.6 years (Statistics Canada, 2004a). The median retirement age in Canada is 61, compared with 65 twenty years

The authors would like to thank Jason Stahl and Minja Pjescic for their contributions to this paper.

ago.[1] As a result, retirements of 25 to 30 years are becoming increasingly common.

Another important structural change is working in retirement. Working in retirement may mean delaying retirement past the traditional retirement age. It may mean moving to part-time work for one's current employer, or retiring and taking employment, either full-or part-time, with another employer or in another field. Fuelling this trend is the recent nationwide movement towards the abolition of mandatory retirement regulations. In fact, the labour force participation rate among Canadians 65 to 69 has already increased significantly in recent years, from 11.5% in 1990 to 17.8% in 2006.[2] There are compelling arguments that the incidence of working in retirement will increase substantially in the years ahead as Canada's population ages. Indeed, Canadians are already attuned to this future likelihood. In the survey supporting the 2007 Fidelity Retirement Index, 63% of respondent households expected at least one member to work in retirement (Fidelity Investments Canada, 2007b).

Attitudinal changes in retirement include the tendency of many Canadians to carry debt into retirement, increasingly active lifestyles for those in retirement and rising aspirations and expectations regarding lifestyle among those approaching retirement (Fidelity Investments Canada, 2006, 2007a). Carrying debt into retirement would have been almost unthinkable a generation ago. It is now becoming almost commonplace. Like the increasing amount of anecdotal evidence, particularly from the financial advisors with whom we have regular communication, Fidelity's survey data reveal that a substantial proportion of people approaching retirement do not plan to downsize their lifestyle when they retire, which indicates increasing expectations regarding lifestyle in retirement (Fidelity Investments Canada, 2007b).

Another important change is the gradual lessening in the role of defined-benefit pensions and the increasing role of defined-contribution

---

[1]Statistics Canada, Table 282–0051, labour force survey (LFS) estimates retirement age by class of worker and sex; Canada; median age; total, all retirees; both sexes (years).

[2]Statistics Canada, Table 282–0002, LFS estimates by sex and detailed age group; Canada; participation rate; both sexes; 65 to 69 years (rate).

Peter Drake and Colin Randall

pension plans in saving and investing for retirement.[3] It is doubtful that many members of defined-benefit pension plans spend much time thinking about retirement income replacement rates. However, the increased individual responsibility that flows from defined-contribution plans is likely to raise interest in this matter.

It is important to note that both structural and attitudinal changes to retirement are ongoing. Future retirees are likely to face both the conditions resulting from presently known trends and those resulting from trends that are not yet evident.

In the financial planning community, there are well-known and accepted norms for retirement income replacement rates. This "conventional financial wisdom" suggests that replacement rates of 60% to 70% of pre-retirement income are adequate. These broadly accepted norms assume that there will be some downsizing of lifestyle in retirement and/or that some expenses experienced during working life, such as educational expenses or mortgage repayment commitments, will cease and not be replaced by other expenses.

The Research Question

Is the 60% to 70% retirement income replacement rate dictated by conventional financial wisdom still appropriate, in view of the structural and attitudinal changes to retirement? If not, what is the appropriate rate?

The Research

Our first step was to review the rationale behind the conventional financial wisdom. To our surprise, we found that there was almost no Canadian research or documentation supporting the 60% to 70% rate. Extensive discussions with analysts in financial institutions, consulting firms and

---

[3]Statistics Canada, Table 280–0016, RPPs and members, by type of plan; Canada; total of registered pension plans; total defined-benefit plans; members, both sexes (percent), and total of defined-contribution plans; members, both sexes (percent).

government departments produced consistent acknowledgement that the 60% to 70% considered as the accepted norm is not supported by documented research. For example, the federal government's Human Resources and Social Development Canada Website has the following statement in an online publication, "Rule of thumb! Many financial planners say that you will need about 70 percent of your current (pre-tax) earnings to maintain your standard of living in retirement" (HRSDC, 2006).

With little or no documentation on the widely accepted conventional wisdom in Canada, we needed to assemble evidence relevant to actual financial needs in retirement. One approach is to look at spending in retirement, for which there is some statistical evidence. For example, work by Raj Chawla of Statistics Canada notes that, at least in the early years of retirement, spending falls off much less rapidly than income (Chawla, 2005). While Chawla's article notes that people in retirement apparently adjust their spending to falling income levels, the question remains as to whether falling spending in retirement reflects voluntary changes in spending patterns or reductions forced by falling incomes.

There have been some studies produced in the United States, such as one by Aon Consulting and Georgia State University (2004), which do make detailed assumptions regarding how income needs may change in retirement, based on potential changes or reductions to expenses. There are also data from the US Department of Labor indicating that household expenditure, when adjusted for household size, does not experience the substantial decline at retirement that conventional wisdom suggests (US Department of Labor, 1999–2005). Additionally, according to a US survey of households' anticipated and actual changes in consumption at retirement, 35.5% of retired households reported spending levels at retirement similar to those experienced immediately prior to retirement, and another 11.5% reported spending levels that were higher than in pre-retirement (Hurd and Rohwedder, 2005). While the remaining households (53%) reported a reduction in spending at retirement, the survey work points to the considerable heterogeneity that exists in spending levels among retired households.

Even though there is ample US data to support this apparent diversity in retirement spending levels, its relevance in Canada is muted because of significant differences in the conditions surrounding planning for retirement in the United States and Canada. Among these is the necessity for the

Peter Drake and Colin Randall

average American couple to set aside a large sum, in the order of US$200,000 or more, for health-care costs in retirement.[4]

Fidelity Investments Canada has gathered some evidence through surveys of Canadians who are both working and retired. In the survey that provided the data for the Fidelity Retirement Index (discussed later), 37% of non-retired respondents indicated they expected to maintain their lifestyle in retirement, 36% expected to cut back and 27% either were not sure or had not thought about the question (Fidelity Investments Canada, 2007b). Other Fidelity surveys point to Canadians' increasing willingness to carry debt in retirement. Results from a nationwide survey conducted by the Strategic Counsel for Fidelity in 2006 (the Fidelity 2006 Retirement Survey) found that nearly a third (31%) of retirees surveyed reported carrying a mortgage on a home into retirement (Fidelity Investments Canada, 2006). A similar survey conducted by the Strategic Counsel for Fidelity in 2007 (the Fidelity 2007 Retirement Survey) found that 55% of respondents in the higher-income brackets ($80,000 or more) indicated they maintained or increased their spending in retirement compared to their spending pre-retirement (Fidelity Investments Canada, 2007a). The incidence of this was lower as pre-retirement income declined. The statistical evidence is consistent with the increasing amount of anecdotal evidence from financial advisors suggesting their clients increasingly do not intend to reduce their lifestyle in retirement; some indicate that they plan to raise their lifestyle. All of this evidence gives reason to rethink the conventional financial wisdom on retirement income replacement rates.

Rethinking Retirement Income Replacement Rates: Defining the Exercise

The challenge was twofold. One was to determine a new retirement income replacement benchmark reflecting the changes to retirement. The second was to determine a benchmark that would not be in any way prescriptive, either of spending or of lifestyle in retirement. The changes in retirement

---

[4]Fidelity estimates that in the absence of employer-sponsored retiree health-care coverage, a 65-year-old couple retiring in the United States in 2007 will need approximately US$215,000 to cover medical costs in retirement. Fidelity Investments, March 2007.

mean that it is just as easy to envision a retirement in which retirees are able and willing to spend less than in their pre-retirement phase (for instance, in a case where large financial burdens such as mortgage payments and education costs are eliminated, and no new substantial expenses take their place) as it is to envision a retirement in which retirees desire or need to maintain pre-retirement expenditures in order to continue to meet previous financial obligations and/or to meet new ones. For those who are elderly and wish to remain in their own homes, there is a wide range of potential changes to their financial liabilities, from virtually nil, for those fully able to look after themselves and their dwellings, to considerable, for those who need substantial or total care and assistance in maintaining their dwelling. A second consideration is our view that the financial services industry should not dictate the rules either for preparing for retirement or for lifestyle in retirement. Rather, it should provide information and benchmarks that individuals are free to use, modify or reject.

We concluded that the appropriate benchmark is the retirement income replacement rate that will enable a retiree to maintain the same total level of spending in retirement as in the pre-retirement years. It is important to note that we specify total spending, with no reference or implication as to specific spending patterns. Total spending in retirement may include offering financial assistance to a child or grandchild for educational purposes. It may include increased contributions to charitable causes. It may include leaving a legacy to family or to charity. While it seems highly likely that for many, spending patterns in retirement will differ from those in the immediate pre-retirement period, such speculation is intentionally excluded from our considerations. Another point to note is that we did not specify the length of the pre-retirement period on which to determine pre-retirement earnings. The rationale for this is that among a large population group in an age of apparently increasing labour mobility, there is no inherent reason to assume that lifetime earnings continue to increase during the working period or that they reach a peak in the years immediately prior to retirement.

Peter Drake and Colin Randall

Retirement Income Replacement Rates: The Methodology

Pre-retirement income was divided into four components:

- contributions to retirement savings (presumed to be 10% of gross earnings),[5]
- contributions to employment insurance and to the Canada/Quebec Pension Plan,
- personal income taxes, and
- the remainder, which constitutes total spending.

When a person retires from employment, it can be assumed that contributions to retirement savings, employment insurance and the Canada/Quebec Pension Plan cease. This leads to a lower total income need that, with a number of age- and pension-related tax credits, usually results in a decline in the retiree's personal income tax liability. Thus, the components of income in retirement are total spending at the same level as pre-retirement and sufficient additional income to cover personal tax liability.

The next step was to calculate the gross income required to support the same total level of spending as in the pre-retirement period, and the relevant income taxes. In calculating specific retirement income replacement rates, we assumed retirement at age 65 and, for the purpose of determining personal tax liability, that work and retirement take place in the same province or territory.

The calculations were made for both single persons and couples, with pre-retirement incomes ranging from $20,000 to $200,000 annually. We also calculated the role that public retirement benefits — C/QPP and OAS/GIS — play in replacing pre-retirement income. A more rigorous version of the methodology is:

---

[5]Canadians age 25 to 64 who saved in a registered plan and who earned $10,000 or more per year contributed approximately 10.6% of their net income, on average, to an RRSP and/or RPP (Statistics Canada, 2004b).

$$\text{Income}_{\text{pre}} - \text{Tax}_{\text{pre}} - \text{Public Plans}_{\text{pre}} - \text{Savings}_{\text{pre}} = \text{Consumption}_{\text{pre}}$$
$$\text{Consumption}_{\text{pre}} + \text{Tax}_{\text{retire}} +/- \Delta \text{ Consumption}_{\text{retire}} = \text{Req'd Income}_{\text{retire}}$$

Where

$\text{Income}_{\text{pre}}$: Pre-retirement Income (pre-tax)

Tax_{pre}: Pre-retirement taxes

$\text{Public Plans}_{\text{pre}}$: Pre-retirement public benefit plan contributions

$\text{Savings}_{\text{pre}}$: Pre-retirement savings

$\text{Consumption}_{\text{pre}}$: Pre-retirement consumption

And

$\text{Tax}_{\text{retire}}$: taxes payable in retirement

$\text{Consumption}_{\text{retire}}$: Consumption in retirement

$\text{Req'd Income}_{\text{retire}}$: Required retirement income (pre-tax)

Retirement Income Replacement Rates: The Results

The accompanying figures show the retirement income replacement rates required to maintain pre-retirement spending in retirement, for annual pre-retirement income levels from $20,000 to $200,000, both for single persons and couples. The figures also show the proportion of retirement income covered by government benefits, namely Canada/Quebec Pension Plan (C/QPP) payments and Old Age Security/Guaranteed Income Supplement (OAS/GIS). Not surprisingly, there are differences in the required income replacement rates for single persons and couples, owing to certain economies of scale inherent in being part of a couple (for instance, we have assumed the use of pension income splitting). Thus, the required income replacement rates for single persons (who account for approximately one-quarter of persons retiring between the ages of 55 and 69[6]) cover a range of 77% to 88%. The range for couples (who account for approximately three-quarters of retirees age 55 to 69[7]) is from 73% to over 100%. In general, the results show that depending on one's household situation, most Canadians will need to replace somewhere between 75% and 85% of their pre-retirement income, if their goal is to maintain their pre-retirement spending levels in retirement.

---

[6]Statistics Canada, Table 051–0010, Estimates of population, by marital status, age group and sex; Canada, [multiple series].

[7]Ibid.

Peter Drake and Colin Randall

Figure 1: Retirement Replacement Rates — Individual Retiring at 65
(By level of pre-retirement income)

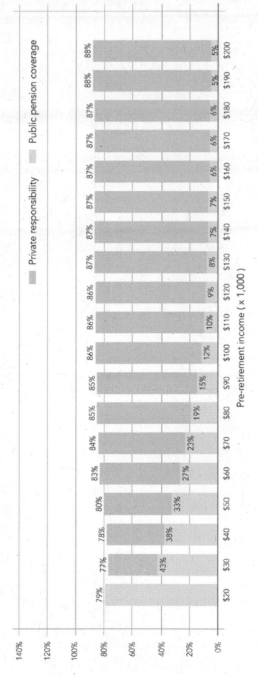

Pre-retirement income (x 1,000)

Notes: Replacement rates at each income level represent the median for all provinces and territories. All results fall within +/- 2.5% of each median. The representative individual is assumed to retire at age 65. Replacement rates are calculated by solving for the level of pre-tax retirement income needed to replace 100% of the individual's pre-retirement consumption in retirement. Pre-retirement consumption is determined by subtracting the applicable taxes, CPP/QPP contributions, EI premiums and savings from gross pre-retirement income. Public pension coverage includes an approximation of CPP/QPP, OAS and GIS benefits, according to income. OAS and GIS figures are clawed back according to 2007 rates. Federal and provincial tax brackets for 2007 are used. Tax credits, where applicable, include the basic personal amount, credits for CPP/QPP and EI, the pension credit, age credit and certain province-specific credits for low-income individuals. Provincial surtaxes and premiums have been included, where applicable. Figures have been rounded. Exact results will vary by province and individual circumstances.
Source: Fidelity Investments Canada ULC.

Figure 2: Retirement Replacement Rates — Couple Retiring at 65
(By level of pre-retirement income)

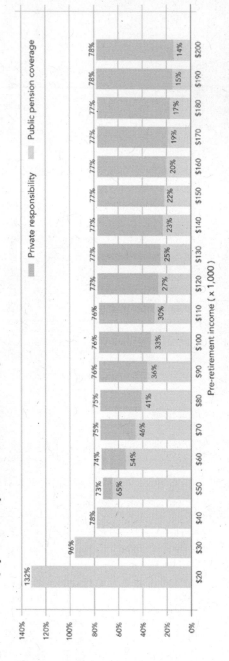

Notes: Replacement rates at each income level represent the median for all provinces and territories. All results fall within +/- 5.0% of each median. Both individuals of the representative couple are assumed to be age 65 at retirement. Replacement rates are calculated by solving for the level of pre-tax retirement income needed to replace 100% of the couple's pre-retirement consumption in retirement. Pre-retirement consumption is determined by subtracting the applicable taxes, CPP/QPP contributions, EI premiums and savings from gross pre-retirement income. Public pension coverage includes an approximation of CPP/QPP, OAS and GIS benefits, according to income. OAS and GIS figures are clawed back according to 2007 rates, and 2007 federal and provincial tax brackets are used. For the purposes of calculating taxes, all employment earnings are attributed to one spouse only. In retirement, pension splitting is applied to private retirement sources according to the measures laid out in the 2007 Federal Budget. All provinces and territories are assumed to allow pension splitting. In the absence of pension splitting, required replacement rates will be generally higher, all else being equal. Tax credits, where applicable, include the basic personal amount, credits for CPP/QPP and EI, the pension credit, age credit and certain province-specific credits for low-income individuals. Provincial surtaxes and premiums have been included, where applicable. Figures have been rounded. Exact results will vary by province and individual circumstances. Source: Fidelity Investments Canada ULC.

Also not surprising is the fact that at the lowest end of the pre-retirement income spectrum, public benefits replace all or substantially all of pre-retirement income. For a single person earning $20,000 annual pre-retirement income, public benefits cover the entire required 79% retirement income replacement rate. At a $50,000 annual pre-retirement income, public benefits cover approximately one-third of that amount. For couples, public pension benefit coverage is considerably higher. For couples earning $20,000 annual pre-retirement income, public pension benefits replace 132% of pre-retirement income. For couples earning $60,000 annual pre-retirement income, public benefits cover 54% of that amount. As levels of pre-retirement income increase, public pension benefits play an increasingly less significant role, to the point where they account for only 5% of pre-retirement income at the highest pre-retirement income in the exhibits for single persons, and 14% for couples.

The increased incidence of working in retirement noted earlier raises the question as to the role it will play, relative to increased saving and investment, in enabling retirees to reach their desired retirement income replacement rate. According to a presentation delivered at the Queen's Retirement Conference, research from Statistics Canada indicates that working in retirement is one technique used to achieve retirement income replacement rates well in excess of the conventional wisdom (LaRochelle-Côté, Myles, and Picot, 2008). Yet, there is also evidence to suggest that working in retirement may not be the important source of retirement income that some suppose. In the Fidelity 2007 Retirement Survey, retirees were asked whether their actual retirement occurred before, after or at the time they planned to retire (Fidelity Investments Canada, 2007a). The group that retired earlier than planned accounted for 63% of the total. Moreover, the top three reasons that Canadians reported their retirement were: deterioration of health, job downsizing and loss of enthusiasm for their job. The first reason amounts to involuntary retirement, the second means at least temporary involuntary retirement and the third borders on involuntary retirement.

What Percentage of Pre-Retirement Income Are Canadians Actually on Track to Replace?

The Fidelity Retirement Index, which measures the median working Canadian's expected income replacement rate at retirement, was developed in 2007 and released in late October of that year. Although this is the first time the Index has been calculated for Canada, Fidelity affiliate companies around the world have produced similar indexes for Japan, Germany, the United Kingdom and the United States. The Index projects the median retirement income replacement rate for Canada as a whole, as well as for the provinces of British Columbia, Alberta, Ontario and Quebec, the Prairie region (Saskatchewan and Manitoba) and the Atlantic provinces.[8]

As Figure 3 shows, the national Index score is 50, meaning that Canadians are on track to replace 50% of their pre-retirement income. There are differences in Index scores among the provinces/regions.

Older Canadians are better prepared for retirement, that is, they have a higher projected retirement income replacement rate than younger Canadians. Specifically, the median score for respondents age 25 to 40 was 44%, while the median score for respondents age 55 and over was 59%. These differences are not surprising and presumably reflect the fact that savings and investment priorities generally shift away from non-retirement areas towards retirement planning as retirement looms larger on the horizon.

A second significant difference in financial preparedness for retirement was between respondents who receive financial advice and those who do not. Nationally, the median Index score for those who do not get financial advice was 46%, compared to 54% for those who do. These results were consistent across each age group, with the age 25 to 40 group registering a median score of 42% with no financial advice and 49% with advice. The age 41 to 60 group median score was 51% without financial advice and 58% with financial advice. For those age 55 and older, the score was 53% without advice and 64% for those who get financial advice.

On the international front, Canada ranked ahead of Japan (47%), equalled the United Kingdom (50%) and lagged behind Germany (56%) and the United States (58%). The most surprising result to us was that Canada trailed the United States so significantly. The explanation may lie in two areas: people in the United States are conscious that they are required to shoulder a very significant part of the burden of saving and investing for retirement, and a significant part of their retirement savings is set aside for potential health-care costs, something that is much less necessary in Canada. Note too that caution must be used in comparing the Index constructed by Fidelity in Canada and those made by Fidelity affiliates in other countries, because the methodologies are not precisely similar in each country.

---

[8]The Appendix at the end of this paper provides a description of how the Fidelity Retirement Index's retirement income replacement rates were calculated.

Peter Drake and Colin Randall

Figure 3: Fidelity Retirement Index™

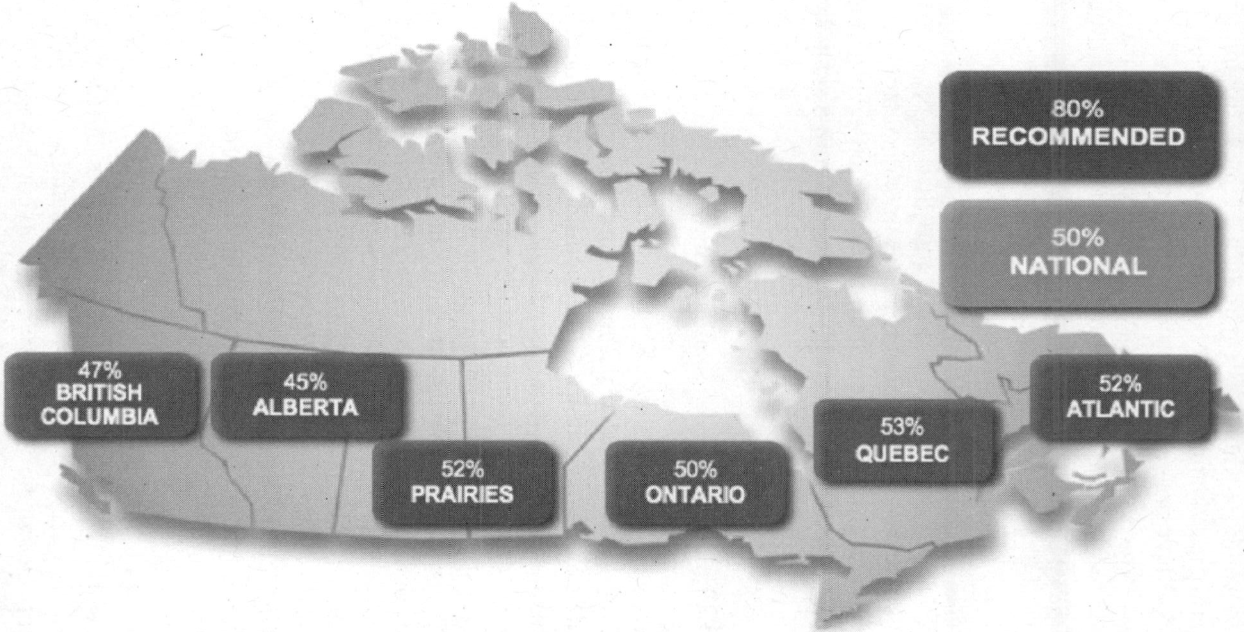

Notes: Figures are projected median retirement income replacement rates determined using a proprietary methodology. Capital market returns used to create the Index were calculated at a 50% confidence level. This is representative of an average market outcome.

Source: 2007 Fidelity Retirement Index Survey sponsored by Fidelity Investments Canada ULC and conducted by Richard Day Research Inc., Evanston IL, February 2007.

The 2007 Retirement Index results revealed that at the median, there is a considerable gap between the projected retirement replacement rate and what is required for those who wish to maintain their level of pre-retirement spending in retirement. Nationally, 9% of Canadians are on track to replace at least 80% of their pre-retirement income, while 17% are on track to replace at least 70%. As would be expected, the younger age group — age 25 to 40 — scored lower in this category, at 6% and 11%, respectively. Older people, age 55 and older, scored considerably higher than the national median, at 15% and 31%, respectively.

The Index is a "snapshot" in time, and future indexes, which Fidelity intends to construct each year, may be influenced by changes in a number of variables. The most significant of these is the actual saving for retirement being carried out by respondents, but changes in other factors, such as the age of retirement and economic assumptions related to inflation, wage growth and market returns, can also influence its future direction.

Future Research

Fidelity Investments Canada intends to continue its retirement research program, including a 2008 Fidelity Retirement Index.

There is a need for more research on spending in retirement. We need to know much more, not only about spending over the course of retirement but also about spending patterns and how they differ from spending in other periods in life, especially in the pre-retirement period. Another large gap concerns the relationship between income and spending in retirement. Additional research on spending in retirement may not be possible without the cooperation of Statistics Canada, since duplication, or extension, of the current Survey of Household Spending seems by far the best way to improve on the information presently available.

At the same time, it is unlikely that any research can answer the question as to what is the single, ideal retirement income replacement rate. Although a 75% to 85% income replacement benchmark provides a useful touchstone for retirement planning in Canada, there will always be wide variations in the determinants of retirement income replacement rates: salary while working, ability to allocate financial resources to retirement savings, financial needs in retirement and financial wants in retirement. From our point of view, the optimum research outcome would be to provide a sufficiently wide range of clear information that individuals can use to optimize their own retirement income replacement rates, whatever those might be.

Peter Drake and Colin Randall

APPENDIX: The Fidelity Retirement Index

How the Index Was Constructed

The basis for the Fidelity Canadian Retirement Index was an online survey of 2,257 individual Canadian households carried out in February 2007. Respondents were required to be over the age of 25, earning at least $20,000 per year and not retired. If partnered, the partner was also required to be not retired (homemakers and students were accounted for as being not retired). The survey was carried out by Richard Day Associates, the firm that has done the relevant survey work for Fidelity Retirement Index in the United States. Sampling was carried out by Survey Sampling International under contract to Richard Day International.

The survey included questions about the respondent's age, retirement savings accumulated to date, regular contributions to retirement savings, portfolio allocation, pension plan participation and expected retirement date. We provided the relevant assumptions regarding projected wage growth, inflation, interest rates and market returns. A proprietary, stochastic asset liability modeling (ALM) engine was used to project the respondents' data to calculate their expected pre-retirement income and income in retirement, the latter including Canada/Quebec Pension Plan and Old Age Security payments. The projected pre-retirement and post-retirement income levels took account of the age at which the respondents stated they intend to retire.

Canada/Quebec Pension Plan payments were assumed to be taken at the age of retirement, though not before or after ages 60 and 70, respectively, in keeping with the plans' guidelines. Old Age Security payments were assumed to be taken at age 65. The results of the individual projections were aggregated into a national index (median) and also into provincial/regional/metropolitan indexes.

References

Aon Consulting and Georgia State University. 2004."Replacement Ratio Study —
A Measurement Tool for Retirement Planning". Chicago, IL: Aon Corporation.

Chawla, R.K. 2005. "Shifts in Spending Patterns of Older Canadians", *Perspectives on Labour and Income*. Catalogue No. 75–001–XIE. Ottawa: Statistics Canada.

Fidelity Investments Canada. 2006. *2006 Retirement Survey*. Conducted by the Strategic Counsel.

_____. 2007a. *2007 Retirement Survey*. Conducted by the Strategic Counsel.

_____. 2007b. *Fidelity Retirement Index Survey*. Conducted by Richard Day Research Inc. Evanston, IL.

Human Resources and Social Development Canada (HRSDC). 2006. "Canada's Retirement System: Simply Stated", November 6. Available at http://www.hrsdc.gc.ca/en/isp/common/hrsdc/ris/simple.shtml.

Hurd, M. and S. Rohwedder. 2005. "The Retirement Consumption Puzzle: Anticipated and Actual Declines in Spending at Retirement", RAND Working Paper. Santa Monica, CA: The RAND Corporation.

LaRochelle-Côté, S., J. Myles, and G. Picot. 2008. "Income Security and Stability During Retirement in Canada". Analytical Studies Research Paper Series No. 306. Ottawa: Statistics Canada.

Statistics Canada. 2004a. *Deaths 2004*. Catalogue No. 84F0211XIE. Ottawa: Statistics Canada.

_____. 2004b. *Retirement Savings Through RRSPs and RPPs*. Catalogue No. 74–507–XCB. Ottawa: Statistics Canada.

US Department of Labor. 1999–2005. *Consumer Expenditure Surveys, 1999–2005*. Washington, DC: US Bureau of Labor Statistics.

Design Features, Strengths and Limitations of Defined-Benefit Plans

Stephen Bonnar

In this paper I discuss some of the features of defined-benefit (DB) plans, and their strengths and weaknesses. Specifically, I address the traditional single-employer plan, which would include that covering federal civil servants, including my employment pension plan, as well as most, but not all, of the employment pension plans of those of you.

There has been significant discussion and debate about these kinds of plans over the last while. What has really been driving the debate is declining coverage. When you look at broad statistics across the country, coverage in defined-benefit plans has dropped from roughly 44% to 34% of the workforce over the period 1992 to 2004.

So why are we unable to reform the country's defined-benefit legislation or system in order to ensure that these types of plans continue to be viable options for employers? In an environment where you will be putting a target on your forehead if you try and make balanced changes where it will only affect less than 34% of your voters, there is not a lot of incentive for politicians to do that. I would submit that this is part of the answer to the question.

If we go beyond that and look at the drop in coverage, we are really looking at averages. These averages mask two different things. In the public sector, the coverage has dropped, but from 92% to 79% over that same period of time. The issue in my view has been much more in the private sector, where that coverage rate has dropped from 29% to 21% — roughly speaking, there has been a one-third drop in coverage over that 12-year period. That begs the question, what have sponsors been running away from?

With that in mind, let me take you through some examples of plans. Towers Perrin conducts an ongoing survey of all benefit plans provided for salaried employees of a number of companies, almost 300, in Canada. I have segregated the plans into three groups. First, let me describe what I would call the "typical" public sector plan. It provides a benefit for each year of service of about 2% of highest-average earnings, with some integration with government pensions. This goes to the point that was raised earlier: after 35 years, somebody who chooses not to retire from the public service is giving up roughly 70% of pay that they could be receiving from the pension plan. The plan requires fairly high levels of participant contributions, generally has a commitment to preserve the pension payment in retirement against erosion due to price inflation, and also typically has very generous early-retirement subsidies. We heard before about the public service plan retirement target of age 55 with 30 years of service. While they are not all the same and do have different provisions, you might think of payment of an unreduced pension at 85 points or in the 85-to-90-point range, where you earn a point for each year of age and a point for each year of service.

Let me contrast that with the typical private sector pension plan provided for non-unionized employees. This plan no longer requires employees to contribute. So it is fully paid for, at least currently, by the employer. It provides a lower level of benefit, as you would typically expect given that there is no employee participation in the cost of the plan. The average benefit for each year of service is a little less than 1.5% of average earnings near retirement. That benefit is generally sitting on top of government pensions as opposed to integrated with government pensions like the public sector plan. There is, generally speaking, no indexing commitment. On the other hand, there is often, though not always, some ad hoc approach to providing inflation protection, but typically at levels that over periods of time might replace less than half of CPI erosion. And as you can imagine, in an environment of lower levels of inflation, the time between increases to replace part of inflation erosion has been lengthening. These plans typically still have some early-retirement subsidies. They might in general provide an unreduced pension somewhere around age 62.

These two types of plans provide pensions that are earnings-related pensions. There is also a large segment of the private sector workforce that is covered for pensions under a unionized arrangement, often providing benefits on a flat dollar basis. If you do a little bit of work, analyze what that flat dollar is relative to wage rates, and express that as a percentage of pay, you might get something a little above 1% of pay. Those plans do not require employee contributions. They typically do not have an indexing commitment, but they have a fairly regular pattern of negotiated increases and very generous early-retirement subsidies.

I think as an aside I'd say that it is the middle segment — the non-union private sector — that is really where the coverage levels seem to be going lower and lower. And generally speaking, coverage appears to be among employers who also have largely unionized workforces, so the non-unionized salaried employees participate in plans almost by virtue of the fact that the unionized portion of the employee group has some pension coverage.

Let me consider the attraction of defined-benefit plans before addressing some of their weaknesses. We have already heard some discussion of their main attraction: the pooling of risk: longevity risk and investment risk. You may argue whether a pension plan is where the risk should be taken, but the defined-benefit plan does allow for considerable risk pooling. It also provides for economies of scale. You can contrast the costs of a defined-benefit pension plan with those that an individual incurs when buying mutual funds that might have a management expense ratio of 150 to 250 basis points or wholesale pooled products within defined-contribution (DC) arrangements of 80 to 150 basis points. If you think of very large plans, OMERS or the Ontario Teachers Plan, they are probably running both investment management and all administration for something on the order of 20 basis points. I am prepared to be challenged on that, but 20 to 30 basis points sounds about right.

Defined-benefit pensions facilitate workforce planning. They can be used as a tax-effective way to facilitate workforce reductions. Also, employers often, at least in the past, have offered these arrangements because they believed that they helped to attract employees. We have recently done a study about the drivers of attraction, retention, and engagement of employees. And unfortunately for me, having a pension plan ranks rather low on the level of drivers for attracting employees; it is number 11 in our study. My colleagues in the compensation practice like to point out that pay is number one.

What are the weaknesses of defined-benefit plans? Arguably, one of the biggest weaknesses is lack of clarity of the deal. What is the specific arrangement? We heard earlier today that the typical view from the employer side is that they own 100 cents of the dollar of the deficit, but only some proportion of any surplus. Yes, surpluses can be used for contribution holidays and the like, but there is no expectation that a 100-cents-on-the-dollar surplus provides full value to the sponsoring employer. It is certainly one view in current discussions. You can also think of competing views around the negotiating table, the financial status of the plan certainly enters into talks as to what is or is not affordable in terms of any potential settlement.

Finally, there are two points. The deal itself, in order to have an effective, ongoing DB pension system, needs to be made clearer. And within that clarity, the risks and rewards of financing the plan need to be balanced; the rewards need to accrue to those who take the risks, but the risks do need to be defined better. The key question is who really takes the risk for funding plan deficits:

- employers by way of additional pension contributions;
- employees by way of potential adverse changes to plan provisions, or worse yet, layoffs; or
- some combination of the two?

In my experience, very few plans have answered this question well.

Stephen Bonnar

Defined-Contribution Plans in Canada and Possible Design Improvements

Dave McLellan

In this paper, I will try and avoid the debate of defined-benefit (DB) versus defined-contribution (DC) pension plans. In fact, I'm going to come from another perspective, recognizing the fact that over half of Canadians do not have an employer-sponsored savings program whether it is defined contribution or defined benefit. My comments are from the employer's perspective: Do I offer nothing? Do I offer a group Registered Retirement Savings Plan (RRSP) to my employees? Or do I offer a defined-contribution pension plan? I would like to cover some ground looking at these options.

One caveat before I get going — if someone had told me ten years ago that we would have CAP guidelines today, I would not have believed them. The CAP guidelines[1] have moved us a long way from a regulatory perspective, and I want to make that point now because, as I may make some contradictory comments, please remember I am very impressed with the job of the regulators. I think they have a very difficult job and I think they are doing it very well.

As an employer I have choices: Do I provide a group RRSP or a pension plan (or nothing)? I will start with a group RRSP, as many of us as retail investors have exposure to the basics of an RRSP. In a group context, the RRSP does look a little bit different. It has been suggested that in the

---

[1]Capital Accumulation Plans put forward by the Joint Forum of Market Regulators in May 2004 on behalf of the Canadian Association of Pension Supervisory Authorities, the Canadian Council of Insurance Regulators, and the Canadian Securities Administrators.

DC world, one buys a retail mutual fund at retail prices and this is a bad option for investors. But generally, that is not the case. Eighty percent of the DC market, particularly RRSPs and pension plans, allow investors the opportunity to purchase group segregated funds, a product that is built specifically for them. As an investment, they are utilizing institutional investment pools at the same or better prices than one would get through a DB program. And where mutual funds are the investment vehicle, they are generally getting deep discounts from retail prices. I would challenge the notion that in a group RRSP one buys a retail product at retail prices, even if, in fact, the investment vehicles are sometimes mutual funds.

At the end of the day, as an employer going the group RRSP route, there is one major drawback, and that is when an employer puts contributions into a program, the employer loses a degree of control over that money. This is because employer contributions into an RRSP program become employment income (of the employee), and it is very difficult for the employer to restrict what an employee does with that money down the road. So if the employee chooses to withdraw that contribution, it is difficult to restrict the employee's access, even if the money is intended to provide a nest egg at retirement.

From a practical perspective, I can tell you that in the group RRSP market, there is always a loud sucking noise every year, particularly just after RRSP season, when people withdraw RRSP contributions. What is most frustrating are the really "astute" individuals who realize that they can take employment income and rather than have a marginal tax rate applied to it, they can direct it to their RRSP, *then* withdraw it and only attract a 10% withholding tax (of course they'll owe the difference a year from now and still have no retirement savings). The group RRSP market has not grown to the extent our industry would like, and this lack of control is a big reason for it. To address this issue, plan sponsors will often marry a deferred profit sharing plan (DPSP) with that group RRSP. This allows the employer to direct their contributions to the DPSP so that a portion of the contributions are limited from being withdrawn. To my mind, this is a novel way to get the outcome the sponsor wants, but I do not think DPSPs were designed to act as retirement savings vehicles. Looking at the RRSP from a regulatory perspective, it would be great if plan sponsors had a little more control.

This leads me to defined-contribution pension plans. As a pension plan, employers have far more control over what happens with the monies in a DC pension plan. But that is a double-edged sword. During employment, certainly you want to restrict any money coming out of the plan, and that is

Dave McLellan

exactly what happens. Once the employee leaves your company, though, most employers have mixed emotions about retaining these members in the plan. If you think about DC, the employer's primary commitment is to contribute the money and to create an environment where it can be invested prudently; the employee's primary commitment is to understand the choices available to them and then invest that money wisely in saving for retirement. Well, once someone is no longer with the firm, what is the employer's responsibility to them to ensure they are continuing to be educated and that they are investing wisely? You could argue there is no responsibility, but yet, by regulation, the employer is forced to allow these individuals to stay in the plan.

What I am seeing with employers in certain industries that have had DC pension plans for 10 and 20 years, is that the lion's share of the members in the plans are no longer employees, although the majority of the assets in the program are very much held by current employees. Unfortunately, the result is a pension plan with significant costs and ongoing liabilities related to former employees.

This really is just one example of the fundamental issue with DC pension plans, which may be a little more controversial — there really is no DC pension legislation in Canada. From my perspective, what we have is DB pension legislation turned sideways and applied to a very different product with a very different set of risks. What I would very much like to see is somebody starting with a blank sheet of paper and saying, "OK, what do we need to put in place to make a DC pension plan viable from an employer's perspective and have all the security from an employee's perspective?" I think we would end up in a different place, probably something as simple as an RRSP with specific funding requirements, which allows employers to limit employees' withdrawals from the program and does not require employers to maintain the program indefinitely for former employees.

All this leads me to my last point, which is that the CAP guidelines give us a wonderful start. The CAP guidelines talk to the responsibilities of employers, employees and service providers. Here are some general themes. The CAP guidelines give employers instruction to make sure they are providing appropriate investment options and plan structure for their employees given the nature of their employee group as a whole, that they provide employees appropriate information about the plan and the investment options, and that the employees have access to education and investment decision-making tools. Employers may also give plan members access to advice. This is all wrapped up by requiring the plan sponsor to monitor their whole program.

Today, the CAP guidelines stop short on a couple of fronts. First of all, they are a framework; they do not explicitly tell plan sponsors what to do and not to do (and maybe that is a good thing). Second, the CAP guidelines do not give employers any kind of safe harbour or comfort that they are limiting the potential for future litigation. So when it comes to the decision to provide no retirement program or something substantial, many employers are reluctant to sign up for a long-term unknown liability. If you were an employer, would you take on a contingent liability that triggers 30 years from now with respect to an employee that might not have worked for you in 27 years?

Here are some of the new things that are going on:

- *Auto-enrolment.* One-third of employees never bother to sign up for their DC programs. In a DC pension plan, you can force their monies in, but for non-pension plans like RRSPs this often means one-third of employees do not take advantage of a company benefit that helps them save for retirement.
- And for those who don't enroll but have money flowing into the program or those who do not know which investments to choose, "default" investment options are a necessity. Relatively new to Canada are *target date retirement funds*, which help people into an appropriate investment mix right from the beginning with the mix becoming more conservative over time. No active decisions are required on the part of the employee.
- A *last issue/opportunity* is in situations where there are matching programs from employees — you put in a dollar and your employer will put in a dollar — up to 40% of employees never take the employer up on this offer of free money. Included in this bucket are employees who take employers up on the offer, but not to the maximum. For example, they put in 3%, when the employer's willing to match up to 5%. Clearly, there is a disconnect.

What we see in the United States are *auto-increase programs*. You sign up to join the program at 3%, and every year or every second year, that will increase. It is 4%, 5%, 6% of your salary — unless you opt out. This is an opportunity for people to go on autopilot, increasing their contributions as their salaries also increase.

As a final observation, I will not come out and say that a DC plan is better than DB. Certainly, every product has its place. But I do want to make sure that the 50% of employers out there who are not sponsoring programs today have viable options. I think there is a place for DC plans amongst those options, and there is a place for DC-specific regulations to help make it happen.

Recent Legal Decisions and Regulatory Changes and their Implications for Design Structure of Pension Plans

Marcel Théroux

The short answer to the question of regulatory change is that regulators and the courts are doing a very bad job in the pension regulatory area in Canada.

I am a lawyer by training, but am not afraid of numbers. And when I look at the numbers, I see this dichotomy between the non-unionized private sector and the public sector. I recently gave a presentation to a number of young lawyers who are making career choices and I showed them two slides. One was the public sector coverage rate — that is, the percentage of the members of the public sector who are in a pension plan — and is 84.3%, according to Statscan. In the private sector, it is 13.3%, almost the exact mirror image. And of that 13.3%, we have 9.3% — that is, 9.3% of the total private sector, non-union, paid workforce that belongs to a defined-benefit (DB) plan. But of course, these are not true DB plans; these are frozen, stagnant, dying, comatose DB plans — not all of them, but a great percentage of them. Although this is anecdotal evidence and I will leave it at that.

I wish to point out that there is no defined-contribution (DC) specific legislation in Canada. We have one pension statute that differentiates very poorly, if at all, between DB and DC plans. In most common law provinces, we have DB statutes where, until they were told by the Supreme Court of Canada what a pension plan was, it was not clear. In Quebec there is a civil law tradition, and it is possible to read one of the opening sections: "A pension plan is a contract, and it is funded by means of a trust". One struggles mightily to find any such clarity in any common law statute. And that, in answer to the introductory question on regulatory change, is the main source of the problem: an imperfectly, inexpertly expressed deal or contract. What is the contract that is sought to be enforced? What exactly is the deal between labour and management? And because the legislation is mute, we have left the task to the courts — the poor, maligned courts — which have had to fill in the gaps in this matter.

Now, the fact that the courts got it wrong is really not their fault. After all, they examined the documents and they saw a trust; they had two ways to go, and they went trust. They did not take into account the fact that a pension trust is not a classic trust; it has attributes and promises and undertakings that will affect our future generations and not only the current generation. All of that was ignored by the courts because — a little note on legal process — courts do make law, but they make very bad policy. They are very good at filling in the gaps of certain statutes where the rules are well articulated and clear. They have a very good interstitial function. When I say they don't make policy, they of course do in the constitutional area, but that can be left for another forum.

The way the system works is, the courts are asked to decide a dispute. They do decide that dispute. But in so doing, they leave a trail of vapour, of fumes if you will. They make the rules to allow other courts to decide similar disputes. And depending on how positivistic or realistic the court is, they can leave more or less rules as precedent. And the common law grows by accretion. The more of these instances that there are, the more rules that are derived. It is an inductive process.

This does not work very well for pension plans because pension plans are long-lived. It does not work very well, again, because only an incomplete expression of what a pension plan is is found in the legislation. Though the courts found that there was a trust, the trust dominates a contractual promise. And that has tainted the entire process of judicial decisions. Now, my labour colleagues would vehemently disagree with this statement. But let me just put the management hat on and say that that has tainted the entire process. The trust analysis has resulted in the class action bar clamouring in order to find ways and means to attack pension structures because of their failure to strictly adhere to trust rules. Pension plan disputes have been found to be the ideal setting for class action suits — a large number of plaintiffs with no necessary requirement for large individual claims; litigation costs which, until recently at least, were payable from the pension trust fund regardless of the outcome of the litigation; and, of course, in the event of success, the lovely contingency fee.

Marcel Théroux

One other comment I would like to make is the issue of retrospectivity or retroactivity, the power that the courts have with respect to retroactive statutes. When dealing with a constitutional case, all of a sudden the courts decide, for example, that same-sex marriages are okay. Well, they do not insult our intelligence by saying, it was okay back in 1982. They say, "alright, we've decided it's now okay, and we're going to do this prospectively. We're going to allow the legislatures a year or 18 months to get their houses in order, and then we'll apply these rules prospectively". That power simply doesn't exist in the private law system.

The Supreme Court recently decided the case of Monsanto. This was a pension plan case involving the interpretation of the Ontario statute, looking at it in the late 1990s, with a trust created in the 1950s. With all the events that had transpired, the court decided that yes, since 1969, the Ontario statute really had provided that whenever you had a corporate reorganization, you had to distribute the pension surplus. You can quarrel with that or not. It may be a fine decision; I really do not care to comment. But the difficulty with the decision is that they did not say: "You will apply it from the date of this decision, the late 1990s." Instead, they said the decision will apply from 1969. Total, retroactive, retrospective legislation was made that no one had foreseen was coming down the chute, and there was no mechanism in order to defuse the chaos that was thereby created.

Having said all this, I should now make some comments about recent case law. The class action bar, and I am not a member of the class action bar, has suffered some reversals of late because the courts have decided to backpedal furiously. The fact that there is a 9.3% DB coverage rate in the non-unionized private sector, is perhaps relevant, but what we have seen in the last year or two are common sense pronouncements like: "You can use an existing surplus in a DB plan to take a DC contribution holiday". "You can pay reasonable plan expenses from the fund". "You can reopen a closed DB pension plan and add new employees who can participate in a DC plan that has been added to it". You would have thought that these propositions were self-evident. Nevertheless, two cases, Kelly and Sutherland, that stand for those propositions, are dated 2007. It will come as no surprise that they are both under appeal.

Another case, the Rogers case, is a case of a closed down pension plan in British Columbia where there were two members or so left — I'm exaggerating for effect — there were very few remaining members. There was a surplus in the plan. So they thought it would be a good idea to get together — after all, there were only two of them — and see if they could get the surplus. Remember I said that trust law was the operative doctrine. Well, there is a doctrine in trust law that says, if all the beneficiaries get together, you can close the trust. This went all the way up to the Supreme Court of Canada. Mr. Rogers is a very stubborn man; he could not stand that particular result. And he was vindicated because the Supreme Court came up with this startling proposition: a pension trust is not a regular trust. And that occurred precisely in 2006. What has happened in the Rogers case is that the Supreme Court also said, "get these pension cases away from us. Give them to the regulators". And the regulator has reopened the Rogers plan and allowed other members to come into it. I am sure there will be either an appeal or a judicial review in that matter as well.

Summary of Discussion

Morley Gunderson asked whether the panel have any insights into how employer-sponsored pensions will change as mandatory retirement is increasingly being banned legislatively? Do we have any experience from Manitoba and Quebec, where it was banned earlier in the 1980s? On the other hand, this also happened in the United States. They've changed the features of a lot of the pension plans to serve as a substitute for mandatory retirement so that there are actual penalties to carrying on working. The incentives were such that it didn't pay to keep on working, and that's a substitute for mandatory retirement. Are there any insights into what has happened and what may happen here in response to the ban? **Stephen Bonnar** responded that, at least anecdotally, employers' response to mandatory retirement within their pension plans appears to have been quite minimal in Ontario. If one just centres on Ontario, if someone worked beyond 65, you had to continue to allow them to accrue benefits, assuming they continued to make contributions if those were required. If you go through the arithmetic, there is a disincentive — not a huge one — but a disincentive for postponing retirement. He really doesn't see much of an issue there because most employers appear to be very happy to have their employees, or at least the performing ones, continue to work for them. He believes what has actually happened is that there's been more of an emphasis on performance-management systems — nothing to do, really, with the pension design. A participant added that the same issues don't exist for a DC plan. If you want to keep working, presumably the employer's happy to continue to contribute.

    Malcolm Hamilton made some comments about Fidelity's study of the adequacy of retirement savings and the replacement ratio that's needed.

Most such studies that attempt to figure out retirees' target income levels treat retirement savings as if it was an isolated element of a financial plan. But it isn't. Other major things most Canadians have to deal with are home acquisition and raising a family. So appropriate retirement savings have to be seen as part of an integrated financial planning problem. What the Fidelity study does — this is common and most US studies do the same — is to say it's important for you in retirement to maintain the standard of living you have at age 64. Since the standard of living you have at age 64 is very high because your mortgage is paid off and your children have moved out, you need to try to maintain that very high standard of living. But this is not close to the standard of living they experienced for most of their working lives. **Peter Drake** responded that the issue of young folks having other objectives is obviously true. And certainly the numbers their study found bear it out, that much lower projected retirement income replacement rates are reported for people, say, in the 25-to-40 age group than, say, in the age 55-plus age group. They consciously do not include housing. It's fine to say you've got a $500,000 house and that's going to generate retirement income, but this presumes that either you're prepared to engage in relatively pricey financing in order to generate retirement income, or you're prepared to sell it and move someplace else. There are also non-financial issues that come in — like attachment to neighbourhoods and communities. And their experience is that most people want to stay in their house that they've worked so hard to pay for.

Richard Shillington pointed out that there are tens of thousands of people out there who have not been getting CPP benefits that they were entitled to and only discovered this once they consulted a lawyer or financial specialist. CPP entitlements come from legislation, not through a contract or a trust. **Marcel Théroux** responded that this is quite correct. One may remember the Supreme Court of Canada case that involved the veterans. There was a fund established for those veterans. The government received the money because those veterans were incapable of taking care of themselves. These are World War veterans and perhaps later. The money sat there, in some cases, for 60 years, and even 70 years. Then the government changed the legislation to provide interest, but not on a retroactive basis, just on a prospective basis. It went to the Supreme Court of Canada and the Supreme Court of Canada said, "That's fine." The problem goes back to the much maligned Canadian Charter of Rights and Freedoms, which has no protection for property. And because there's no protection for property, and because our Supreme Court has not fashioned protection for property, our federal Parliament and our provincial legislatures can expropriate your property without compensation. So Théroux would be very wary of expanding the public role of the CPP and retirement savings generally unless they are held to account. There are some good things about trusts, and that is that if it's my money, if it's promised to me, you should pay.

Cliff Halliwell pointed out that getting back to the question of retirement income adequacy, the elephant in the living room here, is the whole issue of future health care costs. A large number of Canadians are not thinking through what the menu of health technology will be when they're older, that they could buy but which the state is highly unlikely to be able to provide for them gratis. That's clearly a big issue. At a previous pension conference, somebody observed that Canadians believe CPP won't be there for them when they're old, but the health care system will be; but realistically speaking, it's the other way around. When he was at Health Canada, they worked out that, because we had a baby-boom generation, we've actually artificially suppressed the health-to-GDP ratio in the economy. At present, baby boomers are largely in good health and at peak GDP-generating years. If they'd never been born — if we just had a normal fertility rate from our parents — we'd actually have a much higher health-to-GDP ratio than we do right now. What that means is that this ratio is likely to start going up substantially. The leading edge of that is going to be the health-human resources pressures in the health-care sector. Indeed, there's truly a problem with lack of data around this. You see most studies of retirement living standards, Fidelity's included, focus on income needs as opposed to expenditures, and that's largely because we can't get good data on longitudinal expenditure or consumption patterns. That would be a prerequisite toward trying to figure out retirement living standards and how we can project them into the future.

Marcel Théroux added that an example of legislative gap is a total absence of any tax-preferred savings vehicle for post-retirement or other medical benefits. We do have rules in the *Income Tax Act* that deal with private health services plans and allow those private health services plans to be funded. And the benefits under those plans are largely tax-free. But we do not allow tax deductibility for the contributions to those funds. He thinks serious consideration should be given to having a type of Roth plan — it's called a Roth IRA plan in the United States. It allows funds to accumulate free of tax, and then to be free of tax when used to reimburse health care costs. This is something that should definitely be on the public policy agenda.

Suzan Kalinowski remarked that a number of years ago, the Department of Finance undertook some research into the long-term implications of health-care costs on public finances. A big driver of health costs in the future will be innovation in the sector. There has been a lot of innovation in this sector over the last decade and this has generally contributed to accelerating cost increases. This said, it's difficult to know how innovation will affect costs in the future. The work here at Finance suggests that public health care costs are affordable over the long term in the face of aging.

She also mentioned that Cliff Halliwell raised another interesting point, and one which has maybe received less attention to date — that is the labour market pressures facing the health sector and how this will affect the ability of the public system to provide adequate care to a growing population of seniors.

Chapter V

The Retirement Process and Macroeconomic Implications

The Emergence of Phased Retirement: Economic Implications and Policy Concerns

Robert L. Clark

Patterns of Retirement: Old and New

In Canada,

> Baby boomers are likely to reach retirement with lower and less stable pensions than in the past. The need to supplement these pensions will certainly be another reason for some people to continue to work. (Stone, 2006)

In the past, retirement has often been a discrete event — a person, typically in their 60s, was working full-time one day and the next day, the worker retired from their career job, left the labour force entirely and became a full-time retiree. Economists, social observers, and policymakers have long questioned whether this abrupt and complete separation from the labour force was optimal for the individual and in the interest of society. For example, most life-cycle models developed by economists predict a gradual decline in hours under most circumstances. However, rigidities in the labour market, differences in full-time and part-time wage rates, and pension rules can produce an environment in which abrupt, complete retirement is the highest value choice for an older worker. The removal of these constraints might spark a new trend towards gradual or phased retirement among older Canadians and Americans.

In a reversal of the long-term trend towards earlier and earlier retirement that characterized the twentieth century, there has been a small increase in the proportion of older persons in North America over the past decade who have chosen to remain in the labour force. Part of this reversal in the trend towards early retirement is that many older individuals have been choosing to work part-time for a few years as a prelude to complete retirement. Part-time employment can occur through a change from one's career employcr to a new or bridge job where the person works few hours or through a more formal program that allows the transition from full-time to part-time work with a career employer. This paper examines the evolution of alternative transitions into retirement with a specific emphasis on formal phased retirement programs offered by companies to their career employees. Phased retirement programs with one's own employer can involve either a pre-retirement reduction in hours or a post-retirement return to work for the career employer at reduced hours. Phased retirement programs are influenced by employer policies and demand for workers, employee preferences, and government tax and retirement policies.

Phased retirement programs and the postponement of complete retirement are now an important component of public debates on national economic policy in both Canada and the United States. Older persons in North America are living longer than their parents and they are also healthier. However, until recently, 50- and 60-year-olds had been retiring earlier than previous generations. With fewer working years and a longer life span, the life stage of retirement lengthened to approximately 20 years in both countries. The continued aging of the national populations has also resulted in a re-evaluation of the need to postpone retirement or increase the labour force participation rates of older Canadians and Americans. For example, persons aged 45 to 64 composed 27.8% of the working age population of Canada in 1981 but had reached almost 39% by 2006 (van Sluys, 2005). In the coming years, retention of older workers in the labour force will be important to maintaining the rate of economic growth, providing an adequate tax base to support general public expenditures, and more specifically helping to maintain the financial stability of national and company retirement plans.

How will employers find the workers needed to produce the desired level of output in the coming years? As the baby boom cohort ages, a larger proportion of the labour force nears and enters retirement. Given past fertility patterns, the rate of growth of the labour force will slow, making it more difficult to hire younger workers. Companies must reconsider their employment and compensation policies and perhaps reorganize production technologies to provide greater and more desirable work opportunities for older workers. Phased retirement plans should be one option that managers consider to retain valuable human capital during a transition period.

How will individuals finance their desired level of consumption in retirement? Older persons may find that prolonging their working life by including a period of part-time work is necessary if they are to achieve the standard of living that they desire in retirement. Part-time work may allow individuals to continue to amass assets for retirement by delaying the use of retirement savings and continued employment might also result in the further accumulation of pension credits. Phased retirement can also be a useful method of reducing the physical and mental demands of working without totally severing one's link to a career. Of course, the desire to remain on the job will differ widely by industry and occupation and the demands that continued work places on an individual.

How will governments finance their national social security programs with aging populations? Providing economic incentives for older persons to remain in the labour force is one method of addressing the long-term funding problems facing national retirement programs. Phased retirees continue to have taxable earnings and thus contribute needed revenues and phased retirees may also postpone the start of their retirement benefits. As governments in all developed countries face the prospect of fundamental changes in the social security programs by raising tax rates or reducing benefits, a more politically acceptable option may be to raise retirement ages or provide more incentives for older persons to remain in the labour force.

In the first decade of the twenty-first century, we find governments searching for methods to reduce the cost of retirement plans, companies struggling to find sufficient trained workers, and individuals trying to achieve an enjoyable retirement period that is growing longer for each succeeding cohort. The confluence of these events has moved phased retirement plans into the forefront of policy discussions. The Canadian and US governments have attempted to remove impediments to companies offering phased retirement programs and workers enrolling in them. Employers have been experimenting with different types of programs to determine their impact on labour productivity and production costs. In this new environment, will phased retirement be the wave of the future?

What Is Phased Retirement?

For the purpose of this paper, phased retirement is defined as a formal program offered by an employer to its workers that allows individual employees to reduce their hours of work in exchange for reduced pay, usually at a prorated rate, say half-time work for half-time pay. These programs can take a variety of forms. Some programs require workers to retire, perhaps giving up seniority and tenure status, and in return, the individual is moved seamlessly into the new status of a phased retiree for a fixed period of time. In other programs, workers do not formally retire but remain on the job with reduced hours and prorated pay. Still other programs require workers to retire and then after a period of formal separation, the worker is re-employed as a part-time worker or phased retiree or perhaps as a self-employed contract worker. Human Resources and Social Development Canada (2004) provides a list of companies and universities that have adopted some type of phased retirement programs.

Phased retirement plans normally specify service and age standards that employees must achieve before they are eligible to enter into phased retirement, for example, age 55 with 20 years of service. Key parameters of these plans that affect their desirability for workers and their cost to employers include: Do phased retirees continue to be covered by company-provided health insurance? Do phased retirees continue to accrue pension benefits? Can phased retirees receive pension benefits while continuing to work? And, what is the relationship between reduced hours and reduced pay?

Phased retirement plans offer advantages and disadvantages to both the employer and the employee. Both parties must assess the pros and cons of altering the retirement process from the traditional abrupt and complete retirement to a transitional period of phased retirement. Employers must consider the cost of retaining older employees on a part-time basis and compare this to any gains in productivity achieved by lowering turnover rates, reduced hiring costs and maintaining the institutional knowledge of older workers. Employees must consider the value of continued earnings and the impact of phased retirement on benefits such as pensions and health insurance. The cost and benefits of phased retirement to both parties is influenced by prevailing government tax policies and employment regulations.

Employers' View of Phased Retirement: Pros and Cons

A 2002 Survey of business, public sector and labour leaders conducted by the Canadian Labour and Business Centre found that phased-in retirement is not prominent on the list of possible solutions cited to growing fears of skill shortages. (Wortsman, 2003)

If phased retirement plans are currently rare, why aren't more employers interested in establishing phased retirement plans? For most of the second half of the twentieth century, large employers adopted retirement policies that encouraged older workers to retire at age 65 or younger. The adoption of defined-benefit pension plans with early retirement incentives, mandatory retirement policies, early retirement windows, and an assortment of other human relations (HR) policies were used to encourage older workers to leave the firm, thus making room for the hiring of younger employees who were often less expensive and more educated. Population and labour force growth insured a steady stream of young persons seeking employment so that employers could readily replace retirees with younger workers who often could be hired at lower wages and who had a new vintage of skills and education. However, the slow-down in the rate of growth of new entrants into the labour force and the pending surge in retirements is forcing employers to reconsider their retirement policies. Some organizations are now facing the loss of a substantial portion of their trained labour force over a very short time period as the baby-boom cohort begins to retire. As a result, many employers are now considering policies that encourage older employees to remain on the job.

A company's desire to retain older workers, either full-time or part-time, depends on their productivity, the need for retaining the institutional knowledge they have gained over years of service, the cost both in terms of cash and benefits, and the availability of young workers. When considering the adoption of phased retirement plans, managers must also assess the impact of having a larger pool of part-time workers on their payrolls. Key issues include whether part-time workers can be successfully integrated into work teams, will phased retirees continue to exhibit a high degree of loyalty and commitment to the company, and will older workers be able to provide the level of productivity needed.

Employers also worry about whether phased retirement prolongs working life by enticing workers who no longer want to work full-time to remain on the job as phased retirees or whether phased retirement programs might actually shorten work life by enticing employees to switch from full-time to part-time earlier in their careers, thus shortening the period of full-time employment. A final issue, which is often articulated by senior managers, is what type of worker will enter phased retirement — highly productive workers or low-quality employees. These concerns will differ across firms, industries, and occupations and thus, we should expect to observe considerable differences in the incidence of phased retirement across sectors of the economy.

Past hiring patterns influence the age structure of an organization or occupation and can directly affect the desire of employers to retain older workers, either full- or part-time. In Canada, the combination of the age structure of the labour force and the early retirement age is most pressing in the public sector. Statistics Canada (2004) estimated that the median retirement age in the public sector in 2002 was 58.1 and that one-third of public employees were within ten years of retirement.[1] How will various governmental units deal with the loss of such a large amount of human capital? In contrast, the median retirement age in the private sector was 61.4 and only 15.6% of the labour force was within ten years of retirement.

In some specific occupations and especially in certain provinces, the potential for the retirement of a large proportion of the skilled labour force is even more dramatic, for example, nursing. The average age of registered nurses, in Canada is now over 44 and it is rising rapidly. In British Columbia, 20% of RNs are over the age of 55. With an average retirement age of 58, British Columbia and other provinces can expect a large number of retirements in the near future (Wortsman, 2003). A key question for public sector employers in Canada is whether phased retirement programs can be effective in enticing older nurses and other employees to remain on the job, at least part time, for longer.

In the United States, phased retirement is becoming more popular and recent changes in government regulations should stimulate more companies to adopt these programs. Currently, the incidence of phased retirement programs varies substantially across industries. A study by Watson Wyatt Worldwide (1999) in the United States found that phased retirement is becoming increasingly common in higher education with over one-third of employers offering a phased retirement program. Other industries and occupations where phased retirement was relatively common include professional, technical, and public administration. Coverage rates in these sectors ranged between 21 and 25%. Most other industries surveyed had only around 10% of employers offering these types of plans. Other more

---

[1]This represents a very large decline from 1987 when the median retirement age was 62.8.

Robert L. Clark

recent studies report large proportions of firms offering phased retirement (Collison, 2003; Bond *et al.*, 2005; and Hutchens, 2007). While the incidence of phased retirement in Canada may be lower, some employers have introduced these programs through the collective bargaining process. Human Resources and Social Development Canada provides a list of Canadian employers that have included formal phased retirement plans in their collective bargaining contracts.

It should be noted that firms have always attempted to retain selected older retirees who were deemed high value to the employer. These workers typically were identified and offered individual contracts to continue their association with the company. In contrast, the phased retirement programs under discussion are more formal plans that are offered widely to all workers or all workers in areas of high need. We do not consider these informal offers of part-time employment to selected retirees to be phased retirement programs. Neither are we considering use of older workers, retired from other firms, as part-time employees as phased retirement programs. Instead, this analysis focuses on formal phased retirement plans that are available to a wide range of older employees of a firm.

Employees' View of Phased Retirement: Pros and Cons

In a recent Statistics Canada study,... almost 30% of those who retired between 1992 and 2002 indicated they would have continued working had they been able to move to part time status. (Conroy, 2006)

It seems obvious that many older persons would prefer a gradual transition from full-time work to complete retirement.[2] If offered the option of entering into a phased retirement program that would allow them to stay in their career job but at reduced hours, receive a reduced but prorated salary, continue to be covered by important employee benefits, and begin receiving a portion of their earned pension, many older workers would find this an appealing option. However, if staying on the current job means continuing to work full-time or if part-time employment requires a change of

---

[2]The Health and Retirement Study of older persons in the United States found that in 1996, over 50% of employed survey respondents age 55 to 65 had preference for gradually reducing their hours of work as they aged (Hutchens, 2007).

employers and results in a lower hourly wage and the loss of certain benefits, then more older workers will opt for total retirement. While there have been few studies of worker behaviour in the presence of phased retirement programs, in general these programs have proved to be popular with workers and employers.

A Statistics Canada study found that just under a third of recent retirees indicated they would have continued working had they been able to move to part-time status. In addition, approximately 70% of Canadian baby-boom pre-retirees reported that they intended to work, at least part-time, in retirement (Conroy, 2006). However, this desire should be contrasted to actual retirement patterns. Statistics Canada found that in 1994, 86% of Canadians who had retired terminated their employment without moderating their employment schedule prior to retirement (van Sluys, 2005). Not only does phased retirement provide a productive use of one's time but it also continues earnings into the retirement period and should enhance the likelihood that individuals will have a successful retirement.

Until recently, most older workers faced the choice of continuing full-time on their career jobs, complete retirement, or working part-time on some other job. In general, part-time jobs pay lower wages and offer fewer benefits compared to full-time employment. Thus total compensation from these part-time jobs represents a substantial decline in the hourly value of working compared to compensation on one's full-time career job. For many older persons, the value of working part-time was below their perceived value of their time so they retired completely.

The offer of enrollment in a phased retirement program with one's career employer will usually have greater value than part-time employment with a new company and may also exceed the value of the person's time in retirement. Of considerable importance is whether phased retirees continued to be covered by company health insurance, whether phased retirement adversely affects future pension benefits, and whether the phased retiree can also receive some or all of their pension while working part-time. The inability to work part-time for a career employer while also receiving pension benefits is a significant impediment to entering phased retirement. Examining respondents in the Health and Retirement Study, Even and Macpherson (2004) concluded that "pensions are associated with a lower chance of switching from full-time to part-time work with a change in employer". Changes in tax law and other regulations in the United States, for example, those included in the Pension Protection Act of 2006, should allow firms to provide for in-service distributions of retirement benefits in the future and make phased retirement plans more likely among American employers.

Robert L. Clark

Several studies have attempted to estimate the characteristics of individuals entering phased retirement compared to those who do not. If we define phased retirement to be a reduction of weekly or annual hours while remaining with the same employer, the likelihood of entering phased retirement increases with age, is more common among white-collar workers, is more common in higher education and the public sector, and is more common among higher income and more highly educated workers (Even and Macpherson, 2004; Hutchens, 2007; Watson Wyatt Worldwide, 1999; Chen and Scott, 2006; and Allen, Clark, and Ghent, 2004).

Phased Retirement and National Economic Policy

If labour force participation by age remains around the present rates, more seniors will likely mean a shrinking workforce. In fact, the overall participation rate could fall as low as 57% by 2025, a considerable drop from its current level of 67%. (Statistics Canada, 2004)

In 2006, there were 26.2 million Canadians aged 15 and over and 67.2% of them were in the labour force resulting in a labour force of 17.6 million. Statistics Canada estimates that the Canadian population 15 and older will increase to 32.2 million in 2026. If only 57% of these choose to be in the labour force, the Canadian labour force will be approximately 18.4 million or an increase of less than a million workers over a 20-year period. During the same period, the total population 15 and over will have increased by 5.2 million. The modest increase in workers combined with a much larger increase in the number of retirees and other persons not in the labour force will place substantial pressure on Canadian retirement programs as the ratio of non-workers aged 15 and over to employed persons rises from 48.9% to 75.0%, or a decrease from just over two workers per non-worker to only 1.3 workers per non-worker in 2026. This is a substantial change in the support ratio and has substantial fiscal implications for the Canadian government.

A slowly growing or shrinking workforce may give federal policy-makers concerns about the impact on the national economy. Fewer workers could mean a declining gross domestic product (GDP). A scarcity of workers will tend to increase labour costs and make Canadian products less competitive. An aging population will increase tax rates necessary to finance any given level of retirement benefits. In the coming years, governments in all developed countries will be forced to re-evaluate their national retirement policies. In a world characterized by aging populations, economic incentives promoting early retirement are unlikely to be optimal national policies. Instead, the Canadian Parliament, the US Congress, and other governmental bodies must re-examine their retirement plans. Consideration should be given to raising the normal and early retirement ages in national retirement plans. In addition, tax and regulatory policies that provide impediments to continued employment should be reviewed.

Both countries have been reconsidering policies and regulations that adversely affect the ability and willingness of older workers to remain in the labour force. Mandatory retirement was once a common HR policy among large employers and in the public sector. However, compulsory retirement policies for most jobs have been illegal in the United States since 1986 and now mandatory retirement policies also seem to be on their way out in Canada, for example, the Ontario legislature made mandatory retirement illegal in the province effective December 2006. In both the United States and Canada, there have been recent initiatives to remove barriers to older workers enrolling in phased retirement plans with their career employers. In the United States, the Pension Protection Act of 2006 allows workers to receive pension benefits while continuing to work, provided that they had reached the normal retirement age specified in their retirement plan or at age 62 (Rappaport and Young, 2007). In Canada, the proposed 2007 federal budget included a proposal to allow employees to start receiving benefits from their defined benefit pension while continuing to accrue further benefits (Canada Revenue Agency, 2007).[3]

The median retirement age in Canada is now slightly less than 61. After declining by almost four years between 1987 and 1997, the median retirement seems to have, at least temporarily, stabilized and actually has increased over the last few years (Statistics Canada, 2004). The retirement age is considerably lower in the public sector, around 59, compared to the private sector, slightly less than 62 (Stone, 2006). A key policy question is whether the adoption of phased retirement policies and the removal of regulatory impediments to entering these programs will be sufficient to entice older Canadians to remain in the labour force.

---

[3]Several provinces have also passed legislation addressing the relationship among earnings of phased retirees, the level of benefits they can receive while in phased retirement, and whether a phased retiree can continue to accumulate future pension credits.

Phased Retirement in Higher Education: Can it Be a Model for the Future?

There have been relatively few studies of the impact of phased retirement plans on the retirement patterns of older workers and whether they have assisted employers in achieving their employment objectives. Over the past decade, I served on several committees that helped develop and implement a phased retirement plan for the 15 campuses of the University of North Carolina (UNC) system. As part of the implementation strategy, I was given access to administrative records for faculty at UNC approximately 15 years prior to the adoption of the program and five years after it was included as an employment benefit. My charge was to document the impact of the program so that university leaders could decide the merits of the program and decide whether to retain the plan or eliminate it. Thus, I was able to assess the change in retirement behaviour after the introduction of the program. This section briefly describes the effect of the introduction of this program and assesses its value as a management tool.

Phased retirement is particularly well-suited for use at colleges and universities. Work assignments are easily divisible, for example, a half-time teaching load or administrative or research assignments. Individual performance in these tasks is not necessarily linked to the individual's relationship or interaction with other faculty members. The academic labour force is also aging rapidly leading to concerns that the universities may have too many elderly professors now, but also a fear that there will be mass retirements in the near future. Can phased retirement be used as an effective employment policy to help universities achieve their institutional goals?[4]

Limited evidence indicates that phased retirement programs are more common in higher education than in other sectors of the US economy (Watson Wyatt Worldwide, 1999). Ehrenberg (2003) reports that research-oriented universities are more likely to offer phased retirement programs as are institutions that offer defined-contribution pension plans. In general, phased retirement plans seem to be a popular employment policy that

---

[4]In a recent paper, Clark and Ghent (2007) explore how employers could use demographic models to project the future size and age distribution of their labour. It also shows how changes in employment and compensation policies can be used to increase or decrease transition rates to enable the firm to alter these projects.

provides significant advantages to the university while providing a new retirement option to older faculty. As a result, an increasing proportion of institutions are offering phased retirement plans and a relatively large proportion of faculty are opting for gradual as opposed to complete retirement.

The University of North Carolina (UNC) adopted a phased retirement plan in 1998. The plan called for faculty to retire, relinquish tenure and in exchange receive a three-year employment contract that provided half-time pay for half-time work. Each phased retiree negotiated a reduced work load with their department head. Their compensation was half of the annual salary in the year before entering phased retirement. The faculty member could start their pension benefits if they chose and received health insurance as a retiree. Faculty could work half-time in both academic semesters or full-time one semester and have no university responsibilities during the other semester.

In a series of papers, my colleagues and I have examined the implications of this plan on the retirement behaviour of UNC faculty (Allen, 2006; Allen, Clark, and Ghent, 2004; Ghent, Allen, and Clark, 2001).[5] Using data for 15 years prior to the adoption of the plan, we developed baseline patterns of retirement. The data indicated that the probability of retiring at various ages depended on the type of pension plan chosen by the faculty, the type of institution where the faculty member was employed, and various other individual characteristics.

The introduction of phased retirement tended to decrease the probability that a faculty member aged 50 and older would completely retire by about one percentage point. This represented approximately a 10% reduction in the full retirement rate among older faculty. However, phased retirement raised the odds that the person would either retire completely or enter phased retirement by about two percentage points. Phased retirement rates were highest at ages 64 and 65 and then again at age 70. It is important to remember that retirement rates among university faculty tend to be much lower than for older workers throughout the labour force and that many American universities have been concerned about the aging of their faculties especially since the ending of mandatory retirement in the mid-1990s. In general, we are observing faculty in their mid-60s making

---

[5]The implications of adopting phased retirement plans in Canada is discussed by van Sluys (2005). Leslie and Conley (2005) review phased retirement programs in American universities.

decisions to retire completely, remain on the job full-time, or enter phased retirement.

Work assignments matter even among the relatively homogenous employment of faculty in a public university system. Phased retirement was much more attractive to faculty on campuses where the main mission was teaching compared to the research-oriented campuses. Faculty at the two flagship campuses of UNC had phased retirement rates of 1.6% while the annual proportion of eligible faculty entering phased retirement on other UNC campuses ranged between 3.2 and 4.0%. Overall, about one of every five retirements was a phased retirement.

After a five-year trial period, the Board of Governors of UNC decided to make the phased retirement plan a permanent component of the employment benefits for faculty. The overall assessment was that this program was popular among the faculty and provided a useful tool for academic administrators. For the most part, the phased retirement program is cost neutral to the university or may actually result in a cost saving. Phased retirees receive half-time pay for half-time work so cost per class taught is the same as if the faculty had remained full-time. Phased retirees receive health insurance as retirees and this insurance is the same that active faculty receive, so there is no change in this cost. Phased retirees do not accumulate future pension credits nor does the university make pension contributions on their behalf, so there is actually a cost saving here (however, phased retirees can begin to receive pension benefits). Of course, the university continues to be responsible for Social Security and Medicare taxes. Thus, on balance, the cost of a retiree entering phased retirement is comparable to the prorated cost of the person remaining as a full-time faculty member.

As older faculty moved into phased retirement, deans and department heads could better plan for future hiring patterns. In general, the plan was considered to be a win-win for faculty and the university. It was a program that was implemented at a very low cost and achieved its objectives. While the direct evidence is sparse, the spread of phased retirement programs across institutions of higher education supports the notion that phased retirement plans provide value to universities and are popular among their faculties. Are these findings applicable to the employers throughout the economy?

Is Phased Retirement the Wave of the Future?

The populations of Canada and the United States are aging due to the surge in births after World War II, the subsequent decline in fertility, and long-term reductions in mortality at older ages. Increasing life expectancy, slowing growth in the labour force, and a higher old age dependency ratio are placing greater stress on national retirement programs. In addition, these demographic trends are also causing concern about their implications for the size of the labour force and potential impacts on national economic growth. In a world of aging populations, governments should not encourage early retirement nor should they create policies that reduce the ability of companies to retain older workers. Instead, national leaders should be considering policies that make work at older ages more desirable and more attainable. One such policy is phased retirement.

In an effort to encourage older workers to remain economically active, employers should assess the costs and benefits of developing phased retirement programs that give their employees the option of remaining on the job, but gradually reducing hours as they age. Such programs will be easier and less costly in some industrial settings compared to others. Thus, we should not expect employers in all sectors of the economy to be equally willing to adopt phased retirement programs. Prior to establishing phased retirement plans, employers need to consider:

- the age structure of their labour force and their projected employment needs over the next decade,
- their ability to hire replacement workers from a more slowly growing labour force,
- age-specific patterns of productive increments and decrements,
- the cost of retaining older workers compared to the cost of new younger employees, and
- the need for team work and the potential loss of institutional knowledge associated with early retirements of a large number of employees during a short period of time.

In many circumstances, I believe employers will conclude that they need new policies in the coming years to attempt to slow the rate of retirements among their older employees and phased retirement will be viewed as a viable option.

Having determined that there is a business need for phased retirement, employers and policymakers must consider what government policies limit the effectiveness and desirability of phase retirement programs. In the United States, the inability of companies to allow older workers to reduce hours and receive a partial (or full) pension while working has been a major roadblock in the establishment of phased retirement plans. One of the objectives of the Pension Protection Act of 2006 was to eliminate this problem. In Canada, the issue seems to have been whether workers who have reduced their hours can continue to accrue future pension credits. Once again, government regulators seem to be moving to reduce or eliminate this restriction which limits the attraction of phased retirement programs.

As in the movie, *A Field of Dreams*, I believe that if we build it they will come — if employers establish phased retirement programs, older workers will enter them and embrace this opportunity to gradually move into retirement. This new transition will enhance their retirement experience and provide additional resources that will enable them to achieve a higher standard of living in retirement. Thus, while many barriers to the successful spread of phased retirement programs still exist, governments are moving to reduce or eliminate the regulatory constraints and companies will soon be forced to consider phased retirement along with other options for retaining older workers. Thus, future employment policies in many sectors of the economy will include innovative variations of phased retirement plans.

References

Allen, S. 2006. "The Value of Phased Retirement", in R. Clark and J. Ma. (eds.), *Recruitment, Retention, and Retirement: The New Three Rs of Higher Education*. Cheltenham, UK: Edward Elgar Publishing. 185–208.

Allen, S., R. Clark, and L. Ghent. 2004. "Phasing into Retirement", *Industrial and Labor Relations Review*, October, 112–127.

Bond, T.J., E. Galinsky, S.S. Kim, and E. Brownfield. 2005. *2005 National Study of Employers*. At http://familiesandwork.org/summary/2005nsesummary.pdf.

Canada Revenue Agency. 2007. *2007 Budget – Questions and Answers*. At http://www.cra-arc.gc.ca/tax/registered/budget2007-e.html.

Chen, Y.-P. and J. Scott. 2006. "Phased Retirement: Who Opts for It and Toward What End?" Washington, DC: AARP Public Policy Institute.

Clark, R. and L. Ghent. 2007. "Strategic HR Management with an Aging Workforce: Using Demographic Models to Determine Optimal Employment Policies". Paper presented at the International Seminar on Applications of Demography in Business, Sydney Australia, October.

Collison, J. 2003. *2003 Older Workers Survey*. Alexandria, VA: Social for Human Resource Management.

Conroy, N. 2006. "The New 'Third' Stage of Life: Semi-retirement is Here to Stay". At http://theconroygroup.com/articles/55plus_retirework_part2.html.

Ehrenberg, R. 2003. "The Survey of Changes in Faculty Retirement Policies". American Association of University Professors. At www.aaup.org/Issues/retirement/retrpt.htm.

Even, W. and D. Macpherson. 2004. "Do Pensions Impede Phased Retirement?" *IZA DP 1353*. Bonn, Germany: Institute for the Study of Labor.

Ghent, L., S. Allen, and R. Clark. 2001. "The Impact of a New Phased Retirement Option on Faculty Retirement Decisions", *Research on Aging*, November, 671–693.

Human Resources and Social Development Canada. 2004. "Collective Agreements and Older Workers", ch. 6 "Transition to Work". At http://www.hrsdc.gc.ca/en/lp/spila/wlb/caowc/11chapter_6.shtml.

Hutchens, R. 2007. "Phased Retirement: Problems and Prospects", *Issue Brief*, Center for Retirement Research at Boston College.

Leslie, D. and V. Martin Conley, eds. 2005. *New Ways to Phase into Retirement: Options for Faculty and Institutions*. San Francisco: Jossey-Bass.

Rappaport, A. and M. Young. 2007. *Phased Retirement after the Pension Protection Act*. New York: The Conference Board.

Statistics Canada. 2004. "The Near-retirement Rate", *Perspectives*, February, 18–22.

Stone, L. 2006. *New Frontiers of Research on Retirement*. Ottawa: Statistics Canada. At http://www.statcan.ca/english/freepub/75-511-XIE/0010675-511-XIE.pdf.

van Sluys, B. 2005. "Current Trends in Retirement: The Implications for the Canadian University Community". Lethbridge, AB: University of Lethbridge. Unpublished paper.

Wortsman, A. 2003. "Phased-in Retirement Options Needed for Skill Shortage Challenge". *A CLBC Commentary*. October.

Some Macroeconomic Effects of Population Aging on Productivity Growth and Living Standards

William Scarth

Introduction

This paper focuses on a basic worry that underpins many of the specific issues that have been addressed by other papers in this volume. The basic concern is that — with fewer workers, and more individuals in retirement, as the baby-boom generation ages — there will be too few people producing the goods and services that the entire population will want to consume. This development is sometimes called a "crisis" (World Bank, 1994), a "crucial" issue (Mintz, 2004) or a "demographic storm that we should worry about" (Fortin, 2006). One of the first in Canada to flag this concern was our Auditor General; the 1998 Report concluded that

> Unless our productivity somehow increases significantly or patterns of
> work and retirement change substantially, the current demographic trends
> suggest that the growth in the economy ... will tail off in the coming
> decades.

Financial support from the SEDAP Research Program and the Dean of Social Science at McMaster is gratefully acknowledged.

No one seems to be prepared to argue that baby boomers will choose to postpone retirement in a dramatic fashion or that immigration rates will rise substantially. As a result, the following question emerges as central: Is there anything about the aging population phenomenon *itself* that can be expected to lead to higher productivity growth? If so, we might be able to defend a more optimistic reaction to the demographic trend. Such optimism would need to be tempered, of course, given our limited inability to explain the productivity slowdown that began in the 1970s. And, while economists' understanding of the growth process has increased a great deal in recent decades, we are still some distance from being able to be confident about offering specific advice to policymakers. It is interesting that some economists have expressed solid optimism on this broad question, suggesting that population aging may raise living standards. For example, Emery and Rongve (1999) refer to the pessimistic view as "much ado about nothing", and in an article with a title that includes "a positive view on the economics of aging", Mérrette (2002) argues that "the negative impact of aging on growth ... need not be severe ... we could even surprise ourselves with ... strong performance as our society becomes older".

It must be frustrating for non-specialists to confront an economics profession with views that encompass such a wide spectrum of views regarding the implications of the aging population for living standards. The purpose of this paper is to provide a brief overview of how economists have addressed the question of aging and growth, and what they tell us about the likely impact of aging on material living standards. The hope is that readers may then be able to reach an independent and informed decision concerning this broad question. Should we embrace the dominant view — one of pessimism? Or should we support the minority view — that cautious optimism may be warranted?

The remainder of the paper is organized as follows. In the next section, the traditional approach to understanding economic growth is reviewed. In the following three sections, alternative versions of "new" growth theory are outlined. In each case, the implications of demographic developments are explained and, in many cases, the results from numerically calibrated versions of the theory are reported. Concluding remarks are offered in the last section.

William Scarth

Traditional Growth Theory

All modern analyses of the growth in living standards start from the base provided by Solow (1956) and Swan (1956). Their simple framework stresses that material well being is limited by what the nation produces, so the initial focus is on the economy's overall input-output relationship — what economists call the production function. It is assumed that output depends on three things: the quantity of labour services employed, the quantity of physical capital (such as machines) that each employee has to work with and the level of technical knowledge. The model takes the rate of growth of both technical knowledge and the population as given (determined by considerations that are not explained within the model). In addition, it is usually assumed that everyone is employed, so there is no difference between total employment and the population. As a consequence, there are only two simple propositions that drive the model's properties. First, it is assumed that households save a given fraction of their income (the nation's total output). Second, it is assumed that firms incur no costs in taking output that is not purchased by households for current consumption purposes, and converting this output into machines (which are then used — with labour — to produce more goods in future years).

The model's properties can be appreciated by considering the two standard thought experiments: First, what happens to living standards (per capita consumption) if households choose a higher savings rate? This question is relevant, given the focus of this paper, since one of the causes of the aging population is rising life expectancy, and an anticipated longer retirement can lead individuals to save more when they are younger. The second thought experiment is: What happens to living standards when there is a lower population growth rate? This question is also relevant since an old population has a smaller number of individuals in the child-bearing years. While considering both of these questions in this paper, I focus most intensively on a third issue: What happens to living standards when the proportion of the population that is not working rises? To answer all three questions, economists focus is on what is called a balanced growth path — a situation in which all aggregates (total gross domestic product [GDP], consumption, the capital stock, the quantity of effective workers) grow indefinitely at the same rate. This is an equilibrium, since along such a path, various ratios — such as the capital-labour ratio — stay constant.

Whether more saving is "good" or "bad" for living standards depends on how much society is already saving. It can be the case that saving is already so high that we have a particularly large capital-labour ratio. In this case, a lot of each year's output must be put aside — to make up for the depreciation of capital — to ensure that the capital stock grows as rapidly as does the population. As a result, there is not much currently produced output left over for current consumption, and increased saving only makes this problem worse. But it can be shown that, as long as total profits exceeds total investment spending (a situation that is true for *all* countries in *all* years of observation, see Abel *et. al.*, 1989; and Scarth, 2007b, p. 220), we can be confident that our country has not become overly capitalized in this sense. In the empirically relevant version of the model, then, more saving is "good" — in a short-term pain but long-term gain sense. Initially, a higher savings rate must come at the expense of lower consumption. But, as the ensuing increase in the nation's capital stock is brought on stream, labour has more capital to work with, total output per person rises, and a higher *level* of per capita consumption is eventually enjoyed. However, since the ongoing rate of increase in technical knowledge is assumed to be independent of anything that goes on within the model, the *ongoing rate of increase* in living standards is *not* affected at all. Both the short and long run are illustrated in Figure 1.

Figure 1: Effects on Per Capita Consumption (C) of Higher Saving

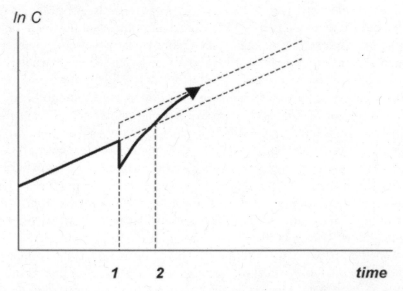

William Scarth

The once-for-all increase in the savings rate takes place at point 1 along the time axis. Had there been no change, per capita consumption would have continued along its exponential growth path (shown here — on a logarithmic scale — as the lower dashed upward-sloping straight line). Initially (between points 1 and 2 in time) the short-term pain emerges, as higher capital accumulation comes at the expense of current consumption. But eventually (beyond point 2 in time), there is enough extra capital to improve labour's productivity, so that overall output, and therefore consumption, is higher. As already emphasized, the *ongoing* growth *rate* of living standards — the slope of the per capita consumption time path — is *not* affected permanently. So in this strict sense, a pro-savings event (such as increased longevity stimulating a desire for a larger retirement fund) does not permanently raise the growth rate. But if all we want to focus on is a period of 30 years or so, it may not be worth stressing this point too much. This is because the growth path for living standards in Figure 1 — the heavy solid line — *is* steeper during the transition between the two balanced-growth full equilibria.

As noted above, the primary focus of our analysis is on the increase in society's dependency ratio that will accompany baby-boom aging. How does this development affect the per capita consumption time path? Answer: it shifts it down in a parallel fashion. Demographers tell us that we can expect about a 10% increase in the overall dependency ratio over the next 30 years. Given this, and the fact that the basic Solow model leaves out considerations such as the particularly high medical expenses that are associated with an older population, the prediction is straightforward: living standards can be expected to fall, in a once-for-all fashion, by about 10% (see Mankiw and Scarth, 2008, p. 232). This outcome is illustrated in Figure 2.

If readers would like to consider this one-time-level outcome in terms of a growth-rate effect that is roughly equivalent, we can note the following. The ongoing annual growth rate of living standards would have to fall by one-third of a percentage point (from an initial annual value of 2%) for 30 years, for living standards to be 10% lower at that 30-year mark. This outcome is illustrated by the flatter solid line between points 1 and 2 along the time axis in Figure 2. So the base-line growth model predicts a serious drop in living standards as a result of the rising old-age dependency ratio.

This prediction has been derived from a very simple framework that has abstracted from several considerations. As a result there are both upward and downward biases in the analysis. Let us, therefore, consider some of

Figure 2: Effect on Per Capita Consumption (C) of Increased Old-Age Dependency

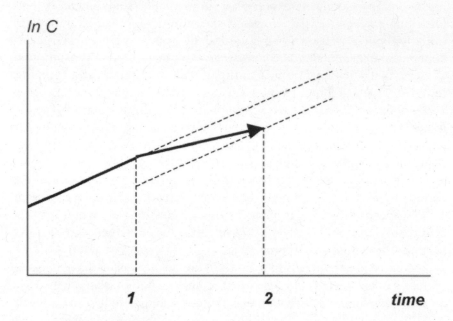

these additional dimensions of the aging population — beginning with two that suggest that our estimate can be considered an underestimate of the overall effects of aging. First, as already noted, the increased importance of higher medical expenses that will be necessary for an older population have been left out. Similarly, the evidence that worker productivity falls as employees age (Guillemette, 2003) has also been ignored. On the other hand, some of the omitted aspects of aging would push the outcome in the opposite direction, so there are reasons for us to consider the numerical prediction given in the last paragraph to be an over-estimate as well. For example, the possible increase in the savings rate that could accompany higher longevity has been excluded. To include this consideration, we need to assume that households are more purposeful. Instead of simply positing that they follow a fixed rule of thumb (always saving a fixed proportion of income), we need to work out what constitutes optimal planning if households can see the demographic change coming in advance. The literature has addressed this issue. It turns out that, *if* future generations are valued on a par with those currently alive (so that despite the overlapping generations of an ever larger number of households, decisions are made

William Scarth

from the point of view that family dynasties live forever), then the core result that was just discussed goes through with *no* modification. Living standards fall by 10% as the dependency ratio rises by this amount. On the other hand, if future generations and immigrants are not so "loved", individuals can be expected to react to the prospect of their working for a smaller proportion of their lives by choosing to save more in their young years. This higher saving leads to a balanced growth path in which workers have more capital to work with, and this partly mitigates the effect of the rising old-age-dependency ratio. Scarth and Jackson (1998) have shown that the net effect on the level of living standards is a more modest 4% reduction in this case. But as Mankiw (2005) has recently remarked, many individuals (even economists) answer interviews to the effect that the most important thing in their lives is their children. Given this, it is not clear that we should put too much emphasis on this less-loved-future-generations version of the model. In short, it is likely that the increased savings effect is small.

There are other ways to alter the model that have the effect of reducing the magnitude of the predicted hit on living standards that accompanies population aging. One is to note that baby boomers will eventually vanish entirely, so the dependency ratio should eventually fall again. Scarth and Souare (2002) have pursued this issue, and it results in the estimated loss in living standards being pulled down a little more — equivalent to about a one-time loss of about 3%. As already noted, another consideration is that the population growth rate will be lower when the population is older, since old people do not have children. In the Solow-Swan analysis, this is "good news" for living standards. The reasoning is straightforward. The capital-labour ratio needs to remain constant for the economy to be in a balanced growth equilibrium. If the denominator of that ratio is increasing at a slower rate, equilibrium requires a smaller growth rate in the capital stock (the numerator of the capital-labour ratio). Thus, lower population growth frees up a larger proportion of each year's newly produced output to be used for current consumption instead of accumulating capital. This freeing up permits higher living standards, and this fortuitous effect of aging acts as a partial counter-balance for the depressing effect that stems from the higher dependency ratio.

The study undertaken by the Auditor General's office argues against our attaching too much significance to this favourable effect of a lower population growth rate. Its authors draw attention to the fact that the part of the population that earns lower incomes depends heavily on government transfer payments. With lower population growth, GDP growth is lower. Since GDP represents the government's tax base, other things equal, governments will have less revenue with which to finance these transfer payments. Thus, those living hand-to-mouth — a subset of the population that is not included in the Solow model — are hurt by lower population growth. Scarth (2007a) has considered a model which includes both forward-looking households who save for the future (that are helped by a lower population growth rate) and hand-to-mouth households (that are hurt by lower population growth). It is shown that lower population growth is desirable according to the hypothetical compensation criterion, since the "rich" are helped by more than the "poor" are hurt by lower population growth. But this reassurance should be interpreted as having only limited appeal. After all, with the increased international mobility that is available to the owners of capital with globalization, it is increasingly challenging for governments to use the tax system to redistribute income towards the hand-to-mouth group within society. All taxes are ultimately paid by unskilled labour if that group cannot migrate to lower-tax jurisdictions while skilled workers and capital can. Scarth (2007b, pp. 195–201) has argued that there is unwarranted pessimism among anti-globalization protesters concerning the scope for governments in small open economies to provide low-income support measures, but nonetheless, it is a mistake to take this challenge lightly. In any event, many policymakers find the hypothetical compensation principle to be of limited appeal if fiscal policy is not likely to be used to turn hypothetical into actual compensation. The final reason to temper our enthusiasm concerning how much lower population growth may compensate for the higher-dependency-ratio aspect of aging is that lower population growth has quite the opposite effect on living standards in one of the "new" growth models that we consider in later sections of this paper.

Let us now take stock of our analysis to this point. Table 1 provides a scoreboard that decomposes the individual effects of the several dimensions of aging, as they have been estimated in calibrated models that are a little more complicated than what has been reported above. While there is no "hand-to-mouth" group in these studies, there are overlapping generations — with the younger generations not fully loved by the older generations, and with the non-working group within the population being limited to the older generations.

We see from the table that the negative effects (of the rising old-age dependency ratio and the higher taxes that will be needed to cover the increases in health-care and public-pension expenses) outweigh the positive effects (of higher saving and lower population growth). The resulting net

William Scarth

Table 1: Estimated Size of some Competing Effects of an Aging Population

Aspect of Aging	Effect on Level of Living Standards
Increase in old-age dependency ratio	Decrease by 8%
Increase in saving for retirement	Increase by 4%
Decrease in population growth rate	Increase by 5%
Increase in tax to finance health/pension costs	Decrease by 8%
Net effect	Decrease by 7%

effect is a one-time, but ongoing, reduction in living standards of about 7%. Whether this is a serious loss or not depends on the eye of the beholder. To have some perspective on this question, it is useful to recall that, when free trade was being debated in the 1988 election, the estimates were that the arrangement with the United States could be expected to raise living standards in a one-time, ongoing, fashion by 3%. That amount of material welfare was considered a very big deal at that time. Consistency in public policy debate would suggest, therefore, that the aging population should be regarded as quite significant, but not a disaster for average living standards.

Of course, Table 1 does not include all possible effects. For one thing, it summarizes the results from analyses that do not allow for a separate "needy" group of households and the associated government transfer payments. We have already noted that this consideration is grounds for additional pessimism concerning the impact of aging on living standards. There is yet another dimension of government policy that has been stressed in the literature on aging, and its omission from Table 1 involves a small bias in the opposite direction. Mérrette (2002) and others have argued that Canada's Registered Retirement Savings Plan (RRSP) program must be considered. In recent years, this program has provided tax breaks for the baby-boom generation. When this group retires, these individuals will have to accept these accumulated savings as current income, and the amount by which this program deprives the government of revenue will be reduced. Other things equal, this development will make it possible for the government to cut tax *rates*. If the tax on "interest" income is thereby reduced, there will be an increased incentive for households to save. The higher saving can boost living standards, so this is a dimension of the aging population that supports optimism. We discuss the likely empirical significance of this consideration in the next section of the paper, and reach the conclusion that it is quite limited. In the meantime, we complete our summary of what traditional (exogenous) growth theory says about aging. As indicated in Table 1, from an empirical point of view, the "good news" developments (higher saving and lower population growth) are roughly cancelled out by one "bad news" development (higher tax rates). This implies that we will not go too far wrong if we continue to focus on the one remaining key dimension of aging — the rise in the dependency ratio. We maintain this focus as we consult what is known as endogenous growth analysis in the remaining sections of the paper.

Before moving on to "new" growth theory, however, it is worth stressing the one key feature of traditional growth analysis that forces that analysis to predict that higher saving can have only a *transitional* effect on the *growth rate* of living standards. This is best appreciated by focusing on households who optimally plan the future time path of their consumption. The standard analysis involves an ever-lasting family dynasty (Ramsey, 1928) that maximizes utility over time. The simplest function that imposes diminishing marginal utility in any one time period is the present discounted value of the logarithm of consumption for all periods into the future, with a rate of impatience (or time preference) applying at a constant exponential rate. To be maximizing utility, such households must arrange their affairs so that their consumption growth rate equals the excess of the rate of return that can be earned on capital over their rate of time preference. Representing this optimizing condition in simple equation terms, we have:

$$n = r(1 - t) - p$$

where n, r, t and p represent the growth rate of living standards, the pre-tax interest rate (marginal product of capital), the tax rate, and the rate of impatience. The intuition behind this behavioural rule is straightforward. It pays households to save only if what the market offers them as compensation for forgoing consumption (the after-tax yield on saving) exceeds the discomfort households feel by postponing consumption (their rate of impatience). So, if the right-hand side of this equation is positive, households do save, and it is the saving that makes positive growth in consumption possible.

Traditional economic analysis specifies that tastes, technology and policy are all determined exogenously (on the basis of outside considerations), and our models are used to determine the remaining items: the resulting economic outcomes. In the present case, parameters p and t specify tastes and policy (respectively), and, in the traditional growth analysis, the productivity growth rate is assumed to be exogenous as well. As a result, the only variable that can adjust to permit households to behave optimally is the pre-tax return on capital, that is, variable r. To see how things work, consider a pro-savings initiative — a lower tax rate. Initially (before any change in r), this policy raises the net return on saving, $r(1 - t)$. So people save more and the nation acquires more capital. But as more and more capital is accumulated, with no corresponding increase in the number of workers, each unit of capital become less productive. (As a simple but telling example, we know that a farmer's rake is not very productive without a worker to use it.) Thus, as time unfolds following the reduction in the tax rate, the pre-tax interest rate gradually falls. The adjustment process is complete when r has fallen by the same amount that $(1 - t)$ has risen. So it is the assumption of diminishing marginal productivity of the man-made input to the production process (capital) that is the driving force behind the proposition that the tax cut cannot permanently raise the growth rate. Modern growth theory is based on the recognition of this fact. All "new" models involve the assumption of constant returns somewhere within the analysis. With this as background, we now consider three versions of new growth theory.

"New" Growth Theory: Human Capital

One revised approach for analyzing growth involves the proposition that newly produced output can be used in three ways, not just two. Current production can take the form of consumption, additions to the physical capital stock, or (the new option) additions to the stock of knowledge (human capital). In equation form, this proposition is given as

$$Y = C + \Delta K + \Delta H$$

where the variables are: Y is output, C is consumption, K is physical capital, and H is human capital. The Δ symbol stands for "change in". The production function is

$$Y = K^a ((1-q)H)^{1-a}$$

where a is a positive fraction and q denotes the proportion of the population that is not working (so $q/(1-q)$ is the dependency ratio). This specification is based on the proposition that, if the individual is not at work, his or her human capital is not available to the production process. The expression defining the marginal product of each form of capital follows immediately from the total product function. Profit maximization involves firms hiring each factor up to the point that the marginal product equals the rental cost that must be paid to households for using their capital. Hence, the following two equations are part of the model: $aY/K = r$ and $(1-a)Y/(1-q)H = w$, where r and w are the rental prices for each factor of production.

Optimization at the household level involves two propositions: that the growth in consumption equals the excess of the after-tax yield over the rate of impatience (as explained above), and that the after-tax yield on both forms of capital be the same. These outcomes can be summarized as $\Delta C/C = r(1-t) - p$ and $r(1-t) = w(1-q)(1-t)$. When the equal-yield and the optimal hiring rules are combined, we have $(H/K) = (1-a)/a$. This outcome can be substituted into the production function, so that it can be re-expressed as $Y = AK$ where $A = ((1-a)/a)^{1-a}(1-q)^{1-a}$.

Given the assumption of balanced growth, the earlier relationships can be summarized as

$$n = \Delta C/C = \Delta K/K = aA(1-t) - p.$$

Since nothing on the right-hand side of this equation changes through time, the prerequisite for an endogenously determined full-equilibrium growth rate is satisfied here. (This is because $\Delta K/K$ equals a constant, not an expression that falls in value as K rises.) As a result, the economy's growth rate is permanently affected by any once-for-all changes that are assumed to take place in the variables that appear on the right. Of particular interest to us is the increase in q (from 0.475 to 0.525) that is predicted by demographers who study the baby-boom aging phenomenon. For reasonable values of the other parameters, this increase in the dependency ratio permanently reduces the growth rate of living standards by a lot — by just under two-thirds of a percentage point.

As we can see in Figure 3, the threat to living standards is more dramatic than what we saw in Figure 2. In the present case, the per capita consumption time path *pivots* down to a lower slope, so that the gap between what we could have enjoyed and what we end up with gets *ever larger* through time. Over a 30-year time frame, this outcome is a reduction in living standards that is about twice as big as we obtained when we based the analysis of the increased dependency ratio on the Solow-Swan analysis.

It is important to have some feel for the sensitivity of this predicted outcome to changes in the model's specification. We consider several. First, as above, we have abstracted from the fact that an older population involves higher health-care costs — that have been estimated at about five percentage points of GDP (Finance Canada, 2003). To this extent, our illustrative numbers are an underestimate of the true outcome. Second, the particular model outlined here assumes that all future generations are loved by the generations that are currently alive just as much as would be the case

Figure 3: Effects on Per Capita Consumption (C) of Increased Old-Age Dependency in the Human Capital Endogenous Growth Model

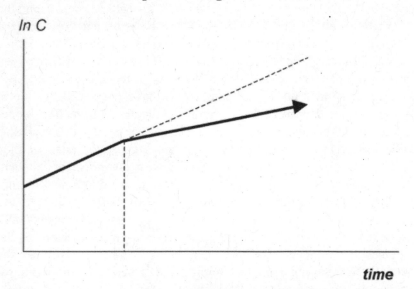

if the current generation never died. Hu (1999), Futagami and Nakajima (2001) and Rafique (2006) have considered more general cases in this regard, thereby allowing for an increased savings effect. In addition, they consider longer life expectancy and lower population growth. They ignore the item that is our major focus — the direct effect of a higher dependency ratio. They find that the favourable lower-population-growth and higher-savings effects combine to yield a higher growth rate equal to about six-tenths of a percentage point. It turns out that almost all of this total outcome follows from the drop in the population growth rate, not the small rise in savings.

What about induced changes in tax rates? To address this issue, we focus on the equations that determine n and A, given earlier in this section. The total differential of these relationships yields:

$$\Delta n = - r\left[((1 - t)(1 - a) / (1 - q))\Delta q + \Delta t\right].$$

To insulate the growth rate from the rise in the dependency ratio (to ensure $\Delta n = 0$), we require a tax-rate change equal to

$$\Delta t = - ((1 - t)(1 - a) / (1 - q))\Delta q .$$

Ilustrative initial parameter values are: $a = 1/3$, $t = 1/4$ and $q = 1/2$, and the demographers tell us that a $\Delta q = 0.05$ can be expected. To keep the productivity growth rate from falling, then, we need a tax rate cut of five percentage points. Mérrette's (2002) analysis indicates that a tax cut of just this magnitude can be expected (if only the RRSP effect is considered). But others, in particular Finance Canada (2003), have pursued this issue in greater detail, and they argue that a tax rate cut that is much smaller — one-seventh of one percentage point — is all that can be expected from RRSP considerations. In their sensitivity tests, the biggest tax-rate cut they estimate is 1.25 percentage points. In addition, we must remember that there is the competing effect on the level of tax rates, the need to finance higher public pension and health expenditure when baby boomers are old. As noted, these expenditures will require about five percentage points of GDP. Thus, there is no way that we can expect tax-rate cuts at all, let alone by the five percentage points that we have seen would be necessary to keep the growth rate from falling in the face of the rising dependency ratio. Indeed, the rising tax rates will be more than enough to cancel out the favourable effects of a higher saving rate and a lower population growth rate. As in the previous section, then, it seems reasonable to argue that we will be erring

William Scarth

a little on the too optimistic side if we proceed with the rough-and-ready assumption that all effects other than the *direct* influence of higher dependency cancel out. In short, this endogenous-growth-rate analysis supports the pessimistic view on aging and growth.

There is one further change in the model that could raise the likelihood that this conclusion could be reversed. The economy can be specified with two distinct parts: a manufacturing sector that produces the consumer goods and the physical capital, and an education sector that produces knowledge (the human capital). With distinct sectors, there are two different production functions. The standard approach is to assume a Cobb-Douglas production function in the manufacturing sector: $Y = K^a(f(1 - q)H)^{1-a}$. This input-output function is the same as we considered above except now there is a proportion f which denotes the fraction of the existing human capital that is employed in this sector. The big difference is the standard assumption that physical capital is not used in the production of knowledge, so the production function in the education sector is $\Delta H = B((1 - f)(1 - q)H)$. According to this specification, the marginal product of using existing knowledge to produce new knowledge, B, does *not* diminish as more knowledge is acquired over time. With the crucial linear growth-rate relationship (needed to have the growth rate permanently affected by developments within the model) embedded in the education sector in this case, it is human capital, not capital in general, that is the "engine of growth". The equal-yields condition is now $r(1 - t) = B(1 - t)(1 - q)$, and the consumption-growth-rate equation becomes $n = B(1 - t)(1 - q) - p$. For illustration, we calibrate as before: initial $r = B(1 - q) = 0.12$ and $\Delta q = .05$. This exercise yields the same estimated effect on the growth rate as we obtained in the one-sector model. However, there may be increased scope for tax policy to counteract this downward pressure on the growth rate in this setting because households have an additional margin of substitution in this case. With the aging population, labour will be scarce relative to physical capital, so wages will be higher and interest rates will be lower. This development creates an increased incentive for individuals to invest in education, and, in this two-sector framework, it is the knowledge sector that is the engine of growth. Depending on how the government allocates the tax-rate changes (on those that apply to wage income, as opposed to income that is derived from physical capital), it is possible that the depressing effect on the growth rate to be smaller in this setting. As a result, it is, perhaps, not surprising that the most optimistic estimate concerning aging and growth comes from Mérrette's study that is based on this two-sector structure.

One final issue might concern readers: the models we have surveyed concern a closed economy — one that has no trading relationships with other countries. Canada is an open economy, so the justification for applying these models to Canada lies in the presumption that the aging-population phenomenon is likely to be quite similar in the United States, and it is customary to use a closed-economy framework for analyzing North America as a whole. We have followed this convention. For readers who find this convention unappealing, it is important to note that open-economy analyses have been derived (Lackie, 2007), and the results support the conclusion that aging can be expected to lower productivity growth by a very similar amount.

"New" Growth Theory: Research and Development

The empirical applicability of the human capital approach to growth has been challenged. As we discovered in the previous section, calibrated versions of these models predict large growth-rate effects following relatively modest changes in tax or savings rates. These predictions do not fit well with cross-sectional evidence. For example, compared with other Organisation for Economic Co-operation and Development (OECD) countries, the United States has low tax and savings rates. Indeed, the national saving rate there has been essentially zero for some time. Yet the United States has the highest productivity growth rate. Another undesirable feature of the human capital model is that it is hard to defend the assumption that all knowledge is inextricably tied to workers. Surely it is the case that, after knowledge about a new invention becomes widespread, all participants in the economy have the ability to exploit this knowledge. This is not made impossible simply because some individuals retire. The research and development (R&D) approach is not open to either of these criticisms.

Aghion and Howitt (1992) have developed a version of the R&D approach that is known as the Schumpeterian paradigm, since it highlights the "creative destruction" that is involved in the innovation process. Their approach formalizes the idea that R&D is carried out by profit-maximizing entrepreneurs, and it involves shifting the location of the linear differential equation (that is necessary for endogenous growth) from the accumulation of capital to the definition of the growth in technology. The rate at which new inventions emerge from the R&D process is proportional to the amount of resources that are devoted to research. An interesting normative analysis of growth policy is possible within this framework since each new invention involves two externality effects: it creates spillover benefits for other producers after the patent period is over and it creates spillover costs in the form of lower profits for the inventor of the previous invention that has then been made obsolete.

It is fortunate that Aghion and Howitt (2007) recently outlined a more accessible version of the Schumpeterian model. Despite the fact that it involves an extension (the addition of physical capital) to their earlier analysis, it is simpler by virtue of the fact that the inter-temporal-optimization underpinnings for the household consumption-savings choice are dropped and replaced by the Solow-Swan specification — a constant savings rate. This change leads to two appealing features: first, it is technically easier to understand and second, the resulting model is a hybrid of the Solow-Swan and the Schumpeterian approaches. In the hybrid, capital accumulation proceeds as it does in the original neoclassical model, but productivity growth arises endogenously as in the creative-destruction framework. Within this setting, the Solow-Swan model emerges as the limiting case of modern growth theory in which the marginal productivity of efforts to innovate is zero.

Readers are encouraged to consult Aghion and Howitt (2007) directly, since it is not appropriate to repeat their analysis in detail here. Instead, I simply report on one straightforward extension that I have pursued. Their model does not permit analysis of an increase in society's dependency ratio since it is assumed that this item is always unity. Instead, using the notation from earlier sections, I replace the unity value with proportion $q/(1-q)$ in all the appropriate equations. After re-expressing the system in change form, I calculate the expression that defines how much the growth rate is affected by an increase in the dependency ratio. Finally, after inserting representation parameter values into this expression I conclude that the annual growth rate can be expected to fall, but only by a very samll amount — by just one-twenty-fifth of one percentage point — as the dependency ratio increases by the amount that demographers predict. Aghion and Howitt have stressed the fact that growth is affected only very slightly by changes in the savings rate in their framework. My extension indicates that the same conclusion applies to the effect of aging on the growth rate. The "good news" aspect of this finding is that this branch of modern growth theory provides some support for a "don't panic" reaction to the prospect of population aging. The "bad news" aspect is that the Schumpetarin approach provides less support for the notion that pro-savings initiatives can be expected to offer significant help in trying to keep the growth rate up as the population ages. This consideration is central to the Canadian policy debate, since the federal government's rationale for establishing its 20% debt-to-GDP-ratio target, to be reached by 2020, is based on the desire to ease the burden of population aging. Two reactions to this concern are possible. First, we can argue that we will not need debt policy to provide a significant cushion for living standards when the baby boomers retire, since (according to this model) the threat to the growth rate of that development is small in the first place. Second, we can remind ourselves that the focus on permanent growth-rate effects in endogenous-growth models tends to distract analysts from the one-time consumption-level effects that are still present within these models. Up to this point, the present discussion is open to this critique. But this is easily rectified. We simply note that — in terms of a negative one-time-level effect on consumption — population aging is still a threat to living standards, and debt reduction can still offer significant relief from this threat in this model. The Scarth-Jackson (1998) analysis was the original motivation for linking the chosen debt policy to the population aging phenomenon. Since that study focused entirely on a level effect, not on permanent growth-rate effects, there is no reason for us to react to the permanent growth-rate effects being tiny in the Schumpeterian approach, by being complacent about aging.

"New" Growth Theory: Population Growth and Limited Natural Resources

The Schumpeterian growth model has its critics as well. Jones (2003) has raised two points. First, the model involves what is known as the scale-effect prediction: the bigger is the *level* of the population, the larger is the productivity *growth rate*. This prediction stems from the simple proposition that the more people there are, the more researchers there are, and so more inventions will emerge from the R&D process. The problem is that data do not seem to support the scale effect; there is no systematic correlation showing that bigger economies have higher growth rates. Jones' second concern is what is known as the knife-edge property of endogenous growth theory. If the engine-of-growth equation is not *precisely* linear, all growth-rate effects become temporary — as in the Solow-Swan framework. According to Jones, it is simply not credible to argue that the processes that generate human capital, or new innovations, are exactly constant-returns-to-scale. This is an especially appealing line of argument if another more easily defended constant-returns relationship can be included in the model. Jones argues that this is possible if we focus on the identities that define the population-growth process.

The amount by which the population grows in any period (abstracting from immigration) is exactly equal to the number of births minus the number of deaths. Denoting the birth, death and population growth rates by b, d and g, and the total population as P, we have $\Delta P = (b - d)P = gP$, which is a truly defensible exactly-constant-returns relationship from which to derive endogenous growth. While it is not necessary to bring non-renewable resources into the discussion, it is tempting to do so — given the current debate on the perceived trade-off between our environmental and higher-growth objectives. It is particularly tempting since Groth (2007) has done this, by building on an early contribution by Suzuki (1976). Non-renewable resources involve another simple identity. Denoting the amount of the resource used each period by R, and the amount of the remaining stock of the resource as S, resource depletion is defined by a simple identity: $\Delta S = -R$. To have a straightforward analysis, Suzuki and Groth make the standard assumption, which is similar to the constant-savings-rate specification in the Solow-Swan framework. Using u to denote the rate of resource utilization (depletion), they assume $R = uS$, and so there is a second constant-returns relationship in the model: $\Delta S = -uS$.

All that remains to be done is to specify the production and capital-accumulation relationships. With proportion $(1 - q)$ of the population working and a Cobb-Douglas specification, we have $Y = K^{\alpha}((1 - q)P)^{\beta}R^{\gamma}$, where all exponents are positive. Groth argues on empirical grounds that ($\alpha + \beta$) may well exceed unity, so we focus on this case. Finally, the capital stock grows whenever current output exceeds total consumption (per capita consumption, c, times the population): $\Delta K = Y - cP$. Assuming a balanced-growth equilibrium, and that we continue to restrict our attention to one-time changes in the old-age dependency ratio, we can show that these relationships imply that the growth in per capita consumption is

$$n = ((\alpha + \beta - 1)g - \gamma u) / (1 - \alpha).$$

For the remainder of this section, we discuss several implications of this result. But first we point out that Jones' analysis is slightly different. It is more complicated since he spells out a particular process for the investment in innovation, but it is simpler since he excludes any consideration of non-renewable resources. Nevertheless, our conclusions about demographic developments are exactly what follow in Jones' study.

The first point is that ongoing growth in material living standards is possible, despite the fact that production involves a non-renewable resource. A doomsday conclusion has been avoided since the Cobb-Douglas production function involves the assumption that no input is absolutely essential. But even still, sustained growth is not assured. It requires increasing returns with respect to capital and labour ($\alpha + \beta > 1$), a "large" population growth rate, and a "small" resource utilization rate. In terms of ongoing growth-rate considerations, an environmentally friendly agenda (a small value for u) leads to higher, not lower, growth in material living standards. In this sense, then, there is *not* a trade-off between our environmental and our higher-growth objectives. This analysis has not been appreciated in recent Canadian debate concerning the environment.

There is a mixed message concerning demographic developments. The good news is that the ongoing growth of living standards is not depressed by an increase in the old-age dependency ratio. The bad news is that the other dimension of the aging population, a lower population growth rate, has very different effects in this growth model. Since the growing population is the "engine of growth" in this framework, lower population growth pulls the growth of living standards down. Unless we can be confident that policymakers should put no weight on this approach to endogenous growth, and I do not believe that we can, then we must now acknowledge that the other approaches to growth may have given us a false impression concerning population growth rates. Except for an undesirable income-distribution consideration — those models supported the view that the lower population growth dimension of the aging baby-boomer phenomenon should be welcomed. If this last class of models has relevance, however, this view can no longer be sustained.

Conclusions

The purpose of the paper has been to survey growth theory, to select simple versions of each approach that can be readily calibrated and applied for direct policy application, and to discover whether a consistent set of conclusions concerning the effect of population aging on material living standards emerges.

Traditional exogenous-growth-rate analysis formed the initial basis of this survey and, within that framework, we paid most attention to four effects. We argued that the unfavourable influences (higher old-age dependency and tax rates) are likely to dominate the favourable ones (higher saving and lower population growth), so that, on balance, aging can be expected to lower average living standards, in an ongoing levels fashion, by about 7%.

Turning to endogenous-growth-rate analysis, we found that the quantitative importance of all four aging effects to be increased, when we based our predictions on the human-capital model. As a result, this analytical framework provides even more grounds for a pessimistic view concerning the impact of the aging population on living standards. Rather different results emerged from the other endogenous-growth analyses. Three of the four aging effects were weaker in both the Schumpeterian and population-growth models. While, by itself, this consideration is grounds for optimism, it was trumped by the other change in prediction. In these models of endogenous growth, the lower-population-growth aspect of aging becomes an unfavourable influence — *not* one of the quantitatively more important favourable influences — on living standards.

Overall, therefore, while our analysis does not support a disaster scenario, we cannot avoid some pessimism. Our main conclusion is that the aging population *does* represent a serious challenge, and those who are concerned about it are not making "much ado about nothing". There is some good news but it is not that living standards will rise. The good news is that the likely magnitude of the hit to living standards may just be manageable. Our public debt-reduction strategy is proceeding well, and with a concerted effort on the tax reform front, more progress in providing the necessary cushion for living standards may be achieved in time. It is discouraging, however, that not all the approaches to growth provide analytical support for all the policy initiatives that are being discussed as responses to population aging.

References

Abel, A., G. Mankiw, L. Summers, and R. Zeckhauser. 1989. "Assessing Dynamic Efficiency: Theory and Evidence", *Review of Economic Studies* 56, 1–20.
Aghion, P. and P. Howitt. 1992. "A Model of Growth through Creative Destruction", *Econometrica* 60, 323–351.

_____. 2007. "Capital, Innovation and Growth Accounting", *Oxford Review of Economic Policy* 23, 79–93.

Emery, H. and I. Rongve. 1999. "Much Ado About Nothing: The Demographic Bulges, the Productivity Puzzle, and CPP Reform", *Contemporary Economic Policy* 17, 68–78.

Finance Canada. 2003. *Tax Expenditures and Evaluations 2003*. At: http://www.fin.gc.ca/taxexp/2003/taxexp03_e.html.

Fortin, P. 2006. "Back to Basics", *Policy Options* (April/May, 59). Montreal: Institute for Research on Public Policy.

Futagami, K. and T. Nakajima. 2001. "Population Aging and Economic Growth", *Journal of Macroeconomics* 23, 31–44.

Guillemette, Y. 2003. *Slowing Down with Age: The Ominous Implications of Workforce Aging for Canadian Living Standards*. Commentary No. 182. Toronto: C.D. Howe Institute.

Groth, C. 2007. "Growth Essential Non-Renewable Resources and Limits to Growth". Working Paper. Denmark: University of Copenhagen.

Hu, S-C. 1999. "Economic Growth in the Perpetual Youth Model: Implications of the Annuity Market and Demographics", *Journal of Macroeconomics* 21, 107–124.

Jones, C. 2003. "Population and Ideas: A Theory of Endogenous Growth", in P. Aghion, R. Frydman, J. Stiglitz, and M. Woodford (eds.), *Knowledge, Information, and Expectations in Modern Macroeconomics*. Princeton, NJ: Princeton University Press.

Lackie, C. 2007. "A Target Debt-to-GDP Ratio with an Aging Population". MA in Economic Policy. Hamilton: McMaster University, Policy Project.

Mankiw, G. 2005. "Comment", *Brookings Papers on Economic Activity*, Issue 1, 316–325.

Mankiw, G. and W. Scarth. 2008. *Macroeconomics*. 3rd Canadian edition. New York: Worth Publishers.

Mérrette, M. 2002. "The Bright Side: A Positive View on the Economics of Aging", *Choices* 8(1). Montreal: Institute for Research on Public Policy.

Mintz, J. 2004. "Is the Debt War Over? What Have We Learned?" in C. Ragan and W. Watson (eds.), *Is the Debt War Over?* Montreal: Institute for Reasearch on Public Policy.

Office of the Auditor General of Canada. 1998. "Population Aging and Information for Parliament: Understanding the Choices", *Report of the Auditor General to the House of Commons — 1998*.

Rafique, S. 2006. "Economic Effects of Declining Population Growth". MA in Economic Policy. Hamilton: McMaster University, Policy Project.

Ramsey, F. 1928. "A Mathematical Theory of Saving", *Economic Journal* 38, 543–559.

Scarth, W. 2007a. "Lower Population Growth and Average Living Standards". Unpublished paper.

_____. 2007b. *Macroeconomics: An Introduction to Advanced Methods*. 3rd edition. Toronto: Thomson Custom Publishing.

Scarth, W. and H. Jackson. 1998. "The Target Debt-to-GDP Ratio: How Big Should It Be? And How Quickly Should We Approach It?" in T. Courchene and T. Wilson (eds.), *Fiscal Targets and Economic Growth*. Kingston: John Deutsch Institute for the Study of Economic Policy, Queen's University.

Scarth, W. and M. Souare. 2002. "Baby Boom Aging and Average Living Standards". SEDAP Research Paper No. 68. Hamilton: McMaster University.

Solow, R. 1956. "A Contribution to the Theory of Economic Growth", *Quarterly Journal of Economics* 70, 65–94.

Suzuki, H. 1976. "On the Possibility of Steadily Growing Per Capita Consumption in an Economy with a Wasting and Non-Replenishable Resource", *Review of Economic Studies* 43, 527–535.

Swan, T. 1956. "Economic Growth and Capital Accumulation", *Economic Record* 32, 145–166.

World Bank. 1994. *Averting the Old Age Crisis: Policies to Protect the Old and Promote Growth*. Oxford: Oxford University Press.

Remain, Retrain or Retire: Options for Older Workers Following Job Loss

Christine Neill and Tammy Schirle

Introduction

As the Canadian population continues to age, so does its workforce. There are concerns among policymakers that stark labour shortages may occur as the baby boomers enter retirement. There are also concerns that an aging workforce is less mobile, less able to adjust to technological change and other shocks to the economy, and may be particularly hard hit by job loss. Policies designed to reduce the costs to older individuals affected by such labour market shocks could potentially improve the adjustment of the economy over the long run, and have been the subject of considerable recent policy interest.

A recent Canadian policy initiative is the Targeted Initiative for Older Workers (TIOW), which has allocated $70 million over two years in funds for community-based training and re-employment programs targeted at older workers — those aged 55 and over. The aim of this program is to help to reintegrate into the labour force those workers who have lost their jobs due to industrial restructuring.

Recently, another option has been circulating in US policy discussions. LaLonde (2007) has made the case for providing wage insurance — similar in concept to unemployment insurance, but with payments made to workers after they find another job if it offers a lower wage than the worker's initial job. LaLonde argues that the losses from a lifetime of lower wages are a considerably higher cost of displacement than temporary income lost due to unemployment, and that those potential losses are not insurable at present.

Both these policies involve substantial targeting of resources to older workers. Is such targeting of resources towards older workers merited or even useful? Could these resources be used more efficiently elsewhere? The goal of this study is to review the existing evidence we have about older workers' experiences following job loss, highlight areas where evidence is lacking, and fill some of the existing knowledge gaps. Currently, little is known about the labour supply and training decisions made by workers who lose their job when near retirement age, or about the consequences of those decisions. Here, we focus on workers who are displaced — they lost their job due to company closure or business slow-down rather than simply being laid off. We begin by presenting evidence on the incidence of job loss among older workers. We then examine several options available to older workers, including the options of retirement, remaining in the labour force or retraining at older ages to improve future labour market outcomes. This is followed by a discussion of these options in the context of various policies available to policymakers.

The Incidence of Job Loss among Older Workers and the Options they Face

Current evidence suggests that older workers are slightly less likely to experience a permanent layoff than their younger counterparts. In Figure 1, we show the layoff rates constructed by Morissette, Zhang, and Frenette (2007).[1] On average, 7% of older male workers (age 50–64) are permanently laid off in any given year.[2] This is consistently lower than the layoff rates for younger men, among whom 8% experience a permanent

---

[1]The figure is based on data found in Table 1a and Appendix Table 1a in Morissette, Zhang, and Frenette (2007). Their results are based on a Longitudinal Worker File sample of individuals employed outside the public sector in firms with at least two employees.

[2]Workers are defined as permanently laid off when they do not return to their former employer in the same year or in the year following layoff (Morissette, Zhang, and Frenette, 2007).

Christine Neill and Tammy Schirle

Figure 1: Permanent Layoff Rates and Displacement Rates

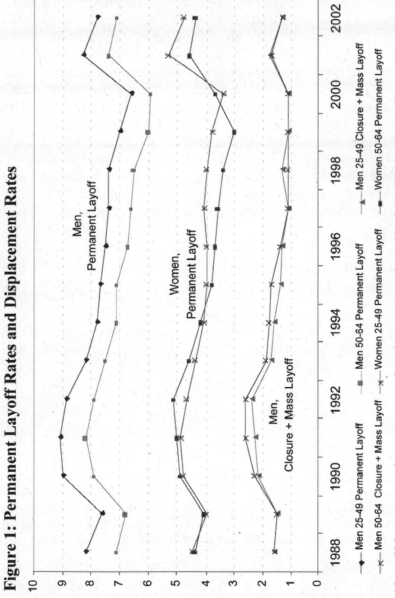

Note: This represents the percentage of workers employed outside the public service in firms with at least two employees.

Source: Table 1a and Appendix Table 1a of Morissette, Zhang and Frenette (2007).

layoff. There do not appear, however, to be such differences between younger and older women. Furthermore, there are no consistent differences in the displacement rates (permanent layoffs due to firm closure or mass layoff) between younger and older workers. Both groups of men experience such displacements at an average rate of 1.6%. It seems likely, therefore, that the permanent layoff rate for younger workers is higher because they are still in the process of finding a position with a good fit between their skills and those required by the job, while older workers are more likely to have found a good match.[3]

Who is likely to become displaced? The first two columns of Table 1 describe the characteristics of older workers who experience displacement from full-time work when over the age of 50 and their counterparts who continue in full-time employment.[4] Displaced older workers are only slightly older, and tend to be among the less-educated workers. It is very unlikely that older public sector, unionized, and high-seniority workers will become displaced. Across industries there are not many differences. There appears to be a higher likelihood of workers in manufacturing becoming displaced, while workers in health-care industries are unlikely to become displaced.[5]

So what happens to these workers following job loss, and what makes them different from younger workers in the same position? Older displaced workers effectively have three options available to them: remain in the labour force; take time away from the labour force and undertake training for a new occupation; or enter early retirement. This last option is not typically available to younger workers, and it is this option that really complicates the decisions of older workers and the policy response. Rowe

---

[3]Jovanovic (1979) provides the classic model of job matching. Here, permanent layoff would become less likely with high seniority as good employer-employee matches are the most likely to survive.

[4]Using the panel data from SLID, individuals are observed over a five-year period and classified as displaced from full-time work if they were separated from a job due to company closure or business slowdown and return to full-time employment in that five-year period. They hold continuous full-time work if over the five-year period they have held the same full-time job.

[5]Note that construction workers and agriculture workers have been omitted from this sample, as separating layoffs due to business slowdown and seasonal work is not entirely clear.

Christine Neill and Tammy Schirle

Table 1: Characteristics of Workers Observed in Full-Time Work Age 50–69, by Work Status Over a Five-Year Period

	Displaced from FT Work (1)	Continuous from FT Work (2)	Displaced from FT, Retired (3)	Voluntarily Retired (4)
Number of observations	1,013	7,046	689	3,186
Wages and Salaries	21,219	39,487	-	-
Age	54.9	52.9	56.1	58.9
Male	0.66	0.64	0.50	0.55
Education				
Less than high school	0.34	0.20	0.35	0.28
High school graduate	0.14	0.18	0.20	0.18
Some postsecondary	0.10	0.09	0.07	0.07
Postsecondary	0.33	0.35	0.31	0.29
University	0.09	0.18	0.07	0.18
"Lost" Job				
Public sector	0.06	0.30	0.08	0.35
Unionized	0.27	0.50	0.21	0.52
Job tenure (months)	90	232	108	214
Pension Plan	0.32	0.59	0.23	0.62
Industry				
Forestry, Fishing ...	0.06	0.03	0.03	0.02
Utilities	0.01	0.01	0.02	0.02
Manufacturing	0.28	0.20	0.23	0.17
Trade	0.17	0.14	0.22	0.11
Transportation ...	0.06	0.06	0.06	0.06
FIRE	0.06	0.06	0.06	0.07
Professional ... services	0.07	0.05	0.02	0.03
Business ... support	0.06	0.02	0.04	0.03
Education	0.02	0.10	0.02	0.14
Health & Soc. Assistance	0.03	0.12	0.06	0.12
Culture & Rec.	0.03	0.03	0.03	0.05
Accomm. & Food Services	0.07	0.02	0.08	0.05
Other services	0.06	0.06	0.09	0.05
Public administration	0.04	0.10	0.04	0.09

Note: Authors' calculations using the Survey of Labour and Income Dynamics. Categories are based on the observation of individuals in full-time employment over a five-year period. Column (1) represents workers displaced from full-time employment who return to full-time employment while workers in column (3) did not return. Column (2) represents workers who remained in the same full-time job for the five years. Column (4) represents workers who voluntarily left a full-time job and did not return in the five-year period.

and Nguyen (2002) have found Canadian workers age 50–65 have much lower re-employment rates following involuntary job separations than the rest of the labour force.[6] Recent Canadian evidence from Gray and Finnie (2007) suggest many older displaced workers immediately enter retirement following displacement, as nearly one-third of older laid-off workers reported receiving a private pension after job loss. Further, education participation rates are lower for older displaced workers — for individuals aged 55–64 at the time of displacement, around 2¼% are undertaking formal education at a postsecondary institution in the year after displacement, compared with 6% of 40–55 year olds.

In the following sections, we examine each of the three options available to older displaced workers in more detail. What are the costs and benefits of each option? While the necessary information is often not available to produce precise answers, we have attempted to provide a discussion of these options with the intention of informing the policy debate.

Remain in the Labour Force

Most workers with a strong labour force attachment will choose to remain in the labour force following displacement. Among full-time workers who are displaced this typically involves the worker enduring a spell of unemployment followed by a return to full-time employment. However, the post-displacement experiences of older workers may differ substantially from the experiences of their younger counterparts.

There is evidence that workers will experience longer spells of unemployment at older ages. In Figure 2, we plot the average weeks of unemployment duration among unemployed men and women for various age groups. Between 2001 and 2006, men aged 55–64 had an average unemployment duration of 31 weeks, ten weeks longer than the average 25–54 year old unemployed man. Older women have similar experiences, with women aged 55–64 experiencing unemployment spells that are on

---

[6]Rowe and Nguyen (2002) find that 60% of job separations among workers age 50–65 were involuntary. Using the Canadian Labour Force Survey, the authors do not observe transitions into retirement following an involuntary job loss. They are able to observe voluntary retirements. Among men age 50–65, 16% of job separations were retirements. Among women age 50–65, 12% of job separations were retirements.

Christine Neill and Tammy Schirle

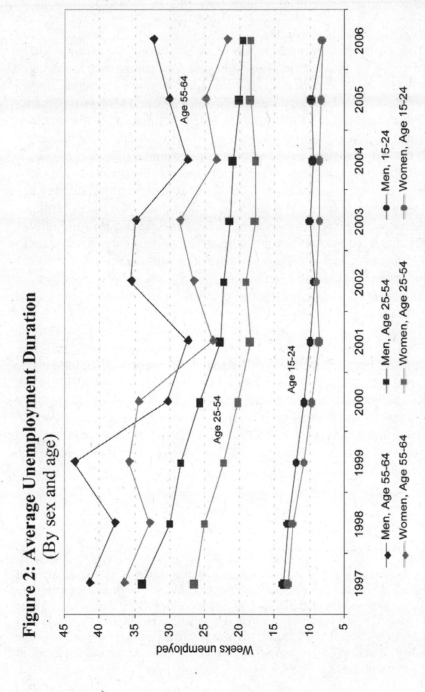

Figure 2: Average Unemployment Duration
(By sex and age)

Weeks unemployed

Age 55-64

Age 25-54

Age 15-24

Legend:
- Men, Age 55-64 (◆)
- Women, Age 55-64 (◆)
- Men, Age 25-54 (■)
- Women, Age 25-54 (■)
- Men, 15-24 (●)
- Women, Age 15-24 (●)

Source: CANSIM II series V2349407, V2349455, V2349479, V2349371, V2349347, V2349299.

average 25 weeks in duration (between 2001 and 2006), seven weeks longer than women aged 25–54. The longer duration of unemployment spells among the oldest workers may in part reflect a greater need for skill upgrading among older workers.

To date, there has been a lack of evidence describing the earnings losses associated with displacement among workers nearing retirement ages relative to those experienced by younger workers. Several studies (including Jacobson, LaLonde, and Sullivan, 1993; and Morissette, Zhang, and Frenette, 2007) have provided evidence that displaced workers face large and persistent earnings losses. Morissette, Zhang, and Frenette's (2007) estimates suggest Canadian high-tenured men displaced between the ages of 25 and 49 face long-term earnings losses in the range of 18%–35% of their predisplacement earnings. Their female counterparts also experience long-term losses between 24% and 35% of their predisplacement earnings. Consistent with the results presented in Jacobson, LaLonde, and Sullivan (1993), displaced workers' earnings begin to fall up to three years prior to displacement. Neither of these studies includes workers nearing retirement age to "ensure that workers' earnings trajectories after displacement are not contaminated by early retirement patterns" (Morissette, Zhang, and Frenette, 2007, p. 13).

To fill this gap in the literature, we have provided estimates of the earnings losses experienced by workers displaced from full-time employment between the ages of 50 and 69. We use data from the Survey of Labour and Income Dynamics, a panel dataset which allows us to observe individuals' characteristics, earnings, the timing and incidence of job separation, and reasons for job separation over the course of six years.[7] Similar to the methods used in Jacobson, LaLonde, and Sullivan (1993) and Morissette, Zhang, and Frenette (2007), the estimates are based on the simple wage regression

$$w_{it} = \sum_{k=-2}^{2} D_{it}^k \delta_k + x_{it} \beta + \varepsilon_{it}$$

---

[7]The sample used to estimate the model is based on the observation of individuals over a five-year period. This sample includes individuals displaced from a full-time job when over the age of 50 and are observed returning to full-time employment. Their comparison group in this sample includes all individuals over age 50 who held continuous employment in the same full-time job over the five years. See the note to Table 1 and Schirle (2007) for a more thorough discussion of sample selection for this model.

Christine Neill and Tammy Schirle

where w_{it} represents the individual i's earnings at time t. The covariates D_{it}^k are dummy variables that represent the event of displacement in the period t-k. The parameter δ_k thus represents the effect of displacement on a worker's earnings k years following its occurrence. The wage equation also includes a set of covariates x_{it} which includes gender, age, education indicators, public sector, and union status, months of job tenure (on the current or lost job) and full set of industry, province and year dummy variables. Schirle (2007) has shown that the self-selection of displaced older workers into retirement does not result in biased estimates of earnings losses.[8] The resulting estimates representing the earnings losses experienced by 50–69 year olds are presented in the first column of Table 2. Comparable estimates for full-time workers age 35–49 and 25–34 are provided in the second and third columns respectively. The loss estimates are duplicated in Figure 3.

The estimates suggest that male workers of all ages suffer substantial and persistent earnings losses associated with displacement, consistent with the existing literature.[9] As expected, the earnings losses of displaced men age 35–49 begin in the years prior to displacement and post-displacement losses are consistently larger than the losses faced by their younger 25–34-year-old counterparts. In contrast, the men age 50–69 do not experience earnings losses significantly different from zero in the years leading up to displacement. Furthermore, and perhaps contrary to expectations, men in the oldest age group are not experiencing larger wage losses than their younger counterparts.[10]

Results for other sub-samples of displaced workers are presented graphically in Figures 4 to 6. First, and consistent with the literature suggesting job loss results in a loss of job-specific human capital, tenure is the key factor in determining an older workers' earnings losses. Estimates suggest that high-tenured men (with more than ten years experience at the

---

[8]Schirle (2007) does, however, suggest that this self-selection into retirement is more generally important when estimating the wage equation in that estimates of the effect of age are biased when selection is not accounted for.

[9]Estimates for a broader sample of workers that include women are not substantially different.

[10]If comparing the loss relative to expected earnings, losses among the youngest displaced workers are only slightly smaller than the losses among the oldest workers.

Table 2: OLS Results Dependent Variable: Annual Earnings

Sample: Male	Age 50–69	Age 35–49	Age 25–34
Displaced			
2 years before	-2263	-7541 ***	-1207
	(6128)	(2249)	(2785)
1year before	-85	-4209 **	-4901 **
	(3700)	(1939)	(2386)
Year of displacement	-12036 ***	-12625 ***	-11011 ***
	(3635)	(1654)	(1803)
1 year after	-14565 ***	-16470 ***	-12549 ***
	(2365)	(1740)	(1897)
2 years after	-10417 ***	-13851 ***	-11375 ***
	(2419)	(1978)	(1969)
Age	-791 ***	60	764 ***
	(165)	(96)	(175)
Education			
High school	2646	878	2659 **
	(1876)	(1077)	(1336)
Some public school	8398 ***	6495 ***	3625 **
	(2759)	(1316)	(1440)
Postsecondary	7218 ***	8412 ***	6495 ***
	(1466)	(1004)	(1174)
University	22050 ***	19746 ***	15102 ***
	(2575)	(1779)	(2301)
Public sector	10033 ***	6010 ***	2550
	(2005)	(1774)	(2655)
Unionized	6883 ***	3320 ***	5424 ***
	(1430)	(917)	(1196)
Tenure	27 ***	39 ***	52 ***
	(5)	(5)	(14)

(Continued - next page)

Christine Neill and Tammy Schirle

Table 2 (Continued)

Sample: Male	Age 50–69	Age 35–49	Age 25–34
Industry			
Utilities	-2879	3403	3681
	(3982)	(3141)	(3489)
Manufacturing	-1785	-4175 **	-2853
	(2920)	(1794)	(2123)
Trade	-14711 ***	-10085 ***	-9431 ***
	(3066)	(1963)	(2084)
Transportation ...	-15867 ***	-11384 ***	-10030 ***
	(3378)	(2079)	(2417)
FIRE	-11991 **	-5100	-8960 **
	(5479)	(3244)	(4520)
Professional ... services	-17552 ***	-11605 ***	-3500
	(4283)	(3123)	(2957)
Business ... support	-17496 ***	-15915 ***	-15343 **
	(4104)	(3712)	(6509)
Education	-20496 ***	-17286 ***	-13083 ***
	(3635)	(2616)	(3964)
Health and soc. assist.	-37819 ***	-23005 ***	-15695 ***
	(3910)	(4187)	(3608)
Culture and rec.	-15218 ***	-9978 ***	-7702 ***
	(4352)	(3509)	(3089)
Accom. and food services	-28267 ***	-24149 ***	-19198 ***
	(4235)	(2400)	(2560)
Other services	-26703 ***	-20954 ***	-12042 ***
	(3551)	(2356)	(2746)
Public administration	-17997 ***	-11537 ***	-5667
	(3432)	(2454)	(3491)
Constant	72989 ***	24078 ***	-137
	(9294)	(4134)	(5417)
Province	Yes	Yes	Yes
Year	Yes	Yes	Yes

Notes: Robust standard errors are in parentheses. Authors' calculations using the Survey of Labour and Income Dynamics. Forestry, fish, oil and gas is the excluded industry category.
***, **, * indicate significance at the 1%, 5% and 10% levels.

same job) experience earnings losses of over $22,000 in the first year following displacement. Low-tenured older men face much lower losses, at just over $10,500 in the first year following displacement.

Second, educational attainment does not appear to be as important for determining the level of wage losses as one might expect. Although individuals with higher levels of education are among the least likely to become displaced, after displacement occurs the earnings losses experienced by high and lower educated workers are not significantly different.[11] Relative to their expected earnings, however, a highly educated worker may expect losses amounting to 23% of their expected earnings while lower educated workers may expect losses closer to 40% of their expected earnings.

Finally, current policies targeting older workers would suggest we expect rural workers or those in smaller communities to experience larger wage losses than their urban counterparts, since urban displaced workers likely have a wider variety of opportunities available to them. The estimates provided in Figure 6, however, suggest that there is no significant difference between the earnings losses of urban and rural displaced workers.[12] Rural workers, however, tend to have lower earnings than urban workers. Here, large and small urban workers are experiencing losses between 30% and 35% of their expected earnings while rural workers are losing close to 45% of expected earnings.[13]

Overall, older workers face large and persistent earnings losses upon displacement. While these losses appear slightly larger than those experienced by the youngest workers, they are not substantially larger than losses experienced by displaced workers between the ages of 35 and 49.

---

[11]Highly educated refers to a worker that has attained more than high school graduation as their highest level of education. To note, as a percentage of expected earnings, the losses of lower educated individuals are higher than those of highly educated individuals.

[12]There is some measurement error in any such estimate since it is not clear how to treat displaced workers who move from rural to urban areas following displacement. In the estimates mentioned here, urban-rural status relates to the time period wages are observed.

[13]Large urban areas are defined as having populations greater than 50,000. The population of a small urban area is between 1,000 and 49,999 while rural areas have populations under 1,000.

Christine Neill and Tammy Schirle

Figure 3: Earnings Losses of Men Due to Displacement
(By age group)

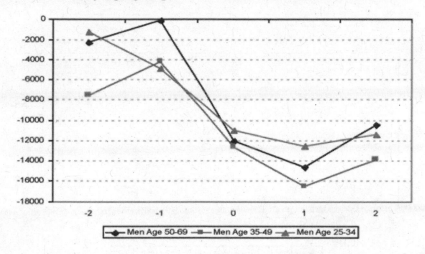

Note: Based on the regression results in Table 2. A person who does not experience displacement expects an earnings loss equal to zero. Here, 50–69 year old men who are displaced will observe annual earnings $12000 less in the year of displacement (t=0), relative to what they would have expected if they continued working full time.

Figure 4: Earnings Losses of Men Age 50–69
(By pre-displacement tenure)

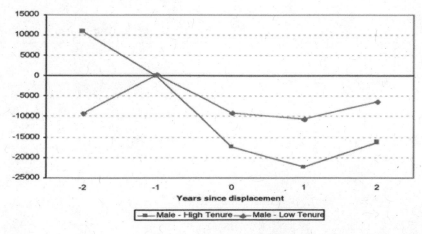

Source: Authors' calculations using SLID. See note to Figure 3.

Remain, Retrain or Retire   *289*

Figure 5: Earnings Losses of Men Age 50–69
(By education level)

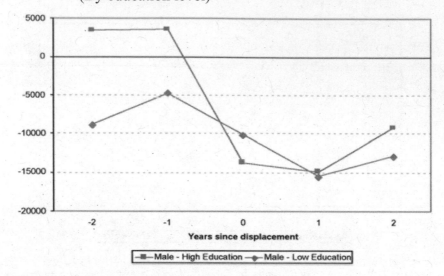

Source: Authors' calculations using SLID. See note to Figure 3.

Figure 6: Earnings Losses of Men Age 50–69
(By urban-rural status)

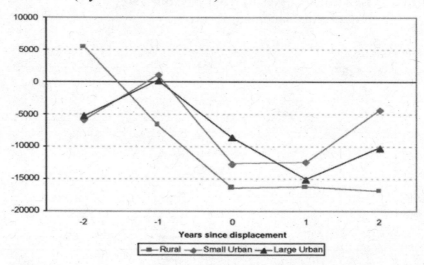

Source: Authors' calculations using SLID. See note to Figure 3.

Christine Neill and Tammy Schirle

Within this group of older displaced men, however, there are relatively larger proportional losses experienced by lower educated, rural workers.

Retrain

For those who are unable to quickly find another job and wish to return to the labour force, retraining may be a desirable option, especially if the skills the worker has acquired over their working life are not easily transferable to other available jobs. There has been an increasing focus on retraining as a way of making a worker more able to integrate into the labour market, and therefore more likely to remain in the labour force. This is reflected in recent policy developments — particularly in the TIOW program, which targets low-skill, older workers and requires training programs of some kind to be provided.

A period after job loss is in many ways an ideal time to undertake training. To the extent that an individual is unable to find a position, the opportunity cost associated with studying is lower. Indeed, individuals who are not currently employed are considerably more likely to be attending a formal program of education than those who are employed (Table 3).[14] However, this difference is less marked for older workers. For those between the ages of 55 and 64, being out of employment less than doubles the probability of engaging in formal education, while it almost triples the probability of studying among younger workers.

Older people are less likely to be studying, regardless of their labour force status. Less than 1% of currently employed individuals over the age of 55 are studying in an educational institution at any given time, compared with 6% of those aged 25 to 39. This pattern has been found in every study of the training or education decisions of adults, including Gower (1997) and Jacobson, LaLonde, and Sullivan (2003), as well as in evaluations of Human Resources and Social Development Canada's (HRSDC) training programs (HRDC, 1999). The consistency of this pattern provides extremely strong evidence to support the theoretical proposition that individuals perceive the

---

[14]This is not true of informal or on-the-job training, a great deal of which is employer provided and financed. Most government training programs in the face of displacement focus heavily on such "informal" programs. The TIOW, for instance, has a required component of help with job scarch, and another training component. The benefits of such programs in productivity and future earnings are not well studied.

Table 3: Percentage of Individuals Attending a Formal Education Program

(By age group and working status)

	Total	Currently Working	Not Currently Working and Last Worked		
			Less than a year ago	More than a year ago	Never
All individuals					
25–39	8.5	6.1	22.3	15.3	22.2
40–55	3.0	2.4	7.9	4.5	7.6
55–64	1.0	0.9	2.0	0.9	1.5
Males					
25–39	7.5	5.1	23.2	22.2	31.1
40–55	2.1	1.6	6.6	4.8	9.1
55–64	0.7	0.6	1.6	0.7	2.8
Females					
25–39	9.5	7.3	21.5	12.8	18.5
40–55	3.9	3.3	9.1	4.4	7.1
55–64	1.3	1.3	2.4	1.1	1.2

Source: Authors' calculations, Labour Force Survey, October 1997–2006.

lifetime benefits of undertaking training or education to be considerably lower when they are older than when they are younger.

It is possible that the reduced likelihood of undertaking education with age is a result of older workers leaving the labour force (retiring) in higher numbers than younger workers. A much larger proportion of the separations of 55–64-year-olds are self-identified as due to retirement — 38.7% of 55–64-year-olds who left their job in the past year and are not currently working said it was due to retirement, compared with 5% of 40–55-year-olds, and essentially no one under 40. However, of all 55–64-year-olds who report that they left work in the past 12 months due to retirement, 1.6% report undertaking some education. This compares with 2.2% of all those who left their job in the past 12 months and have not found a new position. While these are quite different rates, they do not suggest that retirement

Christine Neill and Tammy Schirle

(albeit self-reported retirement) is the main cause of relatively low education participation rates among individuals over the age of 55.

Figure 7 shows age-education participation profiles for four groups: those currently working, those who left a position in the past year, those who are not currently working and who last worked more than 12 months ago, and those who have never worked. These profiles control for characteristics including past education levels, sex, province of residence and year. For all groups, it is clear that older workers are less likely to undertake formal education programs than younger workers. This profile is quite consistent for males and females, though adult women are substantially more likely to undertake further education than are men. The exception to this is women who are not currently employed, and who were last employed over a year ago or who have never been employed. This is particularly true among older employed women, who have education participation rates more than twice as high as those of comparable men. Controlling for the presence of children

Figure 7: Effect of Age on the Likelihood of Studying Relative to 25–29-Year-Olds

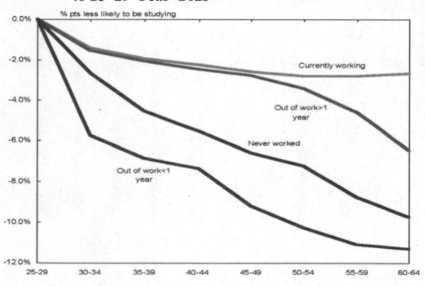

Note: Figures are regression coefficients on the probability of identifying as a student conditional on current employment status. Data are from the October Labour Force Surveys, 1997 to 2006. Regression models include fixed effects for year, province, level of education, and Canada's three largest Census Metropolitan Areas.

affects the female age-education participation profile slightly, but not the male profile.

It is also the case that higher income appears to be associated with a higher propensity to engage in training. Figure 8 shows the relationship between household income and an individual's participation in training by age group. Other than for those with incomes below $20,000, who are more likely to be undertaking full-time training and therefore to be working only part-time, higher income is associated with higher participation in training among all age groups. This relationship casts some doubt on the potential for universal training or education programs to reduce inequalities in educational outcomes that occur earlier in life.

Figure 8: Effect of Age and Income on the Likelihood of Undertaking Any Training

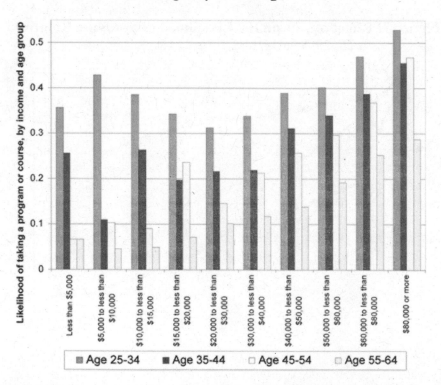

Source: Authors' calculations using the Adult Education and Training Survey.

Christine Neill and Tammy Schirle

We now turn to assessing the extent to which education might benefit older displaced workers. We address three questions. First, can education and training increase the incomes of older workers? Second, can education make up for lost earnings after displacement? Finally, to what extent can policy matter in the education decisions of older displaced workers?

Can education increase the income of older workers? There is considerable research interest at present in the question of the optimal time to provide education to individuals. James Heckman, in a series of papers, makes an argument that scarce education resources are best targeted to children of very young ages, in part because brain development in the early years means that early investments in learning are more efficient and contribute to improved learning later in life.[15] One might be tempted to draw a parallel and argue that among adults — those who are older are likely less quick to learn new skills than those who are younger.

However, there exists little evidence to support such a conclusion. Jacobson, LaLonde, and Sullivan (2003) find no evidence that workers over the age of 35 have less of a productivity boost from a particular study period than workers under the age of 35 — wage increases after a period of study are similar for the two groups. Zhang and Palameta (2006) (in the only Canadian study) show that there are short-run income benefits to older adults (defined as those over 35) from completing a postsecondary certificate. Completion of a college certificate after the age of 35 raises men's hourly wage by 7.6%, and income by 4.5%. On the other hand, there are no such benefits to women, and no benefits to those who do not complete a certificate. As expected, returns to completion of university qualifications are higher than the returns to receipt of a college certificate. While these income increases are about the same for older men as younger men, the returns to younger women are much larger than those for older women. It should be noted, then, that Zhang and Palameta (2006) find no income benefits for anyone completing less than one academic year of post-secondary schooling, and the income benefits they do find are likely well below 8% per year of study.[16]

---

[15]See, for example, Cunha and Heckman (2007) and Heckman (2006).

[16]Completion of a certificate likely takes more than one year. Zhang and Palameta (2006) are unable to examine the returns to a completed year of study, since the data are not sufficiently detailed to allow that.

None of this provides a strong indication that older adults acquire fewer skills while studying than do younger adults. However, there are two additional concerns that suggest training and education is not likely to help displaced workers recover to the point where they can be as well off after the displacement as before. First, the losses in income from displacement due to lost wages typically dwarf the potential benefits of even extended training and education. Second, the older a worker is at the time of displacement, the smaller is the likely length of time in the workforce, which significantly reduces the potential benefits of education.

Can education make up for lost earnings after displacement? LaLonde argues that the up-front spending required for retraining that replaces a substantial portion of a displaced worker's lost earnings is so large that "even if older displaced workers are able to acquire new skills as efficiently as younger persons, it is still the case that their incentives to participate in retraining are less, as are the benefits society receives from their retraining" (2007, p. 17). In what follows, we show calculations of the costs and benefits of undertaking education for displaced workers at several different ages, following LaLonde's (2007) approach.

As discussed earlier, conditional on tenure in a position, older men do not experience larger earnings losses than younger men. The estimates suggest that displacement causes a loss in annual earnings of around $11,000. That is more than a quarter of the average earnings of non-displaced workers. One academic year of education is typically estimated to increase earnings by around 10%. In order to make up for the lost earnings, then, an individual would have to train for at least three to four years.[17] So education and training are very unlikely to provide a practical solution for completely reversing the loss of income due to displacement, particularly for older workers for whom three or more years out of the workforce comprise a very substantial proportion of the remaining working life.

Table 4 provides some rough calculations of the cost of losing a job at various ages (accounting for loss of tenure), and the likely effect of education in raising lifetime incomes. This assumes a nine month training course, costing an individual $5,000 (equivalent to one academic year at a university). For the hypothetical displaced worker, this course would cost

---

[17]These figures are very similar to those in LaLonde (2007), despite using Canadian rather than US data.

Christine Neill and Tammy Schirle

Table 4: Costs and Benefits of Education for Older Displaced Workers

Individual characteristics				
Age	40	50	55	60
Tenure	6	16	21	26
Estimated cost of displacement				
Pre-displacement earnings	35,000	35,520	35,780	36,040
Post-displacement earnings	23,688	23,688	23,688	23,688
Years of working life left	25	15	10	5
Lifetime income lost	196,978	141,250	103,147	56,569
Estimated benefits of education				
Foregone earnings		17,800		
Cost		5,000		
Total cost		22,800		
Annual benefits ($)		2,400		
Discounted lifetime benefits	41,200	28,300	20,200	10,800
NPV (individual)	18,500	5,500	-2,600	-11,900
NPV (total, assume no externalities)	8,500	-4,500	-12,600	-21,900

Assumptions		
	Wages	
	Earnings at age 35	35,000
	Return to tenure	52
	Displacement cost	11,000
	Retirement age	65
	Discount rate	3%
	Effects of education	
	Cost to individual	5,000
	Government subsidy	10,000
	Length of time (yrs)	0.75
	Assumed rate of return	10%

Note: Return to tenure, displacement cost and earnings at age 35 are taken from Schirle (2007). The assumed rate of return of 10% to one academic year of study is at the upper range of the estimates of the benefits of education, and is used by LaLonde (2007). It is well above returns to certificates estimated by Zhang and Palameta (2006) for adult Canadians, particularly on a per year basis.

around $22,800 in lost income and direct costs.[18] Given a post-displacement income of $23,688, plus a 10% increase in salary due to one academic year of education, the lifetime income increase due to the training would only just cover the costs for a worker aged 50 at displacement, and would have negative returns for older workers. Note that this assumes rates of return to education of adult workers higher than those found by Zhang and Palameta (2006) or Jacobson, LaLonde, and Sullivan (2003). Unless there are substantial external benefits to the education, the social benefits are lower, reflecting subsidies to education implicit in the current system.[19]

The fact that a large upfront investment — in terms of both time and money — is required for retraining, then, makes it less viable as an alternative the older an individual becomes. This is reflected in the fact that individuals over the age of 50 are much less likely to be students.

Can policy make a difference? The social cost-benefit analysis is largely affected by the same considerations as the individual cost-benefit analysis. To the extent that there are any social benefits accruing to education, these are smaller the shorter is the future working life of the individual.[20] There are also, however, potential social benefits from individuals remaining in the labour force rather than retiring. If those individuals who receive additional education are less likely to retire, then there may be social benefits in terms of lower dependency ratio and lower public pension payments.

However, for the social cost-benefit calculation to differ markedly from the individual calculation, these effects would likely have to be very large. Unfortunately, there is no information available on the effects of training programs on the probability of retiring from the labour force.

---

[18]If the individual has no alternative job available, then the calculation of the costs of education is lower.

[19]Conservatively, we assume that the total cost of nine months of education is $15,000 — that is, that the government covers two-thirds of the cost, and the individual one-third. Government subsidies to education come principally from direct subsidies to universities and tuition and education tax credits.

[20]There are some social benefits of education that are not directly related to labour force participation — including possible health and citizenship benefits — but there is no evidence of the effect of adult education on these external effects. Since most of the retraining programs focus directly on labour market outcomes, we do not consider these further here.

Christine Neill and Tammy Schirle

In addition, while policy initiatives often target workers over the age of 55, most studies of education and training decisions of older workers define "older" as being over the age of 35. Clearly, it is not reasonable to expect that the lifetime benefits of training and education will be the same for a 55-year-old and a 35-year-old, even if there is no loss of learning ability among older relative to younger workers. The statistics above show that individuals certainly do not consider this to be true.

There is nonetheless interest in providing government assistance to individuals who have lost their jobs in the form of retraining. The TIOW is such a program, which is intended to provide employment search assistance and short-term general training programs to older individuals who formerly worked in a declining industry.[21] The TIOW does not focus on formal retraining so much as basic skill upgrading programs. It is possible that these have larger returns per unit of time than formal academic programs, and may be less costly. These programs may therefore be economically worthwhile where formal education programs are not. It does appear that job search assistance in particular has payoffs in finding employment, although not necessarily high wage employment. LaLonde (2007) argues that re-employment services are less likely to aid displaced workers in the long run than training, because the latter has effects on long-term wages that the former does not. For other forms of training and assistance, however, the evidence is even murkier. Zhang and Palameta (2006) found that incomes typically did not rise after undertaking formal education unless it led to the receipt of a certificate.

To summarize, undertaking formal education is unlikely to be beneficial to individuals over the age of 50, given the shorter time period available to recoup the costs of education. More basic skills upgrading programs are less costly; however, the chances that such training programs could make up for a drop in income of one-quarter to one-third of expected earnings are quite small.

---

[21]While the TIOW is described as a retraining program, targeted at older vulnerable workers, it has several characteristics that suggest it is more targeted at vulnerable communities. In particular, workers from large municipalities who are displaced from their jobs are ineligible for assistance.

Retirement

Given the wage losses faced by older displaced workers and the relatively short time period remaining in the labour force to enjoy the benefits of retraining, many workers may find the retirement option relatively attractive. Consistent with the evidence from Gray and Finnie (2007), several US studies have found lower employment rates among older displaced workers. Chan and Stevens (2001) use the Health and Retirement Study to examine the effects of involuntary job loss on employment outcomes for workers age 50 and above in the United States. Hazard model estimates indicated that even four years after a job loss, the displaced workers' employment rates are 20 percentage points lower than their non-displaced counterparts. They suggest this reflects both a reduction in the rates of return to employment after displacement and elevated rates of exit from post-displacement jobs.

The lower re-employment rates may simply reflect a lack of job prospects for displaced older workers. Hirsch, Macpherson, and Hardy (2000) examine the age structure of hires into different occupations and finds that employment opportunities for older individuals are restricted. Maestas and Li (2006) use a sample of non-workers from the US Health and Retirement Study to examine the job search behaviour and employment outcomes of older workers. They find that only half of older searchers successfully attain jobs. Furthermore their results suggest that 13% of older job searchers become discouraged workers.

The characteristics of older displaced workers who do not return to the labour force are summarized in the third column of Table 1. These individuals are slightly older than the workers who return to full-time employment following displacement. They are not very different in terms of their education levels but, perhaps surprisingly, are less likely to have had a pension plan available in their pre-displacement job. They are also more likely to be female. This might suggest that these displaced workers are "forced" into retirement as discouraged workers rather than choosing this as a most desirable option. The displaced workers who leave the labour force appear to be worse off than their counterparts who voluntarily leave full-time employment for retirement. (Their characteristics are summarized in the last column of Table 1.) These workers are among the higher-educated workers and are much more likely to have left public sector jobs with pension benefits.

Whatever the circumstances under which they decided to enter retirement, displaced workers who take this option will have to stretch a smaller amount of retirement wealth over a longer-than-expected period of time. Several past Canadian policy initiatives — most notably the Program for Older Worker Assistance (POWA) — were designed to provide income support during the gap between displacement and retirement for certain older workers.

Policy Issues

Policy Background

For at least the past 20 years, Canadian governments have been concerned about the plight of older displaced workers. In the past they have implemented several programs specifically targeted at that group. This largely reflects the concern that "among *older displaced workers*, the financial repercussions are progressively worse, the older the workers are when they are laid off" (HRDC, 1999, p. 4).

Canadian government policies with regard to older displaced workers have passed through a number of different phases. POWA was introduced in 1986 at a time when unemployment rates had been high and long-term unemployment rates were high on the policy agenda. The aim of the program appears to have been largely to ensure that displaced older workers were not in financial hardship in the years before they became eligible for pension benefits, and evaluations suggest it successfully achieved that goal. It also potentially helped ease unemployment among younger and prime age workers, by reducing the number of older workers seeking employment.

Clearly, such a program makes sense in times of high unemployment. Its abolition in 1997 was undoubtedly partly due to evaluations that had shown that labour force participation rates of those who claimed POWA were half those of other older workers who had lost jobs but were not eligible for POWA. While this was a key advantage of the program in 1987, it was a disadvantage by 1997 when unemployment rates were falling and older workers were a substantially larger and rapidly increasing share of the labour force. Furthermore concerns about increases in the dependency ratio and fiscal sustainability of public pension programs were on the rise.

Programs established during the 1990s have focused more on the reintegration of displaced workers — among them older workers — into the labour market. The Employability Improvement Project (EIP) was instituted in 1991, and was funded through the EI system. It provided employment development services, including some training elements, and was found to increase weeks worked and annual earnings among older workers (HRDC, 1999). Assessments of such programs typically find that reintegration is facilitated by job search assistance. While it does appear this increases the probability of re-employment, however, there is little evidence that it can make up for lost wages (LaLonde, 1995).

Currently, with unemployment rates at a 30-year low, more emphasis is being placed on training older displaced workers — the recent TIOW being one example. This appears to be in part a result of an increasing concern that slower overall population growth and the increasing share of older workers in the population mean that future increases in the economy's human capital stock are likely to come through education of the current adult population, rather than increasing levels of education among the current youth cohort. This is somewhat odd, coming at a time when the gap between education levels of older workers and those of younger workers is closer than at any time in the past 30 years (see Figure 9).

Do We Need Policies Directly Targeted at Displaced Older Workers?

It is somewhat uncomfortable to suggest that age should play a role in determining government assistance to displaced workers. There are three reasons why this might be important, however. First, older displaced workers themselves as a group systematically choose different options from younger displaced workers — they are more likely to retire and less likely to take advantage of training and education programs. These decisions likely do not reflect simple "barriers" to reintegration into the labour force, so much as they reflect different profiles of lifetime benefits and costs from each path. In this sense, any policy designed to reintegrate displaced workers is likely to have different outcomes for individuals of different ages. Policies targeted at income replacement may, for instance, give younger workers time to find better paying jobs, but provide older workers with a financial bridge to retirement.[22]

---

[22]Of course, not all older workers, nor younger workers, are the same. Some 60-year-olds may be planning to remain employed on some basis for a further 20 years, and some 50-year-olds may wish to retire tomorrow. Any policy evaluation will mostly pick up on average effects. Equally, however, policies have to be designed taking into account a typical response, even when potentially allowing for heterogeneous responses.

Figure 9a: Education Levels of the Canadian Population
(By age group, 1976–1980)

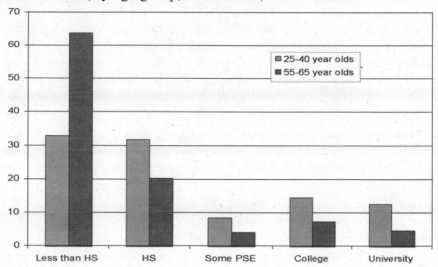

Source: Authors' calculations, Labour Force Survey, various years.

Figure 9b: Education Levels of the Canadian Population
(By age group, 2001–2006)

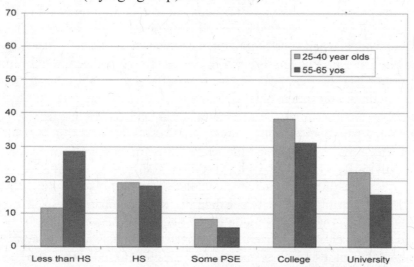

Source: Authors' calculations, Labour Force Survey, various years.

Remain, Retrain or Retire   *303*

Second, the fact that public pensions are available to older workers and those pensions may cause some distortions to older workers' labour market behaviour (see Milligan and Schirle, 2006) makes these older workers different from younger workers. Policy development should account for this and may need to account for those aspects of pension policies that lower labour force participation.

Third, there is a general perception that older workers face losses of a different order of magnitude than younger workers, as suggested by HRDC (1999). There is some dispute as to whether this is the case, however. Consistent with the evidence presented in earlier sections, LaLonde (2007) notes that the per period cost of displacement is not necessarily higher for older workers, since younger workers experience income losses almost as large as those of older workers, and these income losses are also highly persistent. Thus, it is possible that the lifetime loss from job loss is higher for someone who loses that job at age 40, with potentially 25 more years of income earning potential, than someone who loses that job at age 60.

What policies are then ideal in helping older workers adjust after displacement? The answer depends on whether the key goal is to ensure they are reintegrated into the labour market, or whether the goal is to alleviate the personal financial hardship. In general, it is difficult to design policy that would simultaneously achieve both goals. Rather, trade-offs are expected.

Policies designed to help reintegrate older workers into the labour market can scarcely expect to make up for the wages lost due to displacement, even if they incorporate a substantial training and education component. The existing evidence suggests that although some older workers may wish to retrain and begin a new type of job, the vast majority do not consider this a worthwhile investment. Any effort to make training or education a central component of a program is unlikely to be effective, largely due to low interest in retraining among older workers themselves.

Policies implemented to reduce financial hardship have tended to reduce labour force participation rates among older displaced workers. A policy option which may help to boost incomes while minimizing labour supply disincentive effects (associated with past income support policies) is a wage subsidy scheme. In such a scheme, displaced workers would be paid a percentage of the difference between their pre-displacement wages and their post-displacement wages. LaLonde (2007) has suggested such a scheme, funded by payments from currently employed individuals in a way similar to unemployment insurance systems. He argues that for displaced workers, the majority of the costs are not due to wage losses during the short period in which they are typically out of work, but longer run losses associated with lower lifetime wages.[23] Since such a scheme would not make payments to individuals who were not employed, it would encourage, rather than discourage, continued labour force attachment. Studies of the wage subsidy element of Canada's Self-Sufficiency Project show that financial incentives given to welfare recipients can result in both higher incomes and increased labour force participation, especially in the short run (Michalopoulos, Robins, and Card, 2002).

Such a scheme would have its disadvantages, however. First, it would be quite costly to introduce. Second, there are likely to be some distortions to individual decisions on the type of job taken — both pre- and post-displacement. It would constitute an effective transfer from individuals employed in industries that are relatively stable to individuals employed in industries that are relatively unstable. In part, this is an advantage — it means that workers are not discouraged from working in industries that are likely to be in flux, and thus it may encourage dynamism in the broader economy. On the other hand, it may also discourage adjustment in some ways — workers may, for instance, choose to stay at a low paying job in their local community rather than taking a more lucrative job at some distance.[24] Equally, such wage subsidy schemes would reduce the incentive for younger displaced workers to engage in education and training. Indeed, any action which entails upfront costs to achieve longer run wage increases is likely discouraged in the presence of a wage subsidy scheme. Although LaLonde intends this program to principally benefit workers who are middle-aged when they lose their jobs, rather than older workers, it may be less distorting if eligibility is restricted to relatively older workers.

Finally, it is also important to ensure that policy measures account for provisions found in public and private pension schemes. If, for example, older displaced workers are encouraged to take on part-time employment to supplement their earnings, it is important to recognize that this may hamper their eligibility for pensions. A wage subsidy scheme may have important long-term effects on pension eligibility, for instance, if public pensions are

---

[23]Note that this is not an income subsidy, so would not be expected to lead to an increase in individuals choosing to work on a part-time rather than full-time basis.

[24]For instance, a displaced worker in New Brunswick may be less reluctant to move to Alberta for employment if a wage subsidy is available for a relatively low paying local job.

only based on earned income. Here, the wage subsidy scheme may reduce pension eligibility for affected individuals in the long run.

Conclusion

In this paper, we have shown that the costs of displacement for older workers are not substantially greater than the costs of displacement for younger workers. Both younger and older workers are likely to experience large and persistent earnings losses following job displacement. Because older workers have a shorter expected remaining working life, their responses to displacement will systematically involve a higher retirement rate and lower rate of participation in training and education.

In the context of an aging workforce, developing a policy response that will ensure the labour market is able to adjust to economic shocks and encourage older workers to remain active in the labour force is a complex task. There is clearly some tension between the two policy goals of improving the incomes of older displaced workers and maintaining their labour force participation. In this paper, we have focused on two possible options: providing income support or education and training programs. Each has disadvantages. Pure income support policies can have serious disincentive effects, and when used in the past have led to lower labour force participation among older workers. Education and training programs might at first glance appear to be promising, since they may increase the flexibility of the labour force and could improve the productivity and incomes of older workers. However, even if substantial education and training is undertaken, it is not likely to be able to make up for the earnings losses associated with displacement, especially once foregone wages are taken into account.

Perhaps the most interesting compromise policy option is a wage subsidy — whether paid directly to workers, or to employers of older displaced workers. There is some evidence from Canada's Self-Sufficiency Project that employment subsidies could support continuing labour force attachment at the same time as they raise incomes. However, the effects of wage subsidies on older workers, who have the option of retirement that is not as readily available to younger workers, are less well understood and deserve further attention.

References

Chan, S. and A.H. Stevens. 2001. "Job Loss and Employment Patterns of Older Workers", *Journal of Labor Economics* 19(2), 484–521.

Cunha, F. and J. Heckman. 2007. "Formulating, Identifying and Estimating the Technology of Cognitive and Noncognitive Skill Formation", *Journal of Human Resources*, forthcoming.

Gower, D. 1997. "Facing the Future: Adults Who Go Back to School", *Perspectives*, Autumn. Ottawa: Statistics Canada.

Gray, D. and R. Finnie. 2007. "Displacement of Older Workers: Re-Employment, Hastened Retirement, Disability, or Other Destinations?" CLSRN Working Paper No. 20. Vancouver: Canadian Labour Market and Skills Researcher Network, UBC.

Heckman, J. 2006. "Skill Formation and the Economics of Investing in Disadvantaged Children", *Science* 312(5782), 1900–1902.

Hirsch, B.T., D.A. Macpherson, and M.A. Hardy. 2000. "Occupational Age Structure and Access for Older Workers", *Industrial and Labor Relations Review* 53(3), 401–418.

Human Resources and Development Canada (HRDC). 1999. *Older Worker Adjustment Programs: Lessons Learned.* Evaluation and Data Development and Strategic Policy. Ottawa: HRDC.

Jacobson, L., R.J. LaLonde, and D. Sullivan. 1993. "Earnings Losses of Displaced Workers", *American Economic Review* 83(4), 685–709.

_____. 2003. "Should we Teach Old Dogs New Tricks? The Impact of Community College Retraining on Older Displaced Workers". Working Paper No. 2003–25. Chicago: Federal Reserve Bank of Chicago.

Jovanovic, B. 1979. "Job Matching and the Theory of Turnover", *Journal of Political Economy* 82(5), 972–990.

LaLonde, R.J. 1995. "The Promise of Public Sector-Sponsored Training Programs", *Journal of Economic Perspectives* 9(2), 149–168.

_____. 2007. "The Case for Wage Insurance". Council Special Report No. 30. NY: Council on Foreign Relations.

Maestas, N. and X. Li. 2006. "Discouraged Workers? Job Search Outcomes of Older Workers". Retirement Research Centre Working Paper No. 2006–133. Ann Arbor, MI: University of Michigan.

Michalopoulos, C., P.K. Robins, and D. Card. 2002. "When Financial Incentives Pay for Themselves: Evidence From a Randomized Social Experiment for Welfare Recipients", *Journal of Public Economics* 89, 5–29.

Milligan, K. and T. Schirle. 2006. "Public Pensions and Retirement: International Evidence in the Canadian Context". HRSDC-IC-SSHRC Skills Research Initiative Working Paper Series No. 2006–A–13. Ottawa: HRSDC.

Morissette, R., X. Zhang, and M. Frenette. 2007. "Earnings Losses of Displaced Workers: Canadian Evidence From a Large Administrative Database on Firm

Closures and Mass Layoffs". Analytical Studies Branch Research Paper Series Cat. No. 11F0019MIE — No. 291. Ottawa: Statistics Canada.

Rowe, G. and H. Nguyen. 2002. "Older Workers and the Labour Market", *Perspectives on Labour and Income* (Catalogue No. 75–001–XIE) 3(12), 23–26.

Schirle, T. 2007. "Earnings Losses of Displaced Older Workers: Accounting for the Retirement Option". CLSRN Working Paper No. 22. Vancouver: Canadian Labour Market and Skills Researcher Network, UBC.

Zhang, X. and B. Palameta. 2006. "Participation in Adult Schooling and its Impact on Earnings in Canada". Analytical Studies Branch Research Paper Series, Cat. No. 11F0019MIE — No. 276. Ottawa: Statistics Canada.

Summary of Discussion

One participant raised the issue of employer preferences for older workers. One issue we haven't heard about so far are the preferences and perspectives of younger workers. One could envision a scenario whereby the implementation of policies to accommodate demands of older workers could create some tension with younger workers, who are facing their own challenges. This underscores the importance of introducing policies to accommodate the preferences of all workers, young and old. **Robert Clark** responded that over the years, he has done a number of papers on trying to get a handle on the optimal age structure of a firm. It turned out to be a difficult question to answer. It depends on workers' lifetime productivity patterns; and it depends on lifetime costs and the role of people who are in the workplace. But what you can show is that the longer people stay on, the promotional prospects for younger workers slow down — whether that's good or bad for the society or for the company is unclear.

Syed Ahsan asked a question of Bill Scarth with respect to modeling a longer working life. As population growth falls, the working life can lengthen. Would this have an effect on savings? If savings were to fall with a longer working life, how would that affect the result of the model? It may have the results of the physical capital going one way and the human capital going the other way. **Bill Scarth** responded that there *are* indeed competing effects, and they both are in the analytics. From a macro point of view, if there are more people retired, there's simply less human capital and therefore, relatively speaking, more physical capital around. So simple demand and supply says there'll be higher rents on the now scarcer human capital. That should be an incentive for people to invest more in human capital, and that would be a cushioning response of society. On the other hand, at the individual level, if a person is expecting to live a longer time in retirement and not collect the returns on the investment in human capital, there's a lower incentive to invest in human capital. Both those competing effects are in that little expression "m" called "messy term".

Richard Disney commented that he did some work a few years ago, on the age composition of occupational hires. One of the most striking things you observe is not really surprising, but it may be a big problem for displaced workers. As you move up the age profile, the fraction of occupations that hire becomes more and more concentrated. In other words, pretty much every occupation hires young people, but as you move up towards 40-year-olds and 50-year-olds, the fraction of occupations that make any hires of older workers is quite limited. So hires become concentrated in fewer occupations. That would seem to be an important issue relevant to thinking about retraining and displacement of older workers. **Tammy Schirle** responded that there is evidence that older individuals are limited in terms of their occupation choices. And that probably does have a lot to do with the fact that in many jobs and in many occupations, there's a lot of on-the-job training that has to go on before a person is fully productive and earning what would be their full wage. This should clearly be further researched.

Richard Disney also offered a couple of HR-type observations. One is that phased retirement sounds really good in principle, but one of the things that seems tricky about moves into part-time or phased retirement or part-time work is that the job definition has to be established. The amount of output you get from people varies by quite a large amount. Some people can enter a phased retirement without moving out of their full-time position at all. Therefore, the phased retirement is partly related to the nature of the job and the nature of the variability of the output you get out of different workers.

A second observation is that HR policies may reflect the preferences of senior executives and hence the organizational behaviour of CEOs or people at the top, and whether they want to push workers out to make room for their own appointments. It's quite convenient for them to have DB plans that force people out at what seems to us, as retirement economists, a very early age because they want to transform and have newer, younger people in who are younger than themselves, who will do what they're told, and back them up and so on.

Malcolm Hamilton noted that in the private sector in Canada, when you sit down and talk to organizations about phased retirement, there are two obstacles that almost always arise. The first is they have a bulge in the workforce for the baby boomers. The fact is, introducing phased retirement, at most, shifts the leading edge of the exodus. You don't, by introducing phased retirement, prevent the boomers from retiring. At best, you shift it along a couple of years. You blur the leading edge and you blur the trailing edge and shift it a couple of years as well. But when they look at it, the bottom line is that there's still a period out there where they're going to lose a lot of workers. And the phased retirement doesn't eliminate that; it only shifts it a little. So the question is, what's the advantage of introducing phased retirement if there is still going to be this problem? Maybe they should just deal with it rather than spending a lot of time shifting it down the curve. The second problem organizations quickly run up against is that they almost invariably conclude that they want the majority of potentially eligible workers to retire as early as possible. But there is a minority — and it can be a sizeable minority — that they're interested in retaining. So they're almost never interested in an indiscriminate phased retirement program open to all workers for all time. They're much more interested in something that's more narrowly targeted at the people they actually want to retain. This very much inclines them in the private sector towards the retire-and-selectively-rehire model as opposed to, let's tell everybody we've got phased retirement and see who stays around. **Robert Clark** agreed that each company will have to evaluate their own policies and their own production and cost functions and figure out what works best for them. He thinks that overall, for society and for many industries, the desire will be to retain workers to a later age, and phased retirement will be an integral part of those policies.

John Kesselman raised the question of what do we know of the possible causes of the typical large drop in earnings of displaced workers. He suggested three possible explanations. One could be the loss of specific human capital, specific to the previous job or employer. Another reason could be the loss of deferred compensation. That is where employees may have been paid less than their productivity early in their tenure with an employer and they're being overpaid, in some sense, later in their career to command their loyalty and diligent work with the employer. The third one might be a form of age discrimination related to any future employers' perceptions of ability based on age or perhaps based on an objective calculation of the costs of hiring and training for someone who will not be there for many years based on age. Being able to distinguish and establish the relative importance of these alternative causes is key because they may have different policy implications.

Leroy Stone questioned the notion that you should simply set aside the access to training and education of the older ages because it's not worth it. When you look at the benefits from training from the perspective of promotion of active aging, he wonders whether the concept of returns to human capital shouldn't be broadened so that they aren't simply a matter of how much output or how much compensation you get in return for the cost of the education or training. Might the returns be defined in a broader way, in terms of promoting dimensions of active aging and general quality of life at older age that don't get measured very well within the standard concept of returns to training and education?

Chapter VI

Panel on Risk and Pension Investment Strategies

Longevity Risk and How to Manage It Effectively

Malcolm Hamilton

Longevity is not like other risks where one starts by asking whether the risk can be avoided. In the case of longevity, this may be viewed as an insensitive question — in particular when addressing an audience of seniors. When one talks about the risk that seniors might live too long, seniors have a hard time appreciating the problem or why anyone would worry about it.

In this paper I will look at longevity risk from three different perspectives. I will talk about defined-benefit (DB) pension plans which, as David Dodge wrote, have an exposure to beneficiaries living longer than expected. I will then discuss how individuals view longevity risk. Less than half of our workforce participate in DB pension plans; so what do the other half do when they get to retirement and have to deal with the "risk" of living too long? I will then address longevity risk from the government's perspective. Since I have never worked in government this will be an outsider's view of how government *should* look at longevity risk.

Defined-Benefit Pension Plans

Longevity risk has become a big issue for UK pension plans while remaining a small issue for pension plans in Canada and the United States.

Why is this? Is it because Brits are living longer than Canadians and Americans? I don't think so. Is it because Canadian and American actuaries have done a better job than British actuaries in preparing pension plans for longevity risk? I do not see any evidence of this. Is it because British actuaries have done a better job than Canadian and American actuaries in figuring out how long people are likely to live? Quite possibly.

Perhaps the most important factor is the decline of the DB pension plan, which at this point is more advanced in the United Kingdom than it is in Canada. In ongoing pension plans, investment risk dominates longevity risk. The risk of poor stock market returns or declining interest rates is so large that longevity risk does not appear on the radar screen. But when plan sponsors start looking at pension plans as arrangements that might wind up in the foreseeable future, they often reduce or eliminate investment risk and the longevity risk comes to the fore. So if Canada follows the United Kingdom, our DB pension plans will begin to see themselves as entities that might wind up in the not-too-distant future and longevity risk will become as important in Canada as it is in the United Kingdom.

There are two quite distinct wind-up risks. The first is the risk that your pension plan's mortality differs from the average. Most pension plans calculate their wind-up liabilities assuming that, if they had to annuitize their pensions, they would get standard rates. Some groups have much better than average mortality — universities, for example. As a rule, they make no provision for "super standard" mortality in estimating their wind-up liabilities and they may be both disappointed and surprised by the cost of actually discharging the wind-up obligations of their pension plans.

The other major risk is the unknown rate of future mortality improvement. Actuaries use a standard improvement scale called the AA scale. It is not clear where it came from or how reliable it is. It probably underestimates, in particular for women, the rate of mortality improvement that we can expect. Most pension plans either make no allowance for mortality improvement or they make a partial allowance based on the questionable AA scale. As soon as they try to persuade an insurance company to take the liability from them, they discover that insurance companies make a full allowance for future mortality improvement. This can materially increase the cost of winding up the pension plan.

I know of one large Canadian public sector pension plan that was able to collect 35 years of pensioner mortality experience. This was examined by experts at the University of Waterloo. To make a long story short, the rate of improvement in mortality was faster than the AA scale and the pension liabilities will be increased by 3% to 5% as a consequence. In a world where your annual investment gain or loss is 8% of the pension fund, a one-time 3% to 5% increase in liabilities is manageable. But if you are an organization trying to figure out what it's going to cost to wind up your pension plan, an unexpected 5% increase in the cost is somewhere between inconvenient and intolerable as the organizations most likely to be winding up their pension plans are the organizations least able to absorb unexpected cost increases.

I should note that the cost of winding up a pension plan is particularly sensitive to rates of mortality improvement at advanced ages — 85 to 95. These are often the ages at which the improvement scales are the least reliable — we just do not have decades of reliable experience for elderly female pensioners. Even if we did, we cannot be confident that past rates of improvement are good predictors of future rates of improvement. Consequently, it may be some time before the full extent of the longevity risk to which DB pension plans are exposed is fully appreciated.

Finally, even if a Canadian pension plan made a heroic effort to measure and understand longevity risk, there is not much that it can do about it. Until pension plans start winding up in larger numbers there will not be an efficient annuity market in Canada. Nobody knows what would happen today if a pension plan needed to buy $1 billion of annuities, in particular $1 billion of indexed annuities. The price is unlikely to be attractive.

Individual Retirement Savers

Individuals do not know when they are going to die. They hope it is going to be a very long time from now. Some people may worry about outliving their money, but most worry more about dying young and having their money outlive them.

Low-income seniors derive most of their income from government programs. I suspect that the bottom half of the retired population (measured by income) has a very large percentage of its income coming from Canada Pension Plan (CPP), Old Age Security (OAS), Guaranteed Income Supplement (GIS), etc. The benefits are payable for life and they are fully inflation protected. There is little longevity exposure for this group. The federal government and the Canada/Quebec Pension Plans underwrite the longevity risks.

At the other end of the income spectrum we find the affluent seniors. Affluent seniors often realize soon after retiring that they are unlikely to need all of their savings. They continue to save. They give away money. They are very comfortable passing longevity risk to their heirs. If they live long, their heirs inherit less. If they die young their heirs inherit more. This is probably how it should be and affluent seniors are unlikely to spend much time managing longevity risk on behalf of their heirs.

The people in the middle are the ones who should be buying annuities to manage longevity risk. But they do not. They are not interested in annuities. They would rather live frugally. To manage longevity risk they assume that they will live a very long time. They do not encroach on capital. They do not sell their houses. They just live modest lives. Often their net worths increase until the day they die. They sense, accurately in my view, that even if they do live into their 90s or 100s they are unlikely to spend much at these ages. So middle-income Canadians manage longevity risk in the traditional Canadian way. They live frugally. They err on the side of caution. The older they get the less they spend. And when they die, they leave surprisingly large estates.

Government

Government has many longevity exposures. It is the sponsor of the country's largest, richest employee pension plans. It has an even larger exposure to longevity as the payer or guarantor of social security pensions. It is a tax collector and it is the underwriter of the health-care system. From the government's perspective, a long working life is a good thing; a long retired life is a bad thing. Working people are sources of funds and retired people are users of funds. If people live longer and work longer, public finances are not at risk. But if people live longer without working longer or, worse still, if people live longer and work less, governments will be under pressure.

Canadians are living longer, but do they live the extra years as young Canadians or as old Canadians? Are we adding years to our youth, to our old age, or both? The assumption that the boomers make, and are encouraged to make, is that if people are living five years longer then they must be young five years longer. While it is easy to understand why aging boomers want to believe this, evidence in support of this conclusion is hard to find.

Demographers are beginning to make a distinction between life expectancy and healthy life expectancy. It is easy to measure life expectancy, but it is hard to measure healthy life expectancy without making difficult judgements about when people's health deteriorates. A UK study looking at the period between 1981 and 2001 concluded that healthy life expectancies were increasing at about half the rate of life expectancies. The relationship between the two is important. If life expectancies increase by five years and healthy life expectancies increase by five years, it is not unreasonable to think that the retirement age should increase by five years. Population aging then becomes a solvable problem, albeit solvable by doing some things that are politically unpopular. On the other hand, if life expectancies increase by five years and healthy life expectancies remain the same, it will be difficult to increase the retirement age by five years. If people are living longer as sick old people, it will be difficult to extend working lives and population aging will not be solvable by simply encouraging people to retire later.

I attend many meetings where people assert, axiomatically, that the solution to population aging is to tie the retirement age to life expectancies in some obvious way. With due respect, it is not that simple. The age at which you die says little about the age up to which you can reasonably be expected to hold a job or the age up to which you can reasonably be expected to find a job if you have the misfortune of being unemployed. The assumption that increasing the retirement age solves all problems is, I fear, a dangerous over-simplification.

Pension Plan Investment Strategies by Major Pension Plans in Canada

Sterling Gunn

I think most everyone here is familiar with the Canada Pension Plan (CPP). So here I will discuss briefly the objective of the CPP Investment Board (CPPIB), the organization charged with investing CPP funds. I will talk about some of the choices that we are confronted with in developing our investment strategy, how we hold ourselves accountable while pursuing our investment strategy, and how we measure outcomes and success.

The objectives of the CPPIB are clearly set out in its enabling legislation: to maximize returns, without undue risk of loss, having regard for the factors influencing the funding of the CPP. The Stewards initially set the CPPIB to pursue a passive investment strategy, investing in public market indexes to harvest market returns.

There is an alternative mandate, another stylized choice, to be active managers extracting excess returns out of the marketplace over and above the passive returns that are available in an index. That is the choice we have made as an organization. You can think about what led to that choice, and I'll get into that in a few moments. But I think fundamentally what we are saying is that we feel confident enough that we can add value over and above the passive alternative that was available to the fund stewards ten years ago.

Let me compare these two strategies. A low-cost, passive strategy harvests returns from the market place — you need not be particularly knowledgeable about the markets to do that. The alternative strategy is trying to add value relative to the passive strategy, which requires skill. We made the choice to build an organization that maximizes the potential of our strategic advantages through our own skills and those of our partners. We chose not to be simply a set of deep pockets where others use our assets to capture excess returns. We have chosen to apply our skills, and those of our partners, to capture additional value for our fund.

We have developed a four-tiered investment strategy. The first tier is a passive strategy reflecting the risk-and-return appetites of the stewards, represented by a reference portfolio expected to harvest the returns needed to fulfill our mandate. This reference portfolio provides our stewards with a point of comparison. So at any time, you can look at the reference portfolio and say, that could have done the job; How are we doing compared to that? The reference portfolio is a critical piece of the strategy, because its existence acknowledges we are active managers tasked with out-performing the reference portfolio.

Once we accept the fact that we are active managers, the question is, where are we going to find that additional value? Can we create that additional value efficiently, more efficiently than the returns that are generated by the reference portfolio? There are a number of alternatives available to us. Remember that the reference portfolio is a low-cost strategy involving very, very liquid assets, earning whatever returns the market will give. We then build on top of that and say, there are other opportunities, less liquid asset classes, strategies that may require skill in order to capture additional value. We refer to the less liquid asset classes, those not explicitly included in the reference portfolio, as "better beta" asset classes.

For example, for the passive reference portfolio, you might invest in a combination of a few low-cost indexes such as the S&P 500, or the TSX or a bond index. There are other asset classes where you need to work to become a little more familiar with them, assets like real estate, or infrastructure. You cannot just buy these assets readily in the marketplace, and yet you expect they will improve your portfolio through diversification and additional returns. These are the "better beta" opportunities we seek as part of our value adding strategy.

Over and above better beta, we look for active investment strategies, investment strategies that require skill. To be effective you need some advantages in the marketplace, advantages you can lever through skill to extract additional value from the market.

These, then, are the first three components of our investment strategy: a reference portfolio, to which we compare and measure our actual value-added and the risks that we are taking. Then we add better beta opportunities, the asset classes that we think will provide additional risk-adjusted returns. And finally we look for alpha opportunities, strategies that require skill to add additional value.

Why would we go through all this effort? Why would we sit down and claim we are going to add value? Because these activities can improve the sustainability of the CPP. If you review the chief actuary's work and look at his analysis, additional returns earned by the CPPIB *do* contribute to the sustainability of the CPP. Every year the chief actuary estimates the steady state contribution rate and compares it to the legislated contribution rate. He deems the plan sustainable so long as the steady state rate does not exceed the legislated rate.

By adding value, we help lower the steady state contribution rate. It is a relatively simple exercise in theory; but complicated in execution. Based on the chief actuary's analysis, 50 basis points of excess returns over a long sustained period reduce the steady state contribution rate by roughly 25 basis points. How this additional value might be used is an entirely different question. The key thing is that directionally and materially, the value added makes some difference.

We believe we have a number of competitive advantages. Some of these advantages are structural, and some of them are choices that we have made. Our anticipated steady influx of cash over the next decade means we can make very long-term commitments to the marketplace. The OCA estimates fund flows will be net positive until about 2019, or roughly ten years. This means we have a patient pool of capital and can invest in relatively illiquid asset classes such as in real estate, infrastructure and other long-term commitments. This long-term commitment has real value for the partners that we deal with in the marketplace. Not everyone has that advantage. Other funds may have to maintain a more liquid balance sheet and be less able to make such long-term commitments.

The other structural advantage is the certainty of our assets. As a mandated, contributory plan, we have a pretty clear idea of when money will be arriving for the next 15 to 20 years, and the size of our asset base. And we can lever that certainty by considering commitments of a size that most organizations cannot make. And yet those commitments will not dominate our portfolio. We currently have around $120 billion worth of assets. The chief actuary forecasts that we will have roughly $250 billion in another eight years, and about $380 billion by about the year 2021. So it is possible for us to make what appear to be large investments today and not have them dominate our portfolio in the future.

We have also made some choices about how we will manage our organization. One important choice for us is a total portfolio approach, a top-down approach. You can contrast that with some other organizations, which may choose to give X dollars to one asset class and another amount to another asset class. And not a lot of work may go into figuring out how those things come together, which is ultimately what you have to do to figure out if you are efficiently funding your plan. Our choice has been more top-down, so when we look at investment strategies and at asset classes, we are always asking: What is the marginal contribution to risk and return to the total portfolio? Because we know it is the total portfolio that ultimately drives the performance of the fund.

The other advantage we have, because of our size, is that we are an attractive to world-class partners. They could be attracted to us just because we are a large pool of funds. And in fact, we could be a partner of choice simply because they could take money out of our deep pockets. But we are building our organization so that we will be a *smart* partner and make sure that the value created comes to the fund and is shared with the fund. But working with us remains an attractive proposition to the better players in the marketplace.

Finally, we are also building our culture — a culture of accountability built around integrity, high performance and partnership. We believe these principles are also advantages. Those words may sound superficial, but when you try to live and breathe them every day, it has a material effect. Our organization is attractive because these principles are an integral part of our culture.

I have talked about the total portfolio approach. One further thing that's related to this approach — related directly to risk and the investments' risks — is that you cannot rely on the simple labels that are applied to asset classes. This may sound obvious, but people often throw around words like *infrastructure* and *real estate* and *equity* and *debt*, and you might think, that's 90% of the story, we're done, we can all go home. But the reality is, you need to look through these labels. If you are purchasing infrastructure, or if you are purchasing real estate, you need to really understand what drives the value of that asset or that asset class. That's a fair amount of work because these things are not transparent; it is not necessarily easy to do.

We ask ourselves: What is this investment going to do for my total portfolio? And only then can you really assess whether or not you have made a contribution to the sustainability of the CPPIB.

This is the core of our investment strategy — start with a reference portfolio, which is a viable alternative to the stewards of the plan, and then add value by pursuing a more active strategy by investing in better beta and alpha strategies. We believe this investment strategy will meet our objectives, and contribute to the sustainability of the CPPIB.

Managing Investment Risks Over the Long-Term

Graham Pugh

In this paper I will discuss the investments' risk management strategy at OMERS. One of our approaches to managing investment risk is to deal with it in our asset mix strategy. Sterling Gunn talked about managing alpha and beta — and, for a pension plan, it is important to decompose the returns in any fund or asset class into beta and alpha. And let's be honest with ourselves: the risk in the alpha component is a flea compared to the risk in the beta component, which is the elephant. We have chosen to sort out the elephant in the room through our asset mix strategy.

I would like to provide some background on OMERS and talk about the process we go through to come up with our asset mix. We are extending the duration of our asset mix by moving into the non-public (or illiquid) asset classes in a significant way. Then I would like to discuss how we improve our portfolio efficiency through our asset mix strategy.

One of the bigger issues facing pension plans, which are looking to further invest in non-public asset classes, is the regulatory quantitative restrictions currently in place. OMERS is seeking to extract the liquidity premium from the non-public asset classes — namely real estate, infrastructure and private equity. One of the reasons for doing that is the regulatory rules that are currently in place imposed on us by the Pensions Benefit Act (PBA).

OMERS has been cited as a great example of a multiple-employer defined-benefit (DB) pension plan. We were formed in 1962. In 2006, the OMERS Act was revised to have two boards of directors. We have the

Sponsors Corporation, which is responsible for plan design, benefits and the setting of contribution rates. There are 14 members on that board consisting of seven employee and seven employer representatives. The second board is the Administration Corporation. This group is responsible for the administration and investments of the fund. Again, there are 14 members on that board consisting of seven employee and seven employer representatives.

We are a DB plan for local governments in Ontario. Some examples of the members of the OMERS plan include the City of Hamilton, Toronto Hydro, Hydro One Brampton as well as the police officers and fire fighters of Ontario. Some of the employers can actually opt out of our plan. Hydro One Brampton, for example, could leave the OMERS and go into the Hydro One pension plan. Because of the ability of some of these employers to opt out, we have to provide service to our clients in a slightly different way than many other pension plans. We have assets of slightly over $50 billion; 365,000 members; about 100,000 retirees and a little over 900 employers. So it is a fairly complex pension plan, but one that, I think, is a great example of multiple-employer DB plans.

As indicated, we are continuing our move into the illiquid asset classes. We want to have 42.5% of our mix in the illiquid assets — 10% in private equity, 20% in infrastructure and 12.5% in real estate, with the remainder of the 57.5% in public markets — equities, fixed income and real return bonds (RRB). So how did we come up with this asset mix?

In determining our asset mix, we go through a traditional mean-variance optimization. First, we identify the asset classes to be considered, identifying the expected return, the expected volatility and the correlation structure of those asset classes. A mean-variance optimization analysis gives you various choices to look at but does not identify the amount of risk a particular plan or fund should have. Stochastic projections of your actuarial assumptions, return assumptions, volatility and correlation assumptions and liquidity requirements in terms of the demographics of your plan, help identify the risk-return trade-offs and how much risk you want to take on. Then the question becomes: At what comfort level does management or the board say no, we don't want any more risk in the fund? Then, of course, there is the regulatory landscape to consider.

The mean-variance optimization can only get you maybe 50% of the way there. The rest of the qualitative and judgement issues are what really define the asset mix and, I think, make or break the performance of the fund.

At the end of the day, and even with the best modeling intentions, the actual asset mix is typically below the efficient frontier. This is because most plans are usually in transition to a long-run asset mix or economic focus has changed since the last asset allocation exercise. The question is then: How do you get from that point, below the efficient frontier, to some point on the efficient frontier? And of course, the black box gives you no indication of how to get there or where on the efficient frontier you should be. It is mostly judgement and qualitative assessment that helps guide a plan to an appropriate asset mix.

Generally, the liability matching portfolio in DB plans is typically close to 100% RRBs. It might be a mix of RRBs and some fixed-income instruments, but generally, it is very close to 100% RRBs. We all know that we cannot go out and invest 100% in RRBs as there just isn't enough in circulation in the market. Furthermore, doing so would typically lock in a funding deficit. Thus you need to invest in equities and non-public asset classes.

However, in doing so, you create a mismatch in the duration and timing of cash flows between the assets and liabilities of the plan. As a result of this mismatch, you need to manage the fund accordingly to ensure you can meet the pension promise over the sustainable future. You really have to look closely at the demographics of your plan to see when cash flows are required. So even when you think you have nailed down an efficient asset mix, you then have to look at stochastic projections in terms of what the potential cash flows could be. This helps guide you in terms of what the asset classes can provide for liquidity depending on when you need that liquidity.

Another piece to consider is the opportunity cost. Once the plan does get to its long-run asset mix target, there is an opportunity cost of forgoing potential investment opportunities. If a particularly favourable investment comes your way, it is difficult to move the pension ship off course to take advantage of those opportunities. So each plan needs to find a way to be able to be flexible enough so that there are not lost investment opportunities. As the large plans move into the illiquid asset classes, in order to take advantage of the liquidity premium not provided by public markets, they will need to ensure cash flows of those assets match the requirements of the liabilities.

And finally, there are regulatory issues to deal with. The regulatory landscape in Canada is different from other jurisdictions. For example, public DB pension plans cannot have any more than 5% of its assets in one real estate or Canadian resource property; it cannot have any more than 15% of its fund in aggregate in Canadian resource properties; it cannot have any more than 25% in aggregate in real estate and Canadian resource properties combined; and finally, while it can have 100% ownership in a company, it cannot actually have any more than 30% of the shares eligible to elect board members. So we can have 100% ownership of the investment but only up to a 30% share of the ability to elect board members in that company.

These rules date back to 1985 and they have not been substantially updated since then. But because of these rules and because of the need to increase duration in DB plan assets, it does place additional costs on those pension plans seeking to increase duration by investing in non-public assets. Pension plans have to set up complicated legal structures to be able to deal with these sorts of investments, and it is a costly endeavour to do that. OMERS has made this point in its submission to the Arthurs expert commission on pension reform.

As indicated, our pension investment rules are out of step with other jurisdictions. The United States, the United Kingdom and Australia operate under a "prudent person rule". Risk management techniques have improved dramatically over the years and have reduced the need for these quantitative restrictions. In the early days, I think the PBA rules were put in place as a risk mitigant. Risk management has evolved into not imposing restrictions on the dollar amount of investment you can have in any one investment or asset class, but it is now the amount of risk you can have in the total portfolio. So it is not a matter of limiting ourselves to 5% in any one Canadian resource property, for example; it is now looking at the fund as a total package.

Pension plans are no longer passive investors. Large pension plans have many investment professionals who actively manage these asset classes. This was not the case 20 years ago when these rules went into practice.

I believe that reducing the regulatory burden here would result in more investment opportunities for pension plans. It would help us to more effectively manage investment and actuarial type risks such as longevity risk. Pension plans look at longevity risk in an asset-liability framework in terms of what stochastic projections would imply about potential risks to increases in longevity. Again, if we could reduce the regulatory burden in Canada, I think it would permit Canadian plans to more effectively compete on a global stage. Some of these burdens put us at a competitive disadvantage with other jurisdictions. And because of the size of OMERS, for example, we do have to think globally in terms of investment opportunities. At the end of the day, eliminating these regulatory restrictions will result in more investment opportunities and greater pension security.

To sum up, our main approach to managing investment risks is to manage our asset mix relative to the objectives of the OMERS plan. We do that through an extensive asset mix study and through stochastic projections of the investment, actuarial and demographic assumptions. Then we layer on management's views as to where the greatest returns are likely to come from in the next decade to develop an asset mix with high probability of meeting the pension promise on a sustained basis.

Summary of Discussion

Armine Yalnizyan commented that we have had a tradition now for the last 12 years of paying down public debt instead of rolling it over. And CPP traditionally used to be the capital pool that financed our public infrastructure needs. There were low-interest loans given to subsidiary levels of government that then invested in the things that communities needed. Some estimates three or four years ago have put it that we had a $100 billion deficit in required infrastructure. She now wonders if as CPP and plans like OMERS start investing in real estate and infrastructure and require a higher rate of return than what we used to have by lending to subsidiary levels of government, this is, in fact, actually managing risk for the retirees that are baby-boomer-aged but passing on the costs to the next generation. That higher rate of return that is coming, is coming at the price of higher taxes being paid by residents all over the country — in particular, the working group. She wonders if, by protecting the income flow required by the baby boomers as they retire and by abandoning the traditional role of the CPP pool of capital for financing subsidiary levels of governments' capital requirements, we're actually doing ourselves a disservice.

    Cliff Halliwell observed that when he was at Health Canada, they did some number-crunching to look at where Canada was getting the gains in life expectancy. And interestingly, historically, the large gains in life expectancy didn't do that much to dependency ratios because the gains were coming out of reductions in infant mortality. The gains were coming from not killing yourself as a teenager in an automobile accident. The gains were coming out of not falling into the works at the mill when you were 33 or not coughing your lungs out at 42. Looking forward, this could be somewhat different. We're going to have to be cognizant of the fact that, increasingly, we're seeing gains in life expectancy, but we're still having a debate about whether we're expanding morbidity or contracting morbidity — which is the proportion of time spent in good and poor health. We're going to have to understand that a lot better.

Halliwell then asked a question pertaining to the whole process of portfolio management — finding all these wonderful rates of return in a world where a lot of people seem to feel that the world is awash in an excess of savings relative to the actual investment opportunities, in part driven by extraordinarily high savings rates in India and China and elsewhere. He wonders whether the fundamental balance between savings and investment opportunities globally might limit the scope for wonderful returns.

Malcolm Hamilton shares this concern to the following extent. What we've seen in the last 10 or 15 years are dramatic reductions in real and nominal interest rates. Bond prices have been bid up in Canada and right around the world. In part, this seems to be the result of Canada's fiscal policy: we used to be a big borrower and now we're retiring debt. We're retiring debt at the time when our population's supposed to be doing a lot of saving and when we've got a lot of seniors pushing into ages where they're supposed to be looking for low risk and high returns. So there seems to be an imbalance there. The thing that concerns him, though, is the institutional response, which he thinks is very rational but a little worrisome. The institutional response is, if safe investments and low-risk investments won't produce the kind of return we're accustomed to, we must pursue exotic investments or risky investments because we need to get the same return even if the market isn't providing it the way that it used to. This'll turn out to be a winning strategy or a great tragedy. He knows these organizations are extremely well run. But you've got to be careful if, at the heart of the decision-making, the idea is, we need to earn real 4 or 5 no matter how much risk that suggests we have to take.

Sterling Gunn responded that, if you were to run a pension fund on an asset-only basis and simply looked at target returns, then indeed, you would probably be running a great disservice. What he has been speaking about is the fact that the real risk that they are trying to manage is the sustainability of the fund. That means that certain exogenous choices have been made about how to fund the plan. In the case of the CPP, the choice is a contribution rate of 9.9%. They are then supposed to manage those funds the best way they can. And they've decided the best way is to maximize the sustainability of the plan. It doesn't mean they pursue an absolute target for returns, but it does mean that they look at the risks associated with the total package of liabilities and assets, and try to find the best mix.

Derek Hum asked Malcolm Hamilton what he thought of a suggestion that was once debated in Sweden when they were worrying about their citizens living too long and being too healthy. They proposed a bill — which he believes was subsequently passed — that indexed the age of eligibility for their various government-sponsored defined-benefit plans to the estimated age of mortality. So if the population wcrc going to live five years longer, all of a sudden the age of eligibility for their various government plans would also kick in five years longer. That was the basic principle. He wondered whether that seemed a reasonable way for government programs to manage — though not totally solve — the longevity risk. **Malcolm Hamilton** responded basically, that he opposed that approach. He was not opposed to the idea that, if people are living longer healthier lives, it's reasonable to expect them to work longer. But he rejected the notion that, because life expectancy goes up by three years, people are living healthier lives to the tune of three years. That may be true; but it may also not be true. He does not think that longevity at this point tells us very much about the age up to which people can reasonably be expected to work. Logically, it's hard to see how the fact that the age at which you die moves from 80 to 82 means you can now hold a job until 70 instead of 68.

Peter Hicks asked a related question about the basic premise of bringing compression of morbidity into the discussion. It is clear that we do not do nearly enough research into the kinds of physical capacity and particularly mental capacity (depression and things like that) which play a huge role in the policy debate around work and retirement. These are huge factors that are often overlooked. When we look at age of retirement, he is unaware of any literature that suggests there's any serious expansion of morbidity in the period between, say, 50 and 69, which encompasses the effective age of retirement. **Malcolm Hamilton** followed up that what we really need is some way of getting at the age up to which people can work. Healthy life expectancy isn't probably exactly right. But he thinks it's more right than life expectancy. The fact is, this is a complicated thing. He doesn't have a magic-bullet solution, but tying it to life expectancy because it's convenient actuarially for costing purposes, or it's convenient for the government in doing fiscal planning is not the road they should go down. Ultimately, these programs are supposed to support the population, not vice versa. The notion that the government has a financial need and everyone should work longer — he doesn't buy that. If everyone can, that's good.

But just suggesting that everybody has to do it, or should do it, or must be able to do it because it would be convenient for government if it happened is not convincing.

Another participant remarked that it seemed to him that the real issue with a DB plan is not how much risk you want to take on, but how you deal with the downside risk — that is, the risk of not meeting the discount rate that the actuary has used to discount the liabilities. Your goal is not just to beat the benchmark but to make sure that the surplus of the fund is positive. How do you manage this downside risk, which is not a symmetric objective function? **Sterling Gunn** responded that that's actually part of what a later study in this volume will be talking about. At the end of the day, the Chief Actuary has some kind of a test for the plan overall. The way we manage that risk is to try to account for how that test interacts with our activities as investors. What we try to accomplish is to minimize the probability that we'll fail that test. So the Chief Actuary has some kind of discount rate that he applies to the net cash flows of the plan, and the object of the fund is to try to backfill any gaps in the net liabilities. So he has a test, and CPP designs a strategy that tries to minimize failing that test. That's fundamentally what they do.

Chapter VII

Pension Rules and Retirement

Working While Receiving a Pension: Will Double Dipping Change the Elderly Labour Market?

Kevin Milligan and Tammy Schirle

Introduction

Receiving a pension while working often attracts great public controversy, especially when it involves tax dollars. A recent episode in Ohio in which government employees were collecting a pension while continuing on the public payroll generated the following strongly-worded reaction:

> "I find the whole practice by and large very offensive, and there is no shortage of people in Hamilton County who I think have frankly scammed the system for their own benefit, which is just wrong", Commission President Todd Portune said.
> *Cincinnati Enquirer*, Tuesday August 28, 2007

So-called "double-dipping" is also controversial in Canada. In 2005, a Toronto Member of Parliament (MP) complained about former MP and Royal Canadian Mint President David Dingwall:

> Toronto MP Jim Karygiannis said Dingwall already gets an MP's pension and that's all he deserves. Dingwall sat in Parliament from 1980 to 1997 as a Liberal MP and cabinet minister. "He was in here for 16, 17 years.

He's got a pension. We can't double-dip. It's a healthy pension",
Karygiannis said.

> *CTV News*, October 5, 2005.

There are three potential sources of the public outrage over double-dipping. First, there may be a concern that the total lifetime pension payout to these recipients may be higher than if they waited to initiate their pension until they stopped working. Second, some might worry that a pension recipient ought to retire in order to "free up" a job slot for a new employee. Third, if one views a pension as a gift of a beneficent employer, then continuing to work could be seen as an abuse of the payer's goodwill. No matter whether these arguments survive more serious scrutiny, they do appear influential in determining public opinion.[1]

Many economists, on the other hand, might view double-dipping from a less critical perspective. In the standard personnel economics view, pensions are a form of deferred compensation.[2] Once rights to the deferred compensation have accrued to the employee, the timing of the payments is for the most part irrelevant.[3] That is, the decision of when to consume the accumulated wealth of deferred compensation in theory should be largely irrelevant for decisions about how much and whether to work.

In a fascinating turn of events, recent changes in the labour market appear to have swung policy pressures in the direction of the standard economists' position. Persistent, low unemployment levels combined with the coming retirement of the baby-boom generation have led to concerns

---

[1]The first concern is irrelevant if pensions are actuarially adjusted for early uptake or if a worker who has reached his or her maximum pension entitlement returns to work when the alternative would be to draw the same pension while not working. The second concern represents the classic "lump of labour" fallacy and should be dismissed. The third concern suggests that pensions are something other than deferred compensation; that employees did not already implicitly pay for their pensions through lower wages when younger. The empirical evidence (e.g., Hutchens, 1987) supports the notion of deferred compensation.

[2]See, for one example, Lazear (1990).

[3]One argument for paying pensions only after retirement is to ensure worker effort in the final years of employment (e.g., Carmichael, 1989). However, if pension rights already have been accumulated based on past performance, they will be received independent of worker effort going forward. So, for pension rights that are unconditional on future performance, the timing of payment is irrelevant in the absence of liquidity constraints.

Kevin Milligan and Tammy Schirle

about labour shortages. One policy response to perceived labour shortages is to attempt to extract more labour supply from the existing population, through means such as encouraging later retirements or more work in the pre-retirement period. Previously in bad taste with the public, double-dipping has now become the flavour of the month.

The recent federal budget embraced this approach. Citing a need to plan for an aging workforce and to keep experienced workers in the labour market, the 2007 federal budget announced plans to change the regulations to allow what was called "phased retirement". One channel through which the federal government affects pension provisions is the Income Tax Act. Only those pension plans satisfying the requirements set out in the regulations to the act may qualify for the advantaged treatment of a Registered Pension Plan. Until now, the regulations have prohibited benefit accruals after the day of retirement.[4]

New regulations were included in the Bill C-28 (Budget and Economic Statement Implementation Act, 2007) which received Royal Assent on December 14, 2007. An addition to Section 8503 of the Regulations provided an exemption for "additional benefits" under certain conditions.[5] The key conditions are:

- The plan must be a defined benefit plan.
- The benefit being paid must be no more than 60% of the full benefit to which the employee is entitled.
- Employees must be 60 years of age, or age 55 and entitled to a full, unadjusted pension if the employee retired.

---

[4]Section 8503(3)b of the Income Tax Regulations reads:
"Benefits are not provided under the provision ... to a member in respect of a period that is after the day on which retirement benefits commence to be paid to the member under a defined benefit provision of ... the plan ..."
Moreover, the first item in Section 8502 describing the Primary Purpose of the section reads (emphasis added):
"The primary purpose of the plan is to provide periodic payments to individuals *after retirement* and until death in respect of their service as employees."

[5]This discussion follows the summary provided by the Canada Revenue Agency at http://www.cra-arc.gc.ca/tax/registered/budget2007-e.html.

There is no condition on how much work is allowed while receiving the pension benefits, so the work could be full-time or part-time.

While these new regulations might give employers some additional flexibility, it is not clear how wide the impact of these measures will be. Only 32.6% of the labour force is currently covered by a registered pension plan, and a growing (although still small) proportion of these are in a defined contribution plan. Moreover, the law firm McMillan Binch Mendelson (2007) noted in their review of the 2007 budget that only a "… limited number of plan sponsors … provide full unreduced pensions at age 55". This suggests that only a fraction of the 32.6% of Canadians in Registered Pension Plans will actually be eligible to take advantage of this new phased retirement policy.

To directly evaluate the impact of this policy change, one would need detailed information on pensions, work, and preferences about retirement. We do not know of any data that would allow that depth of analysis. Instead, in this paper our goal is to provide some analysis on the potential impact of the policy more indirectly. We do this by attempting to answer the following three questions: How much do the elderly actually work? How strong is the current joint incidence of work and pension receipt? Do the retired actually want to work more? The answers to these questions may be useful in understanding the extent to which changes in pension regulations may increase employment among the elderly and near-elderly. In what follows, we provide evidence on each of the three questions. The paper then closes with a discussion of the evidence and the prospects for policy on employer-provided pensions to influence the broader labour market.

Long-Run Trends in Elderly Employment and Pension Coverage

We begin by laying out the long-run trends in elderly and near-elderly employment. Using the Labour Force Survey, we construct a consistent time series of employment rates for males and for females from 1976 to 2006. We use three age groups: age 55–59, age 60–64, and age 65–69. Figure 1 displays the graphs for males. All three lines follow the same broad U-shaped trend with a trough in the mid-1990s. Schirle (2008) finds that a leading explanation for the rebound in male employment is a desire for

Figure 1: Employment Rates of Men
(By age group, 1976–2006)

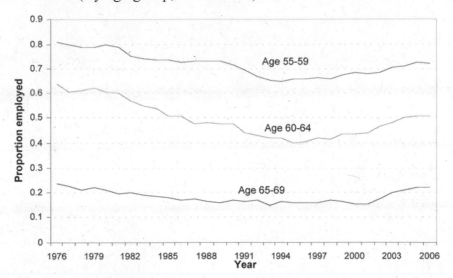

Source: Labour Force Survey, authors' calculations.

joint retirement with spouses. For the age 55–59 group, employment rates decline moderately from over 80% down to around 70%. The decline among the 60–64 year olds is stronger, as the employment rate drops by more than one-third from 64% in 1976 to 40% in 1995. Finally, while there is also a slight rebound for the 65–69-year-old men, the overwhelming impression from this graph is that few men work past age 65.

Figure 2 shows the employment rate for females in the same three age groups. The female employment rates are everywhere lower than males of the same age. The time trend in all three age categories is quite flat until the mid-1990s. Schirle (2008) shows that this increase in female employment largely reflects cohort differences in lifetime labour market participation — the women arriving in near-elderly ages in the late 1990s were those who were at the vanguard of the increase in female labour market participation in the 1960s and 1970s.

Next, we turn to the trends in pension coverage. We graph the proportion of the labour force (age 15+) who are currently members of a Registered Pension Plan (RPP), and then break out the proportion in defined benefit plans and defined contribution plans. The result appears in Figure 3. From 38.5% in 1978, the coverage rate has dropped to 32.6% in 2006.

Figure 2: Employment Rates of Women
(By age group, 1976–2006)

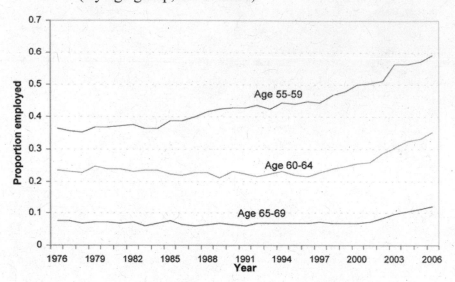

Source: Labour Force Survey, authors' calculations.

Figure 3: Percentage of the Labour Force Age 15–69 Covered by Registered Pension Plans

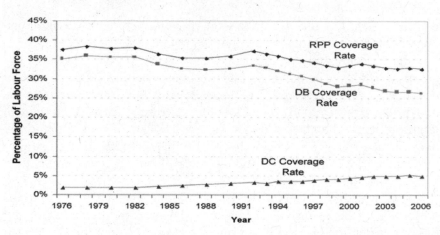

Source: Authors' calculations using CANSIM II series V2062810, V31200437, V31200455 and V31200461.

Kevin Milligan and Tammy Schirle

While the large majority of members are in defined-benefit plans, the proportion in defined-contribution plans has more than doubled over the last 30 years. It is important to remember that this measures membership at one point in time. Milligan (2005) shows the cross-cohort pattern of pension coverage using the 1999 Survey of Financial Security. In that data, coverage peaks when workers are ages 49–51 at a little over 50%. Moreover, an additional 10% of the sample had pension entitlement from a past employer.

Taking this evidence together, the last decade has shown an increase in work among those in the near-retirement years, but a decrease in those enrolled in defined-benefit pension arrangements.

The Joint Receipt of Pension Income and Earnings

How strong is the current joint incidence of work and pension receipt? Using the 2003 Survey of Labour and Income Dynamics (SLID), we present the proportion of individuals with positive income in the form of wages or retirement pensions at each age, from age 55 to 69, in Figure 4. Consistent with the employment rates presented in Figures 1 and 2, the proportion of individuals earning a wage or salary declines steadily with age. As these individuals leave employment, many pick up a retirement pension. On average, 11% of individuals age 55–69 received both retirement pension income and wage income in 2003.[6] The joint receipt of wages and pensions appears most likely between the ages of 61 and 65.

This does not imply, however, that 11% of these individuals are simultaneously receiving wage income and retirement pension income. Rather, it partly reflects the fact that incomes are reported on an annual

---

[6]It is important to note that the variable recording retirement pension income in SLID (pen42) includes income from registered pension plans and superannuation and annuities. This excludes RRSP withdrawals and includes RRSP annuities and RRIF withdrawals. As such, we might be slightly overstating the proportion collecting a retirement pension from an employer, in particular if individuals under the age of 69 are converting their RRSPs to RRIFs. Comparisons made with evidence in other surveys suggest this does occur, but quantitatively the occurrence is negligible for the purposes of this study.

Figure 4: Wage and Retirement Pension Receipt
(By age, 2003)

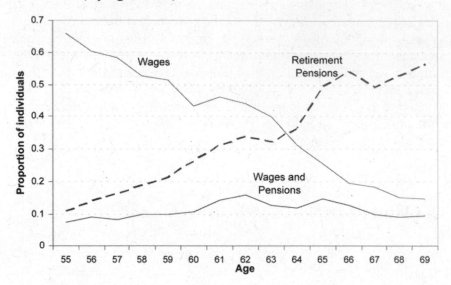

Source: Survey of Labour and Income Dynamics, authors' calculations.

basis and that people enter retirement throughout the year. That is, employment and retirement may be sequential but in annual data for the transition year both employment income and pension income will appear. In Figure 5 we display a series of monthly labour force participation rates within the sample of individuals who received both wages and pensions in 2003.[7] In January 2003, their participation rate was nearly 50%. By December 2003, the participation rate of this group had fallen to under 40%. This suggests that the actual proportion of Canadians receiving both employment income and pensions is on the order of 0.40*0.11 = 4.4%. Based on recent population estimates, this represents less than 211,000 individuals or less than 1% of the Canadian population age 15–69.[8]

---

[7]As a measurement issue, the monthly participation rates represent a great deal of churning in the labour market as well as individuals staying in permanent employment through the year.

[8]Based on the 2006 population estimates from Statistics Canada (2007).

Kevin Milligan and Tammy Schirle

Figure 5: Monthly Labour Force Participation Rate
(Individuals age 55–69 reporting wages
and retirement pensions, 2003)

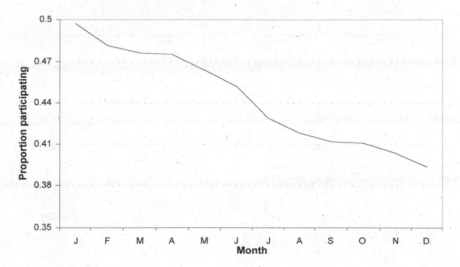

Source: Survey of Labour and Income Dynamics, authors' calculations.

What characterizes the individuals likely to receive both wage and retirement pension income? In Table 1 we present the results of a simple logit model used to predict the likelihood of joint wage-pension receipt among 55–69 year olds. The dependent variable here is a one-zero indicator for having both wage and pension income. Reported in the table are both logit coefficients and the implied marginal effects. The marginal effects can be interpreted as the change in the probability of having both types of income associated with each of the regressors, relative to the excluded category.

The results yield few surprises. Consistent with the results in Figure 4, individuals between the ages of 61 and 66 were most likely to receive both pensions and wages in 2003. At age 65, individuals are predicted to be 10.4 percentage points more likely to have joint pension and wage income than are 55-year-olds. Education is also a significant predictor of joint wage and pension receipt, as individuals with a university degree were 12 percentage points more likely than individuals with less than high school graduation to receive both pension and wages in 2003. Similarly, men and native-born

Table 1: Logit Regression Results. Dependent Variable: Individual Reports Both Wage and Pension Income

	Coefficient	Marginal Effect		Coefficient	Marginal Effect
Age			Education		
56	.274 (.221)	.033 (.027)	High School Graduate	**.527** (**.132**)	**.047** (**.014**)
57	.133 (.230)	.015 (.026)	Post-Secondary	**.661** (**.105**)	**.091** (**.020**)
58	.406 (.237)	.051 (.031)	University degree	**.825** (**.131**)	**.120** (**.027**)
59	.419 (.222)	.053 (.029)	Region		
60	.444 (.229)	.057 (.030)	Atlantic	.128 (.152)	.015 (.018)
61	**.821** (**.222**)	**.119** (**.034**)	Quebec	.433 (.155)	.055 (.024)
62	**.912** (**.222**)	**.136** (**.036**)	Ontario	**.483** (**.143**)	**.044** (**.013**)
63	**.758** (**.224**)	**.108** (**.034**)	Prairies	.226 (.155)	.027 (.020)
64	**.686** (**.232**)	**.095** (**.034**)	Male	**.767** (**.088**)	**.062** (**.012**)
65	**.923** (**.224**)	**.138** (**.036**)	Immigrant	**-1.058** (**.176**)	**-.077** (**.016**)
66	**.734** (**.232**)	**.104** (**.035**)	Married	.039 (.102)	.004 (.011)
67	.567 (.250)	.076 (.036)	Constant	-3.773 (.252)	
68	.419 (.253)	.053 (.034)			
69	.527 (.246)	.069 (.034)			

Notes: The sample is from SLID 2003, including individuals age 55–69. N=10607. Standard errors are in parentheses. Marginal effects are evaluated for a 55-year-old married male in Ontario with high school graduation. For indicator variables, the omitted groups are: Age 55; Education: less than high school graduation; Region: BC. Bold indicates the coefficients are significant at 1% level.

Kevin Milligan and Tammy Schirle

Canadians are more likely to receive both forms of income, in part reflecting the higher likelihood of these groups to have access to a pension. Across provinces, individuals in British Columbia are the least likely to receive both pension and wages while those in Ontario are the most likely.

The above evidence makes clear that very few Canadians currently work while receiving a pension. By our estimates, only 4.4% of workers were also in receipt of pension income. Of course, there may be a latent desire to work while receiving a pension that cannot be realized because of the limitations in the current pension regulatory framework. So, this evidence could either be interpreted as showing that the policy change would not matter or that it is necessary in order to unlock a latent desire to work. To distinguish between these possibilities, we turn in the next section to evidence on the desire of older workers to continue working.

Do Retirees Want to Work?

The previous section reported evidence that only around 4% of Canadian elderly workers are currently receiving both employment income and a pension. This may suggest that new policy initiatives in this area will not meet with large-scale demand. On the other hand, it is also possible that many who are currently retired or currently working in this age range would have chosen a phased retirement if it had been available. If given the opportunity to enjoy their pension while continuing in employment, how many retirees would want to continue working? While it is impossible to quantify this precisely, we have turned to the 2002 General Social Survey which asks retirees of their preferences for retirement and the circumstances under which they would have continued working for an employer instead of retiring. A similar analysis by Schellenberg, Turcotte, and Ram (2005) of the same data focused on why those who returned to work did so. They find that the plurality (38%) of respondents returned to work because of financial considerations. They also find that 45% of those who did return to work returned on a part-time basis.

We focus in our analysis on three questions: why respondents retired, the circumstances under which they would have continued working, and the desired intensity of post-retirement work. The responses are summarized in Table 2.[9]

When asked why they retired, the most popular reasons among retirees indicates that most people really want to leave their jobs. The most common reason for retiring is that individuals simply want to do other things (63% of 60–64-year-olds). Many retirees appear to wait until they have enough years of pensionable service to collect their pension (over 47%) or retirement was financially possible (over 69%).

There is some indication that not all retirements are entirely voluntary. For example, 25% of 55–59-year-old retirees were offered early retirement incentives and 27% of 65–69-year-olds left their jobs because there was a mandatory retirement policy. Over one-fifth of retirees left their job because their health required it. These individuals did not have the opportunity to enjoy any double-dipping arrangements.

When asked about the circumstances under which retirees would have continued to do paid work, there is some indication that a minority of individuals are interested in some sort of phased retirement or double-dipping arrangements. Roughly one-quarter of retirees report they would have continued to work if they could work fewer or shorter days without affecting their pension. Similarly, roughly one-quarter reported they would have continued working if they could work part-time. The behaviour of these retirees appears to be consistent with their stated preferences. Among those who said they would continue working if they could have worked part time, 39% of 55–59-year-olds were either in employment or looking for employment at some point after their retirement. This participation rate is reasonably higher than participation among individuals who did not express interest in continuing to work part-time.[10]

To summarize, the survey evidence strongly indicates two findings about the attitudes of recently retired Canadians about work. First, the majority of retirees prefer to be retired than to have continued working. Second, among those who would consider working, part-time work options carry considerable favour.

---

[9]The sample includes any individuals who report they have ever retired. Rather than using their age in 2003, we code the age at the date of their first retirement. The responses provided are related to individuals' first retirement only.

[10]To note, those who said they would have continued work if they could work fewer days were also more likely to claim they would continue work if their health were better.

Kevin Milligan and Tammy Schirle

Table 2: Retirement Preferences

	Age of First Retirement		
	55–59	60–64	65–69
Why did you retire?			
– employer offered an early retirement incentive	.25	.16	.03
– employer had a mandatory retirement policy	.10	.12	.27
– new technology was introduced	.05	.05	.04
– health required it	.26	.25	.20
– completed years of service for pension	.47	.48	.49
– were unemployed and could not find a job	.06	.05	.03
– retirement was financial possible	.67	.69	.66
– needed to care for a family member	.09	.09	.08
– wanted to stop working	.57	.63	.62
– no longer enjoyed your work	.15	.13	.09
– wanted to do other things	.43	.41	.40
– job was downsized	.15	.11	.05
Would you have continued to do paid work if ...			
– you were able to work fewer days without affecting your pension	.26	.22	.26
– you were able to work shorter days without affecting your pension	.24	.20	.24
– your vacation leave was increased without affecting your pension	.17	.13	.19
– your salary was increased	.19	.16	.21
– mandatory retirement policies had not existed	.09	.10	.22
– your health had been better	.25	.24	.19
– you could have worked part time	.25	.23	.28
Post-retirement labour force participation			
– would have continued part time	.39	.28	.32
– would not have continued part time	.21	.13	.12
– would have continued with fewer days	.40	.28	.25
– would not have continued with fewer days	.21	.13	.16

Note: GSS samples of individuals who had ever retired.

Discussion

In this paper, we have investigated the empirical relevance of double dipping — collecting a pension while still working. We find that employment among the elderly and near-elderly is not currently very high, although it has been growing over the last decade. Pension coverage, in contrast, has been falling. Among those with earned income, we find that the share also collecting a pension is quite small; on the order of 4% of the elderly labour force. Finally, in survey responses on attitudes about work and retirement, we find that most expressed a preference to stop work when they retire and many of those who wanted to continue would seek a part-time arrangement.

We are now in the position to offer a tentative answer to the question posed by the title of the paper. Even if a reform such as the one featured in the 2007 federal budget were to double the proportion of elderly workers who double-dipped, the impact on the elderly labour market would not be large. This is further diminished by the reported desire of those who might seek continued work to do so only on a part-time basis. From the data we have available, therefore, we conclude that the 2007 budget measures will have at best a very modest impact on the elderly labour market and almost no impact on the aggregate labour market.

The reform, however, is a step in the right direction. If one views pension entitlements as deferred compensation or wealth, individuals are made better off by having access to it to consume as they wish whether they continue to work or not. Increases in labour market flexibility for the elderly may indeed help to expand the work capacity of the Canadian population. If successful, even on a small scale, the reform may clear a path for a more substantial liberalization of pension rules.

References

Carmichael, H.L. 1989. "Self-Enforcing Contracts, Shirking, and Life-Cycle Incentives", *Journal of Economic Perspectives* 3(4), 65–83.

Cincinnati Enquirer. 2007. "Commissioners Want 'Double-Dip' Ban". August 28, Internet edition.

CTV News. 2005. "Some Liberals Outraged over Dingwall Severance". CTV News online, October 5.

Hutchens, R.M. 1987. "A Test of Lazear's Theory of Delayed Payment Contracts", *Journal of Labor Economics* 5(4), Part 2, S153–S170.

Lazear, E.P. 1990. "Pensions and Deferred Benefits as Strategic Compensation", *Industrial Relations* 29(2), 263–280.

McMillan Binch Mendelson. 2007. "Impact of Budget 2007 on Pension Plans and Retirement Savings Arrangements", *Pensions and Employee Compensation Bulletin*, March. At http://www.mcmbm.com/Upload/Publication/ImpactonPensionPlans.pdf.

Milligan, K. 2005. "Lifecycle Asset Allocation and Accumulation in Canada", *Canadian Journal of Economics* 38(3), 1057–1106.

Schellenberg, G., M. Turcotte, and B. Ram. 2005. "Post-Retirement Employment", *Perspectives on Labour and Income* 6(9). Catalogue No. 75–001–XIE. Ottawa: Statistics Canada.

Schirle, T. 2008. "Why Have the Labour Force Participation Rates of Older Men Increased Since the Mid-1990s?" *Journal of Labor Economics* 26(4), 549–594.

Statistics Canada. 2007. "Population by Sex and Age Group". At http://www40.statcan.ca/l01/cst01/demo10a.htm, September 17.

Mandatory Retirement and Incentives in University Defined-Benefit Pension Plans

John Burbidge and Katherine Cuff

Introduction

On 12 December 2006, Bill 211, the Ending Mandatory Retirement Statute Law Amendment Act, came into effect in Ontario. By amending the Ontario Human Rights Code to prevent discrimination on the basis of age for all persons over the age of 18, this act effectively eliminated the use of mandatory retirement in all Ontario universities and, more generally, in the province of Ontario. Individuals working in academia now have the right to work beyond 65.[1] What will be the effect of this act on academic labour markets?

We thank Chris Gunn and Evan Meredith for research assistance, Robin Boadway and other participants of the JDI Conference on Retirement Policy Issues in Canada for helpful comments, and the Social Sciences and Humanities Research Council of Canada for financial support.

[1]Employers who can demonstrate that age is a bona fide occupational requirement may receive exemption from the act and thereby enforce mandatory retirement (Ontario Human Rights Commission, 2007). Such occupational requirements are unlikely to apply to the university sector.

One might be inclined to think that this act would have no significant effects on labour markets for academics. For decades after 1960, male labour force participation rates at older ages fell and although female labour force participation rates at older ages increased over this time period, the overall rates were still low. So, perhaps there might be a very few who, when given the option to work beyond 65, would choose to do so, but, with the continuing trend to retire earlier, the few would become an insignificant percentage of the older population.

This paper questions this view. We use the last ten years of the Canadian Labour Force Surveys (LFSs) to show that there are significant groups, particularly men with higher levels of education, who may decide to continue in their jobs beyond age 65. In addition, we argue that the trend to retire earlier may have reversed for all education groups, that, in the future, an increasing fraction of men and women may choose to stay in their jobs beyond 65. A comparison of Manitoba and Quebec, which abolished mandatory retirement in the early 1980s, with the rest of Canada shows that a much smaller proportion of the labour force retires in the neighbourhood of age 65 in Manitoba and Quebec.[2] If it is true that the abolition of mandatory retirement has changed the labour force behaviour of older workers in Manitoba and Quebec, and is likely to change labour force behaviour in Ontario and other provinces, then it is of some interest to know who will choose (or has chosen) to work beyond 65 and what inducements universities might have to offer these individuals to persuade them not to work beyond age 65.

Previous work examining the incentives to retire have often focused on wealth-maximization models which ignore any utility individuals may receive while they are retired. In these papers, the benefit accruals under different pension plans, or equivalently, the change in the present value of benefit entitlement if an individual works one more year are calculated. Any positive accrual is a financial incentive for the individual to work another year. In fact, the implicit subsidy rate on continued work

---

[2]Changes in Quebec's employment standards legislation effectively banned mandatory retirement in 1983. The removal of mandatory retirement in Manitoba resulted from a series of court challenges to the Human Rights Act and become effective by 1982.

can be defined as the ratio of a positive accrual to the individual's current year labour earnings.[3]

In this paper, we model not only all of the (after-tax) financial incentives but also the utility individuals may derive from retirement, by extending the consumption-retirement model in Burbidge and Robb (1980). In their paper, they showed how to adapt the standard one period consumption-leisure utility maximization model to understand pension and retirement behaviour. In the standard consumption-leisure model, individuals face a decision about how to allocate their time between work and leisure. The opportunity cost of another hour of leisure is the wage rate. An increase in the wage rate has two effects: a substitution effect and a wealth effect. The substitution effect encourages the individual to work more, holding wealth constant, since the opportunity cost of leisure is higher. A higher wage rate also increases wealth which, in turn, affects the work decision. Typically, it is assumed that people with higher wealth work less, that is, leisure is a "normal" good. Consequently, for an individual with a higher wage rate, the substitution effect encourages more work, the wealth effect encourages less work, and *a priori* it is unclear which effect will dominate.

In the context of retirement, one can approximate the opportunity cost of another year of retirement by the gap between a person's annual earnings and annual pension benefits, and also approximate "wealth" by the discounted present value of earnings and pension benefits.[4] Earnings trajectories differ across and within disciplines in academia. Consider two individuals: individual A has a higher earnings trajectory than individual B. Individual A will have higher lifetime wealth which according to the wealth effect would encourage A to retire earlier. But if pensions are roughly proportional to earnings, A will have a higher opportunity cost of retiring one year earlier and, according to the substitution effect, would retire later than B. Predicting the effects of the abolition of mandatory retirement requires establishing which effect is

---

[3]See, for example, Gruber (1997) and Baker, Gruber, and Milligan (2003) on the retirement incentives of the Canadian public social security programs and Baker and Benjamin (1999a, 1999b) on the effect of these programs on labour market participation. Similar approaches have been used to uncover the financial incentives to retire in employer-sponsored private pension plans in Canada (Pesando and Gunderson, 1988; Gunderson, 2001).

[4]Note that in most defined-benefit plans working another year also changes pension benefits.

Figures 3 and 4 repeat the exercise for men and women aged 65–69. Again, we observe similar upward trends in these percentages for both older men and women starting in 2001. These percentages are particularly noteworthy as most of these workers are over the age of mandatory retirement.

Figure 3: Percentage of Men, Aged 65 to 69, Working Full-Time by Education Level

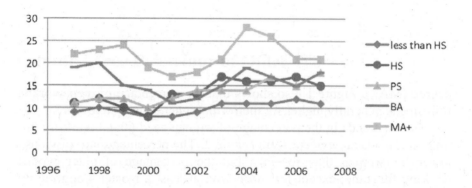

Figure 4: Percentage of Women, Aged 65 to 69, Working Full-Time by Education Level

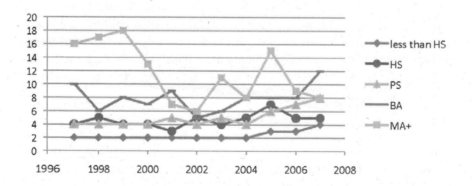

John Burbidge and Katherine Cuff

To get some sense whether the abolition of mandatory retirement has influenced the employment rates of older workers, we can compare these rates in Manitoba and Quebec with the rest of Canada.[7] Manitoba and Quebec both eliminated the use of mandatory retirement in the early 1980s. Figure 5 contrasts the percentage of older men, with at least a master's degree, working full-time in both Manitoba and Quebec versus the rest of Canada. The percentage of men aged 60–64 working full-time is lower in Manitoba and Quebec than in the rest of Canada, whereas the percentages of men aged 65–69 are about the same in Manitoba and Quebec as the rest of Canada. This suggests that, near age 65, fewer men

Figure 5: Manitoba and Quebec versus the rest of Canada, Males with at least an MA

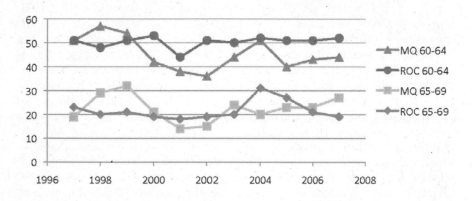

[7]Shannon and Grierson (2004) look at the impact of the elimination of mandatory retirement in Manitoba and Quebec on the employment of older workers in those provinces. Using provincial variation in mandatory retirement restrictions over the period 1976–2000, Shannon and Grierson compare the employment rates of 65–69 year olds in Manitoba and Quebec to the employment rates of two different control groups — 65–69 years olds in other provinces where there is mandatory retirement and 60–64 years olds in Manitoba and Quebec — before and after the policy changes. They do not find any significant effects of the elimination of mandatory retirement on the employment rates of older workers. They suggest, however, that the trend towards early retirement over this time period may have mitigated any positive employment effects from the elimination of mandatory retirement.

with at least a master's degree leave full-time employment in Manitoba and Quebec than in the rest of Canada. It seems likely that the 1980s abolition of mandatory retirement in Manitoba and Quebec may have contributed to this difference.[8]

If the trend towards early retirement is reversing then the elimination of mandatory retirement might have some real effects. Who will decide to retire in academia? What changes in university pension plans might induce them to retire at 65? To answer these questions, we extend the consumption-retirement model of Burbidge and Robb (1980) and use the model to simulate a typical defined-benefit pension plan.

---

[8]Using annual survey data collected from Canadian universities, Worswick (2005) compares the age distribution of faculty employed at universities with mandatory retirement to those without. He shows that the percentage of faculty over the age of 65 is higher at universities without mandatory retirement and the rate at which faculty aged 64–65 leave a university with mandatory retirement is 30 to 35 percentage points higher than the exit rate at a university without mandatory retirement. These findings are consistent with those using US data (Ashenfelter and Card, 2002). Worswick (2005) is not, however, able to track those faculty who left their university, and therefore it is not clear whether these individuals have truly retired or simply pursued employment in a job without mandatory retirement, possibly in Manitoba or Quebec. Were the migration patterns of older workers affected by the elimination of mandatory retirement in the provinces of Manitoba and Quebec? To answer this question, we used the public census data from 1981 and 1991 to focus on individuals over the age of 51 who are likely to be thinking about their retirement options. We compare the movement of individuals in the labour force between Quebec/Manitoba and the rest of Canada before and after the elimination of mandatory retirement in these two provinces as well as compare their movement to two control groups; those over the age of 51 and not in the labour force and those aged 37 to 45 and in the labour force. Overall, there was increased movement of all individuals in 1991 relative to 1981. The total number of individuals moving out of Quebec and Manitoba in both years, however, is extremely small. Consequently, it is difficult to infer any statistically significant effects on migration but it is instructive to describe what occurred. Larger samples of census 20% should be available over the next little while in the Statistics Canada Research Data Centres and with these larger datasets an extension of this empirical investigation could shed some light on this question.

Theoretical Framework

We employ a life-cycle model based on Burbidge and Robb (1980) to analyze an individual's decision to retire where the retirement decision is assumed to be discrete and permanent so individuals do not re-enter the labour market once retired. Following Burbidge and Robb (1980), we abstract away from any family considerations and focus solely on an individual's decision to retire.[9] Further we ignore any bequest motive on the part of the individual.[10] The individual is assumed to be 50 years of age at time 0 and acts as if he will live until time T. The individual has preferences over consumption and leisure time that can be represented by a separable utility function. Leisure can be varied only by changing the age of retirement. Further, leisure is normalized to zero when the individual is working and to unity when the individual is retired. We assume that there is a constant minimal amount of consumption required when the individual works and a constant but lower minimal amount of consumption needed when the individual retires. We could interpret these different levels of minimum consumption requirements as differ-

---

[9]We do not attempt to model to decision of family size or any joint household decisions, including joint labour force participation or retirement decisions. Clearly, spousal considerations could be important in an individual's retirement decision (see the work of P.-A. Chiappori and his co-authors, for example, Chiappori, 1988; Bourguignon and Chiappori, 1992; and Bourguignon, Browning, Chiappori, and Lechene, 1994).

[10]There are two types of bequest: intentional and unintentional. The former arises when the individual obtains some utility from the wealth he or she bequeaths. If utility were additively separable in the amount of the bequest, then the marginal trade-off between annual consumption and years of retirement (as described in the model of this section) would be unaffected by bequests and thus the bequest motive would give rise only to a form of income effect. Of course, it is possible that individuals could differ in their bequest motive, or equivalently, differ in their preferences for bequests and consequently could make different consumption/retirement decisions, all else equal. Unintentional bequests, on the other hand, arise when individuals face uncertainty over their lifetime. We assume that the individual acts as if he or she will live to a particular age. It is possible, of course, that the individual does not live to this age and consequently leaves a bequest. Following Burbidge and Robb (1980), we assume that the subjective discount rate is constant over time. Alternatively, we could allow for time-varying subjective discount rates reflecting differing mortality rates over the lifetime without affecting the main insights of the model and simulations.

ences in home production. For example, while working, individuals are likely to incur additional costs such as commuting or travel costs and higher food costs. When the individual retires he or she receives a constant pension benefit which depends positively on the number of years of full-time work.[11]

The individual chooses a lifetime stream of consumption and the number of years to work to maximize discounted lifetime utility subject to a budget constraint which depends on initial wealth at time zero, the stream of earnings net of any taxes and pension contributions from full-time work and the stream of pension benefits after retirement. It turns out under a separable utility function, consumption is constant while the individual works and constant, at a lower level, when the individual is retired.[12] This implication matches the data quite nicely. Burbidge and Davies (1994) show that controlling for family size using adult-equivalence scales, consumption is roughly constant while individuals work and then drops significantly when they retire but still remains relatively constant over the retirement period.[13]

Given the above analysis, we can think about an individual having preferences over consumption while working, consumption while retired and number of years of retirement. We denote these preferences by the following utility function

$$V(C_w - \overline{C}_w, C_r - \overline{C}_r, R - \overline{R}) \tag{1}$$

where $\overline{C}_w > \overline{C}_r$ are the minimal consumption amounts while working and retired, respectively and $\overline{R} \geq 0$ is some minimum number of years of retirement. The individual's budget constraint is

$$\int_0^N e^{-rt} C_w dt + \int_N^T e^{-rt} C_r dt = W_0 + \int_0^N Y(t) e^{-rt} dt + \int_N^T P(N) e^{-rt} dt \tag{2}$$

---

[11]We assume that the interest rate is constant and equal to the subjective discount rate.

[12]See Appendix for details.

[13]The more-standard hump-shaped consumption profile describes families with children.

John Burbidge and Katherine Cuff

where r is the interest rate, R is the number of years the individual is retired, and $N = T - R$ is the number of years the individual works. The individual's initial wealth at time 0 is W_0 and $Y(t)$ is the individual's (exogenous) earnings net of any taxes and pension contributions in that year if working. When the individual retires, she receives a constant pension benefit P which depends positively on the number of years of full-time work, N, and therefore depends on the individual's decision about when to retire. The interest rate r is assumed to be constant. The last two terms of the individual's budget constraint are the present value of the individual's lifetime earnings and pension benefits. We assume that increases in years of retirement reduces the present value of the individual's lifetime earnings. The actual shape of this function will, however, depend on the specific pension rules.

The individual maximizes utility subject to this budget constraint by choosing annual consumption while working and while retired, and the number of years of retirement. We solve this problem in two steps. First, taking R as given, the individual chooses consumption to maximize the present value of lifetime utility subject to the budget constraint. Combining the first-order conditions on consumption, given R, yields

$$\frac{\partial V / \partial C_w}{\int_0^N e^{-rt} dt} = \frac{\partial V / \partial C_r}{\int_N^T e^{-rt} dt} = \lambda . \tag{3}$$

where λ is the multiplier on the individual's budget constraint and can be interpreted as the increase in utility from a marginal increase in the lifetime resources. For a given number of years of retirement, the individual chooses a consumption bundle that equates the marginal benefit of consumption while working to the marginal benefit of consumption while retired. The marginal benefit of consumption is equal to the increase in utility from a marginal increase in consumption or the marginal utility of consumption in either state (working or retired) divided by the presented value of the resource cost of a marginal increase in consumption in either of the two states, that is, the discounted stream of an increase in consumption while working and while retired. The above condition, together with the budget constraint, yield the optimal levels of consumption while working and while retired as a function of the number of years of retirement and the other parameters of the model: $C_w(R; W_0, \overline{C}_w, \overline{C}_r, \overline{R})$ and $C_r(R; W_0, \overline{C}_w, \overline{C}_r, \overline{R})$. It is worth noting that consumption is a normal good so any increase in the individual's initial wealth or increase in the exogenous stream of earnings while working will increase consumption for a given number of years of retirement. Explicit expressions for these optimal consumptions as a function of years of retirement can be determined under assumed functional forms.[14]

The second step is to use these optimal consumptions as a function of years of retirement to obtain utility as a function of R only. The individual then chooses the number of years of retirement to maximize utility subject to the budget constraint. This yields the following optimality condition:

$$\frac{\partial V / \partial R}{\lambda} = e^{-rN}\left[(Y(N) - P(N)) - (C_w - C_r) - P'(N)\left(\frac{1 - e^{-r(T-N)}}{r}\right)\right] \quad (4)$$

The left-hand side is the individual's marginal willingness to pay, at age 50, for an additional year of retirement. The right-hand side can be interpreted as the price of an additional year of retirement. The cost of an additional year of retirement comprises three terms. The first term represents the difference between labour earnings and pension benefits. The second term is the difference in consumption levels while working and while retired. The third term is the discounted stream of changes in pension benefits from working one less year.

We use the above model as the basis for our simulation work. Although the model does not capture what are clearly some important determinants of the retirement decision, in particular health shocks, we believe it does a reasonably good job of capturing important aspects of what we observe in the real-world, particularly the relatively flat consumption streams controlling for family size. We use simulations to study the effects of changes in pension rules on the individual's decision to retire.

---

[14]See the Appendix for an example with a Cobb-Douglas utility function and with a utility function exhibiting aversion to consumption inequality over the lifetime.

Simulations

We begin by outlining the assumptions we made regarding the institutional features of the representative university defined-benefit pension plan.

Assumptions

Representative University Defined-Benefit Pension Plan

We model a typical defined-benefit pension plan of a Canadian university.[15] The rules of the plan are as follows: working members are required to contribute 4.25% of their annual salary up to the current Year's Maximum Pensionable Earnings (YPME) and 5.75% of their annual salary less the YMPE. Once the individual reaches the normal retirement age of 65, he or she can retire with a full pension. The pension benefit is equal to 1.4% of the worker's best average salary (BAS) up to the average YMPE, times the number of years of pensionable service plus 2% of the worker's BAS in excess of the average YMPE times pensionable service. Members might also retire early with full pension benefits if they reach the special retirement date which is a function of the member's age and their years of participation in the pension plan. For example, under a rule of 80, members whose age plus years of pensionable service equals or exceeds 80 can retire with full pension benefits. Members can also retire early with a reduced pension any month in the ten-year period before reaching the normal retirement age of 65. Pension benefits are reduced by 0.5% for each month the actual retirement date precedes the normal retirement date. Finally, plan members who end their employment after two years of participation in the plan can receive a lump-sum amount equal to two times the member's required plan contributions plus the net interest earned on their contributions.

---

[15]Goss (2007) surveys the faculty pension plans at 52 Canadian universities. Close to half of the universities have defined-benefit pension plans and the benefit formulas used in the plans are all very similar. When calculating the expected replacement ratio of the defined-benefit plans, however, Goss shows that differences can arise across plans as a result of differences in the indexing of pension benefits for inflation and the length of the guarantee period of pension benefits. We return to these issues when we discuss our results.

Income Tax System

We use the 2006 Federal and Ontario tax schedules to calculate tax payable.

Income

Individuals are assumed to have been working and covered by the university pension plan since the age of 30. They are currently 51 years of age. They have accumulated some wealth which reflects their personal savings. We assume that interest income is not taxed so that if individuals are saving while working then they are saving in income-taxed sheltered vehicles such as housing or registered education or savings plans. There is no lifetime uncertainty or at least individuals plan as if they will live until 80 years of age. The earnings profile is based on the career-progress merit system at McMaster University and University of Waterloo. To reflect the observation that earning profiles tend to be steeper early in one's career, individual earnings are assumed to grow over time with the greatest growth occurring in the first 20 years of work, then slowing down for the next ten years and then even slower growth thereafter.

Preferences

Following the theoretical model described above, we assume individuals have preferences over consumption while working, consumption while retired and years of retirement. We consider different specifications of utility functions, including requiring minimum levels of consumption and number of years of retirement. We also consider cases where annual consumption is constant throughout the individual's lifetime and where consumption streams differ over the lifetime. We do not, however, allow for preferences to change over time. As well, following the theoretical model, we assume individuals use exponential discounting and therefore ignore the possibility that individuals may use other forms of discounting which could give rise to regret over their retirement decision.[16]

---

[16]Diamond and Koszegi (2003) consider the retirement decision when individuals use quasi-hyperbolic discounting.

Results

As noted above, the simulation model is based on the defined-benefit pension plan used at McMaster University and the University of Waterloo, the earnings profile is representative of the earnings profile at McMaster and Waterloo, the income tax system is the Canadian personal income tax system as it existed in 2006, and individuals care about consumption while working, consumption when retired, and years of retirement. We made the plausible assumption that annual consumption expenditure in retirement is 90% of annual consumption while working. We calibrate individual preferences so that the optimal retirement age is 62 for the individual on the higher earnings profile who is earning one and a half times the median earnings. Using the simulation model, we were able to determine the impact on the individual's optimal retirement decision of various changes in both the university pension plan and the individual characteristics. Following is a summary of our results.

Who Decides to Retire Early?

Now looking at an individual on a lower earnings profile there would be both substitution and wealth effects. Switching to the lower income individual, the wealth effect would tend to make the person work longer and the substitution effect would tend to make the person retire earlier. In our simulations, a person whose earnings are one-half of the median earnings will choose to retire at age 69. In other words, in our simulations, the wealth effect dominates the substitution effect. This person would choose to retire at 65 with mandatory retirement but, when mandatory retirement is abolished, will choose to retire at age 69. An implication of this result is that, with the elimination of mandatory retirement, it may be individuals with the lower earnings trajectories who choose to work beyond the normal retirement age of 65. Of course, this assumes preferences are constant across individuals with different age-earnings profiles.

Buy-Outs

Mandatory retirement may or may not be binding for individuals. For those for whom it is binding, the employer might want to provide an incentive for these individuals to retire. The simulation allows us to calculate how much one would have to increase the pension at age 65 to induce the person to retire at 65, when otherwise he would choose to retire at age 69. It turns out in our context that it required a 20% increase in pension benefits at age 65 to induce the low-earnings individual to choose to retire at age 65.

Inflation Risk

Inflation gives individuals an incentive to delay retirement when pension benefits are linked to their final few years of earnings and pensions are not indexed for inflation.[17] Not surprisingly then, when we consider inflation persistence, the optimal retirement ages went up. With uncertainty over inflation it seems possible that individuals might want to re-optimize at every point in time or at least try to determine their option value of working one more year. We leave this line of research for future work.

Changes in Pension Plan Provisions

We also consider various changes to the university pension plan. In particular, we considered different early retirement provision rules. Changes in these rules, for example, a move from a rule of 80 to a rule of 81, had no effect on the optimal retirement age. Given our assumptions, individuals were generally not taking these early retirement provisions and consequently small changes in these provisions had no effect. If the rule was increased substantially, then the individual's retirement decision would be affected. Anecdotal evidence suggests individuals do take early retirement and further they continue to work at other jobs. This suggests that individuals differ with respect to their outside employment opportunities and that this can affect their decision to retire early. Retiring so early as to qualify only for a reduced pension was never optimal. Again, without outside employment opportunities the individual's budget set is always smaller under a reduced pension.

Changes in the contribution rates and pension benefits had the expected effects on the retirement decision. Increases in pension benefits

---

[17]Goss (2007) shows that whether the pension benefits are indexed for inflation affect the replacement ratio of the pension plan. This suggests the financial incentives to retire will also depend on whether benefits are indexed, partially or fully, to inflation. Goss is not, however, looking at the retirement decision. In his simulations, he assumes that all individuals begin work at age 30 and retire at 65.

reduced the optimal retirement age and increases in contribution rate increased the optimal retirement age.

Conclusion

Using the most recent Canadian Labour Force Survey data, we have shown that the trend towards early retirement is reversing, particularly for persons with higher levels of education. Consequently, the recent elimination of mandatory retirement in Ontario is likely to have real effects in the academic labour market. To investigate such effects, we use the consumption-retirement model of Burbidge and Robb (1980) as a basis to simulate the retirement behaviour of individuals following typical university age-earnings profiles in the context of the Canadian personal income tax system and a representative university defined-benefit pension plan. Our analysis shows that, controlling for consumption-leisure preferences and outside options, it will be the individual on the lower earnings trajectory who would wish to work beyond 65. Further, we show that it would require large increases in university pension benefits for these individuals to persuade them to retire by age 65.

Appendix

Theoretical Model

Following Burbidge and Robb (1980), at time zero, $t = 0$ the individual is assumed to be 50 years of age and acts as if he will live until time T. The individual has preferences over consumption at time t, denoted by $C(t)$, and amount of leisure at time t, denoted by $L(t)$. We also allow for the possibility that there is some minimum required amount of consumption needed to survive each period t, denoted by $\overline{C}_t \geq 0$. Preferences can then be represented by the following utility function $U(C(T) - \overline{C}_t, L(t))$ where U is increasing, at a decreasing rate, in net consumption. The minimal amount of consumption is assumed to be constant when the individual works and to be constant, possibly at a different level, when the individual is retired. Denote these minimal consumption amounts by $\overline{C}_w$ and $\overline{C}_r$, respectively. Leisure can be varied only by changing the age of retirement. Further, L is normalized to zero when the individual is working and to unity when the individual is retired. Let N be the number of years the individual spends working full-time. The individual is retired for $R = T - N$ years and the age at retirement is $50 + R$.

The individual chooses consumption in each period, $C(t)$, and the number of years to work N (or, equivalently the number of years of retirement) to maximize their discounted value of utility subject to their lifetime budget constraint. The individual's discounted value of utility is given by

$$\int_0^N U(C(t) - \overline{C}_w, 0)e^{-\delta t} dt + \int_N^T U(C(t) - \overline{C}_r, 1)e^{-\delta t} dt \quad (5)$$

where δ is the constant subjective discount rate. The individual's lifetime budget constraint is

$$\int_0^T C(t)e^{-rt} dt = W_0 + \int_0^N Y(t)e^{-rt} dt + \int_N^T P(t)e^{-rt} dt \quad (6)$$

where W_0 is the individual's initial wealth at time 0 and $Y(t)$ is the individual's earnings if they work in period t net of any taxes and pension contributions in that time period. When the individual retires, they receive a constant pension benefit P which depends positively on the number of years of full-time work, N. The interest rate r is also assumed to be constant and for simplicity assumed to be equal to the subjective discount rate, δ.

Let λ be the multiplier on the individual's lifetime budget constraint. Maximizing (5) subject to (6), yields the following optimality conditions:

$$U_c(C(t) - \overline{C}_w, 0) = \lambda, \quad t \in [0, N] \quad (7)$$

$$U_c(C(t) - \overline{C}_r, 1) = \lambda, \quad t \in (N, T] \quad (8)$$

From the above conditions, we have that $C(t) = C_w$ for $t \in [0, N]$ and $C(t) = C_r$ for $t \in (N, T]$. Consumption is constant while the individual works and constant, possibly at a different level, while the individual is retired.

John Burbidge and Katherine Cuff

Given $U_{cc} < 0$, we have the following result:[18] if utility is separable in consumption and leisure, $U_{cL} = 0$, then

$$C_w - \overline{C}_w = C_r - \overline{C}_r \qquad (9)$$

Under a separable utility function, $C_w > (<) C_r$ if $\overline{C}_w > (<) \overline{C}_r$. Burbidge and Robb (1980) consider separable utility when $\overline{C}_w = \overline{C}_r = 0$ so that consumption is constant over the individual's lifetime. We could interpret different levels of minimal consumption requirements as differences in home production. For example, while working individuals are likely to incur additional costs such as commuting or travel costs and higher food costs, so $\overline{C}_w > \overline{C}_r$ and consequently, $C_w > C_r$.

Cobb-Douglas Utility Function

Suppose, for example, utility is given by:

$$(R - \overline{R})^\alpha (C_w - \overline{C}_w)^{\beta(1-\alpha)} (C_r - \overline{C}_r)^{(1-\beta)(1-\alpha)} \qquad (10)$$

where $\alpha \in (0,1)$ is the utility weight on years of retirement and $\beta \in (0,1)$ is the utility weight on consumption while working. Define *M(R)* as the present value of the individual's lifetime earnings where we assume that $M'(R) < 0$. Further, define $\delta_w = \int_0^N e^{-rt} dt$ and $\delta_r = \int_N^T e^{-rt} dt$. Under this specification, we have

$$C_w = \frac{\beta}{\delta_w}(W_0 + M(R) - \delta_r \overline{C}_r) + (1-\beta)\overline{C}_w, \qquad (11)$$

$$C_r = \frac{1-\beta}{\delta_r}(W_0 + M(R) - \delta_w \overline{C}_w) + \beta\overline{C}_r. \qquad (12)$$

---

[18]If $U_{cL} > (<)0$, then $C_w - \overline{C}_w < (>) C_r - \overline{C}_r$.

How consumption changes with years of retirement is ambiguous.[19] To see this, note that

$$\frac{\partial C_w}{\partial R} = \frac{\beta}{\delta_w} M'(R) - \frac{\beta}{\delta_w^2} \frac{\partial \delta_w}{\partial R} (W_0 + M(R) - \delta_r \overline{C}_r) - \frac{\beta}{\delta_w} \frac{\partial \delta_r}{\partial R} \overline{C}_r \quad (13)$$

$$\frac{\partial C_r}{\partial R} = \frac{1-\beta}{\delta_r} M'(R) - \frac{1-\beta}{\delta_r^2} \frac{\partial \delta_r}{\partial R} (W_0 + M(R) - \delta_w \overline{C}_w)$$
$$- \frac{1-\beta}{\delta_r} \frac{\partial \delta_w}{\partial R} \overline{C}_w \quad (14)$$

The first term in both expressions is a wealth effect and is negative. Working one less year reduces the present value of lifetime earnings and pension benefits, and reduces consumption while working and while retired. The second term is a price effect. An increase in R reduces the discount rate applied to consumption while working and increases the discount rate applied to consumption while retired. In other words, consumption today is relatively less expensive than consumption tomorrow. Therefore, the individual will substitute away from consumption while retired to consumption while working so the second term is positive in the first expression and negative in the second expression. The last term is an income effect arising from the change in relative prices because of minimum consumption requirements. As mentioned, the price of consumption while working (retired) has gone down (up). The resources required to purchase the minimum amount of consumption while working (retired) has gone down (up). This reduces (increases) the resources available for consumption while working (retired). The last term is negative in the first expression and positive in the second expression. Although we cannot determine how either consumption level changes with a change in R we can say that an increase in the years of retirement increases the difference between consumption levels.[20]

---

[19]It is straightforward to determine how these consumption levels depend on the various parameters.

[20]This follows simply from subtracting the second expression from the first expression and using the fact that $\partial \delta_w / \partial R = - \partial \delta_r / \partial R$.

We could also consider the case in which preferences are represented by

$$(R - \overline{R})^{\alpha} \min \left\{ \beta(C_w - \overline{C}_w), (C_r - \overline{C}_r) \right\}^{1-\alpha} \tag{15}$$

Under this specification, individuals are averse to consumption inequality over their lifetime and for a given R will optimally choose C_w and C_r such that

$$\beta(C_w - \overline{C}_w) = (C_r - \overline{C}_r) \tag{16}$$

Substituting this condition into the budget constraint, we can solve for the optimal consumption levels as a function of R.

$$C_w = \frac{W_0 + M(R) + \delta_r(\beta\overline{C}_w - \overline{C}_r)}{\delta_w + \beta\delta_r} \tag{17}$$

$$C_r = \frac{\beta(W_0 + M(R)) + \delta_w(\overline{C}_r - \beta\overline{C}_w)}{\delta_w + \beta\delta_r} \tag{18}$$

If $\overline{C}_w = \overline{C}_r = 0$ or if $\beta\overline{C}_w = \overline{C}_r$, then the ratio C_w / C_r will be constant and equal to β. Otherwise, the ratio will depend on the actual level of consumption as well as the minimal required levels of consumption. Again, how consumptions change with the number of years of retirement is ambiguous.

References

Ashenfelter, O. and D. Card. 2002. "Did the Elimination of Mandatory Retirement Affect Faculty Retirement", *American Economic Review* 92, 957–980.

Baker, M. and D. Benjamin. 1999a. "How Do Retirement Tests Affect the Labour Supply of Older Men?" *Journal of Public Economics* 71(1), 27–51.

_____. 1999b. "Early Retirement Provisions and the Labor Force Behavior of Older Men: Evidence from Canada", *Journal of Labor Economics* 17(4), 724–756.

Baker, M., J. Gruber, and K. Milligan. 2003. "The Retirement Incentive Effects of Canada's Income Security Programs", *Canadian Journal of Economics* 36(2), 261-290.

Bourguignon, F. and P.-A. Chiappori. 1992. "Collective Models of Household Behavior: An Introduction", *European Economic Review* 36, 355–365.

Bourguignon, F., M. Browning, P.-A. Chiappori, and V. Lechene. 1994. "Incomes and Outcomes: A Structural Model of Intra-Household Allocation", *Journal of Political Economy* 102(6), 1067–1097.

Burbidge, J. and A.L. Robb. 1980. "Pension and Retirement Behaviour", *Canadian Journal of Economics* 13(3), 421–437.

Burbidge, J. and J. Davies. 1994. "Household Data and Saving Behavior in Canada", in J. Poterba (ed.), *International Comparisons of Household Saving*. Chicago: University of Chicago Press, 11–56.

Chiappori, P.-A. 1988. "Nash-Bargained Household Decisions", *International Economic Review* 32, 791–796.

Diamond, P. and B. Koszegi. 2003. "Quasi-Hyperbolic Discounting and Retirement", *Journal of Public Economics* 87, 1839–1872.

Goss, A. 2007. "Can Professors Afford to Retire? Evidence from a Survey of Canadian University Pension Plans", *Journal of Pension Economics and Finance* 6(2), 187–226.

Gruber, J. 1997. "Social Security and Retirement in Canada", NBER Working Paper No. 6308. Cambridge, MA: National Bureau of Economic Research.

Gunderson, M. 2001. "Income Security Programs: Simulations of Incentive Effects of Private and Public Pensions", Strategic Evaluation and Monitoring Evaluation and Data Development Strategic Policy Paper No. SP-AH086-05-01E. Ottawa: Human Resources Development Canada.

Kieran, P. 2001. "Early Retirement Trends", *Perspectives on Labour and Income* 2(9), Catalogue No. 75-001-XPE. Ottawa: Statistics Canada, 7–13.

Marshall, K. and V. Ferrao. 2007. "Participation of Older Workers", *Perspectives on Labour and Income* 8(8), Catalogue No. 75-001-IPE. Ottawa: Statistics Canada, 5–11.

Ontario Human Rights Commission. 2007. "Factsheet: The End of Mandatory Retirement". At http://www.ohrc.on.ca/en/resources/factsheets/end mandatoryretirement, accessed 16 October 2007.

Pesando, J. and M. Gunderson. 1988. "Retirement Incentives Contained in Occupational Pension Plans and their Implications for the Mandatory Retirement Debate", *Canadian Journal of Economics* 21(2), 244–264.

Shannon, M. and D. Grierson. 2004. "Mandatory Retirement and Older Worker Employment", *Canadian Journal of Economics* 37(3), 528–551.

Statistics Canada. 2007. *The Daily*, 21 June.

Worswick, C. 2005. "Mandatory Retirement Rules and the Retirement Decisions of University Professors in Canada", Analytical Studies Branch Research Paper No. 11F0019MIE, 217. Ottawa: Statistics Canada.

CPP Sustainability: A Stochastic Liability Model Analysis

Rick Egelton and Steven James

This chapter is part of the presentation on "Sustainability of the CPP's 9.9% Contribution Rate" at the October 26-27, 2007, conference by Rick Egelton and Sterling Gunn of the CPP Investment Board. The portion of the presentation by Sterling Gunn on "Developing the Asset Liability Model for the CPP Investment Board" is more technical and can be found on the JDI webpage at http://jdi.econ.queensu.ca/ .

The views in this presentation reflect work in progress and do not represent the official views of the CPP Investment Board.

In 1995, the CPP fund was projected to be exhausted by 2015...

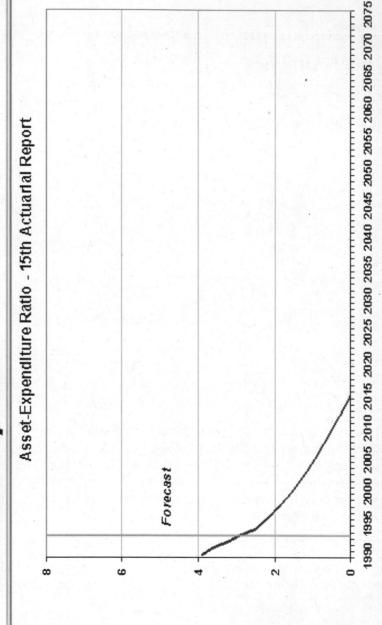

Asset-Expenditure Ratio - 15th Actuarial Report

Forecast

Rick Egelton and Steven James

...and the contribution rate to rise to 15½% by 2030

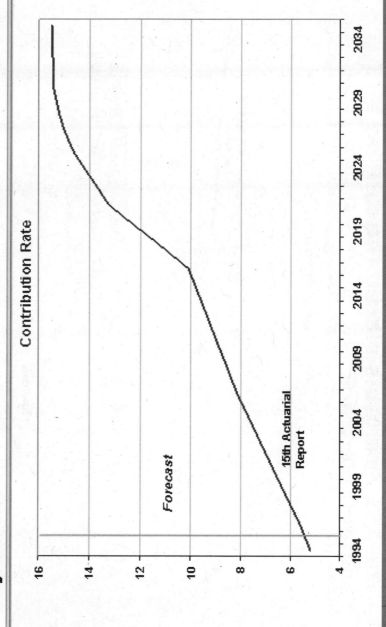

Contribution Rate

Forecast

15th Actuarial Report

The 1997 reforms placed the CPP on a sustainable track

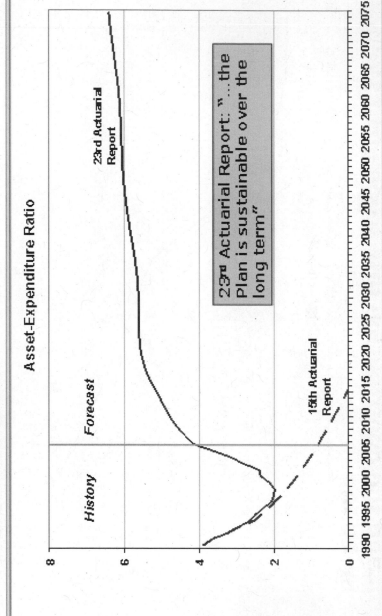

Asset-Expenditure Ratio

History

Forecast

15th Actuarial Report

23rd Actuarial Report

23rd Actuarial Report: "...the Plan is sustainable over the long term"

Rick Egelton and Steven James

...and ensured a much lower long run contribution rate

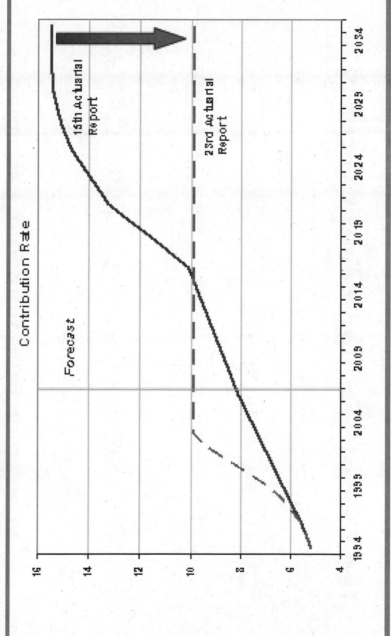

Contribution Rate

Forecast

15th Actuarial Report

23rd Actuarial Report

1994 1999 2004 2009 2014 2019 2024 2029 2034

4 6 8 10 12 14 16

The CPP offers high benefit security...

CPP: public, mandatory

☐ Very low default risk

⋀ Future benefits backed by assets and future contribution base

Private Employer-Sponsored Defined Benefit

☐ Sponsor default risk

⋀ Need to be fully-funded in case plan terminates

Rick Egelton and Steven James

The CPP contribution rate is sustainable if assets equal or exceed liabilities...

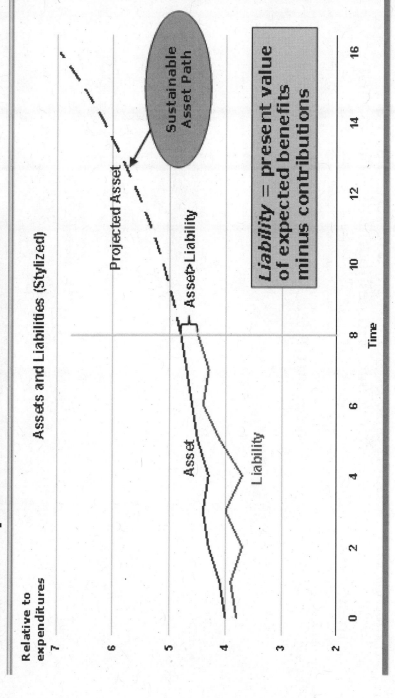

Relative to expenditures

Assets and Liabilities (Stylized)

Projected Asset

Sustainable Asset Path

Asset

Liability

Asset>Liability

Liability = present value of expected benefits minus contributions

Time

...but a contribution and/or benefit adjustment may be required if adverse economic and demographic shocks push the liability above the asset...

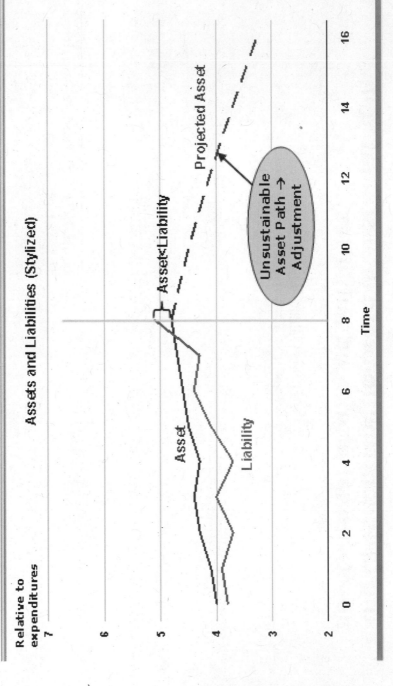

Relative to expenditures

Assets and Liabilities (Stylized)

Asset

Liability

Asset<Liability

Projected Asset

Unsustainable Asset Path → Adjustment

Time

Rick Egelton and Steven James

...or if an adverse asset return shock pushes the asset below the liability

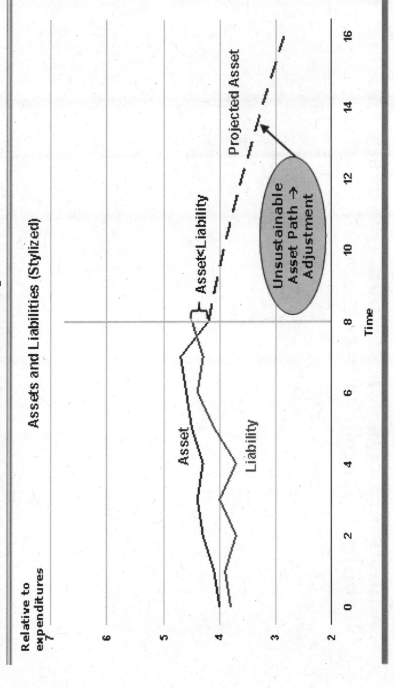

Relative to expenditures

Assets and Liabilities (Stylized)

Asset

Liability

Asset<Liability

Projected Asset

Unsustainable Asset Path → Adjustment

Time

Adjustment risk is less when the asset and liability are positively correlated...

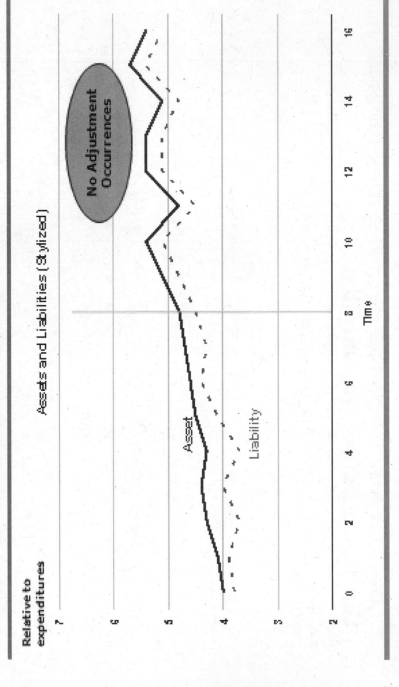

... and higher when they are negatively correlated...

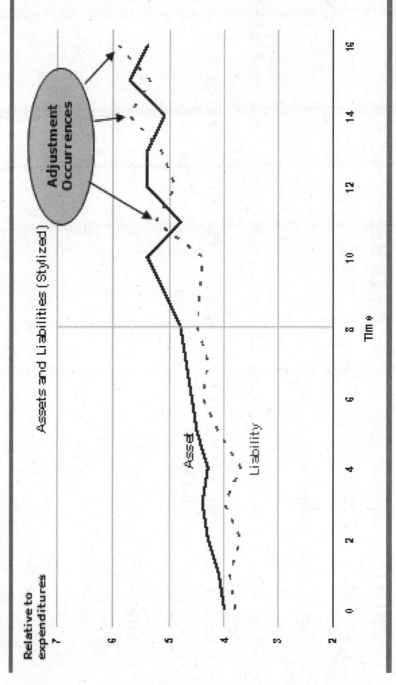

CPPIB investment strategy is designed to reduce adjustment risk

Statutory mandate

☐ achieve a maximum rate of return without undue risk of loss, having regard to the factors that may affect the funding of the CPP and the ability of the CPP to meet its financial obligations

Implementation

☐ portfolio that addresses projected CPP liabilities

☐ investment activities that enhance risk-adjusted returns

Rick Egelton and Steven James

The *stochastic liability model (SLM)* models CPP liability dynamics and risks...

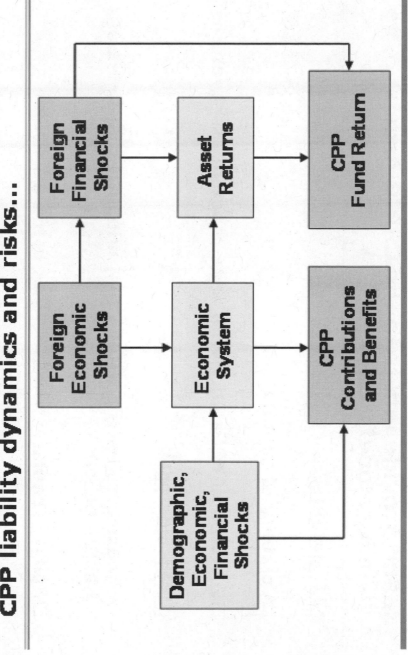

...and provide inputs to the CPPIB Asset-Liability Model (ALM)

SLM outputs

☐ Volatility of liability

☐ Correlation of liability with wide range of asset returns

ALM framework

☐ Choose reference portfolio that minimizes an index of adjustment risk

☐ update regularly as assets and liabilities evolve

Using the SLM we generate 10,000 sample paths to 2160

☐ Stochastic fertility, mortality, net migration

☐ Stochastic productivity and demand

> Canada and U.S.

☐ Stochastic asset returns

> Global equities and bonds

Key OCA23* Economic and Fund Return Assumptions

☐ Mean long-run productivity growth = 1.3%

☐ Mean long-run inflation = 2.5%

☐ Long-run real fund return = 4.2%

*Office of the Chief Actuary,
23rd Actuarial Report on
the Canada Pension Plan
as at 31 December 2006

Rick Egelton and Steven James

Older population share rises with widening confidence band after 2035

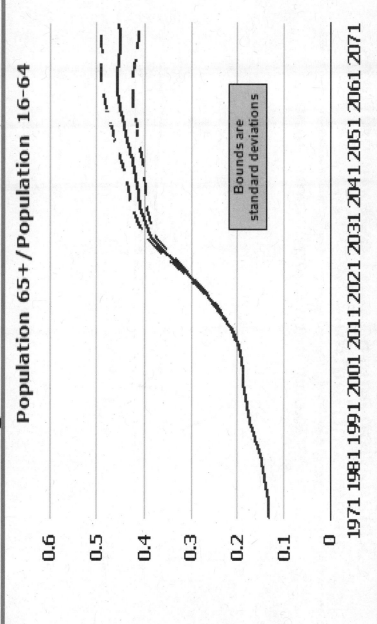

Population 65+/Population 16-64

Bounds are standard deviations

0.6 0.5 0.4 0.3 0.2 0.1 0

1971 1981 1991 2001 2011 2021 2031 2041 2051 2061 2071

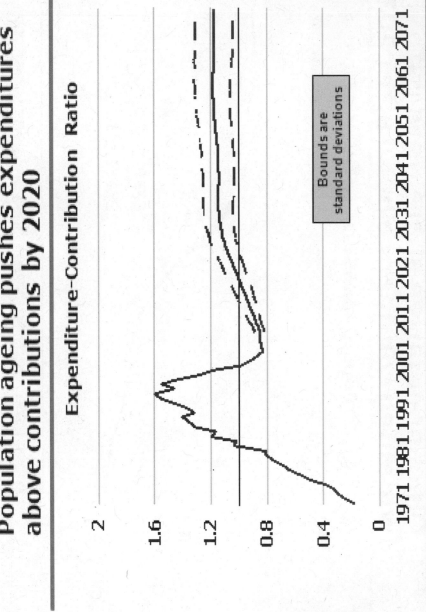

Population ageing pushes expenditures above contributions by 2020

Expenditure-Contribution Ratio

Bounds are standard deviations

2 1.6 1.2 0.8 0.4 0

1971 1981 1991 2001 2011 2021 2031 2041 2051 2061 2071

Rick Egelton and Steven James

Asset-expenditure ratio rises and confidence band widens steadily as horizon increases

Asset-Expenditure Ratio

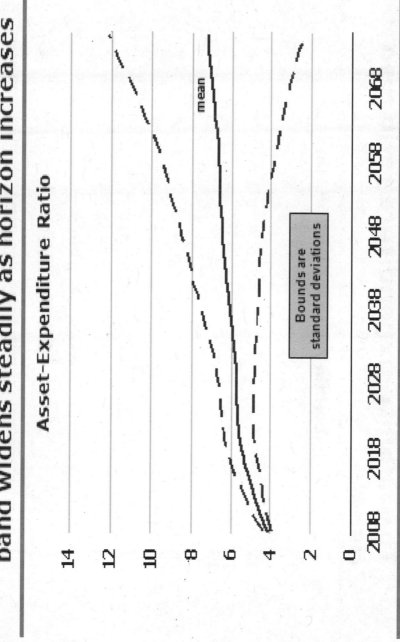

mean

Bounds are standard deviations

14 12 10 8 6 4 2 0

2008 2018 2028 2038 2048 2058 2068

The liability-expenditure ratio also rises

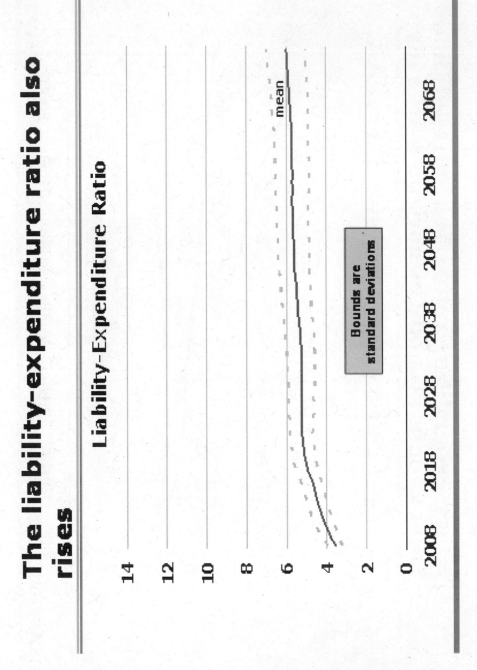

Liability-Expenditure Ratio

mean

Bounds are standard deviations

Rick Egelton and Steven James

Expected assets exceed liabilities, but there is a considerable confidence band overlap

Asset and Liability-Expenditure Ratios

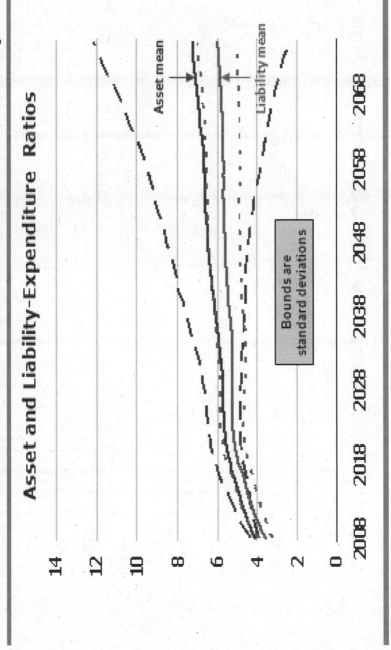

...implying moderately low adjustment risk

Adjustment Risk

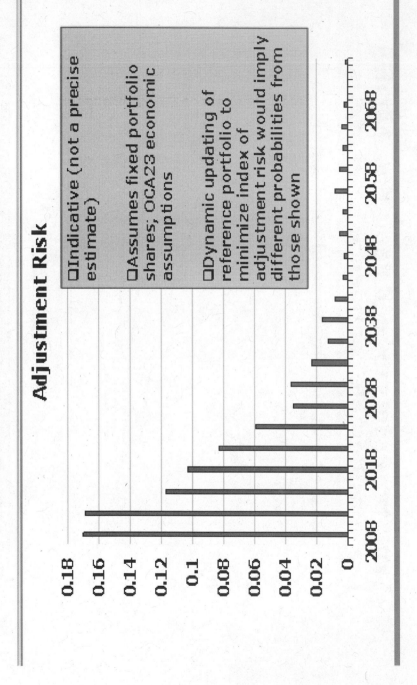

□Indicative (not a precise estimate)

□Assumes fixed portfolio shares, OCA23 economic assumptions

□Dynamic updating of reference portfolio to minimize index of adjustment risk would imply different probabilities from those shown

Rick Egelton and Steven James

Adding 50bp to the actual and expected fund return boosts the asset path and lowers the liability path

Asset and Liability-Expenditure Ratios

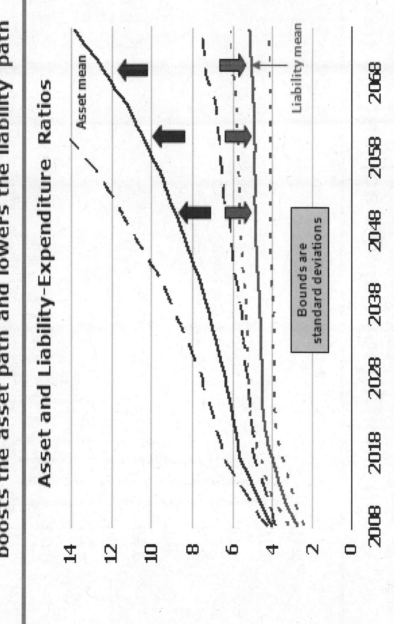

Asset mean

Liability mean

Bounds are standard deviations

2008 2018 2028 2038 2048 2058 2068

0 2 4 6 8 10 12 14

...and significantly reduces adjustment risk

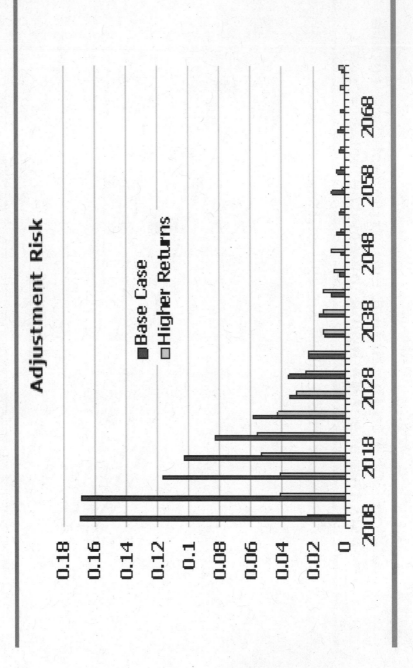

Adjustment Risk

Base Case
Higher Returns

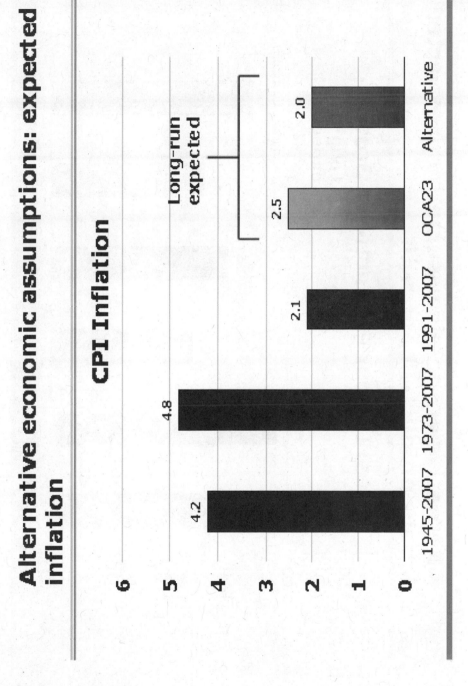

Alternative economic assumptions: expected inflation

CPI Inflation

Long-run expected

4.2	4.8	2.1	2.5	2.0
1945-2007	1973-2007	1991-2007	OCA23	Alternative

Alternative economic assumptions: expected labour productivity growth

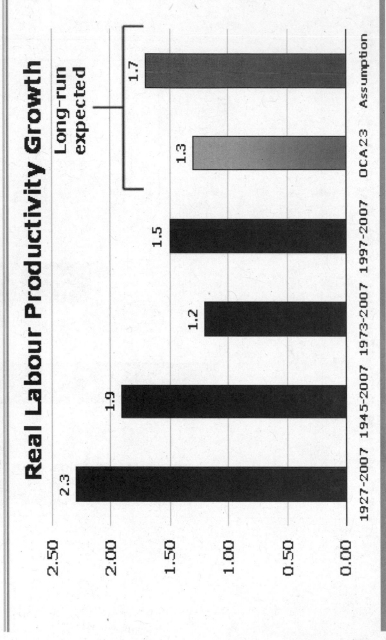

Real Labour Productivity Growth

Higher productivity growth lowers the expenditure–contribution ratio path...

Alternative Economic Assumptions

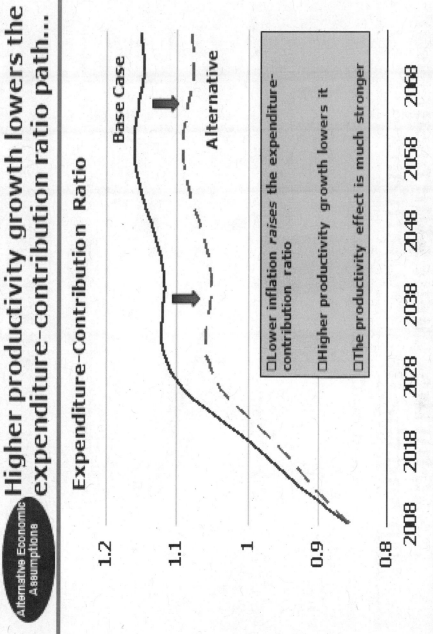

Expenditure-Contribution Ratio

Base Case

Alternative

☐ Lower inflation *raises* the expenditure-contribution ratio

☐ Higher productivity growth lowers it

☐ The productivity effect is much stronger

1.2

1.1

1

0.9

0.8

2008   2018   2028   2038   2048   2058   2068

...and further pushes the asset path up and the liability path down...

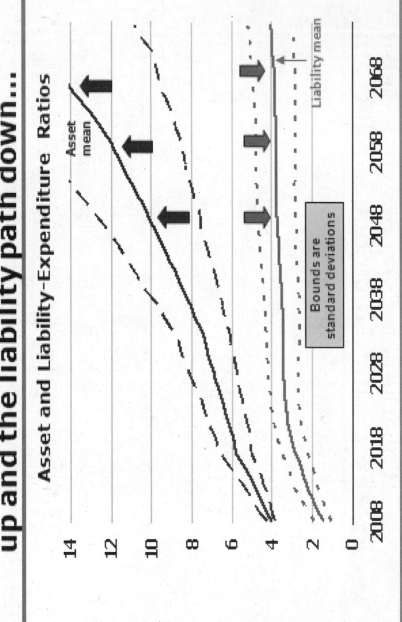

Asset and Liability-Expenditure Ratios

Asset mean

Liability mean

Bounds are standard deviations

14
12
10
8
6
4
2
0

2008 2018 2028 2038 2048 2058 2068

...implying still lower adjustment risk

Adjustment Risk

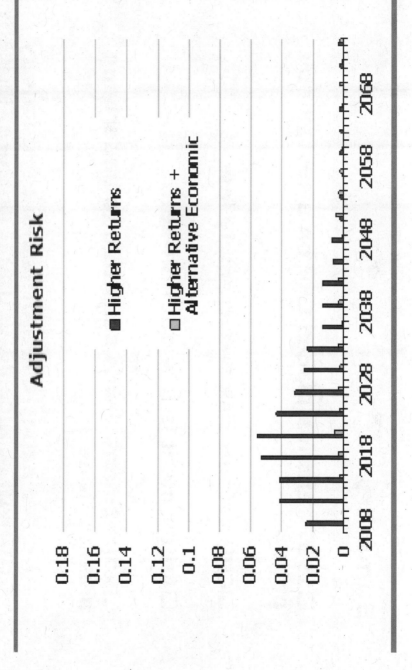

■ Higher Returns

▨ Higher Returns + Alternative Economic

Summary

- 1997 reforms placed CPP on a sustainable path

- CPP default risk is extremely low

- Adjustment is low but non-zero

- Adjustment risk is sensitive to underlying assumptions

  ➢ **Higher expected returns and productivity growth reduce adjustment risk dramatically**

Rick Egelton and Steven James

Summary of Discussion

Jonathan Kesselman observed that the typical situation in American universities, where there's been no mandatory retirement for quite some time, is that low-productivity academics tend to retire early while high-productivity academics tend to stay on. That reflects dimensions that are not in the Burbidge-Cuff model. Low-productivity individuals, perhaps, are in more teaching-oriented institutions, have less interest in research, and may have health factors that come in that make it harder and less desirable to work, while higher-productivity faculty occur in more research-oriented institutions where they may be doing work that is more interesting and challenging. Kesselman also comments that it's useful to see the role of education differentials in the choice of continuing to work by older workers. This helps explain why retirement ages are now creeping up and why we might expect them to creep up a good deal more. If you look at the educational attainment of people, say, 55 to 64 now, they are substantially higher than for workers of that age 10 or 15 years ago. And, in 10 years from now, the educational achievement of those 65 to 74 will be much higher as well. This means that the types of occupations that people are filling are very different than they were 15–25 years ago. A lot fewer of us are in back-breaking work in manufacturing, resource extraction and resource processing. A lot more of us are knowledge-type workers in various degrees, whether it's in academia or the service sectors. He thinks that's going to feed into a continuing rise in typical retirement ages.

Bill Gleberzon made two observations, and one's a kind of challenge. We have talked about phased retirement, but that refers to only one of the tax changes made for seniors in the 2007 budget. Another was pension-splitting, which only affects retired people. It's quite a major change. The other one is extending the age at which you have to transfer, or convert, your RRSP into a RRIF to 71. His hunch is that these latter changes may be a better indicator and promoter of keeping people in the workforce. This is simply because a lot more people have RRSPs and the amount they have in their RRSPs is, generally speaking, rather limited. So he thinks more people will want to, when they have the choice, continue working so they can continue contributing to their RRSP. The other comment is a general observation. Retirement studies have typically looked at people up to age 64. But he thinks the real change is going to come for the group beyond age 64 when the first wave of boomers turns 65. The latter have a completely different attitude towards life. Many of them have not saved sufficiently for their retirement. And many of these people, with mandatory retirement gone, are going to take up that challenge and continue working to a greater extent than the current generations are working. He thinks that this is something that should be on the research agenda for the future.

Armine Yalnizyan remarked on the assumption in the CPP model that productivity increase would affect the expenditure and contribution rates because you'd see a flow-through for wages. But we've had 30 years of rising productivity and 30 years of stagnant real wages. **Rick Egelton** responded that over the long term, productivity growth and real wages should move together. He thinks they have until recently. Lately, what we've seen is a huge surge in corporate profits as a share of GDP to record-high levels. You've had a divergence in terms of productivity and real wages over the last decade. The assumption in the CPP model is that they will coalesce, and he thinks most economic models would suggest that over the long run, productivity gains and real wages are indeed going to move together.

Kevin Milligan responded to the comment from Bill Gleberzon. First, about RRSPs, he agrees the latter's intuition is right for the direction of the impact of the change in RRSP rules — as a result of moving the age at which you must shift funds into a RRIF from 69 to 71. Actually, it was 71 until about 1991 or so, so we have the reverse experiment this time. The ability to accumulate contribution room is in a sense like a wage subsidy, so you can perhaps induce more employment. But the big thing is, there are so few people working at age 69 anyway that he's not sure you're going to see much of an impact.

Chapter VIII

Mandatory Retirement and the Changing Prospects of Retirement

Mandatory Retirement: Myths, Myths and More Damn Myths

Rafael Gomez and Morley Gunderson

Introduction

Mandatory retirement is an important workplace practice in that about one-half of the Canadian workforce are in jobs that have a mandatory retirement policy.[1] Its importance will grow in the future given a number of inter-

Financial Support of the Canadian Labour Market and Skills Research Network is gratefully acknowledged, as are discussions with Lorne Carmichael and James Pesando.

[1] Evidence on the existence of mandatory retirement is mainly indirect and should not be regarded as precise; nevertheless, it is also consistent with figures from the United States before they banned mandatory retirement. See Gunderson and Pesando (1988, p. 33) and Gomez, Gunderson, and Luchak (2002) and other references cited in these studies. A recent survey of larger organizations of 100 or more employees indicates that 52% of Canadian organizations had a company-wide mandatory retirement policy and some others had such a policy for part of their workforce (Hewitt Associates, 2003). The restriction to larger firms may slightly overstate the extent of mandatory retirement for the workforce as a whole (Kesselman, 2004, p. 9). The fact that half of the workforce works in jobs with a mandatory retirement policy does not mean that half will involuntarily retire because of the policy. Many may die prior to the policy and others may prefer to

related demographic factors: the proportion of older workers in the workforce is increasing, given the aging baby-boom population and declining fertility rates[2] as well as the fact that youths are spending longer acquiring education;[3] older workers are working longer as the trend towards early retirement is being reversed;[4] and their health and longevity is improving so that they have a longer potential remaining lifespan for continuing to work.[5]

Until recently, mandatory retirement was allowed in all Canadian jurisdictions except Manitoba and Quebec (both banned in the early 1980s) and even in those jurisdictions the extent of the ban was not complete. For example, a court decision in Quebec allowed people to be terminated at the age of 65 on the grounds that only those up until the age of 65 had their employment protected.[6] In Manitoba, university professors were exempt from the ban and were still subject to mandatory retirement. There is also a perception — one of the many myths — that the federal government also banned mandatory retirement. The reality is that the federal government voluntarily moved away from mandatory retirement for its civil servants, but this is an option that can be followed by any employer.

---

retire at that time. Others may work with their organization after they "officially" retire, and others may work with other organizations.

[2]By 2021, for example, workers age 55 and over are expected to constitute 20% of the workforce compared to 14% in 2005 (Martel *et al.*, 2007). By 2020, workers age 50–64 are expected to constitute 25% of the workforce compared to 15% in 1980 (United Nations, 2002). Demographic issues around mandatory retirement are also outlined in Ibbott, Kerr, and Beaujot (2006).

[3]The longer education period of youths is documented and discussed in Beaujot (2004).

[4]The reversal of the trend towards early retirement in Canada is documented and discussed in Gomez, Gunderson, and Luchak (2002), Lowe (2005), Marshall and Ferrao (2007), Milligan (2005), and Schirle (2007).

[5]Improvements in health and longevity in Canada are outlined and discussed in Chen and Wayne (2000), Crompton (2000), and Hogan and Lise (2003).

[6]*Parent v. The Gazette,* 81 D.L.R. (4th) 689 (A.Q.) (1991).

In a series of mandatory retirement decisions in 1990, the Supreme Court of Canada refused to override the right of provinces to allow mandatory retirement. The court argued that mandatory retirement was "demonstrably justified in a free and democratic society" because its social benefits (for reasons outlined subsequently) exceed its social costs, including its possible infringement on the rights of some particular individuals. This placed the decision back in the hands of individual provincial governments. In 2005, Ontario followed Quebec and Manitoba and banned mandatory retirement (effective 2006) and others are following suit. In essence, the trend is in the direction of legislatively banning mandatory retirement.

Whether that decision is right or wrong, it is an issue that is not well understood. As we have indicated elsewhere in a typically Canadian "kinder and gentler" manner, the issue is "not as simple as it seems" (Gunderson and Hyatt, 2005). Or in a more aggressive tone: "The debate over whether to ban mandatory retirement is one of the most misunderstood discussions in the area of labour and social policy" (Gunderson, 2004, p. 1). And now in an even more aggressive manner: "myths, myths and more damn myths". One can only imagine our next subtitle.

The purpose of this paper is to set out those myths in the debate over mandatory retirement, and to provide what we perceive to be the realities. Prior to that discussion, some basic background facts will be provided to help frame the discussion.

Some Background Facts

The background facts are based mainly on the 2002 Workplace and Employee Survey (GSS Cycle 16) the most recent cycle to have included questions on retirement.[7] They include information on: reasons for retiring and the factors associated with those reasons; factors that would have facilitated the continued employment of those who retired; and reasons for returning to work after retirement. Many of these facts will be drawn on in our subsequent discussion of the realities surrounding mandatory retirement.

---

[7]Schellenberg and Silver (2004) use this GSS to analyze the congruence of retirement preferences and experiences.

Reasons for Retiring

In descending order of their relative importance, the reasons that retirees gave for retirement were (percents summing to more than 100% since multiple responses were possible):

- financially possible 59.7%
- wanted to stop working 55.5%
- wanted to do other things 39%
- qualified for a pension 38.6%
- health 28.4%
- early retirement incentive 13.3%
- no longer enjoyed work 12.8%
- job downsized 11.3%
- mandatory retirement 11.1%
- care for a family member 11%
- unemployed 4.8%.

This highlights that individuals retired for reasons that could generally be considered as voluntary such as wanted to stop working, wanted to do other things, financially possible, qualified for a pension, early retirement incentives and no longer enjoyed working. Health reasons and care for a family member can also be generally regarded as voluntary, in response to those personalized constraints. Involuntary reasons are less prominent and include the job being downsized (11.3% of respondents) and being unemployed (4.8%), although even here retirement may be a viable alternative for older persons. Even the number who responded that they retired due to mandatory retirement (11.1%) appears low given that about half of the workforce appears to be in jobs with a mandatory retirement policy. Furthermore, the 11.1% figure is likely an *extreme* upper limit of the proportion of the workforce who retired *involuntarily* because of mandatory retirement, since the mandatory retirement date could correspond with their preferred age of retirement. Retiring because of a mandatory retirement policy does not mean that the decision was involuntary. This is supported by the empirical evidence[8] that banning mandatory retirement has not had a substantial effect on older workers continuing in employment.

---

[8]Reid (1998) and Shannon and Grierson (2004) for Canadian evidence, with references also to US evidence.

As indicated in the more detailed discussion in Gomez and Gunderson (2005) retiring due to mandatory retirement was more prominent for males and persons with higher education, better health, full-time work, urban locations and higher income households. These are characteristics generally associated with more advantaged as opposed to vulnerable workers.

Factors that Would Have Facilitated Continued Employment

In descending order of their relative importance, the factors that would have facilitated the continued employment of persons who retired were (percents summing to more than 100% since multiple responses were possible):

- better health 27.3%
- part-time work 23.1%
- work fewer days 22.9%
- work shorter days 21.0%
- better pay 16.4%
- vacation leaves 13.0%
- no mandatory retirement 10.5%
- suitable care giving 5.8%

Better health tops the list, but this is followed closely by reduced *work-time* arrangements that are under the control of employers. Many retirees would have continued if they could have reduced work time in such forms as part-time work, fewer days per week, fewer hours per day and longer vacations or leaves. This highlights that if employers want older workers to continue working to offset the labour and skill shortages associated with the impending retirements of the large baby-boom cohort, flexible work-time arrangements are a viable mechanism. Of course, this entails a Catch-22 situation: in order to get older workers to continue working, employers should enable them to work less. But this is part of a phasing into retirement that is likely in the interests of all parties, in part to avoid the all-or-nothing pattern that is otherwise common.

The fact that only 10.5% suggested they would continue working if there were no mandatory retirement suggests again that this is not a substantial constraint for most. Again, this does not imply that they would prefer not to have the policy of mandatory retirement. They may well prefer the policy for reasons outlined subsequently, but say that they would have continued working if the policy did not exist.

Returning to Work after Retirement

Almost one-quarter (22.6%) of persons who ever retired had returned to work after retiring. For those who returned, the most prominent reason for returning was financial (43.9%) followed by did not like retirement (22.4%), with returning because of improvements in health being uncommon (5.2%), as was the case for care-giving no longer being required (2.9%). Females were more likely to return because it was no longer necessary to provide care-giving. Divorced persons were more likely to return for financial reasons while widows were more likely to return because care-giving is no longer needed, possibly reflecting the fact that they were providing care until their spouse deceased. Immigrants who arrived before 1970 and in the 1970s were less likely to have to return to the labour market for financial reasons while those who arrived in the 1980s and 1990s were more likely to have to return for financial reasons, likely reflecting the greater difficulty that more recent cohorts of immigrants have had assimilating into the labour market. Retirees in Quebec and Manitoba were much less likely to return because they did not like retirement. Since these were the two jurisdictions that banned mandatory retirement this likely reflects that fact that persons in those provinces would be less likely to retire if they felt they would not like retirement.

Myths and Realities about Mandatory Retirement

These background facts provide evidence to guide some of our discussion of the myths and realities about mandatory retirement. We fully recognize the dictum scrawled in a washroom stall: "reality is for those who can't face drugs". Nevertheless, we continue undaunted under the rationale that: "reality is for those who have fallen victim to the myths". What are the myths and the realities?

Mandatory Retirement Means Having to Retire from the Labour Force

Mandatory retirement is often erroneously regarded as government or other policy that requires individuals to retire from the labour force at some predetermined age such as 65 when public pensions such as the Canada/ Quebec Pension Plan (C/QPP) are normally received. The Ontario government's Speech from the Throne on April 30, 2003, announcing the government's intention to ban mandatory retirement, for example, stated: "[The government] will also introduce legislation to allow more seniors to remain active in the workforce — retiring at a time of their own choosing, not an arbitrarily *government appointed time*" [emphasis added].[9] *The Globe and Mail* stated: "CPP [Canada Pension Plan] should be more flexible so that it *allows* people to stay in the workforce past 65 if they want to and are able" [emphasis added, highlighting that the implication is that the CPP does not allow people to work past 65].[10]

The reality is that mandatory retirement policies are private contractual arrangements between employers and employees that terminate a particular contractual arrangement invariably at the age when the employer-sponsored occupational pension plan normally becomes available. In some cases, termed *compulsory* retirement, re-contracting can occur and a new contractual arrangement can be worked out that allows the person to continue working for that employer. In other cases, termed *automatic* retirement, the parties pre-commit to not allowing re-contracting. Mandatory retirement is part of a collective agreement or formal personnel policy and not part of any government policy or public pension policy that prohibits individuals from working past age 65 or any age. As discussed subsequently, government laws and policies only allow or disallow private parties from entering into arrangements that involve mandatory retirement.

Mandatory Retirement is an Employer Policy Forced on Employees

There is often the perception that mandatory retirement is a policy that benefits only employers, enabling them to shed their expensive and unproductive older workers. This image is highlighted by phrases like "forced" retirement or "involuntary" retirement.

---

[9]Hon James K. Bartleman. "Speech from the Throne," April 30, 2003, <http://hansardindex.ontla.on.ca/hansardeissue/37-4/l001.htm> (October 15, 2004).

[10]Heather Scoffield, "Rethink CPP's Age-65 Rule," *The Globe and Mail*, April 21, 2004, p. A1.

The reality is that mandatory retirement can serve a number of positive functions for *both* employers and employees. Otherwise it would not be part of collective agreements negotiated by powerful unions and generally defended by unions as in the interest of their members. Nor would it be part of formal personnel practices where individual employees often have considerable individual bargaining power.

Possible rationales for mandatory retirement have been enumerated in detail elsewhere.[11] As such, they will only be summarized here, emphasizing how they can be in the interests of *both* employers and employees.

Mandatory retirement can facilitate deferred or back-loaded compensation in longer-term contractual arrangements whereby workers are underpaid relative to their productivity when they are younger and overpaid relative to their productivity when they are older and more senior with the organization. Importantly, such a deferred compensation package implies nothing about the relationship between productivity and age; whatever that relationship it simply implies that people are paid less than their productivity when younger and more when they are more senior with the organization. Mandatory retirement provides a termination date to such a contractual arrangement (Lazear, 1979) with the equilibrium condition being that the expected present value of the overpayment period just compensates for the underpayment period. Without a termination date, the equilibrium could not be sustained because the overpayment period could continue for an undefined period.

Deferred compensation can be an optimal compensation scheme for employers for a number of reasons. It can deter shirking and induce work effort from employees, and foster loyalty and commitment, since the deferred compensation is like the employer holding a "performance bond" to be returned to the employee conditional upon good performance (Lazear, 1979). For the same reasons deferred compensation fosters employees having an interest in the financial solvency of the firm and this in turn can encourage behaviours such as concession bargaining to sustain that solvency. It can reduce quits and unwanted turnover since employees have an incentive to remain with their firm to receive their deferred compensation (Ippolito, 1987, 1991). This reduced turnover in turn provides an incentive for the firm to provide training to their employees since they can recoup their training investments (Carmichael, 1983). Deferred

---

[11]Rationales for mandatory retirement are outlined, for example, in Gunderson and Pesando (1980, 1988), Gomez, Gunderson, and Luchak (2002) and Gunderson and Hyatt (2005).

compensation can save on current wage costs and provide a source of internal funds for investment. It can enable employers to periodically monitor and evaluate the performance of their employees and to do so on a retrospective basis, based on past performance which is easy to observe (Prendergast, 1999, p. 47). In a world of asymmetric information, deferred compensation can discourage workers who privately know that they will be poor performers or "lemons" from applying since their poor performances will be revealed over time (Salop and Salop, 1976). Since their deferred compensation will be paid in the future, it may also attract employees who are savers and more future oriented, and these may be associated with desirable work characteristics (Ippolito, 1994, 2002).

Survey evidence indicates that employees also prefer such deferred compensation (Frank and Hutchens, 1993; Loewenstein and Sicherman, 1991) for a variety of reasons. It often comes in the form of pension benefit accruals and this provides security in retirement. As well, deferred compensation (especially in the form of pensions) implies deferred taxes, perhaps coming at a time in the life cycle when marginal tax rates are lower. Employees may prefer the periodic and retrospective monitoring and evaluation that is facilitated by deferred compensation. They may value the longer-term employment relationship that tends to be associated with deferred compensation. Employees may also receive higher lifetime compensation to the extent that deferred compensation has positive incentive effects and hence better performance outlined previously.

Employees are also protected from opportunistic behaviour on the part of employers who otherwise may have an incentive to dismiss employees when their wages begin to exceed their productivity. Firms that did this would be disciplined by a loss of reputation that would inhibit hiring new employees into such a deferred compensation system (unless they voluntarily induced older employees to leave through generous early retirement buyouts). They could also be subject to wrongful dismissal claims where the magnitude of any award would be based on any wage loss associated with their being displaced to their next-best alternative employment. When they are covered by a collective agreement, employees are protected by seniority rules as well as unjust dismissal protection through the grievance procedure.

Mandatory retirement can also serve other positive functions for both employers and employees. For employers, it can facilitate succession planning and the costing of age-related fringe benefits such as pensions and disability benefits since the retirement date is known in advance. For the same reason it can facilitate planning for retirement on the part of employees in advance of their known retirement date.

Mandatory retirement can facilitate employee renewal and open job and promotion opportunities for younger persons. It can reduce the need for the monitoring and evaluation of older workers who are approaching the mandatory retirement age and who otherwise may be dismissed for poor performance. Employers and work-teams are more likely to "wait it out" knowing that it is for a finite period. This in turn facilitates "retiring with dignity" on the part of older employees.

Clearly, there are a variety of reasons for both employers and employees as to why mandatory retirement may be part of an optimal compensation policy. It is not simply a policy that mean-spirited employers force on employees. Even if employers do benefit disproportionately more by the policy and it imposes costs on employees, this simply means that employers have to compensate employees for such a disamenity at the workplace. This could occur in the form of compensating wage premiums or perhaps pensions to provide income security in the post-retirement period.[12]

Mandatory Retirement is Forced on Vulnerable and Uninformed Employees

The impression often exists that mandatory retirement is not only forced on employees, but that the employees are vulnerable and uninformed. It is the case that mandatory retirement may be a job attribute that some employees may reluctantly accept even if it is accompanied by higher wages and more generous pensions. But all jobs involve a bundle of attributes that have to be traded off in any decision to accept or leave a job.

Furthermore, as outlined previously in the background material and in the general literature, the reality is that mandatory retirement is generally associated with "good jobs" with higher wages, generous pensions and due process provided at work.[13] Mandatory retirement is generally part of a

---

[12]Canadian evidence on the wage-pension trade-off is provided in Pesando, Gunderson, and Hyatt (1992), which also contains a discussion of the US literature in this area.

[13]The association between mandatory retirement and "good jobs" is documented and discussed in Gomez, Gunderson, and Luchak (2002), Gunderson and Pesando (1988, p. 33), and Pesando and Gunderson (1988 and references cited therein).

Rafael Gomez and Morley Gunderson

collective agreement or formal personnel policy involving an implicit contract of long-term employment relationships. Vulnerable workers, in contrast, are more often part of the "spot market" with no mandatory retirement — but also no pension, collective agreement, personnel policy or job security. They are generally hired and terminated at the will of the employer.

Since mandatory retirement is part of an inter-temporal contractual arrangement where the constraint comes later in the person's career, it is possible that individuals underestimate the constraining effect.[14] It is also possible that they may not be fully informed about the constraint. But these are always issues associated with any inter-temporal contracts such as student loans or mortgages or even marriage contracts. Banning such inter-temporal contracts to "protect people from themselves" (or at least to protect their future self from their current self) seems an over-reaction. The appropriate response would be to ensure that employees are informed of the constraint and possibly that the constraint is accompanied by other benefits at the time it becomes binding. Since mandatory retirement is often part of a collective agreement and invariably twinned with a pension, it is very likely that employees are informed of the policy and they receive the benefit of the pension at the time the constraint binds. As well, court decisions have disallowed mandatory retirement when individual employees were not informed of the policy.[15]

It is the case that employees may prefer that the policy not be in place when the constraint becomes binding, but they have benefited from it earlier and they will benefit by it being banned since they will receive a windfall from any continuation of deferred compensation whereby their wages exceed their productivity. In that vein, the growing voting bloc of "grey panthers" suggests that they may well pressure for banning mandatory retirement.

---

[14]This argument is articulated in Kesselman (2004, 2005) and Krashinsky (1988).

[15]The British Columbia Supreme Court in *McLaren v. Pacific Coast Savings Credit Union,* British Columbia Court of Appeals, 186 (2000), disallowed a mandatory retirement provision on the grounds that it had not been effectively communicated to the employee and the employee had not explicitly accepted it as a condition of employment.

Mandatory Retirement Has a Disproportionate Adverse Effect on Women and Immigrants

Mandatory retirement is often perceived as having a disproportionate adverse effect on women and immigrants — groups that may not have worked sufficiently long in the labour market to accumulate labour market earnings to provide savings for their retirement, or who may not have accumulated the service credits upon which pension benefits are based. For women, this may occur because of career interruptions associated with childbirth and child-raising. For immigrants it may occur because they may be late entrants into the labour market, and more recent cohorts may have had difficulty assimilating into the labour market.

It is the case that women tended not to accumulate the service credits upon which pension benefits are often based and this also reduces their eligibility for subsidized early retirement benefits (Pesando, Gunderson, and McLaren, 1991). However, that effect is dissipating over time as women's participation rate is approaching that of men, and subsidized early and special retirement benefits are becoming less prominent than they were in the 1970s and 1980s when they were used as a form of downsizing — the current issue being one of labour shortages (Conference Board of Canada, 2005). As well, both women and immigrants may have benefited by the job and promotion opportunities that were fostered by retirements induced by mandatory retirement.

Mandatory Retirement Will Foster Poverty amongst the Aged

A further myth is that mandatory retirement will foster poverty amongst the aged since it may inhibit some from continuing working to accumulate savings for retirement (Croll, 1979, p. 26; McDonald, 1995, p. 447).

The reality is that it would be extremely rare to find anyone in poverty who retired because of a formal mandatory retirement policy. As indicated previously, mandatory retirement is associated with good jobs and pensions. Persons who retired from such jobs would not be in poverty except for extremely unusual circumstances.

In fact a legitimate concern is that banning mandatory retirement could exacerbate poverty if it led to a dissipation of the pensions that are invariably twinned with mandatory retirement. Pensions may dissipate because people could be perceived as capable of working indefinitely; there would no longer be a need to provide pensions as a *quid pro quo* for mandatory retirement. Since private pension income is the largest component of income for the elderly, then any dissipation of pensions could reduce their financial security in retirement.[16]

Mandatory Retirement Constitutes Age Discrimination

The most notable attack on mandatory retirement is that it constitutes age discrimination and this is the argument upon which court cases against mandatory retirement have been based.[17] The argument seems appealing since mandatory retirement is an age-related rule that indicates that the person has to retire from a particular job at a pre-specified age, regardless of their performance. The appearance of age discrimination is enhanced by the fact that in jurisdictions where mandatory retirement is allowed, it is done so largely through an age cap or limit in the human rights code at age 65 (Gunderson, 2003). That is, the human rights code which normally protects against discrimination does not apply for employment issues for persons over 65. This appears to say: "discrimination on the basis of age is prohibited — except against persons age 65 and older"! The reality is that this age cap exists to allow mandatory retirement as not being contestable in the courts. But the reality is also that this creates a loophole in that persons 65 and older do not receive normal protection against age discrimination.

Age discrimination is a serious concern and it likely has not received the attention given to other forms of discrimination. As indicated in Ontario Human Rights Commission: "Age cases tend to be treated differently than other discrimination cases, particularly when the case involves retirement issues. The most noticeable difference from a human rights perspective is the lack of moral opprobrium linked to age discrimination which, in comparable circumstances would generate outrage if the ground of discrimination were, say, race, sex or disability" (2000, p. 39). Further-

---

[16]In 2003, retirement income from private pensions averaged $14,100 for the 60% of persons over 65 who had such income. This was over half (56%) of the average income of about $25,100 across all persons age 65 and over (Statistics Canada, 2005).

[17]Legal issues surrounding mandatory retirement in Canada are discussed in Gillin and Klassen (2005), Gunderson (2003) and Ontario Human Rights Commission (2000, 2001).

more, age discrimination is difficult to document empirically (unlike say gender discrimination through pay equity procedures) in part because age is related to so many other factors that can influence wage and employment outcomes (Gunderson, 2003).

The age discrimination argument, however, ignores the fact that mandatory retirement is a mutually agreed upon private contractual arrangement between informed parties where the employees have considerable individual or collective bargaining power. It is part of an inter-temporal contractual arrangement generally made at the time in an individual's life when the discriminatory attribute (age) is not a factor when the contractual arrangement is made. Importantly, the age of mandatory retirement is a characteristic that applies to all who are in that contractual arrangement if they have the good fortune to reach the age in question. If it is discrimination, it is discrimination that our *current* selves are imposing on our *future* selves. This is different from discrimination against *other* groups such as women, visible minorities, Aboriginal persons or disabled persons when discrimination is imposed by majority groups.

Mandatory Retirement Fosters Labour and Skill Shortages

A further argument against mandatory retirement is that it can foster labour and skill shortages at a time when the retirements of the baby-boom population are fostering such shortages. Requiring large numbers of baby boomers to retire at a specific age contributes to such shortages.

The reality is that employers can move away from mandatory retirement if they find that it inhibits them from filling labour shortages. In fact, this does appear to be occurring in the current climate of impending shortages: survey evidence from the Conference Board of Canada (2005, p. 11) indicates that 55% of Canadian companies that have a mandatory retirement policy intend to eliminate that policy in the near future. Firms that follow automatic retirement where they have pre-committed not to continue to employ their retirees can also shift to compulsory retirement (which simply terminates the existing contractual arrangement) and employ them on a new contractual basis. They could also raise the mandatory retirement age. In situations where mandatory retirement is part of the collective agreement, they would obviously have to negotiate these changes with the union, but this is part of the normal give-and-take of the collective bargaining process. If the gains to employers from altering mandatory retirement to facilitate filling labour shortages outweigh the costs, then this would provide the

Rafael Gomez and Morley Gunderson

means to compensate the unionized employees. Furthermore, workers who retire from a particular employer because of mandatory retirement could still remain in the labour force and fill shortages of other employers. In essence, banning employers from having mandatory retirement to help them fill their labour shortages, again appears to be an over-reaction to help employers help themselves. Surely they can do it on their own if it is sensible.

Mandatory Retirement Is Against the Interest of Some Union Members

When mandatory retirement is part of a collective agreement there is often the concern that the union may not represent the interests of all of its members and some individual workers may not want the policy. This is always a concern with respect to collectively provided goods. Workers without children may not want unions to negotiate childcare arrangements. Workers in good health may not want to give up cash wages for health and disability benefits. Young workers may not want to give up cash wages for future pension benefits. Workers who played hockey as youths and lost their teeth as a right of passage in Canada may not want their union to negotiate dental plans. These are part of the normal union trade-offs that are always present.

Again, the reality is that it is an over-reaction for governments to prohibit unions from negotiating provisions like mandatory retirement in return for pension benefits because they want to protect union members from the union. Some protections already exist in that members can bring a "duty of fair representation" complaint against the union if they feel that their interests are not properly being represented. Furthermore, union actions are largely determined by the preference of the median union voter. Since the median union voter is likely to be an older worker, the trade-offs involved in mandatory retirement are likely to be well represented by the union.

Mandatory Retirement Should Be Banned

The arguments and myths outlined above foster the "mother of all myths" — that mandatory retirement should be banned. Individuals should be able to choose their own time of retirement rather than have that decision made by a company personnel practice or collective agreement. Mandatory retirement appears to be against individual choice.

But the reality is that the "pro-choice" argument would allow private parties the choice to enter into contractual arrangements like mandatory retirement because of the previously discussed benefits even though it constrained choices in the future. Banning mandatory retirement is banning the private parties from the option of entering into such contractual arrangements in spite of the mutual benefits.

This highlights that the relevant question to ask with respect to mandatory retirement is *not*: Are you for or against mandatory retirement? Rather, it is: Are you for or against allowing private parties to enter into contractual arrangements that provide mutual benefits, but that can impose constraints like terminating an existing contractual arrangement? It is quite possible to be individually against mandatory retirement at your workplace but be in favour of allowing it to exist, just as it is possible to be individually against abortion, but "pro-choice" in allowing the parties the right to chose. Governments often ban mutually agreed upon contractual arrangements like prostitution or assisted-suicide. But they sanction others like marriage contracts and loan contracts that provide mutual benefits and impose constraints. As such, legitimate trade-offs and difficult decisions are involved. Is mandatory retirement more like prostitution and assisted-suicide or like marriage or loan contracts?

Our perspective is that it is more like the latter and hence should be sanctioned and not banned. It confers mutually beneficial arrangements which is why it is negotiated in situations where the parties have reasonable individual and/or collective bargaining parties. The parties do not need to be protected from themselves by prohibiting them from entering into such arrangements. If these mutual gains from trade are no longer prominent, then the parties will voluntarily negotiate new arrangements that suit their changing needs, as appears to be occurring already.

The current practice of accommodating mandatory retirement by having an age cap in the human rights code of jurisdictions that allow mandatory retirement, however, creates a loophole in that it does not provide the normal protection against age discrimination to persons over age 65. The solution, however, is simple. Remove the age cap so that such persons have the normal protection against age discrimination, but exempt *bona fide* pension plans or collective agreements that have mandatory retirement (Gunderson, 1998, 2004). This will effectively allow mandatory retirement since it invariably is part of a pension plan or collective agreement. But it ensures that the contractual arrangement is allowed only if there is the *quid pro quo* of income security of a *bona fide* pension plan and/or collective agreement. One could also add the requirement that employees be fully informed of the existence of the mandatory retirement requirement, perhaps by signing a formal statement to that effect. If there is concern that collective agreements do not provide adequate protection — and this is not a concern of these authors — then the exemption could exist only if there is a *bona fide* pension plan.

Such an arrangement would allow private contracting in this area, but only if it were accompanied by specific safeguards. In our view, this would provide the appropriate balance in this complex, and often misunderstood, area.

References

Beaujot, R. 2004. *Delayed Life Transitions: Trends and Implications.* Ottawa: Vanier Institute of the Family.

Carmichael, L. 1983. "Firm-Specific Human Capital and Promotion Ladders", *Bell Journal of Economics* 14 (Spring), 251–258.

Chen, J. and J. Wayne. 2000. "Are Recent Cohorts Healthier than their Predecessors?" *Health Reports* 11, 9–23.

Conference Board of Canada. 2005. *Work to Retirement: An Emerging Business Challenge.* Ottawa: Conference Board of Canada.

Croll, D. 1979. *Retirement Without Tears: Report of the Special Senate Committee on Retirement Age Policies.* Ottawa: Supply and Services.

Crompton, S. 2000. "One Hundred Years of Health", *Canadian Social Trends* 57, 2–13.

Frank, R. and R. Hutchens. 1993. "Wages, Seniority and the Demand for Rising Consumption Profiles", *Journal of Economic Behavior and Organization* 21, 251–276.

Gillin, C.T. and T. Klassen. 2005. "The Shifting Judicial Foundation of Legalized Age Discrimination", in T. Gillin, D. MacGregor, and T. Klassen (eds.), *Time's Up! Mandatory Retirement in Canada.* Toronto: James Lorimer Publishers, 45–73.

Gomez, R. and M. Gunderson. 2005. *Costs and Benefits of Workforce Aging and Retirement to Firms.* Ottawa: Human Resources Development Canada.

Gomez, R., M. Gunderson, and A. Luchak. 2002. "Mandatory Retirement: A Constraint in Transitions to Retirement?" *Employee Relations* 24(4), 403–422.

Gunderson, M. 1983. "Mandatory Retirement and Personnel Policies", *Columbia Journal of World Business* 28 (Summer), 8–15.

_____. 1998. *Flexible Retirement as an Alternative to 65-and-Out.* C.D. Howe Institute Commentary No. 106. Toronto: C.D. Howe Institute, 1–16.

_____. 2003. "Age Discrimination in Employment in Canada", *Contemporary Economic Policy* 21, 318–323.

_____. 2004. "Banning Mandatory Retirement: Throwing the Baby Out with the Bathwater", *C.D. Howe Institute Backgrounder* (March), 1–18.

Gunderson, M. and D. Hyatt. 2005. "Mandatory Retirement: Not as Simple as it Seems", in T. Gillin, D. MacGregor, and T. Klassen (eds.), *Time's Up! Mandatory Retirement in Canada.* Toronto: James Lorimer Publishers, 139–160.

Gunderson, M. and J. Pesando. 1980. "Eliminating Mandatory Retirement: Economics and Human Rights", *Canadian Public Policy* 6 (Spring), 352–360.

_____. 1988. "The Case for Allowing Mandatory Retirement", *Canadian Public Policy* 14 (March), 32–39.

Hewitt Associates. 2003. *Mandatory Retirement: Current Practice and Future Directions Survey Report.* Toronto: Hewitt Associates.

Hogan, S. and J. Lise. 2003. "Life Expectancy, Health Expectancy and the Life Cycle", *Horizons* 6, 2–9.

Ibbott, P., D. Kerr, and R. Beaujot. 2006. "Probing the Future of Mandatory Retirement in Canada", *Canadian Journal on Aging* 25(2), 161–178.

Ippolito, R. 1987. "Why Federal Workers Don't Quit?" *Journal of Human Resources* 22, 281–299.

_____. 1991, "Encouraging Long-Term Tenure: Wage Tilt or Pensions?" *Industrial and Labor Relations Review* (April), 520–535.

_____. 1994, "Pensions, Sorting, and Indenture Premia", *Journal of Human Resources* 29, 795–812.

_____. 2002. "Stayers as 'Workers' and 'Savers': Toward Reconciling the Pension-Quit Literature", *Journal of Human Resources* 37, 275–308.

Kesselman, J. 2004. *Mandatory Retirement and Older Workers: Encouraging Longer Working Lives.* C.D. Howe Institute Commentary No. 200. Toronto: C.D. Howe Institute.

_____. 2005. "Challenging the Economic Assumptions of Mandatory Retirement", in T. Gillin, D. MacGregor, and T. Klassen (eds.), *Time's Up! Mandatory Retirement in Canada.* Toronto: James Lorimer Publishers, 161–189.

Krashinsky, M. 1988. "The Case for Eliminating Mandatory Retirement: Why Economics and Human Rights Need Not Conflict", *Canadian Public Policy* 14, 40–51.

Lazear, E. 1979. "Why is There Mandatory Retirement", *Journal of Political Economy* 87 (December), 1261–1284.

Loewenstein, G. and N. Sicherman. 1991. "Do Workers Prefer Increasing Wage Profiles?" *Journal of Labor Economics* 9, 67–84.

Lowe, G. 2005. *Work-Retirement Transitions: A Synthesis Report.* Report for Human Resources and Skills Development Canada.

Marshall, K. and V. Ferrao. 2007. "Participation of Older Workers", *Perspectives on Labour and Income* 19 (Autumn), 31–38.

Martel, L., C. Caron-Malenfant, S. Vézina, and A. Bélanger. 2007. "Labour Force Projections for Canada, 2006–2031", *Canadian Economic Observer* (June), 3.1–3.13.

McDonald, L. 1995. "Retirement for the Rich and Retirement for the Poor: From Social Security to Social Welfare", *Canadian Journal on Aging* 14, 447–451.

Milligan, K. 2005. *Making it Pay to Work: Improving the Work Incentives in Canada's Public Pension System.* C.D. Howe Institute Commentary No. 218. Toronto: C.D. Howe Institute.

Ontario Human Rights Commission. 2000. *Discrimination and Age: Human Rights Issues Facing Older Persons in Ontario.* Toronto: Ontario Human Rights Commission.

_____. 2001. *Time for Action: Advancing Human Rights for Older Ontarians.* Toronto: Ontario Human Rights Commission.

Pesando, J. and M. Gunderson. 1988. "Retirement Incentives Contained in Occupational Pension Plans and their Implications for Mandatory Retirement Debate", *Canadian Journal of Economics* 21 (May), 244–264.

Pesando, J., M. Gunderson, and D. Hyatt. 1992. "Early Retirement Pensions and Employee Turnover: An Application of the Option Value Approach", *Research in Labor Economics* 13, 321–337.

Pesando, J., M. Gunderson, and J. McLaren. 1991. "Pension Benefits and Male-Female Wage Differentials", *Canadian Journal of Economics* 24, 536–550.

Prendergast, C. 1999. "The Provision of Incentives in Firms", *Journal of Economic Literature* 37 (March), 7–63.

Reid, F. 1988. "Economic Aspects of Mandatory Retirement: The Canadian Experience", *Relations industrielles/industrial relations* 43, 101–113.

Salop, J. and S. Salop. 1976. "Self-Selection and Turnover in the Labor Market", *Quarterly Journal of Economics* 90 (November), 619–627.

Schellenberg, G. and C. Silver. 2004. "You Can't Always Get What You Want: Retirement Preferences and Experiences", *Canadian Social Trends.* Ottawa: Statistics Canada, 2–7.

Schirle, T. 2007. "Why Have the Labour Force Participation Rates of Older Men Increased Since the Mid-1990s". Working Paper. Waterloo: University of Waterloo School of Business and Economics.

Shannon, M. and D. Grierson. 2004. "Mandatory Retirement and Older Worker Employment", *Canadian Journal of Economics* 3, 528–551.

Statistics Canada. 2005. *Income Trends in Canada, 1980–2003*, Catalogue No. 75–202–XIE. Ottawa: Statistics Canada.

United Nations. 2002. *United Nations World Population Projections: The 2002 Revisions,* Volume II, *Sex and Age.* New York: United Nations.

The Retirement Prospects of Immigrants: Will it Require a New Social Contract?

Derek Hum and Wayne Simpson

Introduction

An aging population and low fertility rates are acknowledged features of Canada's demographic landscape (see, for example, HRSDC, 2007). Immigration is now seen as a key component influencing the growth of population and the labour force. However, demographical projections typically demonstrate that immigration as a policy tool cannot possibly offset the effects of low fertility and an aging population, since the level of immigration required to do so is simply not feasible (Denton and Spencer, 2005). To a lesser extent, Canadian productivity growth and, con-comitantly, our capacity to fund social benefits for all Canadians also depend on our labour force and immigration. Canada's retirement programs, public and private, will come under strain. In the public sector, Canada's aging population together with continued reliance on pay-as-you go financing of public pensions will strain our ability to maintain benefit levels, stable premiums and flexible retirement timing, or all three. In the private sector, increasing reliance on immigration for population growth and productivity also has implications if immigrants do not easily and

The authors acknowledge financial assistance from the Prairie Centre for Excellence in Research on Immigration and Integration (now the Prairie Metropolis Centre).

quickly integrate into Canada's labour market. For example, Picot (2004) suggests that the new face of poverty in Canada is increasingly "immigrant", and recent work on labour market assimilation of immigrants has established the deteriorating prospects in the wage labour market as well as a lack of training opportunities for immigrants vis-à-vis earlier generations (see Hum and Simpson, 2003; 2004a,b). If immigrants are unable to achieve economic integration in the labour market and increasingly fall into poverty, this bodes ill for their retirement prospects.

These trends have implications (macro and micro) for individual retirement plans and public policies, especially for immigrants. A lower lifetime earnings profile for immigrants implies permanent scarring discomfort in the retirement years. Past savings and asset accumulation, as well as the need for future income, affect the choice of retirement date. It has been noted that Canada's public pensions have a major influence on work incentives (Baker, Gruber, and Milligan , 2003), and private pensions likely have similar impacts on retirement behaviour. Immigrants may have to postpone or forego retirement altogether if pensions are inadequate. On the other hand, there is the suggestion that immigrants may have stronger desires to work, setting aside other factors, so that delay in retirement may be partly a matter of choice.

Canada's commitment to admitting and integrating new immigrants is unyielding and irreversible. Nonetheless, a failure to integrate immigrants into Canada's workforce will, over time, engender long-run costs for Canada's social benefits, including its suite of retirement programs. A new social contract may be necessary if Canada continues to welcome large numbers of immigrants but fails to integrate them in the economy, all the while desiring generous retirement benefits despite sluggish productivity.

This essay compares the retirement prospects of immigrants with their native-born Canadian counterparts (as a benchmark) using census data in addition to SLID (Survey of Labour and Income Dynamics). Based upon estimated structural differences in life trajectories of immigrants and native-born persons with respect to lifetime earnings, we simulate the potential "retirement gap" of both groups at various ages. This is useful for various policy investigations since one might examine, for example, the "gap" at particular benchmark ages; for example, at age 60 (when early Canada Pension Plan [CPP] are possible), or at age 65 (when Old Age Security

[OAS] and Guaranteed Income Supplement [GIS] are possible).[1] Since our primary objective is to provide a basis to inform policy, the main text merely sketches the econometrics of the simulation. Technical details are provided in Appendix A.

The structure of the paper is as follows. The next section outlines how we construct profiles of immigrant earnings by employing various censuses. The challenge is to incorporate data from all available censuses, yet distinguish the earnings profile over time between immigrants and native–born workers. After outlining our econometric approach, we summarize the main results of our estimates. The third section calculates what we term the "retirement gap", a measure that summarizes the difference in career earnings that an immigrant might expect at entry vis-à-vis a comparable native-born worker. The fourth section then re-examines the pension gap with more direct evidence from SLID (Survey of Labour and Income Dynamic) on contributions to registered pension plans and private retirement income. We offer some concluding remarks in the last section.

Immigrant Integration Earnings Profiles and the Pension Gap

Since we have data on earnings for immigrants and native-born workers in Canada for a variety of censuses that span various periods of economic conditions, this poses a challenge. We wish to estimate earnings profiles for individuals over an entire lifetime, yet census data provide information at a single specific point. Consequently, we use the now conventional "quasi-panel" approach.

---

[1]Care must be exercised in employing our general results when discussing specific programs. For example, many elderly immigrants have lower participation rates in OAS because of the residential requirement that one must have lived in Canada for ten years or more before becoming eligible for OAS. Further, two of three immigrants to Canada are visible minority members, and some visible minority groups may have low take-up rates. See an early paper by Hum and Chan (1980) for a case study on the take-up rate of Canada's OAS programs by the Chinese. The present paper is not concerned with program design details and delivery issues.

The census provides annual earnings at time t for immigrants who arrived in cohort i, denoted y_{it}^1, and for native born, denoted y_t^0. We assume these censuses occur k (= 5) years apart. For any cross-section t one can then estimate the predicted earnings difference between immigrant cohorts i and $i+k$ relative to the native born, where the earlier cohort i is associated with longer years since migration, as

$$\hat{y}_{i,t}^1 - \hat{y}_{i+k,t}^1 = \left[\left(\hat{y}_{i,t}^1 - \hat{y}_{i,t-k}^1\right) - \left(\hat{y}_t^0 - \hat{y}_{t-k}^0\right)\right]$$
$$+ \left[\left(\hat{y}_{i,t-k}^1 - \hat{y}_{i+k,t}^1\right) - \left(\hat{y}_{t-k}^0 - \hat{y}_t^0\right)\right] \tag{1)^2}$$

The first term on the right-hand side of equation (1) then captures the difference in the growth of earnings for immigrant cohort i and the native born from census period $t–k$ to census period t. This within-cohort growth measures the extent of immigrant integration of cohort i relative to the native-born comparison group. The second term on the right-hand side of equation (1) captures the difference in growth between cohort i in period $t–k$ and cohort $i+k$ in period t, or across-cohort growth for given years since migration, relative to the native-born counterfactual. The second term represents the bias associated with cross-sectional estimates of within-cohort earnings growth.

Much of the focus in the literature is on five-year growth rates of the earnings of *entering immigrants* in the first five years after entry. However, longer segments of the immigrant integration profiles can be derived from equation (1) for a sequence of census cross-sections. In particular, consider immigrant cohort i that entered r census periods earlier. One can estimate the entry effect, the difference in earnings between the entering immigrant cohort and the native born as $\hat{y}_{t-rk}^1 - \hat{y}_{t-rk}^0$, evaluated for the characteristics of immigrant cohort i. Then the within-cohort growth measures for immigrant cohort i relative to the native born over census periods $t,t–k,...,t–rk$ provide fairly lengthy estimates of the integration profile (the earnings gap for years since migration) for immigrants who arrived a long time ago.

---

[2]This is equation (3) in the Appendix and is found in Baker and Benjamin (1994, equation [8], p. 381), Grant (1999, equation [3], p. 939) and Frenette and Morissette (2003, equation [4], p. 2).

Figures 1 and 2 portray the immigrant integration profile that incorporates the entry and within growth effects at five-year intervals, estimated for a randomly drawn native-born comparison group and a matched native-born comparison group, for the immigrant arrival cohorts from 1976–80 to 1991–95. The vertical axis represents the gap between the mean earnings of an immigration cohort and its native-born counterparts, using OLS regression (the conventional method) and propensity score matching (marked with an M) to determine the native-born comparison group. The first figure uses the sparser Baker and Benjamin (B&B) (1994) specification while the second figure uses the richer Frenette and Morissette (F&M) (2003) specification that includes visible minority (rather than just black) and urban/regional variables (Montreal, Toronto, Vancouver, Quebec except Montreal, Ontario except Toronto, Manitoba, Saskatchewan, Alberta, BC except Vancouver). The F&M specification is only calculated for the censuses from 1986 because visible minority was not defined before then.

We highlight the following results:

(1) *The results are similar for the B&B and F&M specifications*; we therefore refer to the results from the B&B specification in subsequent discussion.

(2) *The entry effects are increasing*; the estimates from the matched comparison group are slightly larger for all cohorts except 1976–80.

(3) *The assimilation (within growth) effects are substantial and do not necessarily suggest that later cohorts will not achieve parity*; for example, the largest entry effect for the 1991–95 cohort is combined with a substantial assimilation effect (about 15%) in years five to ten which, if it continues, would permit parity within 20 years.

(4) *Projections based on particular specifications of the form of immigration integration profile are unreliable* (including our own in Hum and Simpson, 2004b). It is difficult to project assimilation rates because they are not uniform; for example, cohorts IM76–80 and IM86–90 faltered in the first five years (especially with the matched sample) and IM81–85 falters after doing well in the first five years. Contrary to Grant's (1999) projection, her IM81–85 may not achieve parity with the native born.

Figure 1: Immigrant Integration Profiles
   (B&B specification)

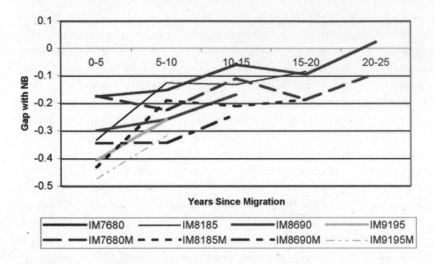

Source: 1981, 1986, 1991, 1996, 2001 Census Public Use Microdata Files.

Figure 2: Immigrant Integration Profiles
   (F&M specification)

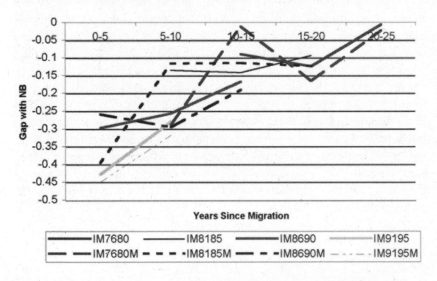

Source: 1981, 1986, 1991, 1996, 2001 Census Public Use Microdata Files.

Derek Hum and Wayne Simpson

Calculation of the Lifetime (Pensionable) Earnings Gap

The immigrant integration profiles depicted in the previous section reflect the percentage gap in mean earnings between an immigrant cohort and that of a comparable group of native-born workers. We now use these profiles, as inexact as they may be for later cohorts, to calculate the cumulative lifetime difference in earnings between these two groups (suitably discounted). This provides an estimate of the "retirement gap" between the two groups and the proportionate difference in pensionable earnings, since absent inheritances, lottery winnings, or other unexpected windfalls, it is the pattern of lifetime earnings (and savings) that determine the economic resources available at retirement.

There are, of course, immigrants who enter Canada late in life, principally through the family reunification and refugee categories, and typically participate little in the labour market. For these immigrants our analysis has little meaning. Rather, our analysis applies to what is now the majority of applicants who are admitted under the points system at a young age. These economic immigrants more and more dominate the evidence regarding immigrant integration because their labour market activity is relatively continuous.[3]

One useful measure might be the net present value of the earnings gap, which would then represent the lump-sum gap in career earnings that an immigrant could expect at entry. This can be expressed as a percentage of the earnings of a comparable native-born worker. If private pension income, and to a lesser extent CPP/QPP income, is closely related to earnings, the lump-sum earnings gap will give a measure of the pension gap between immigrants and the native born.

The logic of our calculation is as follows. Suppose we normalize native-born earnings to $1 per year over a working career of T years and suppose that r is the real rate of interest and discount rate. Then initial native-born earnings will have a present value of $1 and the value at retirement will be $\$1(1+r)^T$. Over T years, the stream of earnings will have a present value of

$$P_{nb} = \sum_{i=1}^{T} \$1 / (1+r)^i \quad \text{and a value at retirement of} \quad L_{nb} = \sum_{i=1}^{T} \$1(1+r)^i .$$

---

[3]We have not attempted to sort immigrants by age at arrival in our analysis, consistent with most of the quasi-panel analyses of immigrant integration patterns. We thank Tammy Schirle for pointing out this limitation of our approach.

Suppose now that immigrants initially earn a proportion $1 - \gamma_0$ of native-born earnings, where $0 < \gamma_0 < 1$ is the entry gap that is eroded with time spent in Canada ($\partial \gamma_i / \partial i < 0$). Parity with native-born earnings ($\gamma_i = 0$) may be achieved at some year i during the work career (or years since migration). Suppose further that a constant portion s of earnings is saved for a private pension, such that an annuity is financed from a retirement earnings pool of sL_{nb} with a present value of sP_{nb}. Then the corresponding present value of earnings for the foreign born will be

$$P_{fb} = \sum_{i=1}^{T} (1 - \gamma_i) / (1 + r)^i \quad \text{and the value at retirement will be}$$

$$L_{fb} = \sum_{i=1}^{T} \$(1 - \gamma_i)(1 + r)^i \quad . \text{Assuming a common savings rate for foreign-}$$

and native-born workers, the retirement earnings pool of immigrants will be sL_{fb} with a present value of sP_{fb} such that the pension gap will be

$$\left[sP_{nb} - sP_{fb} \right] / sP_{nb} = \left. \sum_{i=1}^{T} \gamma_i / (1 + r)^i \middle/ \sum_{i=1}^{T} 1 / (1 + r)^i \right. , \qquad (2)$$

which corresponds to a pension gap at retirement of

$$\left[sL_{nb} - sL_{fb} \right] / sL_{nb} = \left. \sum_{i=1}^{T} \gamma_i (1 + r)^i \middle/ \sum_{i=1}^{T} (1 + r)^i \right. . \qquad (3)$$

Consider the 1976–80-immigrant cohort whose lifetime earnings pattern, relative to the native born, is captured by subsequent censuses to 2001. We adopt the Baker and Benjamin (1994) specification, which is compatible with all previous Censuses to 1976. (The expanded Frenette and Morissette (2003) specification yielded similar results in the cases we estimated.) We use the estimates derived from the traditional OLS estimates first. For this cohort, the estimated immigrant integration profiles imply a pension gap of 11.4% using a discount rate (r) of 5% and a pension gap of 13.1% using a discount rate of 10%. A larger pension gap is to be expected with higher discount rates because the smaller differences between native-

and foreign-born earnings in the future (arising as immigrant integration proceeds) are more heavily discounted.

Our alternative estimates derived from propensity score matching produce a slightly more pessimistic picture of the immigrant integration profile and hence a slightly larger pension gap. For the 1976–80 cohort, we estimate a pension gap of 16.7% at a 5% discount rate and 17.4% at a 10% discount rate.

For other immigrant cohorts, the pension gap is more difficult to estimate because the immigrant integration profile is incomplete. Our approach is simply to "eyeball" the trajectory of the immigrant integration profile for each cohort; this produces the results reported in Table 1 for each cohort from 1976–80 to 1991–95. More sophisticated approaches could be taken but are unlikely to produce very different pension gap estimates since the later earnings are discounted more heavily. Note that our concerns about the reliability of immigrant integration profiles for more recent immigrant cohorts are less important in our exercise, since earnings later in the working lifetime have a less important role in pension income accumulation; that is, our results are largely driven by the earnings gap in the early years after entry and this gap is clearly growing for more recent immigrant cohorts.

As might be expected, the rising initial earnings disadvantage (entry effect) for more recent cohorts produces a growing pension gap. The OLS estimates suggest that the pension gap has doubled from 11% to 22% between the 1976–80 and 1991–95 cohorts, compared to the matching estimates that indicate the gap increasing from 17% to 28%, for a discount rate of 5%. With a discount rate of 10%, the OLS estimates again suggest a doubling of the pension gap from 13% to 26%, while the matching estimates suggest an increase from 17% to 33%. Our results in Table 1 quantify the growing prospective pension gap. This growing pension gap should not be much of a surprise since it is a mirror of the declining labour market fortunes of more recent immigrant cohorts.

Evidence on the Pension Gap from SLID

Previous sections have been guided by census data. We now examine more direct evidence on the pension gap with data from the Survey of Labour and Income Dynamics (SLID) 2002 Public File. SLID is designed as an overlapping six-year panel to capture labour market activity and financial

Table 1: Estimated Pension Gaps as Percentage of Native Born

	Discount rate (%)	IM7680 (%)	IM8185 (%)	IM8690 (%)	IM9195 (%)
OLS estimates	5.0	11.4	17.5	21.0	21.7
	10.0	13.1	20.4	23.5	26.3
Matched estimates	5.0	16.7	26.4	26.7	27.9
	10.0	17.4	29.2	29.3	32.6

Source: Estimates of immigrant earnings profiles from the Canadian Censuses of 1976, 1981, 1986, 1991, 1996 and 2001 plus imputed ("eyeballed") estimates of the profile over a working career of 25 years.

and income information for two panels of individual respondents in each survey period. In particular, SLID provides what amounts to tax record information for Registered Pension Plan (RPP) contributions as well as private pension income for respondents identified by immigration status, age and sex. Consequently, SLID is a valuable data source in addition to the census information. We restrict our analysis to males to be consistent with our earlier evidence.

We ask two questions. First, is there a difference in RPP contributions for immigrant and native-born men, *who are not retired* (have no pension income), by age? Second, is there a difference in private pension income between immigrant and native-born men *who have retired* (are drawing pension income) by age? We restrict our retirement group to those over the age of 55.

Figure 3 provides non-parametric estimates of RPP contributions by age for immigrant and native-born men.[4] It is clear that there is a pension contribution gap at almost all ages, beginning at very early ages and increasing to age 50, then declining. A small RPP contribution advantage for immigrants occurs after age 70. This does not appear to reflect a difference in rates of labour force participation between immigrant and

---

[4]Those who responded, "don't know" to the question on immigrant status are deleted from our analysis. This group is, however, quite large in SLID. The non-parametric estimates are derived from locally weighted regressions that use the tricube weighting function in STATA8.0 LOWESS.

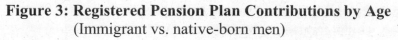

Figure 3: Registered Pension Plan Contributions by Age
(Immigrant vs. native-born men)

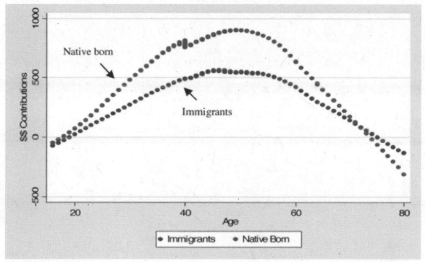

Source: SLID 2002 Public File.

native-born men after age 65, but rather a higher rate of contribution by immigrants who remain in the labour force — perhaps motivated by a desire to "catch up" for low contributions earlier in life.

Figure 4 provides similar evidence for private pension plan income. Immigrants declare less private pension income at almost all ages, consistent with the lower RPP contribution rates shown in Figure 3. Of course, immigrants drawing pensions likely arrived much earlier than those who are now working and making RPP contributions in Figure 3. Nonetheless, the private pension income gap is considerable: At age 60 (when early withdrawal of CPP is permitted), the gap is about $2,500 or 10% of the average native-born private pensions at that age. At ages 65 (the traditional benchmark age) and 69 (when withdrawal of pension monies is often mandatory), the pension gap is about $5,000 or 21–22% of the average native-born private pension at these ages. This gap is consistent with our estimates using the censuses of the differences in lifetime earnings between immigrant and native-born men. To rephrase the matter slightly, at certain conventional benchmark ages when retirement decisions must be considered, immigrants will have approximately 10% less income if they

Figure 4: Private Pension Income by Age
(Immigrant vs. native-born men 55 years and older)

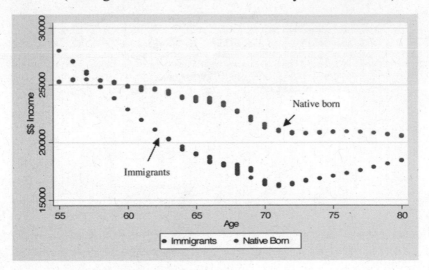

Source: SLID 2002 Public File.

attempt "early retirement" at age 60, and 21–22% less if they choose to delay retirement.

It must be remembered in all this discussion that earlier immigrant cohorts had more success with economic integration than the present generation, and therefore our estimate of the integration profiles embodies immigrant experiences that reflect this better integration performance. Since the current cohorts of immigrants who are still working have greater immigrants earnings gaps compared to the native born, our results predict that this pension gap will only continue to grow over time. This will pose a tremendous challenge for public policy in Canada, not only respecting the design and funding of our public pension programs, but also respecting our enduring legacy of efforts to assist and integrate immigrant workers.

Derek Hum and Wayne Simpson

Concluding Remarks

Canada's commitment to admitting and integrating new immigrants is part of this nation's historical social contract. We hold out for new Canadians a promise of economic success that converges to that enjoyed by all other Canadians. But unlike the cohorts that entered in the 1960s, immigrants to Canada within the last three decades have not fared as successfully. And over time, a continuing failure to integrate immigrants into the workforce will incur long-run costs for Canada's social benefits, including its suite of retirement programs.

This essay compares the retirement prospects of immigrants with their native-born Canadian counterparts employing data from the census and SLID. Census data cover the entire population but represent a snapshot at a single moment. Because our interest is in the lifetime income profiles of individuals, we employ a quasi-panel approach by combining several census datasets to estimate an economic integration time path. We also examine data from SLID. SLID is a useful data source because of its wide variable set (including government transfers) and panel nature. We employ matching methods to determine an appropriate comparison group (based on demographic characteristics, etc.) in the census datasets in order to compare immigrant earnings with native-born earnings. Based upon structural differences in life trajectories of immigrants and native-born persons (used as a benchmark), we calculate what we term a "retirement gap", defined as the net present value of the earnings gap between immigrant and comparable native-born individuals. This retirement gap represents the lump-sum gap in career earnings that an immigrant can expect at entry, expressed as a percentage of the earnings of a comparable native-born worker. We believe the retirement gap measure provides a reasonable basis to inform retirement policy in Canada respecting both immigrants and native-born individuals.

Appendix A
Towards Robust Economic Modeling of Immigrant Integration

Introduction

Key to our discussion of the "retirement gap" between immigrants and native-born workers is the estimated lifetime career earnings of these two groups. This Appendix discusses in greater detail the econometric complexities involved in this exercise, and our approach to the issues.

In the absence of experimental evidence, researchers regularly use non-experimental data. The *modus operandi* involves specification of a linear regression model with a set of critical explanatory variables that vary across agents and which, in the case of panel data, vary over time as well. Any misspecification involving the omission of relevant variables will introduce bias when they are correlated with included explanatory variables, as is normally the case in non-experimental data. Misspecification may include errors in the functional form.

Recognition of these potential specification pitfalls typically leads to specification searches in which a variety of models are estimated. The scientific hope is that the impact of the critical variables is robust, that it varies little as the specification of additional explanatory variables is altered. This hope is often not realized, leaving considerable doubt about the issue under study, the validity of published research, and the prospect for further analysis of non-experimental evidence to resolve the question. Ho *et al.* (2006) refer to this problem as "model dependence".

Recent research in program evaluation has provided new insights to the search for robust models, or models that eliminate the problem of model dependence. The basic evaluation problem is to estimate the impact of a program by comparing the behaviour of the program group with an appropriate comparison group. This literature demonstrates that important sources of bias arise but can be eliminated by careful statistical matching of the program and non-recipient groups, based on their observed characteristics, and assessment of what valid comparisons are supported by the data.

The argument for statistical matching to select appropriate comparators and produce robust model estimates is potentially more general. In this appendix we review the arguments for applying this approach to estimating the performance gap between immigrants and the native born, or immigrant integration. We review the relevant empirical literature and methods used to estimate immigrant integration. Our re-analysis of this evidence using matching estimators forms the basis of our results in the main text.

Model Dependence and Matching

The problem of model dependence in the context of regression models applied to non-experimental data arises from the literature on program evaluation. Suppose that you have a non-experimental dataset with an identifier of program participation. Evaluators wish to answer the question: What would have been the effect on those who took the program if they had not taken it? This measure of program impact is the "average treatment effect on the treated". The problem with this question is, of course, that we cannot observe someone as both a recipient and a non-recipient of the program at the same time. The standard solution is to use the non-recipients to estimate what the outcomes would have been for the recipients had they not taken the program. The identifying assumption is that the mean outcome of non-recipients is identical to that of recipients had they not taken the program, conditional on whatever characteristics we can observe about these groups that affect the outcome. But this may not hold, leading to bias in the estimation of the average treatment effect.

Heckman *et al.* (1998) show that there are three sources of selection bias with this approach. One bias arises from lack of "common support" when either the distribution of observable characteristics for the program group does not overlap the distribution of observable characteristics for the non-recipient group or vice versa. A second bias arises from "differential weighting" of the observable characteristics in the program group and non-recipient group samples where there is common support. The third bias is "true selection bias" which arises from unobservables and remains even when common values of the regressors for both the program group and an appropriate comparison group are used. True selection bias cannot be eliminated, but the sources of bias arising from lack of common support and differential weighting can be eliminated by careful statistical or propensity score matching of the program and non-recipient groups to eliminate differential weighting and to assess what valid comparisons are supported by the data available. Essentially, this involves relatively straightforward estimation of a model of program participation for the entire sample of program participants and non-recipients, based on their observed characteristics. This model yields "propensity to participate" scores which can be used to match program participants with one or a weighted average of non-recipients that have comparable predicted participation probabilities. The adequacy of the match can be assessed by balancing tests, which examine the similarity of the properties of the samples of participants and matched non-recipients. Heckman *et al.* (1998) and others have found that matching estimators, which then estimate program impacts non-parametrically from the refined samples of participants and non-participants, can provide more accurate estimates of program impacts in certain circumstances.

Application to Immigrant Integration

We apply the above approach to analyze the labour market performance of immigrants over time relative to their native-born counterparts, or what we term immigrant integration. Our "program impact" is simply "immigrant status" with a specified number of years in Canada. Our counterfactual or comparison group is the native born; that is, we use those born in Canada to estimate what the outcomes would have been for the immigrants had they been born in Canada.

To be specific, let y represent earnings. Then y will depend on a set of observable characteristics, x, and, for immigrants, an immigrant status function, $\gamma(h)$, where h represents years since migration. Let D be a dummy variable identifying our samples of immigrants ($D = 1$) and native born ($D = 0$). Then we can write our linear regression model to estimate immigrant integration effects in the form:

$$y^i = x^i \beta^i + \gamma(h)D + \varepsilon^i , \quad i = 0(D = 0), 1(D = 1) \quad (1)$$

That is, we can estimate immigrant integration effects by estimating $\gamma(h)$ from regression analysis of equation (1) if the identifying assumption that the mean labour market outcome of the native born is identical to that of immigrants had they been born in Canada, conditional on observable characteristics, is valid.

A body of empirical research has emerged in Canada following Borjas' (1985) pioneering quasi-panel approach to the analysis of immigrant integration in the United States. Borjas showed that immigrant integration tends to be overestimated in cross-sectional studies when unobserved differences among immigrant cohorts, or what Borjas terms cohort quality, is declining. This bias from cross-sectional evidence can be corrected by using a series of cross-sections of individual workers over time to separate immigrant integration within cohorts from differences across immigrant cohorts.

There are three comparable studies of immigrant integration in Canada that adopt Borjas' quasi-panel analysis. Baker and Benjamin (1994), analyzing the 1971, 1981 and 1986 censuses, estimate very low, and even negative, rates of growth of log earnings within immigrant cohorts. Adding the 1991 census, however, Grant (1999) estimates a rapid convergence for the 1980s immigrant cohort that implies parity within ten years. Using all censuses from 1981 to 2001, Frenette and Morissette (2003) find little evidence to suggest that the earnings growth of immigrants who landed in the 1990s will be sufficient to ever achieve parity with their native-born counterparts. These results have left a succession of analysts to wonder what might explain the rapid changes in immigrant fortunes through the last three decades of the twentieth century.[5]

Public use microdata files from the census provide a series of cross-sections which classify immigrant cohorts by period of immigration. Thus, researchers rewrite equation (1) to replace the specific immigrant integration profile $\gamma(h)$ with a set of cohort-specific intercepts, $\delta^1_{i,t}$, which identify immigrant cohort i in census time period t :

$$D = 1(immigrants): y^1_t = x^1_t \beta^1_t + \sum_i \delta^1_{i,t} + \varepsilon^1_t$$
$$D = 0(native\ born): y^0_t = x^0_t \beta^0_t + \delta^0_t + \varepsilon^0_t$$

(2)

The intercept term δ^0_t is common to all native born. The equations in (2) can be estimated for each census cross-section. From these equations, researchers can extract estimates of the predicted (log) earnings of

---

[5]Attempts to explain the changes in immigrant integration across cohorts include McDonald and Worswick (1998) and Green and Worswick (2003), using non-census data, and Abdurrahman and Skuterud (2003) and Frenette and Morissette (2003) using census data. At this point, we are not concerned with the analysis of what is causing changing immigrant fortunes but rather with the robustness of the estimates of immigrant integration on which this literature is predicated.

immigrants by cohort and time period and estimates of the predicted earnings of the native born by time period. For any cross-section t one can estimate the predicted earnings difference between immigrant cohorts i and $i + k$ relative to the native born, where the earlier cohort i is associated with longer years since migration, as

$$\hat{y}^1_{i,t} - \hat{y}^1_{i+k,t} = \left[\left(\hat{y}^1_{i,t} - \hat{y}^1_{i,t-k}\right) - \left(\hat{y}^0_t - \hat{y}^0_{t-k}\right)\right]$$
$$+ \left[\left(\hat{y}^1_{i,t-k} - \hat{y}^1_{i+k,t}\right) - \left(\hat{y}^0_{t-k} - \hat{y}^0_t\right)\right] \tag{3}^6$$

Then the first term on the right-hand side of equation (3) captures the difference in the growth of earnings for immigrant cohort i and the native born from census period $t - k$ to census period t. This within-cohort growth measures the extent of immigrant integration of cohort i relative to the native-born comparison group. The second term on the right-hand side of equation (3) captures the difference in growth between cohort i in period $t - k$ and cohort $i + k$ in period t, or across-cohort growth for given years since migration, relative to the native-born counterfactual. The second term represents the bias associated with cross-sectional estimates of within-cohort earnings growth. Borjas showed that, since across-cohort growth is positive when cohort quality is declining,[7] cross-sectional estimates of immigrant earnings growth will overestimate within-cohort growth, or true immigrant integration.

---

[6]This equation is found in Baker and Benjamin (1994, equation [8], p. 381), Grant (1999, equation [3], p. 939), and Frenette and Morissette (2003, equation [4], p. 2).

[7]That is, earlier cohort i does better than later cohort $i + k$ for given years since migration in relation to their native born counterparts. This declining cohort quality is broadly consistent with a shift in region-of-origin immigration patterns in North America from Europe to South Asia over the last four decades, if South Asian immigrants bring linguistic, work and social skills that are less valuable to the North American labour market.

Derek Hum and Wayne Simpson

Limitations and the Case for Matching

The focus, then, will be on estimates of within-cohort growth represented by

$$\left[\left(\hat{y}_{i,t}^1 - \hat{y}_{i,t-k}^1\right) - \left(\hat{y}_t^0 - \hat{y}_{t-k}^0\right)\right] \tag{4}$$

Predicted earnings in equation (3) or (4) are based on the estimates of equation (2) evaluated for some common bundle of characteristics. The convention is to evaluate predicted earnings at the mean sample characteristics for immigrant cohort i in period t, $\overline{x}_{i,t}^1$. In that case, given the estimates of $\hat{\beta}$ and $\hat{\delta}$ from equation (2), equation (3) reduces to:

$$
\begin{aligned}
\hat{\delta}_{i,t}^1 - \hat{\delta}_{i+k,t}^1 &= [\overline{x}_{i,t} \{(\hat{\beta}_t^1 - \hat{\beta}_{t-k}^1) - (\hat{\beta}_t^0 - \hat{\beta}_{t-k}^0)\} \\
&\quad + \{(\hat{\delta}_{i,t}^1 - \hat{\delta}_{i,t-k}^1) - (\hat{\delta}_t^0 - \hat{\delta}_{t-k}^0)\}] + [\overline{x}_{i,t} \{(\hat{\beta}_{t-k}^1 - \hat{\beta}_t^1) \\
&\quad - (\hat{\beta}_{t-k}^0 - \hat{\beta}_t^0)\} + \{(\hat{\delta}_{i,t-k}^1 - \hat{\delta}_{i+k,t}^1) - (\hat{\delta}_{t-k}^0 - \hat{\delta}_t^0)\}] \\
&= [\hat{\alpha}_{i,t,t-k} + (\hat{\delta}_{i,t}^1 - \hat{\delta}_{i,t-k}^1)] + [-\hat{\alpha}_{i,t,t-k} + (\hat{\delta}_{i,t-k}^1 - \hat{\delta}_{i+k,t}^1)]
\end{aligned}
\tag{5}
$$

where $\quad \hat{\alpha}_{i,t,t-k} = \overline{x}_{i,t} \{(\hat{\beta}_t^1 - \hat{\beta}_{t-k}^1) - (\hat{\beta}_t^0 - \hat{\beta}_{t-k}^0)\} - (\hat{\delta}_t^0 - \hat{\delta}_{t-k}^0)$.

It is well known that decomposition analyses may be sensitive to the choice of base characteristics, $\overline{x}_{it}$ (Horrace and Oaxaca, 2001) which in this case directly affects the computation of $\hat{\alpha}_{i,t,t-k}$. This will no longer be an issue if the native-born comparison sample is chosen to have characteristics identical on average to the immigrant cohort sample.

In a rarely cited paper, Yuengert (1994) finds that this approach to estimating immigrant earnings is sensitive to both the choice of comparison point and the particular specification of earnings used. The comparisons used by Borjas (1985) tend to understate US immigrant earnings relative to the native born while standard Mincerian earnings specifications, linear in education and quadratic in experience, overstate relative earnings for immigrants at the extremes of the education spectrum. These concerns would likely apply to immigrant integration studies for Canada, although perhaps in different ways since immigration patterns differ between the two countries.

Previous Canadian studies have used a random sample of the native born to construct a comparison group of comparable size to the immigrant sample for each census. Baker and Benjamin (1994) use a one-sixth random sample, Grant (1999) uses a comparable (but unspecified) random sample of the native born except for a full sample of blacks, and Frenette and Morissette (2003) use a 20% random sample of the native born. From this perspective, we can ask whether a random sample of the native born provides an appropriate comparison group. In this case, the comparison group is intended to represent what the outcomes for immigrants would have been had they not been immigrants; that is, had they been born and raised in Canada. This requires the identifying assumption that the mean outcome of the native born is identical to that of immigrants had they been born and raised in Canada, conditional on observable characteristics. Intuitively, this suggests that the native-born sample should look like the immigrant sample to provide an appropriate counterfactual. As discussed above, recent literature suggests that a native-born comparison sample matched to the immigrant sample can reduce model dependence and give more reliable estimates of immigrant integration.

This issue might not be important if the characteristics of the immigrant and native-born samples were similar. Authors have consistently observed otherwise, however. Baker and Benjamin (1994, Table 1) show that immigrants tend to be better educated than the native born, although the immigrant advantage is declining over time. Grant (1999, Table 1) finds a reversal of this trend in the 1980s. She also observes that immigrants are older on average with more potential work experience (age minus schooling minus 5), are regionally concentrated in Ontario and British Columbia, and are more ethnically diverse than the native born. Frenette and Morissette (2003, Table 1) find a widening gap in mean education between immigrants and the native born through the 1990s. More immigrants are members of visible minorities, although this information has only been collected since 1986. Moreover, while researchers typically focus on the mean characteristics of their samples, this is not adequate to ensure that the samples "match up" well. There could be dramatic differences in the distribution of characteristics between immigrant and native-born samples whose means are the same. Smith (2006), for example, finds that the mean schooling of immigrants is lower by 1.3 years in the United States as of 2002 but, perhaps more importantly, that immigrants are more highly represented in both the lowest and highest education categories; that is, their years of schooling are more dispersed.

This idea of matching the characteristics of the immigrant and native-born samples is not entirely new. One approach to explain the rapid changes in immigrant fortunes in Canada in the latter part of the twentieth century matches recent immigrants with native-born labour market entrants. Frenette and Morissette (2003), using census data, and McDonald and Worswick (1998) and Green and Worswick (2003), using non-census data, find that much of the change in the prospects of entering immigrants can be explained by similarly dismal prospects for their native-born counterparts entering the labour market, suggesting that at least the estimates of immigrant integration shortly after landing (the entry effect) are sensitive to the choice of comparison group. Frenette and Morissette, for example, find that the immigrant earnings disadvantage at entry has risen only modestly from 7% to 12% over the two decades when arriving immigrants are compared only to native-born entrants, compared to entry effects that rise from 17% to 40% during this period when all native-born workers are used as the benchmark.

The estimates of immigrant integration used in the second section of the main text of this paper are based upon our re analysis using the quasi-panel approach to the census public microdata files from 1971, 1981, 1986, 1991, 1996, and 2001.

References

Abdurrahman, A. and M. Skuterud. 2003. "Explaining the Deteriorating Entry Earnings of Canada's Immigration Cohorts: 1966–2000". Ottawa: Family and Labour Studies Division, Statistics Canada.

Baker, M. and D. Benjamin. 1994. "The Performance of Immigrants in the Canadian Labor Market", *Journal of Labor Economics* 12(3), 369–405.

Baker, M., J. Gruber, and K. Milligan. 2003. "The Retirement Incentive Effects of Canada's Income Security Programs", *Canadian Journal of Economics* 36(2), 261–290.

Borjas, G. 1985. "Integration, Changes in Cohort Quality, and the Earnings of Immigrants", *Journal of Labor Economics* 3(4), 463–489.

Denton, F. and B. Spencer. 2005. *Population Aging and the Macroeconomy: Explorations in the Use of Immigration as an Instrument of Control.* Quantitative Studies in Economics and Population (QSEP) Report No. 398. Hamilton: McMaster University.

Frenette, M. and R. Morissette. 2003. *Will They Ever Converge? Earnings of Immigrant and Canadian Born Workers Over the Last Two Decades.* Research Paper Series No. 215. Ottawa: Analytical Studies Branch, Statistics Canada.

Grant, M. 1999. "Evidence of New Immigrant Integration in Canada", *Canadian Journal of Economics* 32(4), 930–955.

Green, D. and C. Worswick. 2003. "Immigrant Earnings Profiles in the Presence of Human Capital Investment: Measuring Cohort and Macro Effects". Paper presented to the John Deutsch Institute-CIC Conference on Immigration, Queen's University, revised September.

Heckman, J., H. Ichimura, J. Smith, and P. Todd. 1998. "Characterizing Selection Bias Using Experimental Data", *Econometrica* 66, 1017–1098.

Ho, D., K. Imai, G. King, and E. Stuart. 2006. "Matching as Nonparametric Preprocessing for Reducing Model Dependence in Parametric Causal Inference". Cambridge, MA: Harvard University. Unpblished Paper.

Horrace, W. and R. Oaxaca. 2001. "Inter-Industry Wage Differentials and the Gender Wage Gap: An Identification Problem", *Industrial and Labor Relations Review* 54(3), 611–618.

Hum, D. and E. Chan. 1980. "Do Minorities Participate in Canada's Old Age Security Programs: A Case Study of the Chinese", *Canadian Public Policy/ Analyse de Politiques* 6(4), 642–647.

Hum, D. and W. Simpson. 2003. "Job-Related Training Activity by Immigrants to Canada", *Canadian Public Policy/Analyse de Politiques* 29(4), 1–22.

_____. 2004a. "Economic Integration of Immigrants to Canada: A Short Survey", *Canadian Journal of Urban Research* 13(1), 46–61.

_____. 2004b. "Reinterpreting the Performance of Immigrant Wages from Panel Data", *Empirical Economics* 29(1), 129–147.

Human Resources and Social Development Canada (HRSDC). 2007. "Older Workers: Challenges and Policy Issues". Background paper for the Expert Panel on Older Workers. Ottawa: Human Resources and Social Development Canada.

McDonald, J. and C. Worswick. 1998. "The Earnings of Immigrant Men in Canada: Job Tenure, Cohort, and Macroeconomic Conditions", *Industrial and Labor Relations Review* 51(3), 465–482.

Picot, G. 2004. "The Deteriorating Economic Welfare of Canadian Immigrants", *Canadian Journal of Urban Research* 13(1), 25–45.

Smith, J. 2006. "Immigrants and the Labor Market", *Journal of Labor Economics* 24(2), 203–233.

Yuengert, A. 1994. "Immigrant Earnings, Relative to What? The Importance of Earnings Function Specification and Comparison Points", *Journal of Applied Econometrics* 9, 71–90.

Mandatory Retirement Rules and the Earnings of University Professors in Canada

Casey Warman and Christopher Worswick

Introduction

With the aging of the Canadian population, there has been a large amount of debate about the elimination of mandatory retirement. Mandatory retirement rules have particularly important implications for the university sector. With the growth of universities in the 1960s and 1970s in Canada, there were a large number of hires over this period and currently around a third of university professors are over the age of 50. This aging trend is fuelling an ongoing debate in provinces in which universities are allowed to enforce retirement at 65 about whether such a policy should be abolished. Consequently, it is crucial to have a complete understanding of the impact of mandatory retirement rules on the labour market so as to fully comprehend the implications of banning mandatory retirement rules in the provinces in which it is currently allowed. While there is research that

This project was originally part of the research program of the Family and Labour Studies Division, Statistics Canada. The data were provided by the STC Division of Statistics Canada. The authors have benefited from the comments and suggestions of Michael Abbott, Charles Beach, Miles Corak, Jonathan Kesselman, and Daniel Parent as well as the comments of seminar participants at Queen's University, Statistics Canada, University of British Columbia and University of Victoria.

examines the implications of mandatory retirement on the age distribution of professors, little is known about the impact this policy has on salaries.

However, it is very likely that mandatory retirement rules will have implications for the salary structure of professors. While productivity is related to the compensation of the worker, they need not be equal at any given time. In the university sector, as in many other occupations, earnings tend to grow at a faster rate than productivity.[1] Pay schemes, such as deferred compensation, may exist. Such payment schemes may work differently depending on if there is a known end date to the employment. Therefore, employment in the same occupation may provide very different compensation schemes depending on whether or not there is mandatory retirement.

The analysis of this paper uses the existence of interprovincial variation in the ability of universities to force faculty members to retire to identify the effect of retirement behaviour on the salary structure of university professors in Canada. The data used to address these issues come from a yearly census of all university professors in Canada collected by Statistics Canada.

We do find evidence that the salary structure is different at universities with and without mandatory retirement. Examining age-earnings profiles of university faculty, we find that male faculty at universities with mandatory retirement have higher returns to experience at ages 50 to 65 than male faculty at universities without mandatory retirement. This evidence supports the theory that deferred compensation is easier to implement at universities with mandatory retirement relative to universities without mandatory retirement (see Lazear 1979, 1981). Looking at density estimates, we also find evidence that the earnings distributions of male faculty have narrowed at universities that do not have mandatory retirement relative to male faculty at universities with mandatory retirement; however, we do not find the same results for female professors.

---

[1] For example, Krashinsky (1988) noted that at the University of Toronto, professors at age 65 make 2.5 times more than starting professors.

Casey Warman and Christopher Worswick

The Relevant Literature

While there is little research that examines the relationship between mandatory retirement and salary structures, there is some research on the impact of mandatory retirement on age profiles. However, the research on the age profiles has very important implications for our study. In order for there to be an impact of mandatory retirement rules on the earnings profile or distribution of earnings, we likely need for there to be an impact of mandatory retirement rules on the retirement behaviour of workers and on age profiles.

A study by Shannon and Grierson (2004) takes advantage of the intertemporal and interprovincial variation in mandatory retirement laws in Canada. They carry out an analysis of the impact of these rules on the retirement behaviour of older workers in the Canadian labour market using census data from the period 1981 through 1996 and Labour Force Survey data over the period 1976 through 2001. Their results suggest that making mandatory retirement illegal would have little effect on the size of the workforce over the age of 65. Therefore, the elimination of mandatory retirement is not seen by the authors as a way of alleviating the problems attributed to an aging population.

However, it is important to note that the Shannon and Grierson study did not explicitly look at the university faculty segment of the labour force. They argue that the number of people in the broader labour market who are actually constrained by mandatory retirement rules may be small; therefore, the effects of eliminating mandatory retirement on aggregate employment of older workers may also be small. However, one cannot necessarily extend this argument to individual segments of the Canadian labour market such as the segment of interest in this study: university professors. It may be that characteristics of the employment contracts (tenure, union status, work conditions) as well as the preferences of professors themselves make employment past the age of 65 attractive, leading to a large number of professors being constrained by mandatory retirement rules.

Due to a general lack of suitable data, the retirement decision of university faculty members has not received a great deal of attention in the economics literature. One important exception is the study by Ashenfelter and Card (2002) of US faculty retirement patterns. Ashenfelter and Card provide an extensive review of the US history and literature on the impact of the elimination of mandatory retirement (at age 70) in the United States. They argue that the previous US research had indicated that eliminating mandatory retirement for university faculty would not have a major impact on the age distribution at US universities and colleges (for example, see Rees and Smith, 1991 and Hammond and Morgan, 1991). Their research was intended to re-evaluate this view in light of newer data and using more appropriate analytical methods. The data employed by Ashenfelter and Card originate from a special survey carried out on 16,000 older faculty in the United States called the Faculty Retirement Survey (FRS). These data combine payroll records from individual institutions with pension information from the TIAA-CREF pension plan. The survey is based upon older faculty at a random sample of four-year colleges and universities in the mid-1980s. The faculty members are followed for 10 to 11 years overlapping the period of the elimination of mandatory retirement in the United States in 1994. They find strong evidence that the abolition of mandatory retirement (at the age of 70) in the United States led to a substantial increase in the fraction of university professors still working into their seventies. In particular, the retirement rates of 70- and 71-year-olds fell by two-thirds to a level comparable with those of 69-year-old faculty members. They conclude that American universities and colleges will experience a rise in the number of older professors in the future due to the elimination of mandatory retirement.

Worswick (2005) carries out an analysis that is similar to that of Ashenfelter and Card (2002) but using the same Canadian administrative data as are used in this paper. Worswick's identification strategy is similar to that used in the Shannon and Grierson (2004) study. The analysis sheds light on the importance of mandatory retirement rules on retirement behaviour in the Canadian context. Data from the master files of the Full-Time University Teaching Staff Data over the period 1983 to 2001 are employed in the analysis. Worswick (2005) finds that mandatory retirement rules act as a constraint on the decision to keep working beyond the age of 65 for professors at Canadian universities. The age distributions of professors at universities without mandatory retirement and those at universities with mandatory retirement at age 65 are found to diverge over time with a higher fraction of professors over the age of 65 being at universities without mandatory retirement. Using the longitudinal nature of the data, he finds that faculty members have exit rates from the university at age 64 and 65 that are 30 to 35 percentage points lower than those of their counterparts at universities with mandatory retirement. Similar results are found for both men and women; however, the magnitude of this effect is somewhat smaller for women.

Given the large impact that the existence of mandatory retirement rules have on the exit behaviour of workers close to age 65 (Worswick, 2005), it may be the case that the removal of mandatory retirement may influence salary offers and negotiated settlements from collective bargaining. In particular, universities may be prepared to pay salaries to faculty members who are above their productivity if they are close to retirement; however, if the mandatory retirement rule is replaced then the same universities may be unwilling to continue to pay older faculty salaries above their productivity level if there is no clear end in sight. This would likely be the case if there were significant costs associated with either lowering the level (or perhaps growth) of a faculty member's salary in the context of a collective bargaining agreement. Another argument in favour of an effect on salaries of the absence of mandatory retirement was made by Lazear (1979).[2] He argued that deferred compensation may be more difficult to achieve in the absence of mandatory retirement and consequently, there may not exist as high a return to experience for older workers in the absence of mandatory retirement. This would suggest that age-earnings profiles should be flatter at places without mandatory retirement and consequently earnings distributions will be more compact than would have otherwise existed with mandatory retirement.

Mandatory Retirement Regimes in Canada

In Canada, the rules related to the retirement of university professors have varied considerably both over time and across institutions. In the university sector, the rules related to retirement fall under provincial jurisdiction allowing for variation across provinces. Gunderson (2003) provides a review of the recent history related to mandatory retirement in Canada and concludes that only two provinces actually ban mandatory retirement, Manitoba and Quebec. In the case of Quebec, mandatory retirement was banned through provincial employment standards legislation in 1983 (see also Kesselman, 2005). In the case of Manitoba, the banning of mandatory retirement in 1982 resulted from a series of court cases (see Flanagan, 1985, for a detailed discussion). In 1996, a special provision allowed universities in Manitoba and their employees to negotiate mandatory retirement rules. However, while the University of Manitoba and the University of Winnipeg

---

[2]There is large literature which discusses the pros and cons of mandatory retirement. For example, see Gunderson and Pesando (1988), Krashinsky (1988) and Kesselman (2005). See Carmichael (1988) and Hum (1998) for a discussion of the role of tenure on the pay structure of professors.

did eventually enact some form of mandatory retirement, it did not happen until after the period covered by our data.[3]

However, these are not the only sources of variation in retirement rules related to age at retirement. In provinces where there is no legislative ban on mandatory retirement, individual institutions and faculty associations or unions can choose to include mandatory retirement rules in their collective agreements. In most cases, these rules stipulate that faculty members must retire before the beginning of the academic year following their 65th birthday. However, exceptions exist. The University of Saskatchewan has had mandatory retirement at age 67 over the period relevant to the data used in this study. Some institutions have had a few regime changes over the period. For example, both Carleton University and York University switched from having mandatory retirement at 65 to having it at age 71 and 70, respectively, to having mandatory retirement at age 65 again by the end of the sample period. As well, while the University of Alberta and the University of Lethbridge both have mandatory retirement, the University of Calgary does not.

This study focuses on the impact that mandatory retirement rules may have on the earnings of professors. We compare the age-earnings profiles and the earnings densities of workers employed at universities with mandatory retirement at age 65 versus those working at universities with no mandatory retirement. Given the time frame of 1983 through 2001, the main source of variation in mandatory retirement rules across professors in the data is due to interprovincial variation in mandatory retirement rules. This variation is used to identify differences in age-earnings profiles and earnings distributions between faculty members who teach at institutions with mandatory retirement and those without.

---

[3]In 2001, the University of Manitoba had mandatory retirement with gradual retirement after age 69. The University of Winnipeg also enacted mandatory retirement at age 69 around the same time (see MacGregor, 2005, for a discussion).

Faculty Sample, Summary Statistics and Methodology

Data from the master files of the Full-Time University Teaching Staff Data over the period 1983 to 2001 are employed in the main part of the analysis.[4] This confidential, administrative database is collected each year by Statistics Canada from each of the universities in Canada. It contains detailed information on each employee's salary, type of appointment (e.g., tenure and rank), years since first appointment as well as personal information such as age, gender and education.

We remove small institutions from the sample based on a cut-off of having less than 100 full-time faculty members as of 2001–2002. In order to obtain a clean measure of the age-earnings profiles, we also remove universities that had policy changes partway through our sample. For example, Carleton and York are removed from the analysis since, as previously discussed, they have a few policy changes during the time period. As well, we do not include the University of Prince Edward Island since they switched to having mandatory retirement in 1995.

We investigate the relationship between salaries and age for university faculty according to whether their university had mandatory retirement or not. To the best of our knowledge, this type of analysis has not been carried out before. Ashenfelter and Card (2002) did not report results of this kind and this may be due to the fact that their datasets were designed to overlap fairly closely to the timing of the removal of mandatory retirement. Hence, in the US data it would be difficult to identify the impact on the age-salary profiles of the academics affected by the change in rules. In the Canadian data, there are many more years of observations on universities both with and without mandatory retirement being in place. This means that we can investigate the impact on the returns to experience for a large group of Canadian faculty.

We estimate the age-earnings profiles from regression models with the following specification:

$$E_{it} = \beta_0 + \beta_1 Age_{it} + \beta_2 Age_{it}^2$$
$$+ NMR_{it}(\beta_3 + \beta_4 Age_{it} + \beta_5 Age_{it}^2) + \varepsilon_{it} \tag{1}$$

---

[4]We extend the data back to 1970 for the cohort analysis and when we examine the density estimates.

where E_{it} is the individual's annual earnings, Age_{it} is the individual's age and NMR_{it} is an indicator variable for whether the individual works at a university that does not have mandatory retirement.[5] We calculate the age-earnings profiles separately for males and females since it has been found that there are differences in the age-earnings profiles between the two groups (see Warman, Woolley, and Worswick, 2006). In each figure, separate profiles are presented for the case of professors at universities with and without mandatory retirement. In order to prevent policy shifts from influencing the age-earnings profiles, for this part of the analysis, we restrict the time period to 1983 to 2001.

Given that mandatory retirement may have different implications for the contracts of different entry cohorts, we also examine the age-earnings profiles separately by cohorts. We use five-year birth cohorts, with the first cohort being those born between 1930 and 1934 and the last cohort are those born between 1965 and 1969.

We also examine the earning densities of professors teaching at universities with and without mandatory retirement, again separately by gender. Given that the densities are estimated separately by year, we use the full set of data available, 1970 to 2001. This allows us to examine if there were any initial differences in the densities between the two groups of universities prior to the policy changes that occurred in the early 1980s. While there are rule changes among some of the universities during the period displayed (for example, at the University of Toronto, the retirement age changed from 68 to 65 in 1972), the main difference is that Manitoba and Quebec eliminated mandatory retirement in 1982 and 1983, respectively.

Results

We start by comparing the age-earnings profiles of faculty at universities with and without mandatory retirement for females and males separately (see Figures 1 and 2). For both men and women, the returns to an additional year of work experience are lower after the age of 50 for professors at universities without mandatory retirement than for professors of the same

---

[5]The age variable was defined as Age-30 in order to allow for easier interpretation of the β_0 and β_3 parameters.

Casey Warman and Christopher Worswick

Figure 1: Age-Earnings Profiles of Female Faculty: Universities with and without Mandatory Retirement

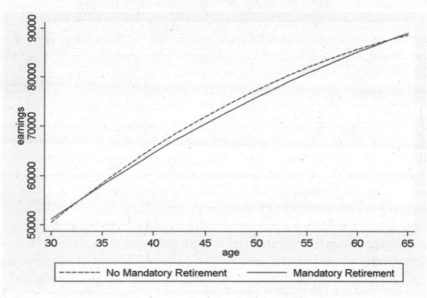

Figure 2: Age-Earnings Profiles of Male Faculty: Universities with and without Mandatory Retirement

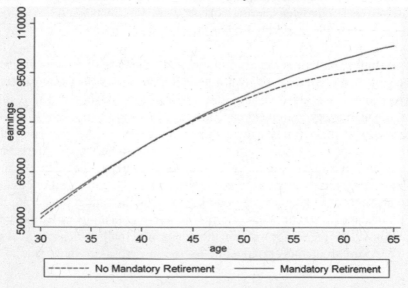

gender at universities with mandatory retirement. The magnitude of this effect is much more pronounced for the case of men than for women. For the case of women, the two profiles are close together but there is evidence of higher earnings for female professors at universities without mandatory retirement during the middle of their careers but virtually no difference at age 30 and at age 65. For the case of men, the two profiles are very close together over the age range of 30 to 50 but a significant divergence occurs at older ages.

Next, we investigate whether these differences in the age-earnings profiles of men and women, according to the mandatory retirement status of the university, vary across time. Equation (1) was estimated using a single cross-section of data taken from selected years of the data: 1983, 1989, 1995 and 2001. Rather than present the actual age-earnings profiles, we present the difference in the profiles across institutions without mandatory retirement and those with mandatory retirement. If no differences existed across these types of institutions in terms of the gender-specific age-earnings profiles, then the predicted curves would be horizontal with a vertical intercept at zero. For the case of female professors (see Figure 3), the trend in these curves indicates a relative decline in the earnings of professors at universities without mandatory retirement (relative to universities with mandatory retirement) over the period 1983 through 2001. These differences are most pronounced at the younger and older ages with a very large drop off at older ages in the 2001 survey. One possible explanation for the sharp shifting down of these curves is that institutions may have offered lower salaries to faculty younger than age 65 so as to be able to finance the relatively higher salaries of faculty choosing to stay on beyond age 65.

A similar pattern is found in Figure 4 for the case of male professors. The general pattern of a downward decline in these curves for most recent cross-sections of data indicates that the male professors at universities without mandatory retirement have not kept up in terms of salaries with the professors at universities with mandatory retirement. As was suggested above, this may result from universities needing to hold some funds back that could have gone towards higher salaries so as to pay the relatively high salaries of faculty who have stayed on past age 65. However, other possible explanations exist such as heterogeneity across the universities with and without mandatory retirement in terms of their overall budgets. Unlike what was found in Figure 3 for women, the position of male professors over the age of 55 does not appear to decline for the last cross-sectional year. The

Figure 3: Differences in Predicted Earnings for Female Faculty Between Universities without Mandatory Retirement and Those with Mandatory Retirement
(Cross-sectional estimates for selected years)

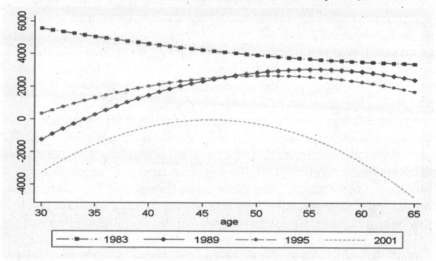

Figure 4: Differences in Predicted Earnings for Male Faculty Between Universities without Mandatory Retirement and Those with Mandatory Retirement
(Cross-sectional estimates for selected years)

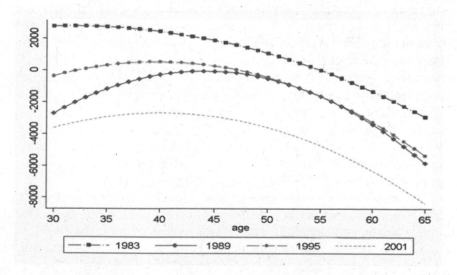

general shape of these curves appears to be very similar across each of the survey years.

The final part of the earnings analysis extends equation (1) to allow for the age-earnings relationship for faculty at both groups of universities to vary by birth cohort. The rationale for this approach is to investigate whether each cohort of professors had a different age-earnings profile at universities without mandatory retirement when compared with the same cohort at universities with mandatory retirement. We extend the data back to 1970 in order to cover a larger number of cohorts. In Figures 5 and 6, predicted age-earnings profiles are presented for male professors at each of the two groups of universities. In both cases, a pattern of cross-cohort decline in earnings over the age range of 30 through 50 is apparent. This indicates that earnings at the same age have been lower in real terms for more recent birth cohorts than for earlier birth cohorts. At the older ages, a different cross-cohort pattern emerges. For faculty at universities with mandatory retirement, the slope of the age-earnings profile is positive and similar to the slope at earlier ages and for the more recent birth cohorts. However, in Figure 5, we see that the age-earnings profiles for these earlier cohorts are flatter over the age range of 50–65 and in the case of the two earliest cohorts dip and have a negative slope between age 60 and age 65. In Figure 7, the differences between each curve in Figure 5 and the corresponding curve in Figure 6 are plotted by birth cohort in order to highlight these differences in the age-earnings profiles across the two groups of institutions. While the patterns are not simple, two general relationships emerge. First, for more recent birth cohorts, professors at universities without mandatory retirement have lost ground for more recent birth cohorts when compared to the predicted earnings of professors from the same birth cohort at universities with mandatory retirement. Second, the returns to experience of professors aged 50 to 65 have declined for more recent birth cohorts of professors at universities without mandatory retirement relative to professors from the same birth cohort at universities with mandatory retirement. This can be seen by the shifting down and the increase in the magnitude of the downward sloping curves for birth cohort 1935–39 relative to 1930–34. In Figures 8, 9 and 10, equivalent profiles are presented for female professors. While differences exist, the overall patterns are very similar to what was found for male professors.

We next examine the earning densities for faculty working at universities with mandatory retirement versus faculty employed at universities that eliminated mandatory retirement in the early 1980s. In order to see how the distribution looks both after and before the rule

Figure 5: Age-Earnings Profiles of Male Faculty by Birth Cohort: Universities without Mandatory Retirement

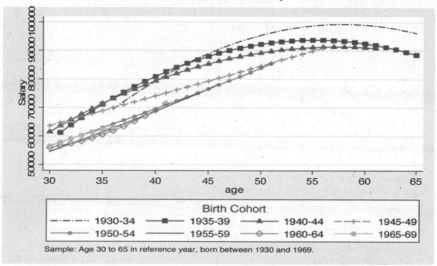

Figure 6: Age-Earnings Profiles of Male Faculty by Birth Cohort: Universities with Mandatory Retirement

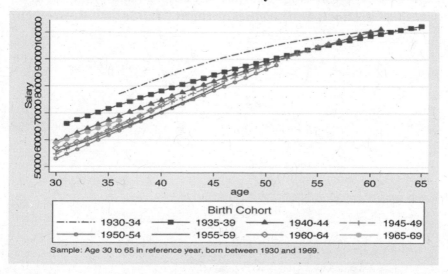

Figure 7: Differences in Predicted Earnings by Birth Cohort for Male Faculty Between Universities without Mandatory Retirement and Those with Mandatory Retirement

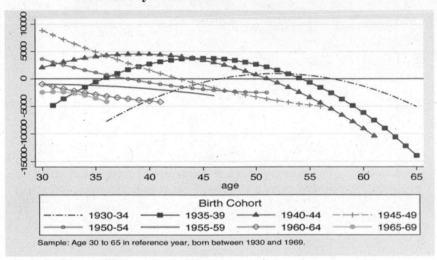

Figure 8: Age-Earnings Profiles of Female Faculty by Birth Cohort: Universities without Mandatory Retirement

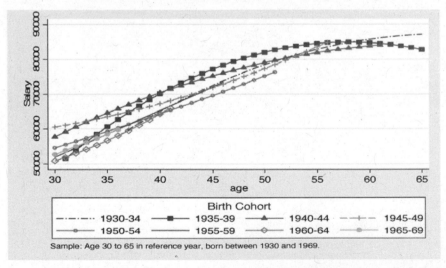

Casey Warman and Christopher Worswick

Figure 9: Age-Earnings Profiles of Female Faculty by Birth Cohort: Universities with Mandatory Retirement

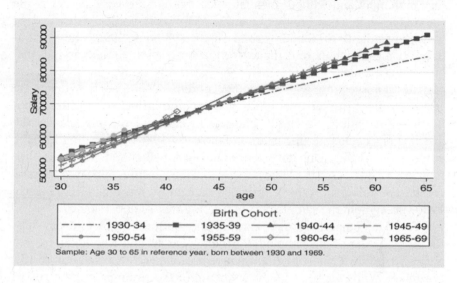

Figure 10: Differences in Predicted Earnings by Birth Cohort for Female Faculty Between Universities without Mandatory Retirement and Those with Mandatory Retirement

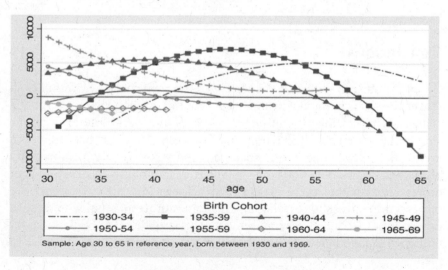

changes, we present the distribution for the full set of available years of data (1970 to 2001). The density of males in both the universities with mandatory retirement and without mandatory retirement are very similar at the start of the sample (see Figures 11 and 12). However, while the distribution widens over the 1970s for both groups, in the 1980s and 1990s, the distribution becomes much more compact for faculty teaching at universities that eliminated mandatory retirement in the early 1980s. Conversely, the salaries of males at universities with mandatory retirement continue to widen in the 1980s. While it is likely that other factors could influence the differences in the distributions, such as budget differences, the change in the distributions occurs starting in around the early 1980s, coinciding with the elimination of the mandatory retirement in Quebec and Manitoba. For females, we do not see the same pattern, and the densities appear to be more compact at universities that eliminated mandatory retirement in the early 1980s throughout the sample period (see Figures 13 and 14).

To aid in comparison of the earning distributions, we plot the densities for the first year of the sample (1970), the year around which there was a change in policy (1983) and the final year of data (2001) (see Figure 15). For males, while we see a slight widening of the earnings distribution of faculty at universities with mandatory retirement, we see a pronounced narrowing of the distribution for faculty at universities where mandatory retirement was eliminated in the early 1980s. For female faculty at universities that eliminated mandatory retirement, we do not see the same narrowing of the earnings distribution that we observe for males.

Conclusions

Given the shift to eliminate mandatory retirement in many provinces in recent years, it is important to understand the full implications of this policy change. While mandatory retirement appears to have little impact on the general labour market (Shannon and Grierson, 2004), it has important implications for some more specific occupations such as university professors (Worswick, 2005). An analysis of the returns to experience of professors over the age of 50 indicates a lower return to experience for professors at universities without mandatory retirement relative to those at universities with mandatory retirement. This was found to be the case for both men and women with the effect being more pronounced in the case of men.

Figure 11: Earnings Density Estimates for Male Faculty at Universities that Eliminated Mandatory Retirement in the Early 1980s

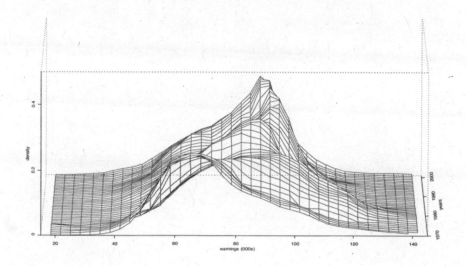

Figure 12: Earnings Density Estimates for Male Faculty at Universities with Mandatory Retirement

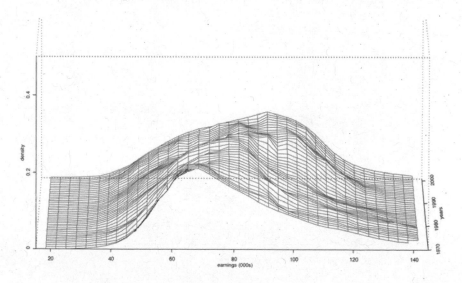

Figure 13: Earnings Density Estimates for Female Faculty at Universities that Eliminated Mandatory Retirement in the Early 1980s

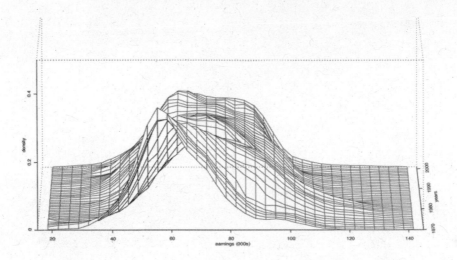

Figure 14: Earnings Density Estimates for Female Faculty at Universities with Mandatory Retirement

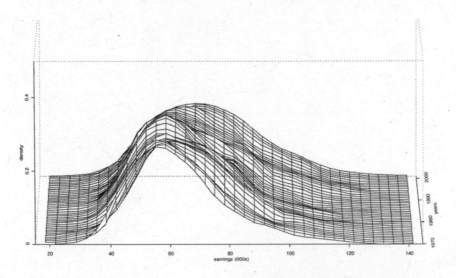

Figure 15: Earnings Density Esimates for Faculty at Universities with Mandatory versus Those that Eliminated Mandatory Retirement in the Early 1980s
(For selected years, by gender)

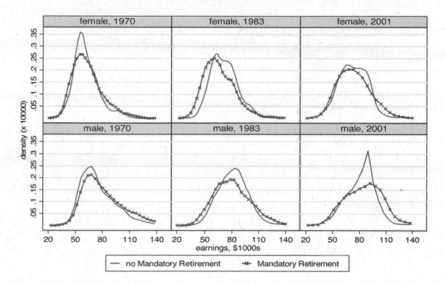

Looking across time, the salary position of both male and female professors in universities without mandatory retirement declined relative to those at universities with mandatory retirement over the age range 30 to 65. This may be due to lower salaries being offered to faculty prior to the age of 65 so as to ensure adequate funds are available to pay the salaries of professors working beyond the age of 65.

An analysis by birth cohort indicates a decline in the earnings of younger faculty at universities without mandatory retirement relative to faculty of the same age and birth cohort at universities with mandatory retirement. In addition, faculty age 50 to 65 at universities without mandatory retirement have lower earnings and lower returns to experience than faculty of the same age and cohort at universities with mandatory retirement. Finally, we do see some evidence, at least for males, that there was a narrowing in the earning densities at universities that eliminated mandatory retirement relative to universities where mandatory retirement was still enforced.

References

Ashenfelter, O. and D. Card. 2002. "Did the Elimination of Mandatory Retirement Affect Faculty Retirement?", *American Economic Review* 92(4), 957–980.

Carmichael, H.L. 1988. "Incentives in Academics: Why Is There Tenure?", *Journal of Political Economy* 96, 453–472.

Flanagan, T. 1985. "Policy-Making by Exegesis: The Abolition of 'Mandatory Retirement' in Manitoba", *Canadian Public Policy* 11(1), 40–53.

Gunderson, M. 2003. "Age Discrimination in Employment in Canada", *Contemporary Economic Policy* 21(3), 318–328.

Gunderson, M. and J. Pesando. 1988. "The Case for Allowing Mandatory Retirement", *Canadian Public Policy* 14(1), 32–39.

Hum, D. 1988. "Tenure, Faculty Contracts and Bargaining Conflict", *Canadian Journal of Higher Education* 28, 47–70.

Hammond, P.B. and H.P. Morgan, eds. 1991. *Ending Mandatory Retirement for Tenured Faculty*. Washington, DC: National Academy Press.

Lazear, E.P. 1979. "Why Is There Mandatory Retirement", *The Journal of Political Economy* 87(6), 1261–1284.

_____. 1981. "Agency, Earnings Profiles, Productivity, and Hours Restrictions", *American Economic Review* 71(4), 606–620.

Kesselman, J.R. 2005. "Challenging the Economic Assumptions of Mandatory Retirement", in T. Gillin, D. MacGregor, and T. Klassen (eds.), *Time's Up! Mandatory Retirement in Canada*. Toronto: James Lorimer Publishers, 161–189.

Krashinsky, M. 1988. "The Case for Eliminating Mandatory Retirement: Why Economics and Human Rights Need Not Conflict", *Canadian Public Policy* 14(1), 40–51.

MacGregor, D. 2005. "The Ass and the Grasshopper: Canadian Universities and Mandatory Retirement", in T. Gillin, D. MacGregor, and T. Klassen (eds.), *Time's Up! Mandatory Retirement in Canada*. Toronto: James Lorimer Publishers, 21–44.

Rees, A. and S. Smith. 1991. *Faculty Retirement in the Arts and Sciences*. Princeton, NJ: Princeton University Press.

Shannon, M. and D. Grierson. 2004. "Mandatory Retirement and Older Worker Employment", *Canadian Journal of Economics* 37(3), 528–551.

Warman, C., F. Woolley, and C. Worswick. 2006. "The Evolution of Male-Female Earnings Differentials in Canadian Universities: 1970–2001". Working Paper No. 1099. Kingston: Queen's University.

Worswick, C. 2005. *Mandatory Retirement Rules and the Retirement Decisions of University Professors in Canada*. Analytical Studies Branch Research Paper Series No. 271. Ottawa: Statistics Canada.

Summary of Discussion

Kevin Milligan poses a question of Gomez and Gunderson concerning age discrimination. He understands the point about private parties engaging in contracts, but we all understand that you can't have a private contract that violates certain norms in our society that are set out in things like the Charter of Rights and Freedoms. You can't have a contract that says, "We don't hire people of certain racial groups, or certain ethnic backgrounds, or religions, or whatever." We've also included in that list of things on which you cannot discriminate, age. The way that he understands rights is that rights are things that should not be subject to majority votes. They should be things that are inherent, that cannot be voted away because 50% plus one voted it down at the union hall, for example. So you seem to have one of two options. Do you think that either age discrimination is something that we shouldn't be protected from? Or do you think that rights should be subject to majority votes? Another participant stated that he didn't think a good argument can be made that the elimination of mandatory retirement interferes with labour market flexibility and freedom of contract. He supports the notion that there shouldn't be discrimination on immutable characteristics such as age and sex and that sort of thing. He thinks that, given the other tools available in the employer's toolbox, the good of maintaining non-discrimination on the basis of age outweighs other considerations.

    Morley Gunderson responded that the real question is not, "Are you for or against mandatory retirement?" The real question is, "Are you for or against allowing people to enter into contractual arrangements or agreements". He feels this is one of those situations where the state shouldn't interfere or should do so only very carefully because these are not contracts where workers are vulnerable. These are contracts with a *quid pro quo*. They're invariably twinned with a pension plan, and workers know it. Or they're part of a collective agreement. He agrees that there are times when union protection may be inadequate. But there are fair-representation laws that workers can bring against the union if they feel that they're not representing their interest well enough. These are problems with all collective enterprises that you enter into. It really amounts to the issue of under what conditions should there be private contracting. He feels it is different from employment standards, which involve protecting vulnerable workers. These people with mandatory retirement policies are in good jobs, well-protected jobs; they're well informed and they have a pension. What unions are concerned about is that this is the thin edge of the wedge for removing pensions from workers and dissipating some of those entitlement policies. But at least this is where the debate should be focused.

Derek Hum pointed out that when you consider the case of Manitoba and the elimination of mandatory retirement at universities, you have to understand the whole package of things. Yes, the legislation removed the ability to make somebody retire at 65. But you should see that as a package in which the rules also allow the university to have mandatory reduction of work load, which is a term we coined because we did not want to violate the notion that you can't retire. We can't make workers retire, but we can mandatorily reduce their work load. In effect, they'll show up in the statistics as not retired, but from the point of view of labour input — from a labour economist's point of view — there's a reduction of work. At the other end, there were people who might otherwise have retired at 65. But if faced with the choice of working full-time or not, they opted for a contractual situation in which they can also reduce their workload pre-65 at a pro-rated salary. Again, they'll show up as not retired. The elimination of mandatory retirement should thus not be interpreted as simply a legislation prohibiting people from retiring at 65. It really was a whole package of things, and that's how it should be interpreted.

A further participant acknowledged that these are costs and benefits of banning mandatory retirement. It's good that you've laid out clearly what the costs are in terms of changes in the compensation package and changes of collective agreements, etc. But again, it comes down to the fact that, when something isn't right, you don't do cost-benefit analysis on it — it's either a right or it's not. There were costs and benefits of banning slavery. But you don't make that decision based on the cost-benefit analysis, necessarily; you'd say, "It's a right or it's not." What is being said is that it's okay to discriminate on the basis of age because there are some costs and benefits to it. But that means you're saying it's okay to discriminate on the basis of age. **Morley Gunderson** responded that he would certainly dispute that as an issue in the sense that what the laws are doing is banning private parties from entering into arrangements where age will become a factor down the road in the future. He normally can't expect to be a woman, he normally can't expect to be a minority and he normally can't expect to be someone else who may be discriminated against. But he knows that he's going to become 65. And he thinks that there *is* a difference, and the Supreme Court recognized that difference. There is a *quid pro quo* here. You get a pension and you're required to retire at 65.

John Burbidge takes issue with Kevin Milligan about discrimination on the basis of age. If you look at the history of social security in Canada, and probably any other country, it's all about discrimination on the basis of age. It's all about younger generations or younger people being concerned about the plight that elderly people were in when we came off the farm and moved to the cities. We didn't have pensions, we didn't have social security, we didn't have all these things. And society, the working generations, came together and decided to tax themselves to pay pensions to those people. It was a straight intergenerational transfer, which is all about what governments do. Look at what governments do; they tax the working-age men and women to pay transfers to the young in the form of education and transfers to the elderly in the form of health care and pensions. He thinks to say that our society has abolished discrimination on the basis of age is nonsense.

Jonathan Kesselman indicated that he doesn't think there's a puzzle here. These are individual contracts between one employee (or a union) and an employer. As has been mentioned, the issue of prohibiting collective agreements that include mandatory retirement is entirely different from discrimination because it affects all of the workers in the work place. It affects the future rights of others who join that company. And it disproportionately disadvantages groups that the Supreme Court often factors into its Charter decisions, groups that have other disadvantages in the labour market perhaps — women who have taken years out from the labour force to raise children, people who've had disabilities that have kept them out of the labour force for an extended period, and perhaps recent immigrants who joined that company. They might join at age 45, 50 or 55. They do not get the full offsetting benefits of accruing this big pension because they might have been there 5, 10 or 15 years, and not 30 or 40 years. They're different in kind from discriminatory differences in compensation.

Contributors

Editors

Michael G. Abbott	Department of Economics, Queen's University
Charles M. Beach	John Deutsch Institute and Department of Economics, Queen's University
Robin W. Boadway	Department of Economics, Queen's University
James G. MacKinnon	Department of Economics, Queen's University

Authors

Stephen Bonnar	Towers Perrin, Toronto
John Burbidge	Department of Economics, University of Waterloo
Robert L. Clark	College of Management, North Carolina State University
Katherine Cuff	Department of Economics, McMaster University
Richard Disney	School of Economics, University of Nottingham and Institute for Fiscal Studies, London
David Dodge	Former Governor, Bank of Canada, Ottawa
Peter Drake	Fidelity Investments Canada Limited, Toronto
Rick Egelton	Canada Pension Plan Investment Board, Toronto
Carl Emmerson	Institute for Fiscal Studies, London
Maxime Fougère	Human Resources and Social Development Canada, Gatineau
Rafael Gomez	London School of Economics and Department of Economics, Glendon College, York University
Morley Gunderson	Centre for Industrial Relations and Department of Economics, University of Toronto
Sterling Gunn	Canada Pension Plan Investment Board, Toronto
Cliff Halliwell	Human Resources and Social Development Canada, Gatineau
Malcolm Hamilton	Mercer Human Resource Consulting, Toronto
Simon Harvey	Human Resources and Social Development Canada, Gatineau

Derek Hum	Department of Economics, University of Manitoba
Steven James	Canada Pension Plan Investment Board, Toronto
Laurence J. Kotlikoff	Department of Economics, Boston University
Yu Lan	Human Resources and Social Development Canada, Gatineau
Sébastien LaRochelle-Côté	Statistics Canada, Ottawa
André Léonard	Human Resources and Social Development Canada, Gatineau
Dave McLellan	Fidelity Investments Canada Limited, Toronto
Kevin Milligan	Department of Economics, University of British Columbia
John Myles	Department of Sociology and School of Public Policy and Governance, University of Toronto
Christine Neill	Department of Economics, Wilfrid Laurier University
Garnett Picot	Statistics Canada, Ottawa
Graham Pugh	Ontario Municipal Employees Retirement System (OMERS), Toronto
Bruno Rainville	Human Resources and Social Development Canada, Gatineau
Colin Randall	Fidelity Investments Canada Limited, Toronto
William B.P. Robson	C.D. Howe Institute, Toronto
William Scarth	Department of Economics, McMaster University
Tammy Schirle	Department of Economics, Wilfrid Laurier University
Wayne Simpson	Department of Economics, University of Manitoba
Gemma Tetlow	Institute for Fiscal Studies, and University College, London
Marcel Théroux	Mercer Human Resource Consulting, Toronto
Michael R. Veall	Department of Economics, McMaster University
Casey Warman	Department of Economics, Queen's University, and Statistics Canada
Christopher Worswick	Department of Economics, Carleton University

Queen's Policy Studies
Recent Publications

The Queen's Policy Studies Series is dedicated to the exploration of major public policy issues that confront governments and society in Canada and other nations.

Our books are available from good bookstores everywhere, including the Queen's University bookstore (http://www.campusbookstore.com/). McGill-Queen's University Press is the exclusive world representative and distributor of books in the series. A full catalogue and ordering information may be found on their web site (http://mqup.mcgill.ca/).

John Deutsch Institute for the Study of Economic Policy

The 2006 Federal Budget: Rethinking Fiscal Priorities, Charles M. Beach, Michael Smart and Thomas A. Wilson (eds.), 2007
Paper ISBN 978-1-55339-125-8 Cloth ISBN 978-1-55339-126-6

Health Services Restructuring in Canada: New Evidence and New Directions, Charles M. Beach, Richard P. Chaykowksi, Sam Shortt, France St-Hilaire and Arthur Sweetman (eds.), 2006 Paper ISBN 978-1-55339-076-3 Cloth ISBN 978-1-55339-075-6

A Challenge for Higher Education in Ontario, Charles M. Beach (ed.), 2005
Paper ISBN 1-55339-074-1 Cloth ISBN 1-55339-073-3

Current Directions in Financial Regulation, Frank Milne and Edwin H. Neave (eds.), Policy Forum Series no. 40, 2005 Paper ISBN 1-55339-072-5 Cloth ISBN 1-55339- 071-7

Higher Education in Canada, Charles M. Beach, Robin W. Boadway and R. Marvin McInnis (eds.), 2005 Paper ISBN 1-55339-070-9 Cloth ISBN 1-55339-069-5

Financial Services and Public Policy, Christopher Waddell (ed.), 2004
Paper ISBN 1-55339-068-7 Cloth ISBN 1-55339-067-9

School of Policy Studies

The Afghanistan Challenge: Hard Realities and Strategic Choices, Hans-Georg Ehrhart and Charles Pentland (eds.), 2009 Paper 978-1-55339-241-5

Measuring What Matters in Peace Operations and Crisis Management, Sarah Jane Meharg, 2009 Paper 978-1-55339-228-6 Cloth ISBN 978-1-55339-229-3

International Migration and the Governance of Religious Diversity, Paul Bramadat and Matthias Koenig (eds.), 2009 Paper 978-1-55339-266-8 Cloth ISBN 978-1-55339-267-5

Who Goes? Who Stays? What Matters? Accessing and Persisting in Post-Secondary Education in Canada, Ross Finnie, Richard E. Mueller, Arthur Sweetman, and Alex Usher (eds.), 2008 Paper 978-1-55339-221-7 Cloth ISBN 978-1-55339-222-4

Economic Transitions with Chinese Characteristics: Thirty Years of Reform and Opening Up, Arthur Sweetman and Jun Zhang (eds.), 2009
Paper 978-1-55339-225-5 Cloth ISBN 978-1-55339-226-2

Economic Transitions with Chinese Characteristics: Social Change During Thirty Years of Reform, Arthur Sweetman and Jun Zhang (eds.), 2009
Paper 978-1-55339-234-7 Cloth ISBN 978-1-55339-235-4

Dear Gladys: Letters from Over There, Gladys Osmond (Gilbert Penncy cd.), 2009
Paper ISBN 978-1-55339-223-1

Centre for the Study of Democracy

The Authentic Voice of Canada: R.B. Bennett's Speeches in the House of Lords, 1941-1947, Christopher McCreery and Arthur Milnes (eds.), 2009
Paper 978-1-55339-275-0 Cloth ISBN 978-1-55339-276-7

Age of the Offered Hand: The Cross-Border Partnership Between President George H.W. Bush and Prime-Minister Brian Mulroney, A Documentary History, James -McGrath and Arthur Milnes (eds.), 2009 Paper ISBN 978-1-55339-232-3 Cloth ISBN 978-1-55339-233-0

In Roosevelt's Bright Shadow: Presidential Addresses About Canada from Taft to Obama in Honour of FDR's 1938 Speech at Queen's University, Christopher McCreery and Arthur Milnes (eds.), 2009 Paper ISBN 978-1-55339-230-9 Cloth ISBN 978-1-55339-231-6

Politics of Purpose, 40th Anniversary Edition, The Right Honourable John N. Turner 17th Prime Minister of Canada, Elizabeth McIninch and Arthur Milnes (eds.), 2009
Paper ISBN 978-1-55339-227-9 Cloth ISBN 978-1-55339-224-8

Bridging the Divide: Religious Dialogue and Universal Ethics, Papers for The InterAction Council, Thomas S. Axworthy (ed.), 2008
Paper ISBN 978-1-55339-219-4 Cloth ISBN 978-1-55339-220-0

Institute of Intergovernmental Relations

The Democratic Dilemma: Reforming the Canadian Senate, Jennifer Smith (ed.), 2009
Paper 978-1-55339-190-6

Canada: The State of the Federation 2006/07: Transitions – Fiscal and Political Federalism in an Era of Change, vol. 20, John R. Allan, Thomas J. Courchene, and Christian Leuprecht (eds.), 2009 Paper ISBN 978-1-55339-189-0 Cloth ISBN 978-1-55339-191-3

Comparing Federal Systems, Third Edition, Ronald L. Watts, 2008
Paper ISBN 978-1-55339-188-3

Canada: The State of the Federation 2005: Quebec and Canada in the New Century – New Dynamics, New Opportunities, vol. 19, Michael Murphy (ed.), 2007
Paper ISBN 978-1-55339-018-3 Cloth ISBN 978-1-55339-017-6

Spheres of Governance: Comparative Studies of Cities in Multilevel Governance Systems,
Harvey Lazar and Christian Leuprecht (eds.), 2007
Paper ISBN 978-1-55339-019-0 Cloth ISBN 978-1-55339-129-6

*Canada: The State of the Federation 2004, vol. 18, Municipal-Federal-Provincial Relations
in Canada*, Robert Young and Christian Leuprecht (eds.), 2006
Paper ISBN 1-55339-015-6 Cloth ISBN 1-55339-016-4

Canadian Fiscal Arrangements: What Works, What Might Work Better, Harvey Lazar (ed.),
2005 Paper ISBN 1-55339-012-1 Cloth ISBN 1-55339-013-X

Our publications may be purchased at leading bookstores, including the Queen's University
Bookstore (http://www.campusbookstore.com/) or can be ordered online from: McGill-
Queen's University Press, at http://mqup.mcgill.ca/ordering.php

For more information about new and backlist titles from Queen's Policy Studies, visit
http://www.queensu.ca/sps/books or visit the McGill-Queen's University Press web site at:
http://mqup.mcgill.ca/

Fax: (877) 864-4272
E-mail: orders@gtwcanada.com